the costs
of the israeli-palestinian
conflict

The Costs-of-Conflict Study Team

For more information on this publication, visit www.rand.org/t/RR740-1

This revised edition incorporates minor editorial changes and an index.

The Costs-of-Conflict Study Team

C. Ross Anthony, Daniel Egel, Charles P. Ries
Craig A. Bond, Andrew M. Liepman, Jeffrey Martini
Steven Simon, Shira Efron, Bradley D. Stein
Lynsay Ayer, Mary E. Vaiana

Library of Congress Cataloging-in-Publication Data is available for this publication.
ISBN: 978-0-8330-9033-1

Published by the RAND Corporation, Santa Monica, Calif.
© Copyright 2015 RAND Corporation
RAND® is a registered trademark.

Cover design. Sean Christensen and Doug Suisman

www.rand.org

To David K. Richards

His courage, vision, and humanity inspired all of us
who had the great privilege of knowing him.

Maps

Map 1
Israel, the West Bank, and Gaza

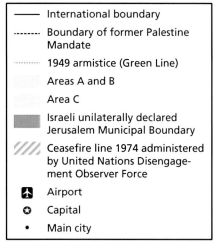

———	International boundary
-------	Boundary of former Palestine Mandate
··········	1949 armistice (Green Line)
	Areas A and B
	Area C
	Israeli unilaterally declared Jerusalem Municipal Boundary
/////	Ceasefire line 1974 administered by United Nations Disengagement Observer Force
✈	Airport
✪	Capital
•	Main city

SOURCE: Adapted from United Nations Office for the Coordination of Humanitarian Affairs (OCHA) Occupied Palestinian Territory (oPt) map.

RAND *RR740-Map1*

Map 2
Israeli Settlements in the West Bank, January 2012

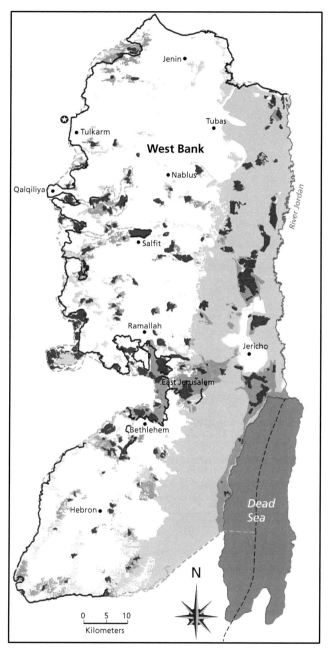

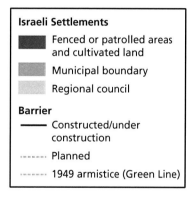

Israeli Settlements

■ Fenced or patrolled areas and cultivated land

▨ Municipal boundary

▨ Regional council

Barrier

—— Constructed/under construction

········ Planned

- - - - 1949 armistice (Green Line)

SOURCE: Adapted from United Nations OCHA oPt map.

RAND *RR740-Map2*

Map 3
Oslo Accords: Areas A, B, and C

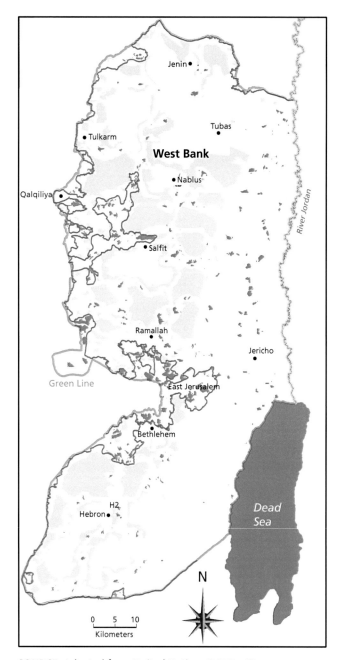

SOURCE: Adapted from United Nations OCHA oPt map.
RAND RR740-Map3

Preface

The study estimates the net costs and benefits if the long-standing conflict between Israelis and Palestinians follows its current trajectory over the next ten years, relative to five other possible trajectories that the conflict could take. The goal of the analysis is to give all parties comprehensive, reliable information about available choices and their expected costs and consequences.

As the regional context for this work is dynamic, we had to choose a date on which to cut off data collection. Data for this analysis were collected from February 2013 through April 2014. Since April 2014, we have tried to incorporate information about certain key events in our discussion, but we have not integrated that information in any systematic way, and it is not reflected in our analytic findings.

This technical report and all related study materials are available on the project website at www.rand.org/costsofconflict. An executive summary (available as a stand-alone document at www.rand.org/t/rr740z1) based on this technical volume highlights the main findings from the analysis.

Economic and political assumptions underpinning the analysis drive important outcomes. We have clearly specified those assumptions in our discussion. However, the project website also houses a costing tool (www.rand.org/cc-calculator), making it possible for users to change key analytic assumptions and explore how the changes affect outcomes.

This work should be of interest to policymakers in Israel, the West Bank and Gaza, and the Middle East more generally; to the international community; to foreign policy experts; and to organizations and individuals committed to finding a permanent and peaceful resolution to the conflict.

The study was supported by a generous gift from David and Carol Richards.

Questions or comments about the work should be sent to the project leaders, C. Ross Anthony (rossa@rand.org) or Charles P. Ries (ries@rand.org).

The Center for Middle East Public Policy

The research described in this report was conducted within the Center for Middle East Public Policy (CMEPP), part of International Programs at the RAND Corporation.

CMEPP brings together analytic excellence and regional expertise from across the RAND Corporation to address the most critical political, social, and economic challenges facing the Middle East today. For more information about the RAND Center for Middle East Public Policy, visit http://www.rand.org/cmepp.html or contact the center director (contact information is provided on the center's web page).

Acknowledgments

Many knowledgeable experts on the conflict, including more than 200 Israelis, Palestinians, Europeans, and Americans, took time from their busy schedules to meet with members of the RAND research team, some repeatedly, as we defined our research objectives and worked through the challenges of devising objective assumptions for present trends projections and our analytical scenarios. We thank them for their patience and wisdom.

We also thank Warren Bass and David Schoenbaum for their work on a concise and balanced history of the conflict from 1967 to the present. While we ultimately decided not to include the chapter in our research report since there is already an extensive literature on the subject, their "history of the conflict" discussion played a key role in informing our research approach and in ensuring that all team members had a firm grounding in the conflict's history over the past half century.

Any project like this should be firmly anchored in reality and stress tested by those who live the trends it purports to analyze. From the outset, therefore, we intended to lay out the evolving research design in a workshop involving Israeli, Palestinian, and European experts with decades of experience and insight. The workshop, held in Athens, Greece, in April 2014, was hosted by the government of Greece and benefited from suggestions, course corrections, and insights of nearly 20 top experts. The research team wishes to thank the Greek Ministry of Foreign Affairs, then-Minister Evangelos Venizelos, and Secretary General for International Economic Cooperation Peter Mihalos for their extraordinary hospitality and support.

We are especially grateful to our technical reviewers, whose wisdom and patience helped to sharpen our analysis and clarify our presentation. We thank Arie Arnon, Keith Crane, David Johnson, Daniel Kurtzer, Karim Nashashibi, Marc Otte, and James Quinlivan for their insights. In addition to his role as a formal reviewer, Keith Crane functioned as an embedded adviser, helping the team address difficult analytic issues and refine critical assumptions. Shanthi Nataraj provided constructive comments on the costing tool, ensuring its accuracy and accessibility. We also thank Shlomo Brom, Hiba Husseini, Dalia Dassa Kaye, Carol Richards, Michael Schoenbaum, Claire Spencer, and Jeffrey Wasserman for informal comments along the way. Shmuel

Abramzon, Sean Mann, and Semira Yousefzadeh provided vital research assistance. Of course, the authors assume full responsibility for the study findings.

Many members of RAND's Office of External Affairs contributed to this document. In particular, we thank Jocelyn Lofstrom for coordinating all aspects of production, including translations and the project website; Sandy Petitjean for her sustained efforts to produce high-quality graphics; and Nora Spiering, whose careful editing greatly improved the clarity of our presentation. We are also grateful for her patience in assembling an integrated draft of the manuscript on multiple occasions to facilitate our work and for managing and verifying the extensive references. In addition, we thank James Torr, who also did considerable work on references. Ingrid Maples provided invaluable administrative assistance at many stages of the project, and her energy and talent for logistics were vital to the success of the Athens workshop.

We wish to thank Michael Rich, RAND's president and chief executive officer, for his unwavering support of this project and the unbiased, objective analysis it seeks to provide.

We are especially grateful to David and Carol Richards. This study would not have been possible without their generous intellectual and financial support. Their commitment to peace in the Middle East remains a source of inspiration to us all.

Contents

Figures

Maps

Figures

Tables

Executive Summary

For much of the past century, the conflict between Israelis and Palestinians has been a defining feature of the Middle East. Despite billions of dollars expended to support, oppose, or seek to resolve it, the conflict has endured for decades, with periodic violent eruptions, of which the Israel-Gaza confrontation in the summer of 2014 was only the most recent.

This study estimates the net costs and benefits over the next ten years of five alternative trajectories—a **two-state solution**, **coordinated unilateral withdrawal**, **uncoordinated unilateral withdrawal**, **nonviolent resistance**, and **violent uprising**—compared with the costs and benefits of a continuing impasse that evolves in accordance with present trends. The analysis focuses on economic costs related to the conflict, including the economic costs of security. In addition, we calculate the costs of each scenario to the international community. Unless otherwise indicated, all costs are denoted in constant 2014 U.S. dollars.

To the degree possible, we consider intangible factors, such as distrust, religion, and the fear of relinquishing some degree of security, and how such factors might affect future pathways.

The study's focus emerged from an extensive scoping exercise designed to identify how RAND's objective, fact-based approach might promote fruitful policy discussion. We reviewed previous research on key dimensions of the problem and, where possible and necessary, we conducted additional research to clarify and define issues. Our overarching goal is to give all parties comprehensive, reliable information about available choices and their expected costs and consequences.

We integrated findings from our fieldwork, the literature review, and our supplemental analyses. Seven key findings emerge from our work:

- A two-state solution provides by far the best economic outcomes for both Israelis and Palestinians. Israelis gain over two times more than the Palestinians in absolute terms—$123 billion versus $50 billion over ten years.
- But the Palestinians gain more proportionately, with average per capita income increasing by approximately 36 percent over what it would have been in 2024, versus 5 percent for the average Israeli.

- A return to violence would have profoundly negative economic consequences for both Palestinians and Israelis; we estimate that per capita gross domestic product (GDP) would fall by 46 percent in the West Bank and Gaza (WBG) and by 10 percent in Israel by 2024.
- In most scenarios, the value of economic opportunities gained or lost by both parties is much larger than expected changes in direct costs.
- Unilateral withdrawal by Israel from the West Bank imposes large economic costs on Israelis unless Israel coordinates with the Palestinians and the international community, and the international community shoulders a substantial portion of the costs of relocating settlers.
- Intangible factors, such as each party's security and sovereignty aspirations, are critical considerations in understanding and resolving the impasse.
- Taking advantage of the economic opportunities of a two-state solution would require substantial investments from the public and private sectors of the international community and from both parties.

Approach

Understanding the costs of the political impasse requires a methodology to compare conditions that Israelis and Palestinians experience today with what conditions might be under alternative assumptions about political conditions. We use a counterfactual approach, which allows us to explore systematically how specific outcomes might have differed if conditions had been different (see Figure S.1).

Figure S.1
Framework for Analysis

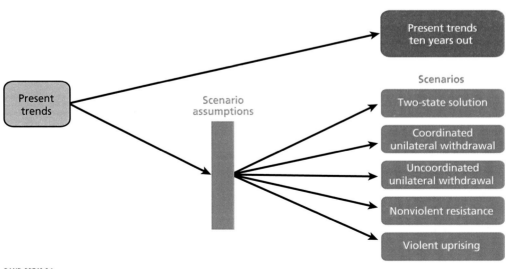

Our base case, which we refer to as "present trends," assumes that economic and security outcomes continue along their current trajectories—i.e., the final status accord issues defined in the Oslo Accords remain unresolved, and there are no significant shocks or changes to economic, demographic, and security conditions. We assume that the impasse remains dynamic, as it has always been, and that conditions, including periodic business disruptions, flare-ups of military engagement, and continued construction of Israeli settlements, continue to evolve along current trajectories.

We use present trends as a baseline reference and compare outcomes, such as GDP or perceptions of security risk, under that reference case to those under five alternative trajectories:

- **A two-state solution**, in which a sovereign Palestinian state is established alongside Israel. Our two-state solution scenario is based on an amalgam of the Clinton Parameters, the Olmert-Abbas package, and the track-two Geneva Initiative.
- **Coordinated unilateral withdrawal** by Israel from a good portion of the West Bank. Our assumptions are based on the work of Israeli nongovernmental institutions, including Blue White Future and the Institute for National Security Studies. The scenario assumes Israeli coordination with both the Palestinians and the international community.
- **Uncoordinated unilateral withdrawal** by Israel from part of the West Bank. We modify assumptions for coordinated unilateral withdrawal to reflect the situation in which Palestinians and the international community do not support Israel's actions or coordinate with it.
- **Nonviolent resistance** by Palestinians in pursuit of their national aspirations. In this scenario, we consider Palestinian legal efforts at the United Nations (UN) and other world bodies, continued support for trade restrictions on Israel, and nonviolent demonstrations.
- **Violent uprising.** In this scenario, we consider the effects of a violent Palestinian uprising, perhaps emanating from Gaza but also including the West Bank and possibly participation from foreign terrorists.

For each scenario, we derive economic and security assumptions based on historical precedent, a review of the existing literature, and conversations with subject matter experts. The scenarios themselves were designed with four core criteria in mind: They should be credible, they must be sufficiently distinct from other scenarios to warrant analysis, they must be feasible in the ten-year time frame for the analysis, and our counterfactual approach must be appropriate for them.

*We use these scenarios as possible alternative futures for analytic purposes, but we make **no prediction** about the likelihood of any of them becoming reality.* Indeed, the reality that evolves is likely to be a mixture of some aspects of all the scenarios presented here. For example, the Gaza war in the summer of 2014, the subsequent recriminations, the

Palestinian diplomatic moves at the UN and its agencies, and the punitive responses from Israel depart from what we originally defined as present trends and seem more akin to our nonviolent resistance scenario.

To avoid ambiguity, we attempt to use terminology precisely. We use the term *Israel* to refer to the State of Israel and to the territory defined by the Green Line. We use *Israelis* to designate Israel's inhabitants in general and *Jewish Israelis* and *Palestinian citizens and residents of Israel* when appropriate to distinguish between these groups. We use the term *Palestine* or *West Bank and Gaza* (*WBG*) to refer to the area of the West Bank and the Gaza Strip as defined by the Green Line. We use *State of Palestine* when appropriate to refer to such a prospective entity, especially with respect to our two-state solution scenario, and *Palestinian Authority* (PA) to refer to the entity set up after the Oslo Accords to administer parts of the West Bank and Gaza. We use the term *Palestinians* to refer to the inhabitants (except settlers) of the West Bank, Gaza, and East Jerusalem.

The counterfactual approach has several limitations. First, the results are driven by and are sensitive to the assumptions. The scenarios we use rely on historical precedent when possible, but we also base assumptions on other available evidence and on discussions with subject matter experts. Second, with certain important exceptions, we conduct this research assuming that changes across each of these different dimensions are essentially independent of the others. Such simplification allows us to sum the results of each change; however, it does not accurately reflect real-world linkages locally or regionally.

We have limited our analysis to ten years—effectively, 2014 through 2024. Both positive and negative effects under each scenario can change dramatically in the long run; thus, our estimates should be considered lower bounds.

Defining Present Trends

The political impasse affects Israelis and Palestinians primarily through its impact on the economic, security, and sociopsychological components of their lives.

Economics

Our analysis of economic performance focuses on GDP, GDP per capita, and public and private expenditures.

Gross Domestic Product. We use historical GDP growth rates to project how the economies of Israel, the WBG, and East Jerusalem are likely to evolve over the next ten years if present trends continue (Table S.1). Because we believe that more recent growth rates are more likely to provide accurate estimates, we use growth rates from 1999 through 2013. This period includes the economic downturn of the Second Intifada (2000–2005), the economic recovery following the Second Intifada, and the economic side effects of Hamas' rise to power in Gaza and several Israeli military operations.

Table S.1
Ten-Year Projections of GDP and GDP Per Capita Under Present Trends: Israel Compared with the West Bank, Gaza, and East Jerusalem

	Israel			West Bank, Gaza, and East Jerusalem		
	Average Growth Rate (1999–2013)	2014	2024	Average Growth Rate (1999–2013)	2014	2024
GDP (U.S.$, billions)	4.1%	$295	$439	3.6%	$13.9	$19.9
GDP per capita	1.9%	$35,900	$43,300	0.6%	$2,890	$3,080

NOTE: Data have been rounded.

The numbers in Table S.1 do not reflect any evolving long-term impact of the July 2014 conflict between Israel and Gaza, which had significant short-term negative effects on both the Israeli and Palestinian economies.

Public and Private Expenditures. In Israel, current government expenditures are roughly 40 to 45 percent of GDP; over the past three decades, public policy has increasingly focused on welfare, social security, education, health, housing, and community services. In an April 2014 survey on the desired order of national priorities, the Israeli public gave top ranking to reducing socioeconomic gaps (47 percent) and second place to creating housing solutions at affordable prices (21 percent). These social sectors account for nearly 70 percent of total public expenditures; proportional and absolute increases have come at the expense of military expenditures and spending on economic services (e.g., direct subsidies, investments in transportation infrastructure).

Israel will face steadily increasing expenditures for social welfare as income disparities continue to grow and the relative sizes of the Haredi (strictly or ultra-Orthodox Jews characterized by rejection of modern secular culture) and the Palestinian citizens and residents of Israel increase. Expenditures for the settlements in the West Bank, including those around Jerusalem, account for more than 2 percent of government expenditures.

Government expenditures for the PA have grown rapidly over the past 20 years, nearly tripling between 1996 and 2012. More than 50 percent of the PA's spending is on defense and administration. Foreign aid continues to be essential for the PA to fund itself. A majority of the PA's self-generated revenue comes from tariffs on foreign imports and value-added taxes on Israeli goods and services, both of which Israel collects. Since the 2006 Palestinian legislative election, Israel has episodically withheld tax revenues for political reasons, most recently in response to the PA's move in January 2015 to join the International Criminal Court.

Security

Israel will continue to face terrorist threats from Palestinian rejectionists, including Hamas; nonstate actors, such as al Qaeda and the Islamic State of Iraq and Syria (ISIS); and other state-supported external forces, such as Hezbollah. Other security concerns include threats to the stability of Israel's Arab neighbors and Iran's potential nuclear and long-range missile capabilities. Although Israel's security threats may increase over the decade, we assume, based on our interviews with security experts and our literature review, that the security environment will fall short of the sustained violent resistance experienced during the Second Intifada between 2000 and 2005. As a result, baseline expenditures for the Israel Defense Forces (IDF) will not change markedly in real terms.

Internally, the PA faces challenges from political and ideological rivals, such as Hamas. Additional threats include violence and vandalism from settlers and military incursions by Israel (e.g., combat operations in Gaza in 2014), both of which have been very costly over the years in terms of lives lost and infrastructure destroyed.

The burden on the Palestinian security apparatus is likely to grow, particularly in a two-state solution; requirements for training, equipment, and infrastructure will expand significantly. But the resources likely to be available to meet these requirements are not guaranteed. Given continued stalemate on the negotiating front, coupled with the measures Israel takes to maintain security—raids, an obvious military presence, checkpoints—episodic violent clashes with Gaza (e.g., in 2008, 2012, and 2014) seem likely to continue.

Sociopsychological Dimensions of the Impasse

Our extensive literature review identified instances in which specific groups have suffered diagnosable mental health consequences of the long, uncertain, and occasionally violent Israeli-Palestinian conflict. In general, the degree of exposure and duration of exposure to violence were key factors driving the incidence of both mental health disorders and violence-related trauma symptoms. The literature has not yet accounted for the possible psychological effects of the 2014 war in Gaza.

How Dimensions of Present Trends Would Change in Each Scenario

In our analysis, we consider how the key dimensions of present trends described above would change under the circumstances captured in our five scenarios.

Economic Dimensions

We considered both direct costs (specific budgetary or financial expenditures related to the conflict) and opportunity costs (lost opportunities for fruitful activity resulting from the conflict).

For Israel, the primary direct costs stemming from the conflict include budgetary expenditures on settlements and security—e.g., military mobilizations. The largest opportunity cost is the impact of perceived instability in Israel on its investment and economic activity. Additional opportunity costs include lost opportunities for trade with the Palestinians and with the Arab world, reduced tourism, and less access to relatively affordable Palestinian labor for work in Israel.

For the Palestinians, including the West Bank, Gaza, and East Jerusalem, direct costs include the destruction of property, security direct costs, reductions in Palestinian labor working in Israel, restrictions on freedom of movement of goods and labor, banking regulations, and stipends for the families of prisoners held in Israel. The opportunity costs are more wide-ranging, mainly stemming from constraints caused by barriers to mobility, trade, and other economic activity, as well as lost economic activity from areas the Palestinians do not control.

Security Dimensions

Israel's security posture includes a range of proactive and reactive mechanisms designed to deter security risks efficiently. Key elements include strategic warning (secured by the IDF in the West Bank and early warning stations in the West Bank and the Negev), tactical warning (including constant border patrols and periodic ground incursions), and a repertoire of proactive tactics designed to degrade potential terrorist infrastructure. Geographical separation between the populated areas of Israel and the Arab states to the east provides a buffer zone. This, coupled with strategic warning, provides strategic depth. Israel maintains the ability to respond rapidly to imminent threats, to preposition forces for deterrence, and to restrict freedom of movement in order to disrupt would-be terrorist activity within the West Bank. Israel uses a combination of such mechanisms to maintain security on the West Bank at relatively low cost to Israel.

In Palestinian security planning, strategic warning, a buffer zone, and strategic depth do not play a role; instead, funding, the requirements for a justice system, and the importance of chain of command are central. Developing responsible internal and external security structures, building basic capabilities, acquiring the essential tools of security, and negotiating authorities within the constrained Israeli framework are among the major challenges to effective Palestinian security.

On the security dimension, the imbalance in power between Israel and the Palestinians is enormous—Israel controls virtually all aspects of security because it believes that Palestinian security forces lack the capacity to address terrorism and did not do so in Gaza. Thus, Israel supports the Palestinian security services or constrains them as it sees fit.

Assumptions for Five Alternative Scenarios

For each scenario, we make a series of economic and security assumptions. Tables S.2 and S.3 describe the economic assumptions for, respectively, the Israelis and the Palestinians. Table S.4 summarizes our security assumptions for each scenario.

Table S.2
Economic Assumptions for Israelis

	Scenario	Two-State Solution	Unilateral Withdrawal		Nonviolent Resistance	Violent Uprising
			Coordinated	Uncoordinated		
Direct costs	1. Security	No change	No change	Defense expenditures increase by 1%	No change	Defense expenditures increase by 3%
	2. Settlement	100,000 settlers leave West Bank with proportional (16%) reduction in annual costs; relocation costs paid for by international community	60,000 settlers leave West Bank with proportional (10%) reduction in annual costs; 75% of relocation costs paid for by international community	30,000 settlers leave West Bank with proportional (5%) reduction in annual costs; 0% of relocation costs paid for by international community	No change	No change
	3. Palestinian services	No change	No change	No change	No change	Israel pays for Palestinian health, education, and social welfare
Opportunity costs	1. Instability and uncertainty	15% increase in investment and labor productivity for 4 years	No change	5% decrease in investment rate for 4 years	10% decrease in investment rate for 4 years	20% decrease in investment, 100% reduction in total factor productivity, 50% reduction in labor market growth for 4 years
	2. Boycott, divestment, and sanctions (BDS)	No change	No change	No change	2% reduction in GDP	No change
	3. Tourism	20% increase	5% increase	5% decrease	10% decrease	25% decrease
	4. Arab world trade	Trade with the greater Middle East triples	No change	No change	No change	No change
	5. Palestinian trade	150% increase	10% increase	No change	No change	15% decrease
	6. Palestinian labor in Israel	Permits increase by 60,000	Permits reduced by 30,000	Permits reduced by 30,000	Permits reduced by 30,000	Palestinian labor in Israel stopped

Table S.3
Economic Assumptions for Palestinians

	Scenario	Two-State Solution	Unilateral Withdrawal		Nonviolent Resistance	Violent Uprising
			Coordinated	Uncoordinated		
Direct costs	1. Destruction of property	No change	No change	No change	No change	$1.5 billion in damage to capital stock
	2. Territorial waters	Access for resource extraction	No change	No change	No change	No change
	3. Palestinian labor in Israel	Permits increase by 60,000	Permits reduced by 30,000	Permits reduced by 30,000	Permits reduced by 30,000	No Palestinian labor in Israel
	4. Freedom of movement	All costs removed	All costs removed	No change	25% increase	100% increase
	5. Access to social services	25% reduction in costs	No change	No change	25% increase in costs	50% increase in costs
	6. Banking regulations	50% reduction in costs	No change	No change	No change	50% increase in costs
	7. Prisoners in Israel	All political prisoners released	No change	No change	10% increase in number of prisoners	100% increase in number of prisoners
Opportunity costs	1. Control of territory	Full control of land vacated by IDF and 100,000 settlers	Full control of land vacated by IDF and 60,000 settlers	Full control of land vacated by 30,000 settlers	No change	No change
	2. Access to water	Unlimited access at market price	Unlimited access at market price	No change	No change	No change
	3. Barriers to trade	50% reduction in transaction costs	10% reduction in transaction costs	No change	25% increase in transaction costs	50% increase in transaction costs
	4. Licensing	Elimination of licensing restrictions	No change	No change	No change	No change
	5. Tourism and travel	Visa restrictions lifted	No change	No change	No change	No change
	6. Dissolution of PA	No change	No change	No change	No change	PA collapses
	7. Investment in public and private infrastructure	Sufficient for all new economic opportunities	Sufficient for all new economic opportunities	Sufficient for 50% of new economic opportunities	No change	No change

Table S.4
Security Assumptions

	Scenario	Two-State Solution	Unilateral Withdrawal		Nonviolent Resistance	Violent Uprising
			Coordinated	Uncoordinated		
Israeli	1. Strategic warning	No change	No change	No change	No change	No change
	2. Tactical warning	Reduced	Reduced	Reduced	No change	Increased
	3. Buffer zone	Reduced	No change	No change	No change	No change
	4. Strategic depth	Reduced	No change	No change	No change	Reduced
	5. Mobility	Reduced	Reduced	No change	No change	Increased
	6. Border security	No change	No change	No change	No change	Increased
	7. Liaison	Increased	No change	No change	Decreased	Reduced
Palestinian	1. Force size	Significant expansion in new mission areas	Increased	Need increased	No change	Significant decrease and/or destruction
	2. Force structure	Significant growth	Increased	Need increased	No change	Reduced
	3. Funding	Increased	Increased	No change	No change	Reduced
	4. Chain of command	Increased	No change	No change	No change	Dispersal of authority; local militias dominate
	5. Liaison relationships	Increased	No change	No change	Reduced	Cut off
	6. Freedom of movement	Increased	Increased	No change	No change	Decreased
	7. Border security	Increased	No change	No change	No change	Decreased
	8. Justice	Increased	Increased	Somewhat increased	No change	No change

For example (from Table S.2), in a two-state solution, Israel would see a 16-percent reduction in the direct costs of the settlements and would benefit from a 15-percent increase in investment because of perceived increased stability in the region. In contrast, in a violent uprising, Israel would see a 3-percent increase in average defense expenditures in each of the ten years (a direct cost) and a 25-percent decrease in tourism (an opportunity cost).

Analogously (from Table S.3), in a two-state solution, the Palestinians would benefit from full control of land and sea, except the Jordan Valley, and a 50-percent reduction in transaction costs due to the removal of trade barriers. In the case of a violent uprising, Palestinians could suffer up to $1.5 billion in direct costs as a result of damage to capital stock and a 100-percent increase in transaction costs due to very stringent restrictions on movement.

Economic Costs and Benefits for Each Scenario

The aggregate economic costs and benefits of each scenario in 2024, compared with outcomes of present trends, are shown in Figures S.2 and S.3 and Tables S.6 and S.7 (presented at the end of this summary). All results compare outcomes in 2024 relative to what the outcomes would have been if present trends had continued. The aggregate economic changes in GDP are reported in Figures S.2 and S.3, which combine the

Figure S.2
Change in Economic Costs in 2024 for the Five Scenarios Studied Relative to Present Trends as a Percentage of GDP

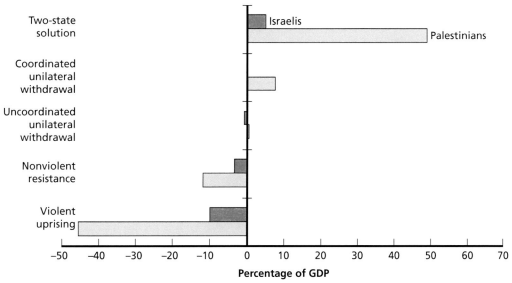

Figure S.3
Change in Economic Costs in 2024 for the Five Scenarios Studied Relative to Present Trends in GDP Per Capita (in U.S. dollars)

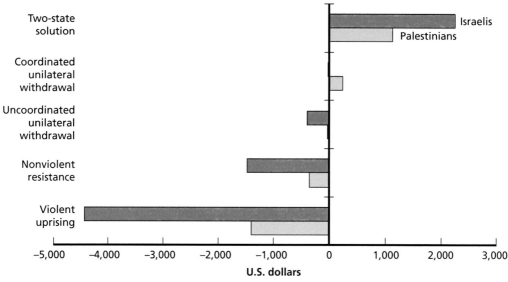

RAND *RR740-S.3*

direct and opportunity cost effects on GDP based on a conservative assumption about the fiscal multiplier.

The **two-state solution** assumes that the Israelis and Palestinians reach a final status accord agreement that is generally based on the Clinton Parameters. Israelis will withdraw to the 1967 borders except for mutually agreed-upon swaps, and we assume that 100,000 settlers will be relocated from the West Bank to Israel. The Palestinians will gain full control of Areas B and C and the ability to exploit the mineral resources there (see Map 1). All trade and travel restrictions on the Palestinians will be lifted, and perhaps as many as 600,000 refugees might return to the WBG in a phased manner. Israeli settlers withdraw from the West Bank except for the agreed-upon swap areas, and the international community pays most of the costs for relocating settlers. Israel's security is guaranteed by the international community, and investment in both Israel and Palestine is forthcoming to take advantage of a new, stable climate and the opportunities that peace brings. Arab country sanctions on Israeli trade are lifted, and Israeli trade with Arab countries increases rapidly.

A two-state solution produces by far the best economic outcomes for both Israelis and Palestinians. However, Israel would benefit more than the WBG in absolute terms. Our analysis suggests that, as a result of the effect of changes in direct and opportunity costs on GDP in the year 2024, Israel's GDP would increase by $23 billion over what it would have been if present trends had continued, while GDP in the WBG would be $9.7 billion larger. The average Israeli would see his or her income in 2024 increased by about $2,200 (about 5 percent), while the average Palestinian's income would rise by about $1,100 (about 36 percent).

Coordinated unilateral withdrawal assumes that Israel coordinates withdrawal from much of the West Bank with the Palestinians, who cooperate, and with the international community; withdrawal is implemented in stages over ten years. We assume that 60,000 settlers would be withdrawn and that the lands they occupied would come under full Palestinian control and be available for full economic use. Seventy-five percent of the cost of settler evacuation would be paid for by the international community and 25 percent by Israel. West Bank checkpoints and other barriers to trade would be greatly reduced, and other transaction costs to international trade would fall by 10 percent. We assume that investment needed to exploit the new economic opportunities would be forthcoming from a combination of the diaspora, international direct investment, and/or donor aid.

Israel's security footprint and costs would change little, while Palestinian security costs would increase significantly to cover expanded responsibilities. Labor permits for Palestinians to work in Israel would be decreased by 30,000 as Israel seeks to disconnect its economy from that of the Palestinians.

Israel experiences little if any economic effect because the various positive and negative factors cancel each other; Palestinians see $1.5 billion growth in GDP by the tenth year, with per capita GDP about 8 percent larger than in present trends, reflecting the economic potential opened up in Area C and reduction in internal and external barriers to economic activity and trade, offset somewhat by a decrease in income as a result of decreased employment in Israel. Direct costs for both parties are relatively small.

The **uncoordinated unilateral withdrawal** scenario is consistent with the belief of many that neither the Palestinians nor the international community is likely to agree to a policy that does not address any of the Palestinians' long-standing aspirations. In this scenario, Israel nevertheless proceeds on its own to cede control of some of the West Bank, but, in this case, only 30,000 settlers will willingly leave areas on the West Bank. In addition, Israel will have to pay 100 percent of their relocation costs—nearly $850 million per annum in total resettlement costs. Although there will be a reduction in some direct Israeli security costs related to the settlements, we expect little overall change in security costs, as the IDF will have more or less the same responsibilities, and there could be increased unrest from both settlers and Palestinians over the ten years examined.

Overall, Israeli GDP, compared to present trends, will fall by about $4 billion in 2024, only a 0.9-percent change in GDP per capita. Palestinians will similarly see a slight 0.5-percent reduction in GDP per capita, with the negative impact of lost Palestinian labor in Israel overshadowing the benefit of a slight increase in economic opportunities in Area C.

The **nonviolent resistance** scenario assumes that the Palestinians take actions to put economic and international pressure on the Israelis. This includes efforts in the UN and the International Criminal Court and boycotts of Israeli products in the WBG. We also assume growth of the BDS movement around the world, but primarily in Europe. We assume that Israel will respond with a number of measures, including reducing the number of work permits issued by Israel to Palestinians to work in Israel by 30,000, increasing internal and external barriers to trade and movement, and periodically withholding payment of taxes that it collects for the Palestinians. In this scenario, security costs for both Palestinians and Israelis are likely to rise. Some feel that the present trends baseline we have defined has already evolved in part into nonviolent resistance.

As a result of increased opportunity costs, nonviolent resistance will cause Israel's GDP to fall by $15 billion below present trends, a reduction of 3.4 percent per capita (about $1,500). Palestinians experience a reduction in GDP of $2.4 billion, or 12 percent per capita (about $370). The drop in Israel's GDP results primarily from reduced international investment and tourism because of perceived instability in the region and from a broader BDS movement in Europe. Palestinians suffer as a result of Israeli destruction of property and retaliation, which increases barriers and transaction costs to trade, and from decreased income because fewer Palestinian workers are in Israel.

In a **violent uprising** scenario, violence erupts—perhaps beginning in Gaza but spreading to the West Bank and possibly involving such foreign actors as Hezbollah in the north. We do not model this scenario as a repeat of the Second Intifada, but how it starts and its ultimate form are hard to project. Israelis would respond with actions designed both to punish the Palestinians and to establish tighter control.

We assume that these actions would cause the PA to collapse; Israel would then have to assume responsibility for essential functions that the PA currently provides, such as security in Area A, and shoulder the costs for health, education, and social services. This is the only scenario in which we modeled the collapse of the PA, but Israeli actions, such as withholding tax receipts and/or the withering of international support, could cause collapse of the PA in any of the other scenarios except a two-state solution.

A return to violence would have strong negative effects on both parties as a result of opportunities lost. As a result of increases in both direct costs and opportunity costs, GDP would fall $9.1 billion for the Palestinians and an estimated $45 billion for the Israelis, as compared to present trends. GDP per capita would fall by 46 percent in the WBG and by 10 percent in Israel. Israel's drop in GDP stems from effects of increased security costs and the effects of an unstable environment on investment and tourism.

Palestinians suffer because of the reduction in trade and economic activity as Israel increases barriers to both, the collapse of the PA, the destruction of homes and infrastructure, and the elimination of Palestinian labor in Israel. Much of the costs resulting from the dissolution of the PA will be in the areas of security, health, and education; Israel will likely have to bear many of these costs, amounting to $2.4 billion per annum as of 2024.

The relative importance of different opportunity and direct costs for the two economies is highlighted in Table S.5, which reports the economic differences between the present trends and each of the five scenarios as of 2024 (i.e., the scenario minus present trends). The economic differences are disaggregated, with the effects of each type of opportunity or direct cost on GDP reported separately. *In each case, a positive number indicates that the economy is wealthier along that dimension for that scenario than in present trends.* In the table, the aggregate changes in GDP because of changes in opportunity and direct costs are broken out separately.

For Palestinians, direct costs include a wider range of restrictions, but they typically reflect external restrictions that the Israelis can place on the Palestinian economy. The largest costs across all the scenarios are the restrictions that Israel can place on the flow of labor, though the destruction of property is expected to be quite large in the violent uprising scenario. The effect of opportunity cost changes on GDP are also larger for the Palestinians; these costs are dominated by restrictions on trade, though the difference between opportunity costs and direct costs is smaller.

The effects on GDP of the changes in opportunity costs far outweigh the importance of direct costs in almost all scenarios, especially with respect to GDP per capita, except in the two unilateral withdrawal scenarios.

Ten-Year Aggregation Across Scenarios

The difference between the economies after ten years in each of the five scenarios captures the difference in only the final year of our ten-year counterfactual analysis. However, these economies will be either richer or poorer across each of the ten years for each of the scenarios. Therefore, we also calculate the aggregate ten-year difference in GDP under the assumption that the effects of changes in costs and benefits of each of the scenarios are realized gradually (Figure S.4).

The two-state solution results in combined ten-year benefits to Israel of $123 billion, or a little less than half of Israel's 2014 GDP; the total benefit for the Palestinians is $50 billion, more than three times the size of their 2014 GDP. The combined total of wasted economic opportunity for both parties is more than $170 billion. Mirroring the year 2024 results, the aggregate ten-year figures in coordinated and uncoordinated unilateral withdrawal are very small. Nonviolent resistance would cost Palestinians $12 billion over ten years and the Israelis $80 billion; a violent uprising would cost Israel $250 billion (slightly less than its 2014 GDP) and the Palestinians $46 billion (more than three times their 2014 GDP).

As was the case for outcomes in the year 2024, the ten-year total economic effects are much greater for the Palestinians than for Israel because the Israeli economy and per capita income are so much larger.

Table S.5
Itemized Economic Differences Between Present Trends and the Five Scenarios in 2024 (changes in GDP in millions of U.S. dollars)

Israelis

	Two-State Solution	Unilateral Withdrawal		Nonviolent Resistance	Violent Uprising
		Coordinated	Uncoordinated		
All Costs					
Total change in GDP from all costs	$22,800	−$180	−$4,010	−$15,000	−$45,100
Direct Costs[a]					
Security	$0	$0	−$130	$0	−$340
Settlement	$90	−$170	−$420	$0	$0
Palestinian services	$0	$0	$0	$0	−$830
Total change in GDP from direct costs	$90	−$170	−$550	$0	−$1,170

Palestinians

	Two-State Solution	Unilateral Withdrawal		Nonviolent Resistance	Violent Uprising
		Coordinated	Uncoordinated		
All Costs					
Total change in GDP from all costs	$9,700	$1,510	−$110	−$2,380	−$9,080
Direct Costs[a]					
Destruction of property	$0	$0	$0	$0	−$750
Territorial waters	$280	$0	$0	$0	$0
Palestinian labor in Israel	$360	−$180	−$180	−$180	−$760
Freedom of movement	$80	$80	$0	−$20	−$80
Access to services	$10	$0	$0	−$10	−$30
Banking regulations	$4	$0	$0	$0	−$4
Prisoners in Israel	$90	$0	$0	−$20	−$180
Total change in GDP from direct costs	$820	−$110	−$180	−$230	−$1,800

Table S.5—Continued

	Israelis						Palestinians				
		Unilateral Withdrawal						Unilateral Withdrawal			
	Two-State Solution	Coordinated	Uncoordinated	Nonviolent Resistance	Violent Uprising		Two-State Solution	Coordinated	Uncoordinated	Nonviolent Resistance	Violent Uprising
Opportunity Costs											
Instability and uncertainty	$9,100	$0	–$2,530	–$5,050	–$39,200	Control of territory	$480	$290	$70	$0	$0
BDS	$0	$0	$0	–$8,780	$0	Access to water	$780	$470	$0	$0	$0
Tourism	$1,120	$280	–$280	–$560	–$1,400	Barriers to trade	$4,300	$860	$0	–$2,150	–$4,300
Arab world trade	$5,580	$0	$0	$0	$0	Licensing	$30	$0	$0	$0	$0
Palestinian trade	$5,580	$370	$0	$0	–$560	Tourism and travel	$770	$0	$0	$0	$0
Palestinian labor in Israel	$1,320	–$660	–$660	–$660	–$2,790	Dissolution of PA	$0	$0	$0	$0	–$2,980
Total change in GDP from opportunity costs	**$22,700**	**–$8**	**–$3,460**	**–$15,000**	**–$43,900**	**Total change in GDP from opportunity costs**	**$6,360**	**$1,610**	**$70**	**–$2,150**	**–$7,280**
						Other costs: Return of refugees	$2,510	$0	$0	$0	$0

NOTE: Data may not match total because of rounding.

[a] In order to translate changes in direct costs into changes in GDP, we assume (1) a fiscal multiplier of 0.5 and (2) that any changes in direct costs are reflected by a 1:1 change in government expenditures.

Figure S.4
Ten-Year Total Combined Change in GDP from 2014 Through 2024 for the Five Scenarios Studied (in billions of U.S. dollars)

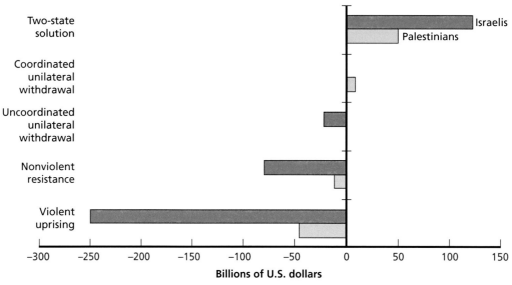

RAND *RR740-S.4*

In a two-state solution, Israel would benefit from increased direct investment in the domestic economy and from new trading opportunities with the Arab world. Israel's only short-run direct benefit from peace results from slightly reduced payments to support the settlements, which we assumed here would be removed from the West Bank with substantial international support; however, many settlement blocs would become part of Israel with agreed-upon border adjustments as per the Clinton Parameters, noted earlier. Palestinian benefits or costs (depending on the scenario) stem from the impacts on trade opportunities, reflected as a reduction or increase in the costs of producing and moving inputs and goods. The biggest direct effect for the WBG in any scenario stems from impact on employment opportunity in Israel. All of the economic results are dependent on and follow directly from our analytic assumptions.

Tables S.6 and S.7, presented at the end of this summary, list the costs and benefits of present trends compared with each of the five scenarios over the period 2014–2024.

Security Outcomes

We examine and calculate direct security costs for Israel and for the Palestinians, as well as their security needs and frameworks. We also examine but do not quantify the increase or reduction in perceived security risk resulting from each scenario. We draw the following conclusions:

- *In the short term, security costs are unlikely to fall significantly for either party under any scenario.* But, under a two-state solution, Palestinian security expenditures would likely rise rapidly as the role of the Palestinian National Security Forces expands substantially both internally and externally. In uncoordinated withdrawal, nonviolent resistance, or a violent uprising, we expect both Israeli and Palestinian security costs to rise.
- *Israel sees unchanged/increased security risks under any scenario.* Any deviation from its current approach to security involves increased uncertainty and greater perceived security risk.

Costs and Investments for the International Community

Each of the five scenarios also has cost implications for the international community—in particular, for the United States and Europe, which have provided financial and political support to both Israel and Palestinians since World War II. The net ten-year cost of each scenario is summarized in Tables S.6 and S.7. Given our counterfactual approach, we report only net changes from the status quo—that is, we assume that large military aid flows to Israel and humanitarian aid to the Palestinians will continue at present trends rates.

Support to Israel

Israel, the largest recipient of official U.S. foreign aid since World War II, has received about $118 billion to date—recently, about $2.6 billion per year. Aid includes defense assistance and a variety of nondefense support, including grants and emergency assistance during economic slowdowns and other geopolitical events. Israel benefits from U.S. budget appropriations related to many other defense programs and various technology transfer programs. Charitable donations from private U.S. organizations and individuals are also a major source of financial support to Israeli institutions; donations are usually made through U.S. tax-exempt organizations. We assume that aid flows to Israel primarily from the United States will continue at current levels.

Funding from the international community to Israel in a two-state solution scenario is primarily to help pay for relocating settlers who move out of the West Bank and the increased security costs that the international community, and the United States in particular, assume as security guarantees in any final settlement. Because the exact nature of those guarantees is unknown, we do not cost them here. In the two-state solution, we assume that funding would total an estimated $30 billion across the ten years; funding would total $13.5 billion in the coordinated unilateral withdrawal scenario.

Support to Palestine

The historical international contribution to the Palestinians has been predominantly development aid and direct budget support. Until the Oslo Accords, U.S. support to Palestine flowed primarily through the UN Relief and Works Agency for Palestine Refugees in the Near East ($1.6 billion between 1950 and 1991). After the Oslo Accords, foreign aid increased dramatically, with expanded support for the PA, which assumed responsibility for many of the social services formerly administered by nongovernmental organizations. After the Second Intifada, the Palestinian economy became very reliant on the direct support of the international community, which has continued.

In the two-state solution scenario, we assume that aid and direct support will continue at similar levels, and we focus on the types of new resources that the Palestinians would require from the international community to take advantage of economic opportunities that emerge in each scenario. Such resources would include a mixture of private and public investment to exploit new economic opportunities in Area C and new trade opportunities. In the two-state solution scenario, we also assume that the international community would provide assistance to fund the new investments that will be needed to repatriate refugees returning to the new Palestinian state from abroad.

In a violent uprising scenario, we estimate that the international community may actually have reduced expenditures. In this case, the flow of aid and direct support from the international community would slow dramatically as Israel assumes the costs for health, education, and social affairs for the Palestinians following the PA's collapse.

Israel will also need significant investment from international and domestic sources to take full advantage of the economic opportunities that peace would bring. We do not try to calculate the amount that would be international in origin: Israel's well-developed capital markets will enable these funds to flow smoothly at market-clearing prices. These funds, the amounts of which are likely to be quite large, are not included in our calculations.

Other Important Noneconomic Factors

Multiple studies (including our own) have demonstrated that the two-state solution is clearly the best solution for both parties, and violence the worst. So why has the Israeli-Palestinian impasse endured? Either the parties do not properly recognize the economic benefits of an agreement, or the economic benefits of an agreement have not been and may not be high enough to outweigh the imputed costs of other factors associated with the present trends, including the perceived costs of such intangible factors as distrust and fear of relinquishing some degree of security.

Based on our literature reviews and interviews, we suggest some of the factors, many interrelated, that may constitute barriers to resolving the impasse. We do not try to assess the relative importance of any one of these factors.

Power imbalance: *Israel, the country with by far the greater power, has a smaller economic incentive to diverge from the present trends. The percentage changes in income for the average Israeli are far smaller than changes for the average Palestinian.*

A singular feature of the Israeli-Palestinian relationship is the power imbalance between the two parties: Israel dominates the region both militarily and economically. This imbalance is true in every scenario.

Economic incentives: *Israelis have less of an economic incentive than the Palestinians do to resolve the impasse.*

Since the Israeli economy and the average per capita income are more than 15 times larger than is the case in the Palestinian economy, absolute changes have a relatively small effect on individual Israelis. The opposite is true for the Palestinian economy. In the case of security, Israel is by far the dominant force in all respects. As noted earlier, because its economy is so much larger than that of the Palestinians, Israel has larger absolute gains from peace or losses from violence, but, in percentage terms, the effect on the average Israeli is much less.

Security management: *Israel has learned how to manage security vis-à-vis the Palestinians at relatively low cost. Diverging from present trends entails significant uncertainty that influences both parties as they consider final status accord issues.*

The scenario of most interest from a security perspective is a two-state solution. For understandable historical reasons, Israel is very risk averse when it comes to security. Any change from the status quo brings uncertainty and, therefore, perceived increased security risk.

The core tenet of Israel's security doctrine is that it must rely only on itself to ensure the state's survival, and not on the United States, although American assistance and relationships with the United States certainly contribute significantly to Israel's security. Israel does not believe that the PNSF can maintain security to Israeli standards without an IDF presence, and Israeli negotiators reportedly have asserted that Israel will not accept international forces as a compensating element. Many in Israel insist on retaining a security corridor and control of the Jordan River and other border crossings. Israel's lack of trust in the Palestinians and its doubt about the international community's commitment to its security appear to outweigh any potential economic benefits that could flow from taking an alternative trajectory.

The Palestinians would presumably be eager to assume new responsibilities in a two-state solution, but Western experts believe that they lack the experience, manpower, and resources to fulfill all of them quickly. Internally, Palestinian security forces would face sharply increased responsibilities, assuming functions currently handled by the IDF, as well as maintaining peace in Gaza. The degree of cooperation from Hamas and other non-Fatah parties will play a critical role in determining the ultimate effectiveness of the security force and arrangements.

Lack of political consensus: *Deep political and religious divisions make it more difficult for either Palestinians or Israelis and their leaders to garner popular support for accepting the compromises required to break the impasse. Subgroups in each population are powerful enough to make change difficult.*

Both Israelis and Palestinians living in the WBG are deeply divided politically and religiously. Fatah and Hamas have significant levels of support in both areas. They also have profoundly different attitudes about Israel and divergent approaches to resolving the conflict, making cooperation between them very difficult. Israel also has many deep and complex political divisions, in part stemming from religious identity and the dominant political perspective of each group.

Lack of leadership: *Neither side believes that it has a partner with which to negotiate peace, and neither side appears to have the leadership necessary to create a new vision and transform it into reality.*

Prime Minister Benjamin Netanyahu has often said that Israel has no partner for peace, a situation many Israelis do not see changing as long as there is a coalition government that includes Hamas. The Palestinians also feel that they lack a partner, and, after Netanyahu's March 16, 2015, declaration that there would be no Palestinian state while he was prime minister, Palestinians have little expectation that Israel under Netanyahu will negotiate a final status accord agreement.

Regional instability: *The Middle East is plagued with upheaval and instability, and there is little on the region's ten-year horizon likely to change this situation.*

The region around Israel in the Middle East has been in chaos for some time, and, for a number of reasons, the political terrain is shifting. The centrality of the Israeli-Palestinian conflict today is receding, overshadowed by the rise of ISIS, the metastasizing Syrian civil war, the collapse of any semblance of governance in Libya and Yemen, Shi'a-Sunni tensions, Egyptian and Gulf State hostility to the Muslim Brotherhood, and Iran's nuclear and regional ambitions. However, the Israeli-Palestinian conflict retains significant sway in Arab public opinion, and periodic outbursts of violence will likely continue, intermittently propelling the issues embodied in the conflict to the forefront of international concern.

Conflicting narratives: *The historical narratives of Israelis and Palestinians, although parallel, are in fundamental conflict with each other. The clash of these narratives, including the increasingly important roles of religion and ideology, significantly enhances the probability that the impasse will continue.*

Fear and mistrust have led Israel to approach the peace process with great caution. Israelis do not trust the Europeans or the international community to stand behind them. They are very reluctant to trust Palestinians in particular and other Arab states more generally. Some Israelis also believe that Israel's destiny is to incorporate all of ancient Judea and Samaria into their state. These feelings make accommodation with the Palestinians exceedingly difficult.

Palestinians seek fulfillment of their long-standing aspirations to national independence and sovereignty. They view East Jerusalem as intrinsically Palestinian territory and Israeli settlements elsewhere in the West Bank as expropriation in violation of established international law. As among Israelis, an important segment of Palestinians frames their national struggle in religious, as well as nationalist, terms. Most Palestinians view Israeli actions as collective punishment or humiliation and subjugation intended to penalize and suppress their national aspirations. Palestinians are deeply pessimistic about whether Israel is negotiating in good faith, noting that the scope and scale of Israeli settlement beyond the Green Line expanded faster after the Oslo Accords than before (see Map 2). Nurturing an environment of mistrust is the fact that Palestinians and Israelis now have little or no direct contact with each other except in the specific context of conflict.

International donor enabling: *The cost of the status quo to both Israelis and Palestinians would be significantly higher were it not for donor aid that has, to some extent, insulated both parties from the total cost of the impasse and lessened incentives to seriously pursue a final status accord agreement.*

Israel continues to receive the world's largest share of official U.S. foreign assistance funding. International aid coming chiefly from the United States, the European Union, and the UN primarily through the UN Relief and Works Agency for Palestine Refugees in the Near East has been a critical component of support for the PA since its formation in the 1993 Oslo Accords.

Where Do We Go from Here?

Key characteristics of Israeli, Palestinian, and international policymaking, strategic thinking, political dynamics, demographics, and social dynamics will shape Israeli and Palestinian relations in the coming years. These trends will be part of a sustained feedback loop, influencing the responses of all parties in ways that reinforce these characteristics. The trends will, in turn, reinforce, perpetuate, and intensify the cycle of action and reaction.

Each cycle will progressively close off options that the parties might have had to break the cycle in potentially favorable ways. As options fade, parties become trapped in circumstances that may be quite far from the outcome they had imagined at earlier stages.

Outcomes projected in our scenarios may already be appearing. The cycle of tit-for-tat moves to pressure the other side has begun in earnest. The PA's UN and International Criminal Court bids were among the assumptions of our nonviolent resistance scenario. In response, Israel withheld Palestinian taxes for four months and has been considering other actions that raise economic costs to the Palestinians. For their part, Palestinians may respond by boycotting Israeli goods and services collectively (this is already a trend, but, in response to Israeli collective action, it may become an official policy). The continuing impasse will also likely enhance the BDS movement and result in a greater economic effect on Israel. The Israelis may, in turn, respond with boycotting Palestinian goods and services. The United States is reassessing its aid to the PA, and some members of Congress have introduced legislation to cut off aid completely.

Six broad trends will exert powerful influences on this cycle of action and reaction:

- *Continued settlement expansion* will make it increasingly difficult and costly to move settlers and resolve the impasse.
- An *open media environment* allows instant communication and worldwide exposure to events as they unfold, making it difficult for parties to disseminate their own interpretations of events.
- *The technology of war and terrorism* will continue to evolve rapidly. With external state actor support, range and guidance systems for terrorist rockets will improve and will be pitted against Israeli improvements in antimissile technology and its Iron Dome system.
- *Public opinion may be shifting.* Young American Jews feel less affinity for Israel and its policies than previous generations and are more apt to criticize its policies. Among British and French publics, strong pluralities report sympathizing more with Palestinians than Israelis. European parliaments, including those in the United Kingdom, Sweden, Ireland, and France, are voting to support recognizing a Palestinian state. The BDS movement has not yet had a significant negative effect on Israel. However, the movement is growing, particularly in Europe,

Israel's largest trading partner, and some Israeli leaders have warned that the movement's effects could have substantial detrimental effects on the economic welfare of Israelis.

- *Regional instability* continues unabated, including the rise of ISIS; civil wars in Syria, Libya, and Yemen; Iran's regional ambitions; and the collapse of governance in Libya and the Sinai.
- *Demographic trends* foreshadow a Palestinian majority in the territory comprising Israel and the WBG—either today or in the near future—and a Palestinian majority in 30 years, even if the population of Gaza is not included. Then, it has been suggested, Israel would face a core policy choice: whether to be a Jewish state with a predominantly Jewish population living side by side with a Palestinian state, a democratic state with a diverse citizenry that is treated equally, or a state without a Jewish majority that comprises the lands known as Israel and all the land between the Jordan River and the Mediterranean Sea.

Some scholars say that, given recent trends, the two sides are marching toward a one-state solution unless Israel opts for unilateral withdrawal, an alternative that also becomes increasingly problematic as West Bank settlements expand. Exactly what the one-state options are and how a single state—even a federation—would operate has not been extensively examined. Research is needed on how—and whether—a one-state solution could be structured in a way that preserves democratic principles.

A potential diversion from the current trajectory could come about if the parties were to radically change the way they currently view the impasse. But, to achieve that, dramatic policy intervention by all would be needed.

We hope our work can help Israelis, Palestinians, and the international community understand more clearly how present trends are evolving and recognize the costs and benefits of alternatives to the current destructive cycle of action, reaction, and inaction.

Table S.6
Summary of the Economic Change of Present Trends for Israel in the Five Scenarios in 2024

	2014	2024 Extrapolation	Two-State Solution	2024 Scenarios			
				Unilateral Withdrawal		Nonviolent Resistance	Violent Uprising
				Coordinated	Uncoordinated		
Population (millions)[a]	8.2	10.2	10.2	10.2	10.2	10.2	10.2
Total GDP (U.S.$, billions)	$295	$439	$462	$439	$436	$424	$395
Change in GDP (U.S.$, billions)	—	—	$22.7	$0.0	–$3.5	–$15.0	–$43.9
Change in GDP (%)	—	—	5.2%	0.0%	–0.8%	–3.4%	–10.0%
GDP growth rate (average)	—	4.1%	4.6%	4.1%	4.0%	3.70%	3.0%
GDP per capita (U.S.$)	$35,900	$43,300	$45,500	$43,300	$42,900	$41,800	$39,000
Change in GDP per capita (U.S.$)	—	—	$2,240	–$1	–$340	–$1,480	–$4,330
Change in GDP per capita (%)	—	—	5.2%	0.0%	–0.8%	–3.4%	–10.0%
GDP per capita growth rate	—	1.9%	2.4%	1.9%	1.8%	1.5%	0.8%
Physical capital (U.S.$, billions)	—	—	—	—	—	—	—
Change in physical capital (U.S.$, billions)	—	—	—	—	—	—	—
Change in physical capital (%)	—	—	—	—	—	—	—
Physical capital growth rate (average)	—	—	—	—	—	—	—

Opportunity costs only

Table S.6—Continued

Combined economic costs	2014	2024 Extrapolation	Two-State Solution	Unilateral Withdrawal		Nonviolent Resistance	Violent Uprising
				Coordinated	Uncoordinated		
Total GDP (U.S.$, billions)	$295	$439	$462	$439	$435	$424	$394
Change in GDP (U.S.$, billions)	–	–	$22.8	–$0.2	–$4.0	–$15.0	–$45.1
Change in GDP (%)	–	–	5.2%	0.0%	–0.9%	–3.4%	–10.3%
GDP growth rate (average)	–	4.1%	4.6%	4.1%	4.0%	3.70%	2.90%
GDP per capita (U.S.$)	$35,900	$43,300	$45,500	$43,300	$42,900	$41,800	$38,800
Change in GDP per capita (U.S.$)	–	–	$2,250	–$20	–$400	–$1,480	–$4,440
Change in GDP per capita (%)	–	–	5.2%	0.0%	–0.9%	–3.4%	–10.3%
GDP per capita growth rate	–	1.9%	2.4%	1.9%	1.8%	1.5%	0.8%
Total ten-year difference in GDP (U.S.$, billions)	–	–	$123	–$1	–$22	–$80	–$250
Total support required from international community (U.S.$, billions)[b]	–	–	$30.0	$13.5	$0.0	$0.0	$0.0

NOTE: Data may not match total because of rounding.

[a] All scenarios assume that any nonsecular increase in Palestinian GDP (e.g., return of refugees) is met with increased investment such that GDP per capita remains constant.

[b] For the Israelis, this includes the total ten-year costs required for supporting the removal of settlers. For the Palestinians, this includes the level of investment that will be required to satisfy the change in opportunity costs, as well as any reductions if the Israelis take over payments for PA functionality.

Table S.7
Summary of the Economic Change of Present Trends for Palestine in the Five Scenarios in 2024

	2014	2024 Extrapolation	2024 Scenarios				
			Two-State Solution	Unilateral Withdrawal		Nonviolent Resistance	Violent Uprising
				Coordinated	Uncoordinated		
Population (millions)[a]	4.8	6.5	7.1	6.5	6.5	6.5	6.5
Total GDP (U.S.$, billions)	$13.9	$19.9	$28.7	$21.5	$19.9	$17.7	$12.6
Change in GDP (U.S.$, billions)	–	–	$8.8	$1.6	$0.1	–$2.2	–$7.3
Change in GDP (%)	–	–	44.3%	8.1%	0.4%	–10.8%	–36.7%
GDP growth rate (average)	–	3.6%	7.5%	4.5%	3.7%	2.5%	–1.0%
GDP per capita (U.S.$)	$2,890	$3,080	$4,060	$3,330	$3,090	$2,740	$1,950
Change in GDP per capita (U.S.$)	–	–	$980	$250	$10	–$330	–$1,130
Change in GDP per capita (%)	–	–	32.0%	8.1%	0.4%	–10.8%	–36.7%
GDP per capita growth rate	–	0.6%	3.5%	1.4%	0.7%	–0.5%	–3.9%
Physical capital (U.S.$, billions)	$27.9	$38.6	$97.0	$48.8	$39.0	$38.6	$38.6
Change in physical capital (U.S.$, billions)	–	–	$58.4	$10.2	$0.4	$0.0	$0.0
Change in physical capital (%)	–	–	151.3%	26.4%	1.1%	0.0%	0.0%
Physical capital growth rate (average)	–	3.3%	13.3%	5.7%	3.4%	3.3%	3.3%

Opportunity costs only

Table S.7—Continued

	2014	2024 Extrapolation	Two-State Solution	Unilateral Withdrawal		Nonviolent Resistance	Violent Uprising
				2024 Scenarios			
				Coordinated	Uncoordinated		
Combined economic costs							
Total GDP (U.S.$, billions)	$13.9	$19.9	$29.6	$21.4	$19.8	$17.5	$10.8
Change in GDP (U.S.$, billions)	–	–	$9.7	$1.5	–$0.1	–$2.4	–$9.1
Change in GDP (%)	–	–	48.8%	7.6%	–0.5%	–12.0%	–45.7%
GDP growth rate (average)	–	3.6%	6.9%	4.4%	3.6%	2.3%	–2.5%
GDP per capita (U.S.$)	$2,890	$3,080	$4,190	$3,310	$3,060	$2,710	$1,670
Change in GDP per capita (U.S.$)	–	–	$1,110	$230	–$20	–$370	–$1,410
Change in GDP per capita (%)	–	–	36.1%	7.6%	–0.5%	–12.0%	–45.7%
GDP per capita growth rate	–	0.6%	3.8%	1.4%	0.6%	–0.6%	–5.3%
Total ten-year difference in GDP (U.S.$, billions)	–	–	$50	$8	–$1	–$12	–$46
Required investment in public and private infrastructure by international community (U.S.$, billions)[b]	–	–	$58.4	$10.2	$0.4	$0.0	–$16.7

NOTE: Data may not match total because of rounding.

[a] All scenarios assume that any nonsecular increase in Palestinian GDP (e.g., return of refugees) is met with increased investment such that GDP per capita remains constant.

[b] For the Israelis, this includes the total ten-year costs required for supporting the removal of settlers. For the Palestinians, this includes the level of investment that will be required to satisfy the change in opportunity costs, as well as any reductions if the Israelis take over payments for PA functionality.

CHAPTER ONE

Introduction

For much of the past century, the conflict between Israelis and Palestinians has been a defining feature of the Middle East. Despite repeated initiatives to resolve the conflict, Israelis and Palestinians have suffered sustained political, social, and psychological upheaval. The conflict between them—sometimes joined by other countries or groups in the region—has periodically flared into violence, sometimes widespread and other times localized. The Israel-Gaza confrontation in late summer 2014 was only the most recent of many eruptions of violence. This episodic violence has cumulative effects. Each outbreak hardens views, complicating and potentially making an eventual solution even more intractable.

In broad demographic terms, the vast majority of both populations has known nothing but some version of the current conflict. As of December 2013, more than 95 percent of the population of the West Bank and Gaza (WBG), and around 90 percent of the Israeli population, were born after the establishment of the State of Israel in 1948. More than 85 percent of the residents of the Palestinian territories, and more than 70 percent of Israelis, were born after Israel occupied the WBG in 1967.[1]

In financial terms, hundreds of billions of dollars have been expended to prosecute, support, oppose, or resolve the conflict in some way. And the sum of such financial expenditures does not begin to capture either the *opportunity costs* of the conflict (alternative ways in which these resources could have been used to enhance the lives of the region's residents) or the *emotional costs* of the conflict.

The conflict solution against which all alternatives are generally measured is a *two-state solution*—i.e., a sovereign State of Palestine alongside the State of Israel. This idea of partitioning an initially undivided territory into Jewish and Arab states predates the State of Israel by nearly 11 years, with the publication of the Peel Commission report in June 1937.[2]

The concept of partitioning entered its modern form of trading "land for peace" with the adoption of United Nations (UN) Security Council Resolution 242 in

---

[1] Authors' calculations using data from U.S. Census Bureau International Data Base (accessed June 2014).

[2] Full text of Peel Commission report found at Jewish Virtual Library, 2015; see also C. Smith, 2001.

November 1967. It continues to be invoked at the highest levels as not just one possible option, nor even the most promising option, but actually as the "only" option for peaceful resolution of the Israeli-Palestinian conflict.[3]

Confidence among the respective populations that such a resolution is possible waxes and wanes with external events.[4] The history of the conflict is studded with efforts to reach exactly such an agreement (see Figure 3.4), but none has been able to overcome the social and political hurdles to achieving a final peace accord. The resulting impasse and ongoing conflict affect all aspects of the lives of Palestinians and Israelis today.

A singular feature of the Israeli-Palestinian relationship is the power imbalance between the two parties: Israel dominates the region both militarily and economically. Both Israelis and Palestinians have similar historical narratives incorporating both injustice and displacement, but their deep religious, political, and cultural differences add another difficult dimension to the relationship. Understanding the feasibility of future policy choices requires understanding the power of these psychological dimensions in shaping current decisions. We consider some of these issues in Chapter Eleven.

The late Anwar Sadat's visit to Jerusalem, the end of apartheid in South Africa, and the fall of the Berlin Wall are salutary reminders that history is indifferent to predetermined outcomes and that even gridlocked highways have exit ramps. However, ongoing events may—and are certainly perceived to—constrain future options. History and its powerful remnants create path dependencies with their own inertia that, over time, become difficult to overcome. Thus, it should come as no surprise that, after the failures of American mediators in the 1990s, 2000, 2008–2011, and 2014;[5] the Second Intifada of 2000–2005; Israel's war with Hezbollah in 2006; wars with Hamas in 2006, 2008, 2012, and 2014; Fatah's defeat at the hands of Hamas in 2006; and the electoral success of Israeli political parties opposed to the two-state solution in 2009, 2013, and 2015, pessimism enjoys a comparative advantage, and optimists are hard to find.

1.1. Purpose of the Study

The purpose of this study is to examine the costs of the impasse going forward relative to alternative possible outcomes so that policymakers can make fully informed decisions. We address three questions:

---

[3]   Keinon, 2014.

[4]   Survey research by the Palestinian Center for Policy and Survey Research, multiple polls, including June 5–7, 2014, and August 26–30, 2014 (Palestinian Center for Policy and Survey Research, 2014b, 2014c).

[5]   American diplomatic efforts during the Bill Clinton, George W. Bush, and Barack Obama administrations are described in Kurtzer et al., 2013; Rabinovich, 2011; Qurei, 2006; Ross, 2005; and Thrall, 2014.

1. What are the net costs and benefits to Israelis and Palestinians if the current impasse endures over the next ten years, relative to several alternative trajectories that the conflict could take?
2. What noneconomic factors surrounding the conflict might influence the parties' assessments of the value of alternative trajectories?
3. What are the longer-term implications—beyond the next ten years—of the impasse for Israel, the WBG, and the international community?

As many studies, including our own, clearly demonstrate, a peaceful resolution of the conflict is the best option economically for both Palestinians and Israelis, while a return to violence is very costly to both sides. Yet the conflict persists. Perhaps the parties do not properly recognize the economic benefits of an agreement, or the economic benefits of an agreement have not been and may not be high enough to outweigh the imputed costs of such intangible factors as distrust, religion, and fear of relinquishing some degree of security. In our discussion, we suggest what some of those factors might be.

1.2. Research Approach

In an initial scoping trip conducted in early 2013, we asked a wide range of Palestinians, Israelis, Americans, and Europeans from diverse political perspectives how RAND could make a meaningful contribution toward resolving the impasse between Israel and Palestinians. The most consistent response was that RAND could play a valuable role by analyzing the true costs of present trends if they endure and comparing those results with the costs of feasible alternative scenarios. Our unique contribution would be to give all parties comprehensive, reliable information about available choices and their expected costs and consequences.

With this goal in mind, we conducted a number of research trips to the region, where we interviewed more than 200 individuals—Israelis, Palestinians, and members of the international community—representing diverse perspectives and goals. The group included intellectuals, academics, representatives from nongovernmental organizations (NGOs), business leaders, security experts, and government officials.[6] We gathered relevant data and identified issues for which additional research was required. We also conducted an extensive literature review on key dimensions of the problem, and, where possible and necessary, we conducted original research to clarify and define issues and derive results.

---

[6]   Those we interviewed included Gazan business leaders and Gazans based in Ramallah who were serving as government officials, but we were not able to gain permission to visit Gaza.

Focus of Our Analyses

We integrated findings from our fieldwork, the literature review, and our supplemental analyses to identify the aspects of the conflict that we would consider. We focused primarily on two aspects: (1) **economics**, including both the performance of the Israeli and Palestinian economies and expenditures associated with the path the two parties are taking as relates to the conflict, and (2) **security**—both direct costs and perceived security risks. We also considered how less tangible factors, such as distrust, religiosity, and fear of relinquishing some degree of security, might affect the conflict.

Methodology

Assessing the costs—especially the opportunity costs—of the impasse requires a methodology for comparing outcomes for Israelis and Palestinians under alternative assumptions about political conditions. For example, one might compare some outcome related to the current economic performance of Israel and the WBG to what that outcome might have been if a two-state solution based on the Oslo Accords had been implemented. We use this approach of assessing "counterfactuals" to consider answers to our three questions.

In an effort to avoid ambiguity in our discussion, we have attempted to define our terminology precisely. We use the term *Israel* to refer to the State of Israel and to the territory defined by the Green Line. We use *Israelis* to designate Israel's inhabitants in general and *Jewish Israelis* and *Palestinian citizens of Israel* when appropriate to distinguish between these groups. We use the term *Palestine* or *West Bank and Gaza* (*WBG*) to refer to the area of the West Bank and the Gaza Strip as defined by the Green Line. We use *State of Palestine* when appropriate to refer to such an entity, especially with respect to our two-state solution scenario, and *Palestinian Authority* (PA) to refer to the entity established after the Oslo Accords to administer parts of the WBG. We use the term *Palestinians* to refer to the inhabitants (except settlers) of the West Bank, Gaza, and East Jerusalem.

Analytic Framework

Figure 1.1 summarizes our analytic framework. We estimate how economic and security outcomes will evolve over ten years through 2024 if the political and economic characteristics of the present trends, including periodic disruptions, flare-ups of military engagement, and continued construction of Israeli settlements, continue along their current trajectories. As we discuss, key inputs to present trends include aspects of the conflict's history, the economic development of Israel and the WBG, and the politics of the region. If the key parameters of the present trends continue on the same trajectory, the impasse continues.

We use the present trends scenario as a baseline reference and then compare such outcomes as gross domestic product (GDP) or perceptions of security under the reference case to those under five alternative trajectories:

Figure 1.1
Framework for Analysis

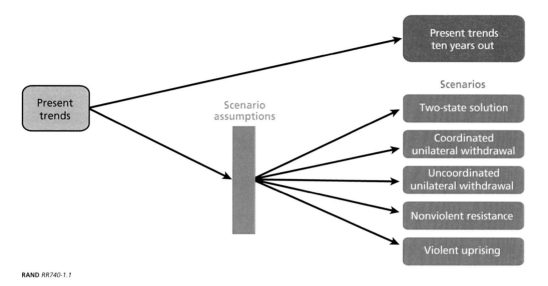

RAND *RR740-1.1*

- **Two-state solution**, in which a sovereign Palestinian state is established alongside Israel. Our two-state solution scenario is based on an amalgam of the Clinton Parameters, the Olmert-Abbas package, and the track-two Geneva Initiative.
- **Coordinated unilateral withdrawal** of Israel from parts or all of the West Bank. Our assumptions here are based on the work of Blue White Future (BWF) and the Institute for National Security Studies (INSS).[7]
- **Uncoordinated unilateral withdrawal.** We modify assumptions for coordinated unilateral withdrawal to reflect a situation in which the Palestinians do not agree to or do not coordinate with Israel's unilateral actions.
- **Nonviolent resistance** by Palestine in pursuit of its national aspirations. The variant of this scenario we consider includes Palestinians' legal efforts at the UN and other world bodies, continued support for trade restrictions on Israel, and nonviolent demonstrations.
- **Violent uprising.** In this scenario, we consider the effects of a violent Palestinian uprising perhaps emanating from Gaza but also including the West Bank and possibly participation from foreign terrorists.

This comparison allows us to gauge the costs and benefits of the impasse by comparing them in a rigorous and systematic way to the costs and benefits of alternative futures.

---

[7] BWF, 2012; Yadlin, 2014b; "Former MI Chief," 2014; G. Cohen, 2014.

In designing each of these scenarios, we derive economic and security assumptions based on historical precedent, a review of the existing literature, and conversations with subject matter experts. The scenarios themselves were designed with four core criteria in mind: (1) They should be credible, (2) they must be sufficiently distinct from other scenarios to warrant analysis, (3) they must be feasible in the ten-year time frame for the analysis, and (4) the counterfactual approach that we use must be appropriate for them. For example, we do not consider a one-state outcome as a potential sixth scenario because our counterfactual methodology requires comparison of distinct Israeli and Palestinian polities over a ten-year time period, and we do not think that achieving a one-state solution is feasible within ten years.

The specific assumptions underlying each scenario are described in detail in Chapter Four. *We use these scenarios as possible alternative futures for analytic purposes, but we make **no predictions** about the likely evolution of any of them.* The reality that evolves is likely to be a mixture of some aspects of all the scenarios presented here. For example, the Gaza war in the summer of 2014, the subsequent recriminations, the Palestinian diplomatic moves, and the punitive responses from Israel belie what we originally defined as present trends and seem more akin to what we have called nonviolent resistance.

1.3. Structure of the Report

Our discussion is organized as follows:

- Chapter Two describes our counterfactual approach in more detail and describes the inputs to the counterfactual strategy.
- In Chapter Three, we define the key outcomes in the areas of economics and security that we anticipated would evolve over the next ten years.
- Chapter Four describes in detail the assumptions underlying each scenario.
- Chapters Five through Nine compare key outcomes if present trends continue with those outcomes in each of the alternative scenarios.
- Chapter Ten summarizes the type of economic support that has been provided to Israel and to the Palestinians since World War II from the United States, Europe, and international bodies, such as the UN, and explores how the support is likely to vary across the different scenarios.
- Chapter Eleven examines some of the important intangible factors surrounding the conflict.
- Chapter Twelve summarizes study findings, highlighting comparisons of the five scenarios and drawing conclusions.

CHAPTER TWO

Analytical Framework

Specific analytical tools and literature differ across the multiple components of our analysis. However, they are all germane to same question: "How do the conditions of present trends evolve over the coming decade compared with how they might evolve under alternative scenarios?" This chapter describes the methodology we use to answer this question.

2.1. Overview of Counterfactual Approach

Understanding the costs of the political impasse requires a methodology to compare conditions that Israelis and Palestinians experience under present trends and what conditions might occur under alternative scenarios. Specifically, we look at the impact on the economy from missed opportunities for greater economic productivity (opportunity costs) and from unproductive expenditures directly attributable to the impasse (direct costs) by following one trajectory rather than another. The focus for our analysis is the next ten years—notionally, from 2015 to 2024. Unless otherwise indicated, all costs are denoted in constant 2014 U.S. dollars.

This counterfactual approach is what we use to explore the cost of the political impasse. Counterfactuals allow us to explore, in a systematic way, how specific outcomes might have differed if conditions had been different.[1]

Figure 2.1 provides a simple hypothetical example. An event (in this case, a violent uprising) with economic costs takes place in year 2. We are seeking to measure the immediate consequences of this economic event—how it impacts GDP, for example. In our hypothetical case, GDP rises along the long-term path until year 2, when the event occurs, and then it falls for a two-year period, during which time it otherwise would have grown. This is shown by the downturn in the red line (the gray line is the status quo base case).

---

[1] Though there were earlier academic precedents in economics (e.g., Fogel, 1964) and security studies (e.g., Churchill, 1931), the counterfactual methodology was first popularized by Hawthorn, 1991.

Figure 2.1
Illustration of Counterfactual Approach: A Violent Uprising

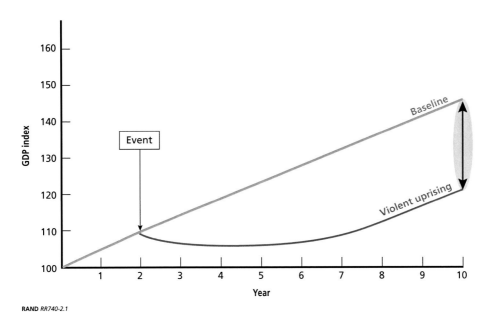

GDP growth returns to normal by the seventh year; however, there is a substantial and persistent difference in GDP after ten years, as shown in the large divergence between the gray and red lines. Specifically, the economy under the conditions of the impasse grows by 45 percent in ten years (base case), while it has grown by only 20 percent in the violent uprising trajectory in the tenth year.

In Figure 2.2, we add an alternative event: a political agreement in year 2. This event has positive impacts: GDP grows more quickly (the blue line) than it does in the base case (the gray line). In this hypothetical example, GDP rises to 160 in the tenth year, about one-third faster than it would have if the base case had persisted.

One might also wish to compare the difference between the outcomes of these two cases. In the baseline scenario of the political impasse, the GDP index has grown from 100 to 145. In the negative trajectory, GDP has grown to 120; in the positive trajectory, GDP has grown to 160. The difference between the gray line and the red line represents the difference between present trends and a violent uprising in year 10. Analogously, the difference between the gray line and the blue line represents the difference between what would happen under present trends and a two-state solution. The arrow highlights the difference between potential GDPs if a political settlement had been achieved instead of a violent uprising having occurred.

The total cost (or benefit) over the ten-year period would be the total of the areas between the baseline and the negative (red) trajectory or between the baseline and the positive (blue) trajectory. The total cost is more difficult to calculate because it requires that we know how the positive and negative trajectories will evolve. They

Figure 2.2
Illustration of Counterfactual Approach: Comparison of Scenarios with Positive and Negative Impacts

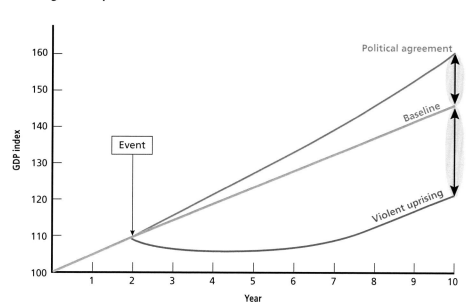

could evolve in various ways. For example, in the case of a two-state solution, it is commonly thought that short-term security costs will rise for both parties before falling. Thus, the positive (blue) trajectory would initially be below the gray baseline before moving above it in the later years.

Our counterfactual approach has several advantages:

1. It provides a unifying framework for exploring ways in which relevant outcomes are likely to be affected by alternative future trajectories of the Israeli-Palestinian conflict.
2. It requires that we clearly articulate the many factors that can influence each of the broad outcome categories.
3. Modeling the scenarios using this approach requires that we precisely state our assumptions about how these factors will be influenced by each scenario; this increases the transparency in our approach.
4. The counterfactual analysis for economics and for direct security costs provides results as dollar values, which are a familiar unit of analysis.

The counterfactual approach also has several limitations: First, the results are driven by and sensitive to the assumptions. The alternative scenarios we use have some historical precedents within this conflict or elsewhere, but we also base assumptions on other available evidence and on discussions with subject matter experts.

Second, with certain important exceptions, we conducted this research assuming that changes across each of these different dimensions are essentially independent of each other. So, for instance, while we explicitly consider how a changing security environment may affect both economic and sociopsychological well-being, in general, we do not attempt to quantify reciprocal effects—for example, how economic improvements affect security. Such simplification is necessary for tractability, allowing us to easily sum the results of each change, but it does not accurately reflect real-world linkages locally or regionally.

Finally, we have limited the time horizon for our analysis to ten years—effectively 2004 to 2014. Both positive and negative effects under each scenario could change dramatically in the longer run.

We now turn our attention to the elements of economics and security that are the inputs to our counterfactual analysis.

2.2. Economic Inputs

The existing literature focuses on the potential economic benefits of a two-state solution. We focus primarily on the characteristics of the political impasse that either create unnecessary expenditures or impede economic productivity as compared with a two-state solution. These characteristics are generally the factors of most relevance to all of the scenarios considered in Chapter Four.[2]

We divide our discussion of economic inputs into direct and opportunity costs associated with the conflict for each economy.

Direct costs are the budgetary or financial costs, whether at the governmental or household level, related to the conflict. They include both expenditures on the conflict (e.g., spending on security) and forgone private or public revenue (e.g., loss of salaries for Palestinian workers in Israel who no longer have access to cross-border employment opportunities because of the conflict). We focus on direct costs incurred since 1999, as this is the reference period we used for calculating present trends.

Opportunity costs are the economic opportunities lost because of the conflict. The primary type of opportunity cost is the lost opportunity for production—whether in a factory, field, or mine—resulting from restrictions placed on international trade, investment, or mobility of people. For each opportunity cost aspect identified, we estimate the magnitude of the change in GDP as a result of the change in availability or

---

[2]   Costs and benefits of both the status quo and alternative scenarios can be quite different for various subgroups in both Israeli and Palestinian society.

flow of resources or goods and services caused by normalized relations between the two economies.[3]

For transparency of analysis, we present direct and opportunity costs separately in our analysis of each scenario. However, we make two additional assumptions that allow us to report an aggregated "economic outcome" for each scenario that combines the opportunity costs and direct costs of each of the scenarios. First, we assume that any direct costs are reflected by a corresponding change in government spending. Second, we assume that the fiscal multiplier for each country is a conservative 0.5— that is, for each $100 in government spending, the GDP of the country increases by $50,[4] and the export-to-GDP multiplier is assumed to be 0.93.[5]

2.2.1. Direct Costs (Expenditures)

The political impasse imposes very different types of direct costs on Israelis and Palestinians. For the Israelis, the primary direct costs are expenditures stemming from the conflict (e.g., direct budgetary expenditures on security and settlements by the Israeli government). These data are typically not reported directly; for several reasons, the Israeli government does not make this information public.[6] However, various domestic and international NGOs have developed estimates on which we draw.[7]

For the Palestinians, the direct costs comprise both additional expenditures and lost revenues attributable to the conflict, including the destruction of property, quotas on Palestinian labor, restrictions on the movement of goods and labor, excess spending on social services, loss of tax revenue, banking costs, and stipends they pay to the families of prisoners held in Israel.

Israeli Direct Cost 1: Costs of Security

The Israeli government spent approximately $16.2 billion on security in 2013.[8] We estimate that just under 10 percent of these total expenditures—approximately $1.3 billion—is directly attributable to this conflict. Based on 1999–2014 data, this estimate includes approximately $800 million in sunk costs and an additional $450 million in variable costs. However, we do not anticipate that these security costs will fall signifi-

---

[3]   A second type of opportunity cost not explored in this analysis is forgone (or realized) new opportunities for consumption of either cheaper or different products.

[4]   Existing estimates from the Bank of Israel suggest that the number is higher, at 0.7, but we assume a conservative 0.5 for both economies (Bank of Israel, 2013).

[5]   Friedman and Hercowitz, 2010.

[6]   In recent years, some members of the Israeli Knesset have pressed for a better accounting of settlement costs, with varying degrees of success.

[7]   UN, 2013, paragraph 9.

[8]   Defense expenditures are 5.7 percent of GDP (Bank of Israel, undated), and GDP data are from Israel Central Bureau of Statistics, undated(b).

cantly in any of our ten-year scenarios, although defense expenditures are assumed to increase during years of conflict, as previously experienced.[9]

There are two types of Israeli security costs. The first is sunk costs, which we estimate to be at most $800 million per annum. This is based on our estimates of $10.8 billion to $12.0 billion for the 1999–2014 time period, which include both (1) one-time investments in military infrastructure or hardware associated with the conflict and (2) one-time expenditures associated with specific operations or military activities. These costs are summarized in Table 2.1.

The variable security costs, the recurring annual expenditures associated with the conflict, account for an additional $450 million per year in government expenditures. The recurring annual expenditures include the maintenance of the separation barrier and a variety of security measures either to protect settlement communities or to

Table 2.1
Security Sunk Costs (in billions of U.S. dollars)

Investment		One-Time Expenditure	
Category	Cost	Category	Cost
Construction of security barrier	$3.2 billion to $3.7 billion[a]	Second Intifada	$0.6 billion to $0.7 billion[b]
Iron Dome	$0.9 billion to $1 billion[c]	Operation Protective Edge	$2.3 billion[d]
Gaza fortification	$0.2 billion to $0.3 billion[e]	Disengagement from Gaza	$2.3 billion to $2.6 billion[e]
		Operation Cast Lead	$1.2 billion to $1.4 billion[e]

[a] The security barrier was constructed by Israel in order to prevent Palestinian West Bank residents from moving uninspected through areas of the West Bank where major settlement blocks had been constructed with the goal of reducing risks of terrorism and violence. As of spring 2013, 525 km of the security barrier had been completed, at an estimated total cost of $2.6 billion, implying that each kilometer had cost roughly $5 million (Busbridge, 2013). When completed, the security barrier is expected to be approximately 790 km long and cost $4 million to $5 million per kilometer (Swirski, 2012, citing Brodet, 2007).

[b] *Haaretz* estimated that the additional cost incurred from troop deployments during the uprising was Israeli new shekels (NIS) 2 billion to 2.5 billion in nominal terms (Bassok, 2003a).

[c] Swirski, 2012. For the cost of Tamir missiles used during operations, see discussion on Operation Protective Edge within the variable security costs discussion in note d below.

[d] These are direct costs only, as reported in Klein, Handelsman, and Sternlicht, 2014. Although this source does not provide an itemized list of costs, it is likely to include the expenditures on the Tamir missiles used for the Iron Dome system—the total bill for the missiles fired is estimated to be as high $90 million (R. Smith, 2014), though the U.S. Congress provided $225 million in emergency funding to replenish the Iron Dome Tamir missile reserves (Sparshott, 2014). Note that Protective Edge had additional opportunity costs, including $1.3 billion in lost economic growth, $440 million in lost tax revenue, $30 million in restitution to communities near Gaza, and $15 million in property damage (Klein, Handelsman, and Sternlicht, 2014).

[e] Swirski, 2012.

---

[9]   We estimate that defense expenditures increase by 9 percent during years of conflict. This is based on comparing defense spending during 2001–2003 and 2000 using data from Bank of Israel, undated.

protect Israel from potential threats originating in the WBG.[10] These annual variable security costs are as follows:[11]

- maintenance of separation barrier: $260 million per year[12]
- emergency security expenditures: $79 million to $91 million per year[13]
- coordination activities: $58 million to $66 million per year[14]
- security in East Jerusalem: $17 million to $22 million per year.[15]

Our estimates of these variable costs do not include any troop-related costs. Israel currently bears the costs of maintaining approximately 10,000 troops dedicated to security for the West Bank.[16] However, as we do not foresee a meaningful change in the size of the Israel Defense Forces (IDF) within a ten-year period in any of our scenarios, we anticipate that any reductions in an IDF presence in the West Bank would be met by a near-identical increase in force size along the Jordanian border or another defensive posture.[17] Thus, although there is a "cost" of paying for these troops, it is not a cost that is relevant for our counterfactual analysis.

Israeli Direct Cost 2: Settlements

The Israeli government also provides a variety of direct and indirect non–security-related economic support to those in settlement communities in the West Bank, including East Jerusalem. Estimates of the number of settlers in 2012 in the West Bank and East Jerusalem are between 500,000 and 650,000, with an estimated 100,000 living to

---

[10] Our estimates do not include expenditures on privately hired security, as we focus only on Israeli governmental expenditures.

[11] The Transportation Ministry budgeted approximately NIS 10 million per year ($3 million) for bus armoring during 2011 and 2012 (Ofran, 2010).

[12] Matar, 2012. Busbridge, 2013, reports a significantly lower estimated of $1.5 million but cites the same source.

[13] Ofran, 2010, estimates NIS 317 million to 319 million ($79 million to $91 million) per year in emergency security expenses for the settlements and communities near the security barrier for 2011 and 2012.

[14] The Israeli budget contains a line item for "coordination of activities in the territories" as part of the first schedule defense budget. For fiscal year (FY) 2013, this item was NIS 101 million, plus NIS 131 million in revenue-dependent expenditure (State of Israel Ministry of Finance, 2013).

[15] The Housing Ministry budget contains an explicit budget line for security in East Jerusalem. The range for this estimate was between NIS 70 million and NIS 76 million per year for 2011 and 2012, or between $17.5 million and $22 million (Ofran, 2010). Ofran, 2010, reports that settlers can be reimbursed by the government for protecting their vehicles from stones. The source of these expenditures (i.e., the ministry responsible) is uncertain.

[16] An existing estimate for the cost of maintaining these troops is $0.6 billion (Bassok, 2003b). Estimates are available only from the period before the Second Intifada.

[17] There are efforts to reduce troop requirements through the use of technological enablers, including unmanned aerial vehicles, unmanned ground vehicles, and fixed defense sites with remote-control weapons, in addition to increased reliance on air defense (Johnson, 2011).

the east of the security barrier.[18] In this study, as a conservative estimate, we have used 600,000 settlers in our analysis, although we recognize that this number has grown rapidly (about 5.3 percent per year) over the decade ending in 2012 and even more rapidly in the past few years.[19] Non–security-related settlement costs are more difficult to estimate than security costs for several reasons. Most importantly, settlement-specific data are generally intentionally obfuscated in Israeli budgetary documents.[20] In addition, settlements are supported through both public and private funding sources (e.g., the Jewish National Fund), so it is often difficult to identify what is being financed through public expenditures. Finally, it is reasonable to expect that some spending on infrastructure, social programs, and other transfer payments would be necessary for the settler population regardless of where they live (i.e., within or outside the Green Line); thus, not all direct spending within the settlements is, strictly speaking, a cost related to the conflict.

We estimate that the Israeli government spends approximately $1.1 billion per year on the settlements. Our estimates are slightly larger than existing estimates that suggest that the annual variable costs for the settlements run from approximately $650 million to $800 million.[21] However, we still believe that our estimates are lower bounds of the actual cost, as individual ministries have a variety of specific programs

---

[18] The estimate of the number of settlers east of the security barrier is from BWF, 2014. According to the UN, 2013, estimations of the current settlement population in the West Bank, including East Jerusalem, range between 500,000 and 650,000. The settler population living in the West Bank (excluding East Jerusalem) has almost tripled since 1993. During the past decade, it grew at an average yearly rate of 5.3 percent, compared with 1.8 percent for the Israeli population as a whole. In his May 24, 2011, speech to the U.S. Congress, the prime minister of Israel mentioned that 650,000 Israelis "live beyond the 1967 lines." Of these settlers, roughly 60 percent are in the West Bank and 40 percent are in East Jerusalem (Fisk, 2010).

[19] UN, 2013.

[20] Gorenberg, 2011, reports respondents as saying that (1) "The [housing] ministry's budget does not make it possible to identify what portion . . . is allocated to Judea, Samaria, and the Gaza District'" (p. 109) and (2) "Total outlay [for settlements] was 'a bigger secret than the [Mordechai] Vanunu affair.'" Rowe, 2008, reports that "calculating an exact figure [for settlement spending] is essentially impossible because the majority of funding is allocated . . . in a state budget that does not distinguish between which funds are channeling to Israel proper and which are being used in the Occupied Territories of Palestine."

[21] Amsterdamski, 2012 (quoted in L. Friedman, 2012), reports a cost of NIS 27 billion over a ten-year period. Peace Now (Ofran, 2010) reports that the total annual financial cost of the settlements for the Israeli government is between NIS 2 billion and 2.5 billion per year. Dror Tsaban estimated an annual cost of NIS 1.85 billion in 2002 (Bassok, 2003b). Bassok (2003b) reported a 2003 estimate of NIS 2.4 billion that included NIS 130 million in 2003 shekels for income tax breaks that no longer exist and NIS 70 million in 2003 shekels for an Oslo grant and intifada grant from the Interior Ministry; they claimed that the costs were relatively constant from 1990 to 2003. Americans for Peace Now, 2012, estimates that the additional costs for settlements in 2012 relative to the Israeli per capita average totaled at least NIS 1.6 billion; this includes all "direct unique expenditures" in the territories plus the additional per capita spending in the territories relative to the Israeli average. In 2005, *USA Today* ("No One Knows Full Cost of Israel's Settlement Ambitions," 2005) reported that government officials had put total settlement expenditures of $50 billion to $60 billion since 1977. *Haaretz* (Bassok, 2003a) reported total settlement costs of NIS 45 billion (approximately $11 billion to $13 billion) from 1967 through 2003.

targeted toward settlers. Because settlement expenditures are not reported by the Israeli government, these costs cannot be fully calculated.

The first major cost is for infrastructure, which we estimate at approximately $700 million per annum. We estimate total settlement expenditures during the 1999–2013 time period as approximately $9 billion; this estimate reflects the cost that would be incurred in order to rebuild equivalent infrastructure. The total value of settlement infrastructure constructed from 1973 to 2009 has been estimated at $19 billion, including[22]

- housing stock (dwellings, houses, and caravans): $12.7 billion[23]
- education facilities: $1.3 billion[24]
- production facilities (agricultural, industrial, and commercial): $1.3 billion[25]
- public institutions: $1.3 billion[26]
- roads and other infrastructure: $2.5 billion.[27]

---

[22] This is based on Arieli et al., 2009, as delineated in the following footnotes. Other estimates give comparable numbers. As an example, the Marco Center for Political Economy estimated the construction costs of Israeli development in the West Bank at $17.4 billion in 2010, 78 percent of which is housing ("Israeli Settlements an Economic Choice," 2010).

[23] Arieli et al., 2009, include 39,483 dwellings at $5.5 billion, 18,462 houses at $6.0 billion, and 5,539 mobile homes at $0.1 billion (stated in 2012 dollars using an expenditure deflator reported in World Bank, 2015b). Americans for Peace Now, 2013, provides a lower estimate of only $50 million per annum in expenditures on housing based on (1) estimated excess spending in the settlements by the Ministry of Construction and Housing and (2) additional spending on relocating an outpost.

[24] Arieli et al., 2009, include 255 kindergartens at $486 million, 237 schools at $505 million, 11 colleges at $156 million, and 24 libraries at $12 million (stated in 2012 dollars using an expenditure deflator reported in World Bank, 2015b). Another source provides a similar estimate of $55 million per annum: Americans for Peace Now, 2013, reports a $40 million budget for the annual construction and development budget of schools in the territories, a $14 million budget for the development of the university in Ariel, and a budget of $30,000 for the Council for Higher Education in Judea and Samaria.

[25] Arieli et al., 2009, include 29 gas stations at $8 million, 140 shopping centers at $191 million, 427 industrial facilities at $760 million, 138 hotels and hostels at $271 million, 133 dairy barns at $388 million, and 54 water towers at $3 million (stated in 2012 dollars using an expenditure deflator reported in World Bank, 2015b).

[26] Arieli et al., 2009, include 656 public institutions at $578 million, 322 synagogues at $143 million, 119 ritual baths at $14 million, 232 sports facilities at $401 million, and 54 shelters at $10 million. The value of 189 public parks covering 844 square miles was not estimated (stated in 2012 dollars using an expenditure deflator reported in World Bank, 2015b).

[27] Arieli et al., 2009, include 775,000 m of internal roads at $1.16 billion; 308,000 m of intercity roads at $889 million; 616,000 m of water, sewage, and canal pipes at $267 million; and 616,000 m of power lines at $27 million (stated in 2012 dollars using an expenditure deflator reported in World Bank, 2015b). Other estimates suggest that this cost could be as high as $150 million per annum. *Haaretz* (Bassok, 2003a) estimated approximately NIS 400 million (in 2003 shekels) in extra road expenditures annually, NIS 80 million (in 2003 shekels) on electricity infrastructure, and NIS 50 million (in 2003 shekels) on water infrastructure. Americans for Peace Now, 2013, reported 2011 expenditures by the Transportation Ministry in the settlements were NIS 307 million or $77 million to $88 million. Peace Now (Ofran, 2010) reported that 2009 budget line items

Assuming that the total sunk cost is directly proportional to the number of dwellings constructed during that period, available data on construction in the West Bank lead to estimates of $9 billion and $21 billion in settlement sunk costs for, respectively, 1999 to 2013 and 1973 to 2013.[28]

The second type of costs is direct noninfrastructure subsidies provided to these communities, which we estimate at an additional $270 million per annum. Variable costs of the settlements can be divided, roughly, into the following categories, with approximate annual values:

- direct support to communities: $180 million[29]
- direct subsidy to exporters: $3 million[30]
- wage subsidies for educators: $60 million[31]
- tourism: $4 million[32]
- solar energy subsidy: $2 million[33]
- health spending: $20 million[34]

---

include subsidized transportation by bus for "other populations" (settlers and Haredim), totaling approximately NIS 31 million ($8 million to $9 million), which had increased to NIS 35 million by 2011.

[28] These estimates are based on the number of dwellings built during the different time frames. From 1973 to 2009, there were a total of 71,328 dwellings; from 1999 to 2013, there were a total of 32,975 dwellings; and from 1973 to 2013, there were a total of 77,375 dwellings built (Israel Central Bureau of Statistics, 2013a, p. 65).

[29] American for Peace Now, 2013, estimates total "overspending" and other costs of the settlements, excluding the Ministries of Education and Interior, at a total of $150 million to $170 million. This included $56 million to $64 million in excess spending to balance budgets. The Interior Ministry also spent NIS 124 million, or $31 million to $35 million, on specific grants in the territories, and NIS 12 million (approximately $3 million) in "Minister Grants."

[30] The state budget included exporter compensation of NIS 11 million in 2011 and 2012 (approximately $3 million) for compensation from loss of revenue caused by European Union (EU) trade policy (Ofran, 2010; L. Friedman, 2012). The EU does not recognize goods from the territories as Israeli under the free-trade agreement.

[31] A teacher living in a settlement receives an estimated 12 to 20 percent more than a comparable teacher working in Israel proper. The higher salary reflects rent subsidies, subsidies for travel expenses related to training, and payment into the training system (UN, 2013). These teachers also receive extra seniority (Rowe, 2008). As nearly 25 percent of employed persons living in the West Bank are teachers, with many of these teachers working in Israel proper, there are nearly 25,000 educators receiving at least $2,400 extra per year. The estimated number of teachers combines the 25-percent number from L. Friedman, 2012, and an estimated 100,000 employed individuals overall in the West Bank settlements (Organisation for Economic Co-operation and Development [OECD], undated). The average salary of a beginning teacher in Israel in 2008 was just over $18,000. Bassok, 2003a, reported a slightly lower estimate of 2003 NIS 100 million for all department programs, and Americans for Peace Now, 2013, reported an estimate of NIS 103 million.

[32] The Ministry of Tourism spent NIS 785,000 to promote tourism in the West Bank in 2011 and invested NIS 17 million ($4 million to $5 million) in three archaeological sites in the territories as part of the Heritage Plan (Americans for Peace Now, 2013).

[33] Americans for Peace Now, 2013, reports that the Israel Electric Corporation, regulated by the Ministry of Energy, purchases solar energy as NIS 1.61 per kilowatt-hour (kWh) in Israel proper, while paying NIS 2.04 in the settlements.

[34] *Haaretz* (Bassok, 2003a) reports the cost at approximately NIS 75 million (approximately $19 million to $22 million) per year as calculated in 2003. Later sources did not report additional health care spending; the reason is unknown.

- other: *unknown value*
  - wage subsidies for social workers: total magnitude not available[35]
  - firm tax subsidy: total magnitude not available[36]
  - water subsidy: total magnitude not available.[37]

The third type of cost is the support provided by the Israeli government to the World Zionist Organization. This organization, which receives its approximate $140 million annual budget from the Israeli government, spends most of that amount on settlements in the West Bank.[38]

Potential Future Israeli Direct Cost: Dissolution of Palestinian Authority

The dissolution of the PA could occur as either a Palestinian strategy to improve long-term conditions in the West Bank and Gaza or as a side effect of ongoing conditions. While this would have drastic impacts throughout the Palestinian economy, many argue that the Israelis would have to assume some share of the total cost of providing health care, education, and other essential services.[39] This direct cost could be substantial, as expenditures by the ministries of social affairs, health, and education account for approximately 40 percent of public expenditures by the PA, or nearly $1.4 billion in 2012.[40]

---

[35] The Ministry of Labor and Social Affairs offers benefits similar to those of teachers in Priority A development areas and slightly smaller levels of benefits for social workers in Priority B areas (three years' seniority, 75 percent reimbursement of travel expenses, and 75 percent financing of employee's contribution to the in-service training fund). Spending on these programs is presumably included in the figures on direct ministry spending listed in direct community subsidies above.

[36] The Ministry of Industry and Trade offers both a grant program and a tax program as investment incentives in Priority A and B areas (Rowe, 2008). Ninety-one current settlements are listed as priority areas for development (UN, 2013). The grant program provides grants of between 15 percent and 24 percent (depending on type and magnitude of investment) of land development and building investment for eligible projects in Priority A areas and 10 percent for Priority B areas. This program also provides discounts on the company tax and dividend tax, depending on the proportion of foreign investment. Alternatively, a company can forgo rights to a grant in exchange for six to ten years of tax exemption (State of Israel Ministry of Industry, Trade, and Labor, undated).

[37] The MA'AN Development Center (2012, p. 20) reports that the magnitude is approximately eight times less per volume unit of water. However, as this is not a comparison between per-unit expenditures for settler households and those within Israel proper and may involve, e.g., alternative conveyance mechanisms, this figure may not be a strict subsidy to settlement consumption of water. Nevertheless, there does appear to be evidence that per-unit costs differ between Israeli and Palestinian populations in the West Bank.

[38] The budget is reported as NIS 500 million (Schlesinger, 2014).

[39] Shikaki, 2014.

[40] Data for 2012 indicate a total of 41.7 percent of nonbudget servicing–related expenditures (World Bank, 2013a). The estimate uses a value of $3.4 billion for total expenditures, as reported in Figure 3.3.

Palestinian Direct Cost 1: Destruction of Private Property and Public Infrastructure
In addition to loss of life, the destruction of Palestinian infrastructure has imposed substantial direct costs on the Palestinian economy. Historically, the destruction of private homes was the primary form taken, with an estimated 20,000 private homes destroyed for military, security, or administrative reasons.[41]

Since the beginning of the Second Intifada, there has been significant damage to public and private nonhousing infrastructure, with at least 10 percent of the productive capital stock destroyed. In the middle of the Second Intifada, in an operation lasting slightly longer than one month (March 29, 2002, to May 3, 2002), Israeli's Operation Defensive Shield caused an estimated $930 million of direct physical damage in the WBG.[42] The three weeks of Operation Cast Lead (December 27, 2008, to January 18, 2009) caused an estimated $1.3 billion in direct damage to infrastructure in Gaza; this included $1.1 billion in damage to physical infrastructure and an estimated $180 million in damage to agriculture.[43] The destruction to physical infrastructure included partial destruction of at least 219 factories, representing a large share of Gaza's limited industrial capability.[44] A third operation, a series of missile strikes against the only power plant in Palestine in response to the abduction of Gilad Shalit, damaged a facility that was a joint investment of a U.S. corporation (Enron) and insured by the U.S. government;[45] note that this power plant was destroyed again during Operation Protective Edge. Israel has maintained that the destruction was accidental.[46] Most recently, Operation Protective Edge caused at least $1.7 billion in damage to physical infrastructure in Gaza, though some estimates of the damage and the reconstruction requirements are substantially higher. There is significant disagreement around these

---

[41]   Estimates are from Dajani, 2005, p. 16.

[42]   This estimate, from the World Bank, 2003, includes damage from October 2000 to December 2002. It estimates the total replacement cost of this damage as closer to $1.7 billion. The West Bank suffered about two-thirds of this damage and Gaza the remaining third. Damage to public infrastructure (e.g., roads, electricity and water networks) accounted for roughly one-third of this damage; agriculture accounted for another third of the total damage; and private buildings, which included both commercial buildings and housing, accounted for another 20 percent. Operations before Operation Defensive Shield accounted for approximately $300 million of this damage.

[43]   Both these numbers are as reported in UN Conference on Trade and Development (UNCTAD), 2010. For the first number, UNCTAD, 2010, cites Palestinian Central Bureau of Statistics (PCBS), 2009. Note that Western donors often bear the economic brunt of these costs—one prominent example was the Gaza Power Plant that was insured by the U.S. government's Overseas Private Investment Corporation (see footnote 45 in this chapter).

[44]   UN Office for the Coordination of Humanitarian Affairs (OCHA), 2009.

[45]   The Gaza Power Plant was American-owned, a joint investment of a U.S. corporation (Enron) and a Palestinian living in the diaspora (Sami Khoury), and insured by the U.S. government (e.g., Wilkie, 2014; "IDF Strike on Gaza Power Plant to Cost US," 2006). A secondary consequence of damage to the plant was a permanent 50-percent reduction in Gaza's independent electricity-generation capacity and increased dependence on Israel (World Bank Technical Team, 2007).

[46]   Ginsburg, 2014.

numbers,[47] and a recent PA report prepared for a donor conference in Cairo in October 2014 estimated the costs of rebuilding Gaza at just over $4 billion.[48]

Palestinian Direct Cost 2: Control of Territorial Waters

The Palestinians depend almost completely on Israel for electricity.[49] The annual direct cost of using Israeli electricity, as compared with using the natural gas available in off-shore waters, is estimated to be $560 million per annum.[50]

Palestinian Direct Cost 3: Quotas on Palestinian Labor in Israel

The growth of the Palestinian economy after 1967 was largely a result of increased integration with Israel's economy. From 1967 to 1987, total employment inside the West Bank and Gaza was almost completely stagnant—all labor force growth came from increases in Palestinian labor in Israel and the settlements. In addition, many Palestinians worked in other countries.[51] As shown in Figure 2.3, by the time of the First Intifada (1987 to 1993), there were nearly 130,000 Palestinian laborers working in Israel, accounting for more than 40 percent of the total Palestinian labor force.

From 1993 to 2000, the Palestinian economy stagnated; economic ties between Israel and the WBG were severely damaged following a spike of violence in 1993.[52] This separation affected the West Bank and East Jerusalem more severely, so that the economic gap between Gaza and both the West Bank and East Jerusalem narrowed.

---

[47] The largest estimates have come from the PA's Palestinian Economic Council for Development and Reconstruction (PECDAR) (e.g., "Scale of Gaza Destruction Unprecedented," 2014), though there is significant dispute about the accuracy of the estimated damage (e.g., Zilber, 2014).

[48] State of Palestine, 2014.

[49] Under the current system, electricity is imported directly from the Israel Electric Corporation. However, some electricity is generated within the West Bank or Gaza using generators run on refined petroleum products, such as diesel fuel. A small share of energy comes from Jordan and Egypt (World Bank, 2007b). Note that limited Palestinian generation is at least partially a result of Israeli policies, including restrictions on efficient power production as a result of restrictions on importing spare parts (ARIJ, 2011, p. 22) and directly damaging Palestinian energy production capability: Damage caused to the Gaza Power Plant reduced its effective production capability from 140 MW to 70 MW (ARIJ, 2011, p. 23).

[50] Natural gas production will save "the Palestinian economy close to $560 million annually" (Palestine Investment Fund, 2010, p. 59). Note that ARIJ (2011, p. 24) reports a slightly lower estimate of $440 million. Inefficiencies in power distribution as a result of the restrictions in Area C (World Bank, 2007b, p. 1) suggest that the total effect may be slightly higher. However, this may be an overestimate, as the Palestinians do not currently have the physical infrastructure to provide electricity at the low cost implied by ARIJ (2011).

[51] Abed, 1990; Shaban, 1993. Interestingly, a committee for "Developing the Administered Territories" that presented its findings in 1967 recommended that "Palestinian labour not be permitted into the Israeli economy while allowing free passage for goods and services between the Territories and Israel" (Arnon, 2007).

[52] The second was the signing of the Oslo Accords in 1993. An economic "peace dividend" was important to these accords, as there was a belief that it would create "political triumph and economic prosperity," a quote attributed to Shimon Peres, for Israel, Palestine, and Jordan (Haberman and Hedges, 1993). However, the benefits of the accords were, at most, modest with Israeli-imposed restrictions possibly playing a major role in the lack of significant benefits (e.g., Eshet, 1999; Calì, 2012).

Figure 2.3
Palestinian Employment in Israel and the Settlements

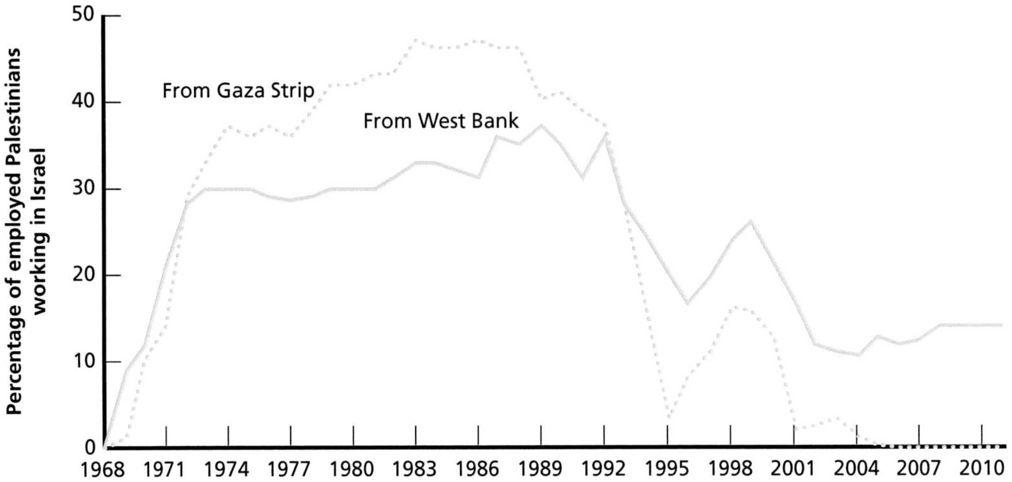

SOURCES: 1968–1994 data are from Farsakh, 2002; 1995–1999 data are from PCBS, 2011a; and 2000–2011 data are from PCBS, undated(g).
RAND RR740-2.3

The stagnation can be attributed in large measure to the dramatic fall in Palestinian labor employed in Israel in 1993, also shown in Figure 2.3, as a result of closures driven by the post–Oslo Accords period of instability. Israel introduced a permit policy in 1991 that allowed only married men who were over the age of 28 and who had received a security clearance from the Israeli military to work in Israel proper.[53] Although an implicit intention of the 1993 Paris Protocol was to have 70,000–100,000 Palestinians working in Israel,[54] the creation of the "closure system" in 1993 dramatically constrained employment.[55] Palestinian employment in Israel recovered somewhat during the late 1990s as the number of foreign and Israeli workers in the building industry dropped.[56] However, employment fell dramatically at the beginning of Second Intifada and the increased restrictions that followed shortly thereafter. The result was that, while Palestinian labor in Israel earned 23 percent of Palestine's gross

---

[53] Regulations on Palestinian labor in the settlements were more lax (Farsakh, 2002, p. 19).

[54] Arnon and Weinblatt, 2001. These authors note that the Palestinians picked a customs union during the Paris Accords over a free-trade agreement because they thought that it would allow for the freer flow of labor.

[55] This closure system was created during the total curfew placed on Palestinian labor during the 1991 Gulf War (Aranki, 2004). Restrictions on Palestinian labor became very tight in 1994 following a wave of suicide bombers.

[56] Farsakh, 2002.

national income (GNI)[57] before the Second Intifada, these workers were responsible for only 10 percent of total GNI in 2012.[58]

Employment opportunities in Israel have been and continue to be critical to the Palestinian economy. However, a potential Palestinian laborer in Israel today faces two major challenges. The first is that the number of work permits issued to Palestinians is capped at 50,000. The second is increased enforcement of restrictions on Palestinian labor mobility; about 70 percent of the workforce was illegal on the eve of the Second Intifada, as compared with approximately 50 percent today.[59] However, despite this increased enforcement and the cap on the number of work permits, there were an estimated 115,000 Palestinians working in Israel and its settlements as of 2013.[60]

The direct cost of these labor restrictions to the WBG is at least $0.5 billion. Using the approach proposed by Akkaya et al. (2008), if we assume that the total number of workers in absolute terms remained constant from 1999 to 2012, then there would have been 153,000 Palestinians working in Israel in 2013 instead of 115,000, and the additional 38,000 workers would have earned an additional $0.5 billion.[61] However, the direct cost of this restriction might be as high as $1.9 billion if we assume that the share of workers working in Israel in 1999 was maintained through 2012 (under such an assumption, there would have been 256,000 Palestinian workers working in Israel in 2012).

These estimates are likely lower bounds: Labor mobility into Israel was already restricted in 1999, indicating that the total potential for employment was likely higher.[62]

---

[57] GNI is a nation's GDP plus net income earned outside the country.

[58] Nominal GNI is from the "Main Economic Indicators" time series data, available from the Palestine Monetary Authority (PMA) website, 2015, and total earnings in Israel is an author estimate using PMA, undated.

[59] While only 46,500 permits were issued in 2000, there were more than 145,000 Palestinians working in Israel and the settlements (Farsakh, 2002). Farsakh, 2002, also reports that 50 to 70 percent of Palestinian workers in Israel were there illegally until the late 1980s but that that number fell to around 30 percent in the mid-1990s. Recent data are from PMA, 2014.

[60] This estimate of 115,000 is based on the PMA reports of a total labor force of 1.15 million persons (PMA, 2014) and the PCBS reports that 10 percent of the labor force is employed in Israel (PCBS, undated[g]).

[61] Akkaya et al., 2008, estimate that an average of $500 million was lost every year during the 2001 to 2005 time frame by comparing total earnings from labor after the Second Intifada and what was being earned before. Cali and Miaari, 2013, estimate $230 million per annum for closures using only data from the West Bank, which is analogous to what Akkaya et al., 2008, found for the West Bank.

[62] The "general closure system" was in force in 1999. Under this system, the number of permits issued, and thus the number of Palestinians legally working in Israel, ebbed and flowed with the political and security situation in the region, though the total number of permits remained roughly stable (Akkaya et al., 2008; Fischer, Alonso-Gamo, and von Allmen, 2001).

Palestinian Direct Cost 4: Restricted Freedom of Movement

A variety of Israeli-imposed restrictions limit the movement of Palestinians within the West Bank and in and out of Gaza. These restrictions are imposed through physical impediments, including checkpoints, road gates, roadblocks, earth mounds, trenches, road barriers, and earth walls; the most recently collected data indicated a total of 542 obstacles, including 61 staffed checkpoints (excluding those along the Green Line), 25 partially staffed checkpoints, and 436 unstaffed physical obstacles.[63] Underlying these physical restrictions is a permit system that controls the movement of Palestinians between Areas A, B, and C and between these areas of the West Bank and East Jerusalem, the Jordan Valley, and the settlements.[64]

The total cost of these restrictions on the movement of goods and labor is at least $185 million per annum. This estimate, from Palestinian Ministry of National Economy in cooperation with ARIJ, includes only the value of lost time for both commuters and shipping companies.[65]

Palestinian Direct Cost 5: Restricted Access to Social and Physical Services

Palestinians in the WBG either partially or completely rely on Israel for hospital care and water for domestic consumption. The total cost of hospital care is at least $40 million per annum. While Israeli hospitals account for approximately 10 percent of referrals from the Palestinian Ministry of Health for specialist hospitals,[66] around 60 percent of these referrals require permits from Israel for Palestinians to access facilities in East Jerusalem, Israel, Jordan, and the West Bank.[67] Challenges faced in acquiring these required transit permits impose a significant direct cost for Palestinians; recent data suggest that 8 to 10 percent of Gazan and 17 percent of West Bank patients miss their medical appointments as a result of either being denied travel permits or the permits not arriving in time to make scheduled appointments, with sometimes-fatal

---

[63] OCHA, 2012b.

[64] This permit system is supported by a Palestinian population registry that allows Israel to issue IDs to Palestinians with specific information about their places of residence, etc. (World Bank Technical Team, 2007).

[65] ARIJ, 2011. These restrictions seem likely to impede internal economic activity as well, though the magnitude of this effect has not been estimated (as far as the authors are aware). However, other sources report that this Balkanization has had a limited, if any, effect on the cost of internal movement of goods as leading shipping companies have optimized their trade routes and now charge a flat rate for all shipped goods regardless of their destinations (RAND interview at Palestinian-American Chamber of Commerce, spring 2014).

[66] The Palestinian Ministry of Health, 2013, Annex 186, reports that 5,113 of the 56,076 referrals by the Palestinian Ministry of Health were for specialist hospitals within Israel (and not East Jerusalem). The costs from these visits are charged directly to the PA. Note that some sources report inflated numbers that include family members of patients ("Increase in Palestinians Treated in Israeli Hospitals," 2013).

[67] This estimate includes, of the total of 56,077 total referrals in 2012, the following: (1) referrals to East Jerusalem for 20,647 West Bank residents and 4,734 Gazans; (2) referrals to the West Bank for 1,475 Gazans; (3) referrals to Jordan for 1,458 Palestinians; (4) referrals to Egypt for 41 residents of the West Bank; and (5) referrals to Israel for 5,114 Palestinians (Palestinian Ministry of Health, 2013, Annex 186).

results.[68] While less than $30 million is spent on Palestinian treatment in Israel per year,[69] the approximately 200,000 Palestinians visiting family members in Israeli hospitals face additional costs.[70] As visitation permits are only single entry, these family-member visits typically span several days or weeks (compared to what otherwise would have been a one- or two-hour commute), requiring overnight hotel stays within Israel and other additional costs.[71]

The reliance on Israel for water for domestic consumption has two types of costs that together account for approximately $70 million per annum. First, many West Bank communities depend on tank trucks for delivery of water because they do not receive adequate water through the agreements with Israel. The total additional cost of tanker-provided water is estimated to be approximately $50 million per annum.[72] The second water-related cost is through health outcomes, with a lower-bound opportunity cost of $20 million. This is due both to the lack of water and to the poor quality of the water that is available.[73] For the West Bank, the World Bank (2009, p. 24) reports an opportunity cost of $20 million from sickness in children alone. The World Bank found that losses from reductions in adult productivity imply that $20 million is a lower-bound estimate. For Gaza, it is believed that the prevalence of poor water quality

---

[68] World Health Organization, 2013. The reported estimate for Gaza is from Table 4, which reports for 2012 (2011) that 6.6 percent (8.0 percent) of permits were delayed and 0.9 percent (2.0 percent) of permits were denied. The reported estimate for the West Bank is from page 15, which reports, using 2012 data from a subset of the Ministry of Health coordination offices, that 16.7 percent of patients were denied permits and another 0.8 percent experienced a delay in getting permits. The World Health Organization, 2013, notes that six Gaza patients died while waiting for permits in 2011.

[69] In 2012, Palestine spent NIS 58 million for 2,525 patients from the West Bank and NIS 46 million for 2,600 patients from Gaza (Palestinian Ministry of Health, 2013, p. 213). There is a common perception that Palestinian patients are overcharged; they are assigned the most expensive rooms and kept in those facilities longer than necessary.

[70] Just over 210,000 health travel permits were issued by the Civil Administration in 2012 (Adoni, 2013).

[71] The magnitude of this cost has not, to our knowledge, been previously estimated. Furthermore, there are extra costs when Israelis approve movement to Palestinian hospitals, such as Makassed Islamic Charitable Hospital located on the Mount of Olives in Jerusalem. In that case, patients' families are restricted to the hospital compound, imposing extra costs on the hospital. Even when patients are ready to be discharged, they must wait for papers to travel back to the West Bank, which are often delayed for some time, imposing extra costs. Because travel back and forth is difficult, patients who should be seen on an outpatient basis are held for longer hospital stays. These inefficiencies increase both financial and human costs of care.

[72] World Bank, 2009, p. 23; the World Bank cites Palestinian Economic Policy Research Institute—MAS (2009), though we were unable to find this cited report.

[73] Although the numbers are disputed between the parties, largely over differences in assumed population, assumptions regarding allocations versus consumption, and the distinction (or lack thereof) of natural freshwater sources versus total water available (including reclaimed water for irrigation), the fact that Israeli per capita consumption is greater than Palestinian per capita consumption does not appear to be in doubt (see, e.g., State of Israel Water Authority, 2012). However, in general, Israel tends to augment its water supplies through desalinization, reclamation, and increases in water-use efficiency through technology, while these techniques are not as widespread in the West Bank and Gaza.

has been exacerbated by import restrictions and has been a significant cause of sickness in children; indeed, nearly one-quarter of disease is Gaza is thought to stem in some way from poor water quality.[74]

Palestinian Direct Cost 6: Lack of Control over Revenues from Imported Goods

The PA relies heavily on taxes and tariffs charged on imported goods. The revenue from these goods, at more than $1.5 billion per annum, accounts for an estimated 70 percent of total revenue and covers more than 80 percent of the costs of public employee salaries (UNCTAD, 2013b).

Under the status quo, as agreed to under the Oslo Accords, Israel controls these revenues and can (and does) withhold them.[75] When revenues are withheld or delayed, the PA must resort to a combination of foreign aid and bank loans to continue paying salaries and other obligations;[76] any interest paid on these loans is a direct cost for the Palestinians.

Palestinian Direct Cost 7: Restrictive Banking Regulations

Restrictions on Palestinian banks are estimated to cost the Palestinian economy approximately $15 million per year.[77] This includes the requirement that Palestinian banks must work through an Israeli bank to clear shekels,[78] must hold large cash collaterals (approximately NIS 1 billion) to access clearing services,[79] and must pay Israeli banks commissions for the service.[80] As there are restrictions on the total amount of shekels that Palestinian banks can clear each day, Palestinian banks often face short-term deficits in Israel that they cannot repay despite having excess shekel cash reserves; they typically have to rely on short-term borrowing to finance these debts. Though

---

[74] Children's health is discussed by the Centre on Housing Rights and Evictions, 2008. The one-quarter figure is from World Bank, 2009, which cites private conversations with World Health Organization personnel.

[75] Most recently, the Israelis restricted these revenues during the Palestinian bid for status in the UN and as a response to the Palestinians' announced intent to pursue war-crime prosecution of Israel in the International Criminal Court.

[76] When revenues were restricted during the UN bid, the PA relied on borrowing from domestic banks, in addition to increased foreign aid, to fund operations (Portland Trust, 2013).

[77] RAND interview with representative from the PMA, 2013.

[78] Unlike the Jordanian and Egyptian banks operating in Palestine, which have their own accounts with the Bank of Israel, Palestinian banks need to purchase shekel clearance services from either Bank Hapoalim or Discount Bank. In the wake of Hamas's takeover of Gaza in 2007, the regulations on the interaction of Palestinian banks with these Israeli banks became more restrictive.

[79] These reserves do not accumulate interest for the Palestinian banks and thus reflect an opportunity cost.

[80] The cost of that commission is typically less than NIS 2 million per annum (Who Profits from the Occupation, 2010).

there has been a recent effort by the PMA in discussions with the Bank of Israel to remedy this issue, the restrictions persist.[81]

Palestinian Direct Cost 8: Support for Prisoners in Israel

An estimated 6 percent of the PA's budget is spent annually providing stipends to the families of prisoners held in Israel.[82] The total annual value of this direct cost is approximately $200 million.[83]

2.2.2. Opportunity Costs (Economic Productivity)

The opportunity costs of the conflict—i.e., the lost opportunities for fruitful economic productivity and subsequent effects on GDP—differ substantially between the Israel and the WBG. For the Israelis, the opportunity costs are related primarily to the effects of perceived local instability on investment. Additional factors include how domestic policies vis-à-vis the Palestinians affect trade with the Arab world, tourism, and access to relatively affordable Palestinian labor. For the Palestinians, the effects are much more wide-ranging and include an extensive variety of barriers to mobility, trade, and economic activity.[84]

Israeli Opportunity Cost 1: Instability and Uncertainty

Israel experienced a rapid rise in foreign direct investment (FDI), and associated FDI-driven GDP growth, following the Oslo Accords and the peace treaty with Jordan.[85] A similar acceleration of GDP growth appeared after a series of economic reforms in 1985, which reduced economic instability by introducing more market-oriented economic policies, including reductions in barriers to international trade.[86] Conversely, in the early 2000s, Israel experienced a three-year recession driven by the violence of the Second Intifada and the bursting of the high-technology bubble in the United States and elsewhere, including Israel.[87] Though economic growth recovered rapidly in the

---

[81]   The Bank of Israel has agreed to accept a total of NIS 300 million every month from seven Palestinian banks. However, this is insufficient to match transaction demand. The result is that companies have to take out loans and pay a 2-percent overnight interest rate to satisfy their customers (RAND interview with PMA official Riyad Abu Shehadeh).

[82]   Ben Zion, 2012.

[83]   PMA data provide an estimated PA budget of US$2012 of $3.2 billion.

[84]   Our analysis does not include the opportunity costs of any internal constraints on economic activity (e.g., land-titling) that could be attributable to present trends, as these opportunity costs are unlikely to change in any of our scenarios.

[85]   Sharaby, 2002.

[86]   The benefits of these reforms were augmented by a large influx of highly skilled immigrants in the 1990s following the collapse of the Soviet Union.

[87]   D. Ben-David, 2011.

wake of that recession, three years of recession meant that the Israeli economy may have lost as much as 15 percent of potential growth.[88]

This recent history illustrates the importance that investment, and the instability and uncertainty that affect investment flows, play in the continued development of Israel's economy. The instability and uncertainty stemming from the ongoing conflict likely constrain both domestic investment and FDI. Fielding focuses on one measure of instability—"politically related deaths in Israel"—and demonstrates that eliminating this violence would significantly increase investment.[89] Fielding's estimates are likely a lower bound for the total attenuation of investment caused by the conflict because they do not capture the cost of overall uncertainty about the future of Israeli lands and property.[90]

Instability can also have secondary consequences, depending on how the international community assigns responsibility for the instability. As an example, during the Second Intifada, Israeli trade with the EU dropped by 10 percent, while trade with the United States was unaffected.[91] Thus, our analysis of the negative impacts of instability should be treated as lower bounds.

Israeli Opportunity Cost 2: Boycott, Divestment, and Sanctions

The boycott, divestment, and sanctions (BDS) movement, initiated in 2005, calls on both Palestinians and the international community to "impose broad boycotts and implement divestment initiatives against Israel similar to those applied to South Africa in the apartheid era."[92] From relatively humble beginnings in the WBG, with a call for Palestinians within the WBG to boycott Israeli-produced goods, the BDS movement spread internationally starting in 2006 and slowly but steadily began to develop support with the international academic, business, and celebrity communities.[93] As an example, in 2010, the EU placed restrictions on imports of goods originating in

---

[88] This value of 15 percent is calculated by comparing what the economy would have looked like in 2005 if the average growth of the second stage (of 2.5 percent) were maintained throughout this period. Horiuchi and Mayerson, 2014, report a much larger estimate of 60 percent as they compare the Israeli recession to a composite control group of countries that had experienced rapid growth.

[89] Fielding, 2003, estimates that reducing the amount of violence from the average (42 Palestinian deaths and 11 Israeli deaths per quarter) would lead to an approximate 2.7-percent increase in nonresidential construction, a 6.5-percent increase in nonresidential machinery and equipment, a 27.9-percent increase in residential construction, and a 14.6-percent increase in investment in residential machinery and equipment. These estimates are based on data for 1988–1998.

[90] This may help explain why Israeli gross capital formation per work-hour is at the low end of the OECD scale (D. Ben-David, 2013).

[91] Schmid et al., 2006.

[92] BDS Movement, 2005.

[93] For early international interest, see BDS Movement, undated. Note that there seems to have been a surge in interest in the BDS movement in the United States in 2014 (authors' estimates based on analysis using Google Trends with the search terms "BDS" and "Israel" in various combinations).

the settlements,[94] and, then, in 2013, it made all settlement-based entities ineligible to receive EU-funded grants, prizes, or financial instruments.[95]

Evidence on the effectiveness of sanctions is mixed, making an assessment of the potential economic effects of the BDS movement problematic. Historically, in terms of an impact on trade, only the most extensive sanctions seem to have a negative impact; neither "limited" nor "moderate" sanctions have any significant trade effects.[96] Analogously, there is no significant evidence that sanctions have a meaningful impact on net FDI. In particular, while there is some evidence that U.S.-supported sanctions reduced FDI from the United States,[97] these sanction-related reductions in U.S. FDI are typically replaced by FDI flows from other countries.[98] Thus, it is perhaps unsurprising that the net effect of the settlement-focused restrictions discussed immediately above, as an example, is reportedly small.[99]

However, there is significant evidence that economic sanctions can have meaningful economic impacts.[100] Financial sanctions, which typically include "delaying or denying credits or grants" and are used primarily against countries with close relations to the sanctioning countries, reduce the sanctioned country's gross national product (GNP) by 1.7 percent, on average.[101] Trade sanctions, which historically have been dominated by export and not import controls, have a more modest effect, at 0.7 per-

---

[94] Melvin, 2012.

[95] In 2004, Israel agreed to a compromise to include city origin on labels partially to assuage concerns about Israeli products grown or manufactured in the West Bank settlements (Schmid et al., 2006). There has also been limited popular support within the United States for enacting similar policies. For example, the American Studies Association voted to boycott Israeli academic institutions in 2013, and Secretary of State John Kerry reported in 2014, "You see, for Israel there's an increasing de-legitimization campaign that has been building up. People are very sensitive to it. There is talk of boycotts and other kinds of things" (Booth, 2014a).

[96] For example, Caruso, 2003, and Hufbauer and Oegg, 2003.

[97] Biglaiser and Lektzian, 2011.

[98] Lektzian and Biglaiser, 2013.

[99] At a microeconomic level, this movement has caused some European businesses and resalers to cease trade with Israeli businesses, especially those that conduct economic activity in the Israeli settlements (Cheslow, 2014). The EU announced that it would not provide Horizon 2020 research and innovation funds to Israeli entities operating in the West Bank or East Jerusalem (Bryant and Llana, 2014). Dutch pension firm PGGM divested from Israel in January 2014, and the State of Germany announced that it would not renew research grants to companies that engage in business outside of the Green Line (Bryant and Llana, 2014). Jordan Valley farmers in the West Bank lost approximately $29 million in revenues because of substitution away from European markets (Bryant and Llana, 2014). As discussed previously, the Israeli government has allocated funding toward reimbursing settlement producers for lost exports.

[100] Financial or trade sanctions were used in 153 of the 204 sanctions initiated during 1915–2000 and studied by Hufbauer et al., 2008.

[101] Estimates are from Hufbauer et al., 2008, and the quoted definition is from the same source on p. 94.

cent of GNP. However, the combined effect of financial and trade sanctions is nearly 3 percent of GNP.[102]

The recent estimate of the potential cost of the BDS movement to the Israeli economy at $3.2 billion, or just over 1 percent of GDP, reported by the Israeli finance minister,[103] is therefore consistent with previous sanctions and is, if anything, an understatement of the magnitude of the potential BDS movement effect.

Israeli Opportunity Cost 3: Restricted Tourism

Tourism in Israel, which generated an estimated $6 billion in 2014, is strongly influenced by the perceived security environment.[104] The annual number of tourists visiting Israel fell by nearly 70 percent during the beginning of the Second Intifada.[105] While the impact of insecurity on tourism has typically been temporary,[106] and although it appears that today's security environment does not affect the industry meaningfully, a return of significant instability would likely again have a substantial effect on Israel's tourism revenue. The recent Gaza conflict provides an important example of this: The 2014 conflict caused the loss of more than $600 million in tourism dollars.[107]

There may also be gains from regional cooperation in tourism, though the estimates of the benefit vary significantly. The lower bound for this effect, based on the realized benefits from Israel's previous peace agreements, is just over $1 billion.[108] However, it is possible that the overall benefit for the Israeli tourism industry is as high as $6 billion.[109] These potential regional tourism benefits are not included in our costing analysis, as none of our scenarios assumes regional cooperation within the ten-year time frame.

---

[102] A third type of economic sanction is asset freezes, though these are unlikely given the close relationship between Israel and the international community (e.g., Hufbauer et al., 2008).

[103] See footnote 34 in Chapter Three.

[104] The one exception to this is domestic demand for hotels, which is relatively unresponsive to security (Fleischer and Buccola, 2002; Krakover, 2005). The estimated $6 billion is based on the Israel Central Bureau of Statistics, which reports that tourism contributes about 2 percent to GDP (Israel Central Bureau of Statistics, 2014) and the overall GDP numbers of $295 billion.

[105] Tourist arrivals to Israel dropped from approximately 2.75 million to under 1 million (Israel Central Bureau of Statistics, 2014).

[106] Getmansky, 2014, found that violence only temporarily affects tourism to Israel.

[107] C. Ben-David, 2014.

[108] Fleischer and Buccola, 2002, reports, based on analysis of the realized tourism benefit from Israel's agreements with Jordan and the Palestinians in 1993 and 1995, that a peace agreement would increase Israel trade by 17 to 20 percent. As tourism contributed around 2 percent to GDP in 2014 for a total of $6 billion, this implies an overall effect of about $1.2 billion (see footnote 104 in this chapter).

[109] Palestine Trade Center (PalTrade), 2006, inflated to 2012 dollars using GDP deflator in World Bank, 2015b.

Israeli Opportunity Cost 4: Restricted Trade with Arab World

Israel's exports to non-Palestinian Middle Eastern markets are estimated to be just over $3 billion, or just over 6 percent of overall exports.[110] Although there has been strong growth in Israeli exports to Middle Eastern markets over the past ten years,[111] the Palestinian territories and Turkey continue to account for the largest shares of Israeli exports to this region.[112] Despite significant opportunity for mutually beneficial trade, trade between Israel and its Arab neighbors is limited, primarily reflecting the deliberate economic policies of the latter. Arab restrictions began in 1945 when the Arab League began a boycott of all financial and commercial transactions with the soon-to-be-established State of Israel.[113]

Today, these restrictions are still in force, though they have been limited in three important ways:[114]

- The Egypt-Israel Peace Treaty in 1979 and the Oslo Accords in 1993 ended the formal direct and indirect boycotts of Israel by Egypt, the PA, and Jordan.[115]

---

[110] Total trade estimates are from Israel Central Bureau of Statistics, undated(b), and based on 2014 nondiamond trade data. Estimates include only Jordan, Egypt, and Turkey, though Gal, 2012, reports some Gulf Cooperation Council (GCC) trade.

[111] Gal, 2012. Israeli exports to Egypt have grown to just below $200 million in 2011 as a result of the trilateral Qualified Industrial Zones agreement, including the United States, and exports to Jordan are now seven times larger (at near $300 million) than in 2000. One objective of the Euro-Mediterranean Partnership formed under the EU's 1995 Barcelona Declaration was free trade among the EU's southern Mediterranean partner countries (e.g., Algeria, Egypt, Israel, Jordan, Lebanon, Morocco, the PA, Syria, Tunisia, and Turkey) (Weizman, 2012).

[112] Turkey is the most important non-Palestinian regional trading partner, accounting for two-thirds of Middle East and North Africa (MENA)-sourced imports to Israel and roughly half of Israeli exports to MENA. Share of imports and author calculations based on Gal, 2012. Author calculations based on Gal, 2012. Political relations between Turkey and Israel were strained in 2010 following the Israeli storming of the *Mavi Marmara*, a ship that was attempting to breach Israel's blockade of Gaza; however, both sides have attempted to maintain strong economic ties, and trade in general is growing between Turkey and Israel (Cagaptay and Evans, 2012). Gal, 2012, also reports that existing estimates understate total trade with Middle Eastern markets as exports to the GCC are indirect through third-party countries and not recorded in official trade statistics. Indirect export volumes to the GCC are estimated to be over $500 million per annum. This estimate is not necessarily universally accepted, however (see Kleiman, 1998).

[113] The primary boycott was a prohibition on trade with any Israeli citizen or the Israeli government. However, countries of the Arab League were prohibited from trading with any agent that trades with Israel (*secondary boycott*) and with any entity that trades with an agent that trades with Israel (*tertiary boycott*) (Fershtman and Gandal, 1998; Weiss, 2013). The Central Boycott Office in Damascus, Syria, maintained the blacklist of companies (Sharon, 2003).

In the early years of the boycott, starting in 1948 and lasting through 1957, Egypt blocked ships with Israeli cargo or destined for Israel from using the canal and began a blacklist of noncompliant ships; this was a primary contributing factor to the 1956 war between Egypt and Israel (Gilat, 1992). By 1968, there were 60 countries and over 2,500 companies on the blacklist, which rose to 69 countries and over 6,000 companies and organizations in 1976 (the last year for which data are available).

[114] In 1994, Morocco and Tunisia established diplomatic relations with Israel but reversed this decision in 2000 with the start of the Second Intifada (Weiss, 2013). However, Algeria, Morocco, and Tunisia do not enforce the boycott (Fershtman and Gandal, 1998).

[115] Weiss, 2013.

- The countries of the Persian Gulf suspended secondary and tertiary enforcement of the boycott following the Madrid Conference in 1991.[116]
- The countries of the GCC ended enforcement of the secondary and tertiary components of the boycott following the Oslo Accords.[117]

The changing character of the boycott has meant that the effective annual opportunity cost has evolved; thus, estimates of this effect vary over time.[118] The net effect of the first 40 years of the boycott, from 1948 to 1988, on GDP has been estimated at $45 billion.[119] Another estimate suggests that the effect of the boycott from 1950 to 1994 was $45 billion to $49 billion.[120] In addition to these direct effects on trade and investment, the Arab boycott has also likely increased Israel's cost for both manufactured goods and energy.[121]

More recent estimates imply a significantly higher opportunity cost from the Arab boycott than the roughly $1 billion in per annum costs suggested by these older studies:[122] The benefit from unlimited free trade with Jordan and Egypt may be as high

---

[116] Weiss, 2013.

[117] Fershtman and Gandal, 1998.

[118] Gilat, 1992, found, overall, that the primary boycott was successful in eliminating trade between the Arab world and Israel, but that the secondary and tertiary boycotts had only limited success. As an example, while Gilat found evidence of the boycott affecting imports from Japan to Israel through 1970 (attributing the effect to the Japanese reliance on oil imports from Arab nations), there was no evidence of a meaningful impact on Europe or the United States. Though there was an intensification of the boycott in 1975, corresponding to the oil embargo and energy crisis, the United States passed antiboycott legislation that prevented American firms or persons from compliance with or participation in the secondary and tertiary boycotts (the Israeli Economic Warfare Authority pushed for this type of policy). Following the peace agreement with Egypt in 1979, the boycott weakened, oil supplies increased, and Israeli trade with the non-Arab world accelerated.

[119] The Israeli Federation of Chambers of Commerce estimated the cost of the boycott over 40 years at $45 billion, driven by the loss of $20 billion in exports, or approximately 10 percent per year, and $24 billion in investment, or approximately 15 percent of total investment ("Arab Boycott Said to Cost Israel $45 Billion over the Past 40 Years," 1992).

[120] Cited in Fershtman and Gandal, 1998; original source not available.

[121] Fershtman and Gandal, 1998, provides a detailed case study of the Israeli automobile market, which suggests a welfare loss of approximately 9.5 percent in terms of higher prices. Sharaby, 2002, provides an analogous discussion of the price of energy.

[122] The current impact of these restrictions may be lower today than historically as the relaxation of the secondary and tertiary boycotts in the mid-1990s increased Israeli trade with Asia and inward FDI (Sharon, 2003). Also, it should be noted that Hufbauer and Schott, 1983, reports a significantly lower estimate for the annual cost for 1983 alone of $260 million.

as $3 billion to $5 billion per annum (in 1996 dollars).[123] The larger effect[124] captured in these more recent studies likely reflects two facts: (1) Israeli exports to the MENA countries are a very small fraction of total imports into those nations, and, on this basis alone, there appears to be considerable potential for increased trade;[125] and (2) unlimited free trade with Jordan and Egypt would allow overland shipping to the wealthy Arab nations of the Gulf.[126]

Israeli Opportunity Cost 5: Restricted Opportunities for Regional Cooperation

In addition to new opportunities for bilateral trade, there are many other regional economic opportunities that Israel forgoes in present trends. These include opportunities for regional tourism and trade (discussed above); benefits from the establishment of regional health facilities, water agreements, and environmental agreements; and new opportunities for Israeli producers and companies in both the energy and water sectors. The magnitude of the potential benefit of these agreements is difficult to estimate, as illustrated below with the examples of energy and water, but could easily rise into the billions of dollars.

Israel's energy sector shifted dramatically in 2010 with the discovery of large offshore reserves of natural gas.[127] How Israel chooses to use this natural gas is still the subject of some debate. There is a potential for a short-term economic dividend, as evidenced by the recent agreement with Jordan for $500 million worth of Israeli natural gas imports, an agreement that could reach $30 billion over a 15-year period,[128] and the growing possibility of either Europe or Asia as a market for Israeli natural gas exports (which would likely require significant cooperation with Arab neighbors).[129] However, others have argued that these natural gas reserves should be kept only or primarily for domestic consumption.[130]

In the water sector, desalination is a prominent example, as Israel—a world leader in desalination technologies—is excluded from an Arab market that is estimated to be

---

[123] This estimate is from Hashai, 2004, who uses the standard "gravity model" of trade for estimation (note that this study was performed using data from the mid-1990s, and this level of exports has not materialized for Jordan or Egypt). PalTrade, 2006, estimated additional export opportunities of $5 billion per year within five to ten years (excluding exports to the Palestinian territories) using a nonquantitative approach.

[124] Note that these numbers were from before the recent civil war in Syria, which could influence these totals a good deal.

[125] Gal, 2012.

[126] In particular, the size of the internal markets and trading networks of these Gulf countries may allow Israeli producers to exploiting economies of scale from a dramatic expansion in the markets that they can access (Tai Keinan, chief executive officer of investment firm KCPS Clarity, in Elis, 2014a).

[127] For example, Bahgat, 2011.

[128] "Israel-Jordan Sign $500 Million Natural Gas Deal," 2014.

[129] For example, Wurmser, 2013.

[130] Shamah, 2013; Popper, Berrebi, et al., 2009; Popper, Griffin, et al., 2009.

as large as $10 billion annually.[131] Though the total opportunity cost of regional peace to this sector is difficult to estimate precisely, the anticipated $1 billion market value of the Israeli desalination firm IDE provides an estimate of the magnitude of this potential sector.[132]

Israeli Opportunity Cost 6: Restricted Growth in Trade with Palestinians

Over half of Israeli Middle Eastern trade is with the Palestinian territories, which have been part of a customs union with Israel since 1994.[133] It has been argued that this customs union ensures that the WBG is a captive market for Israeli exports; therefore, exports to the PA are higher than what might be predicted under normalized political relations.[134] The impact can be seen in the asymmetry in bilateral trade—the WBG supplies less than 1 percent of Israeli imports but is the destination for about 4 to 5.5 percent of exports (though nearly half of these exports are petroleum products and reexports of goods imported from third-party countries).[135] The importance of Israel as a trading partner for the Palestinians is illustrated by a further asymmetry: Israel is the source of approximately 75 percent of PA imports and the destination of 90 percent of Palestinian exports.[136] Exports to the PA fell by almost half in the first stages of the Second Intifada but recovered despite the election of the Hamas government in Gaza in 2007; in 2009, the PA began a boycott of products produced in the Israeli settlements.[137]

The political stalemate has both benefits and costs for Israeli exports. The benefit of the current arrangement is that the mixture of Israeli restrictions on the Palestinian economy protects several domestic Israeli industries from potential competition; further, the current trade regime (customs union) guarantees the Palestinian territories

---

[131] For example, Picow, 2010.

[132] Gabison, 2014.

[133] Trade estimates are from Gal, 2012. Between 1967 and 1994, the WBG was under direct Israeli rule. The Paris Protocol, signed in April 1994 between the government of Israel and the PA, created a formal customs union and the institutions that have governed economic activity in the Palestinian territories since that date (Lavie, 2013).

[134] See, for example, Arnon, Spivak, and Winblatt, 1996. Arnon, 2007, further argues that policies in Area C significantly increase the transaction costs for Palestinian economic activities, which has the effect of protecting Israeli industries and sectors by inflating potential competitors' prices. Under the Paris Protocol, Israeli products are exempt from duty in the Palestinian territories, unlike goods and services from other countries (Lavie, 2013).

[135] Export statistics reported in Merkle et al., 2013, using PalTrade, 2006, were 4.6 percent of exports and 0.8 percent of imports. Trade in the fruit and vegetable sector with the WBG accounts for 20 percent of Israeli fruit exports including citrus and 30 percent not including citrus (reported in Merkle et al., 2013, based on Israel Central Bureau of Statistics, 2012, and Israeli Ministry of Agriculture and Rural Development, 2012).

[136] Gal, 2012.

[137] See Rudoren, 2014, and Gal, 2012.

as a preferential market for Israeli goods.[138] An example is agriculture, in which Israeli control over land and water resources in the West Bank has inhibited the development of agricultural and food processing industries there that could potentially directly compete with Israeli products.

These restrictions hinder Palestinian economic growth and thus reduce the opportunity for growth in Israeli exports to this important trading partner. However, with Israeli exports to Palestine of nearly $3.9 billion,[139] it is clearly an important market. Existing estimates suggest that eliminating all trade and mobility restrictions would lead to a $4.5 billion to $5 billion expansion of Israeli exports to the Palestinians.[140] The enhanced trade and investment opportunities are expected to be primarily within the electricity, fuel, cement, and telecommunication sectors.[141] Some subject matter experts, though, express skepticism that trade with the Palestinians could be significantly expanded because the two economies are already so tightly integrated.

Israeli Opportunity Cost 7: Limited Palestinian Labor in Israel

The Israeli government formally limits the number of Palestinian workers who can work in Israel. Though there are other foreign workers who compete for the same low-skilled jobs in Israel as the Palestinians, there is clearly excess demand for Palestinian labor, as shown by the continued significant numbers of illegal Palestinian workers in Israel.[142] Conditional on security concerns,[143] Palestinian labor is likely to be better for the Israeli economy than other non-Jewish labor, despite the fact that Palestinians

---

[138] Swirski (2008) argues that the lack of Israeli infrastructure and investment in the Palestinian territories, coupled with the trade limitations; restrictions on the movement of people, goods, and services; and permitting policies, reflects a preference among Israeli leadership to protect Israel's domestic industry.

[139] Palestine reported imports of $5.2 billion for 2013 (PCBS, undated[f]), and approximately three-fourths of Palestinian imports are from Israel.

[140] This is based on PalTrade, 2006, which predicts that direct Israeli exports to the Palestinians in goods and services have the capacity to increase by a factor of 2.5 over pre-intifada levels. The estimate of $4.5 billion to $5 billion is based on official export data that report Israeli exports of $3.4 billion for 2008 (Bank of Israel, 2010).

[141] Swirski, 2008. Other sectors, however, may benefit from the conflict. Construction of both buildings and infrastructure in the settlements may be artificially inflated (compared with people who live within the Green Line) due to demand related to noneconomic considerations (Swirski, 2008). In addition, firms operating in settlements with Priority A or B designations likely directly benefit from the incentives related to the National Priority Areas and the ability to hire lower-skilled Palestinian workers, though it is uncertain under a counterfactual of no conflict whether any of these factors would change substantially. Thus, in the absence of the conflict, there would likely be both sectoral winners and losers in the Israeli economy.

[142] Farsakh, 2002, reports that 50 to 70 percent of Palestinian workers in Israel were there illegally until the late 1980s, but that percentage fell to around 30 percent in the mid-1990s. Today, the rate is around 50 percent.

[143] The security-related restrictions on Palestinian labor have "an outstanding track record with regard to security" (Gal, Stern, and Greenapple, 2010, p. 15).

are entitled to the Israeli minimum wage and social security benefits.[144] In addition, Palestinian workers spend the majority of their income on Israeli goods and services.[145] Since Palestinian workers live in the West Bank and commute across the separation barrier to Israel to work, they do not impose the same burden on social programs as foreign workers, who live in Israel proper and use Israeli schools and health facilities.[146]

The primary negative impact of the restriction on Palestinian labor is that it denies Israeli firms access to a relatively inexpensive and well-trained population of laborers willing to work in low-skill industries. Recent estimates suggest that a return to the pre–Second Intifada levels of Palestinian labor in Israel—an increase from today's 80,000 workers to about 140,000 workers—could increase Israel's GDP by approximately 0.3 percent, or roughly $700 million.[147]

Palestinian Opportunity Cost 1: Restricted Control of Territory

The Palestinians face major restrictions on the control of their territory. For the West Bank, the primary restriction is the division of the West Bank into Areas A, B, and C, originally a provisional measure in the Oslo Accords. Area A corresponds to all major population centers, and the PA has responsibility for all civilian and security matters there; Area B covers rural areas in which the PA has civilian control, but military matters are handled by Israel; and Area C is under the full control of Israel's military.

The effect of this provisional measure is twofold. Investment in Area C, which accounts for approximately 59 percent of West Bank land, is complicated by Israeli restrictions on new construction and poorly defined property rights.[148] In addition, Area C subdivides the territory of the West Bank into several dozen checkerboard clusters so that Areas A and B are not contiguous. Thus, even accessing neighboring parts of the same area can be difficult.

---

[144] In October 2007, the Israel High Court of Justice ruled that Palestinian workers in the territories were entitled to the Israeli minimum wage and social benefits (Swirski, 2008). However, enforcement may be lax.

[145] The non-Jewish foreigners who have replaced Palestinians in recent years repatriate significant portions of their incomes to their home countries.

[146] Gal, Stern, and Greenapple, 2010. Ruppert Bulmer, 2003, models how changes in the numbers of Palestinian workers following a change in labor restrictions would affect the number of foreign workers in terms of Israel and Palestinian employment, unemployment, and wages.

[147] Since 2008, the percentage of Palestinians employed in Israel and the settlements has been relatively steady at about 10 percent of total employment (PCBS, undated[d], undated[e]). These estimates are from Flaig et al., 2013, which uses a computable general equilibrium (CGE) model of the Israeli economy. This policy would likely lead to increased income inequality by decreasing incomes for lower-skilled Israeli and foreign workers and increasing incomes for higher-skilled workers.

[148] As an example, World Bank, 2013b, reports that Palestinian agriculturalists have faced significant difficulty in getting permission to build the new infrastructure necessary to intensify agricultural production. B'Tselem, 2013, provides an additional discussion of the licensing restrictions for Area C.

This subdivision of the West Bank restricts the development of higher-value irrigated agriculture, with an opportunity cost of approximately $900 million per annum.[149] This estimate relies on the fact that yields from irrigated land are approximately 20 times larger than yields from nonirrigated land. The estimate assumes that all irrigable lands would be irrigated if it were feasible to do so.[150]

In addition, the restrictions on Area C constrain potential Palestinian resource extraction and tourism investment and raise housing costs. The opportunity cost for resource extraction is more than $1 billion, including the potential development of a Dead Sea mineral extraction industry, with yields as high as $900 million per annum, and marble and stone quarrying, estimated to generate approximately $250 million per annum.[151] For tourism, the opportunity cost is likely smaller, at roughly $125 million to $150 million.[152] The impact on housing is seen in inflated housing prices caused by the artificial scarcity of land; estimates of this effect total approximately $240 million per year.[153]

---

[149] Estimate is based on ARIJ, 2011, and World Bank, 2013b. Nearly all cultivable land in the West Bank has been continuously cultivated since the 1960s (Abed, 1990; Benvenisti and Khayat, 1988; PCBS, 2009a). However, only 24 to 28 percent of the total potentially irrigable land has ever been irrigated. The West Bank currently has about 144,000 dunums of irrigated land. Estimates of potentially irrigable land in the West Bank range from 535,000 dunums (Benvenisti and Khayat, 1988) to 630,000 (Glover and Hunter, 2010).

[150] This estimate relies on the following numbers. First, it assumes that the larger estimate of irrigable land, at 630,000 dunums, is accurate (see Glover and Hunter, 2010). Second, based on World Bank, 2013b, which reports that half of settlement land is under cultivation, it assumes that 93,000 dunums of irrigable land is already being used by the Israelis and will not be relinquished—this is one-half of the 187,000 dunums of land currently controlled by the Israelis. Third, it assumes that the yield, in dollars, of each of the additional 393,000 dunums of newly irrigated land (= 630,000 [total irrigable land] – 93,000 [agricultural land in settlements] – 144,000 [current land irrigated]) is the same as existing irrigated land. Thus, we use the same estimated value differential between irrigated and nonirrigated land of $2,521 per dunum in 2011 dollars used by World Bank, 2013b. Fourth, we assume that any additional water that is required is purchased at the same prices that Jordan pays—at $0.45 per cubic meter (Bar-Eli, 2014)—so that irrigating one dunum costs $260. This returns a total benefit of irrigation of $2,261 per dunum. Fifth, we estimate the upper bound by multiplying this return per dunum ($2,261) by the number of additional dunum (393,000) to get an estimate of $889 million.

Note that other approaches have been used for estimating the opportunity cost. As an example, Gal, Stern, and Greenapple, 2010, estimates the potential agricultural value of the Jordan Valley at $1 billion based on the agriculture productivity of settler farms in Gaza pre-2005.

[151] World Bank, 2013b.

[152] ARIJ, 2011, and World Bank, 2013b, estimate the opportunity cost of restricted tourism around the Dead Sea at roughly $125 million to 150 million based on Jordanian and Israeli tourism revenue. PalTrade, 2006, reports a much larger number of over $1 billion; it assumes that the number of tourists would triple under peace—i.e., the number of tourists would expand from the 1 million before the Second Intifada to 2 million to 3 million—and that Palestinians would be able to extract a greater share of the revenue from tourists to the region. However, it should be noted that the total income from Palestinian tourism before the Second Intifada (in 2000) was only $225 million (PalTrade, 2006, p. 67).

[153] This estimate is from World Bank, 2013b, which derived these estimates in three stages. First, the World Bank estimates a 24-percent inflation in housing prices due to this artificial constraint by comparing changes in the price of housing and the overall change in the consumer price index. Second, using a published demand elasticity

The second major territorial restriction is that Palestinians do not control their own territorial waters, making the development of commercial natural gas deposits all but impossible.[154] Existing estimates suggest that the Palestinian economy would save $560 million per year for the estimated 15-year life of a potential extraction project.[155]

Palestinian Opportunity Cost 2: Restricted Access to Water

Relative to the amount of total sustainable withdrawals from the Mountain Aquifer,[156] the Palestinians face significant restrictions in access to water.[157] Three primary factors contribute to these restrictions. First, water allocations established in the Oslo Accords (a de facto property-rights arrangement) have not been updated meaningfully; thus, the Palestinians have not benefited in any significant way from either the desalination efforts of Israel or the changing needs of the Israeli economy.[158] Second, Israel enforces

---

of housing estimate for a comparable area, it estimates that this 24-percent inflation is equivalent to a 21.7-percent increase in the housing stock. Third, it combines this 21.7-percent increase with the 2011 value of housing to yield an estimate of $239 million in 2011 U.S. dollars.

[154] Natural gas reserves worth an estimated $6.5 billion were discovered within Gaza's territorial waters in 2000. Unilateral development of this resource by a Palestinian consortium is hampered by Israeli restrictions that prevent developers from developing the gas fields and building a Palestinian international export capability. The total benefit of this extraction project is estimated to be $8.5 billion, with the benefiting accruing over a 15-year period (Palestine Investment Fund, 2010).

[155] Palestine Investment Fund, 2010.

[156] The Mountain Aquifer is one of the most significant sources of water for both Israelis and Palestinians (EcoPeace Middle East, undated).

[157] Surface (primarily via the Lower Jordan River and tributaries) and groundwater (via the three-basin Mountain Aquifer) resources are common natural sources of freshwater in the region. There are no enforceable international water law standards when it comes to disputes over common water resources. Palestinian arguments regarding their perceived rights to groundwater resources tend to focus on fair and equitable use and the presumed linkage between land and water (which is not the only possible rights system); Israeli arguments regarding their perceived rights focus on doing no harm in reallocations and historical use (which is also a matter of dispute). This situation is regarded as a major element of the conflict (Zilberman and Carson, 1999).

[158] As part of the Oslo Accords, Palestinians and Israelis agreed (1) to establish a Joint Water Committee responsible for coordinating water issues between the West Bank and Israel and (2) to an interim allocation of water to the West Bank, which has remained in force given the breakdown in negotiations (Israeli-Palestinian Interim Agreement on the West Bank and the Gaza Strip, 1995, Annex 3, Appendix 1, Article 40—the "Water Agreement"). The interim agreement estimated future water needs of the West Bank to be between 70 and 80 million cubic meters (MCM) per year, and Israel was obligated to make 28.6 MCM per year available to the Palestinians. Current allocations, dictated by the interim agreement of the Oslo Accords, were originally designed to last for only an interim period. However, with the unraveling of the peace process and subsequent Second Intifada, final negotiations did not take place. Average available groundwater from the western and northeastern sections of the Mountain Aquifer is 100-percent allocated given current withdrawals, while the eastern aquifer has approximately 78 MCM of available water currently unused in the West Bank (Karner, 2012). The Palestinian share of potential withdrawals in the Western aquifer is approximately 6 percent, and the share of the northeastern aquifer's withdrawals is 29 percent. The Israelis are currently allocated 23 percent of sustainable potential eastern aquifer withdrawals (43 percent of current withdrawals). As such, most groundwater supplied by the Mountain Aquifer is currently allocated to Israel, with de facto property rights enforced by the Israeli authorities. The Israe-

the agreement in the Oslo Accords by preventing the withdrawal of groundwater in the West Bank that is not authorized in the agreement.[159] Third, equipment import restrictions on Gaza have affected the ability of Palestinians there to desalinate available brackish well water.[160]

In addition to the direct costs of water, discussed above, these restrictions create an opportunity cost by constraining agricultural development in the West Bank.[161] Total water supply for the WBG is approximately 300 MCM of water per annum. While this is sufficient to meet the existing municipal and industrial demands of 215 MCM per annum, full irrigation of available irrigable land is estimated to require at least 400 MCM of additional water.[162] The total opportunity cost for agriculture of this restriction has been estimated to be as high as $900 million per annum.[163]

Palestinian Opportunity Cost 3: Barriers to Trade

The WBG has faced significant trade challenges since being integrated into a de facto customs union with Israel in 1967.[164] Though the customs union should have allowed goods to move freely between the territories and Israel, a variety of Israeli policies restrict Palestinian export growth. These restrictions include, among others, nontariff trade barriers to trade and licensing restrictions on Palestinian producers.[165]

---

lis currently sell slightly more than 30 MCM per year to the Palestinians. However, efforts to purchase additional amounts from desalinated waters have run into challenges (Bar-Eli, 2014).

[159] This is done by force. In response to criticism over the allocation of water, Israel claims that it has abided by the terms of the Oslo Accords, that there are illegal hook-ups to the Israeli water conveyance system, that Palestinian infrastructure for conveyance is inefficient, and that the Palestinians have not attempted to treat sewage as per the agreement (see, e.g., Gvirtzman, 2012).

[160] World Bank, 2009, p. 29. In December 2013, as part of a joint agreement between the Jordanians, Palestinians, and Israelis, the Israeli government agreed to increase sales of water to the Palestinians by 20 to 30 MCM ("'Historic' Water Deal Signed by Israel, Jordan and Palestinians," 2013). Given favorable hydrological conditions, the Israeli government was planning to purchase less water from its own (private) desalinization facilities in 2014, as the marginal cost of obtaining water from natural sources is lower (Global Water Intelligence, 2013).

[161] A secondary challenge is the high price of municipal water in some areas. B'Tselem, 2013, reports that there is a significant number of Palestinian villages that do not have access to reliable municipal water lines and must purchase water from contractors for as much as 1,000 percent more than Israeli settlers in neighboring settlements.

[162] ARIJ, 2011.

[163] The higher estimate assumes that all Area C restrictions are lifted and that there is sufficient water to irrigate the estimated 393,000 dunums of additional irrigable land. The estimated requirement for water is based on Glover and Hunter's 2010 estimate of 579 cubic meters of water per year per dunum.

[164] Arnon, Spivak, and Weinblatt, 1997, refers to it as an "involuntary, one-side, impure, customs union" (p. 88).

[165] Arnon, Spivak, and Weinblatt, 1997, Chapter 4, discusses these restrictions and how they hampered the potential benefit of the customs union for the Palestinians. Israel added a variety of nontariff trade barriers (e.g., "transport certificates") and regulations to Palestinian agricultural production to protect Israeli production (p. 91). In addition, Arnon, Spivak, and Weinblatt, 1997, reports that Palestinian entrepreneurs were required to obtain licenses from Israeli authorities "for every economic activity they sought to initiate" (p. 88). Overall,

These trade restrictions have persisted despite attempts by the international community to alleviate them. The Paris Protocol, which was designed to facilitate trade between Palestine and Israel, instead fomented a "closure regime" that saw the introduction of a variety of new internal and external restrictions on the movement of goods.[166] After the failure at Camp David in 2000, which would have created two states and given Palestinians control over their borders, coupled with the effects of the Second Intifada, the burden of these restrictions grew.

Currently, Palestinian producers seeking to export items to Israel or the rest of the world face many restrictions. A variety of restraints (e.g., checkpoints, back-to-back transport arrangements, the absence of a seaport) raise the costs of exporting for Palestinians.[167] "Dual use" import procedures restrict imports into both the West Bank and Gaza of items that "are intended for civilian use but may potentially be used for hostile purpose."[168] Israeli and international businesspeople have difficulty entering the WBG, which complicates the development of business relationships. A related challenge is that the ambiguous international status of Palestinian territory can prevent Palestinian companies from directly obtaining dealerships, franchises, or other subsidiary relationships with foreign companies that have such territorially exclusive relationships in Israel.

The impact of the export restrictions is likely to be very large. A 50-percent reduction in transaction costs, which is estimated to be equivalent to the cost imposed by the variety of export restrictions (and will be modeled in the two-state solution scenario discussed in Chapter Five), could increase Palestinian exports by as much as 50 percent

---

Gazit, 1985, reports, Israeli policies were designed to "prevent the establishment or reactivation of Arab-owned factories that might compete with Israeli products" (quoted in Arnon, 2007).

[166] Arnon, 2007, p. 17. Further, under the Paris Protocol, Israeli products are exempt from duty in the Palestinian territories, unlike goods and services from other countries, so that the WBG is effectively a preferential market for Israeli exports.

[167] These restrictions have become particularly acute in Gaza in recent years (OCHA, 2011a). Note that, before the Second Intifada, trade and transport costs added 35 percent to the cost of domestic goods—while the average premium for the rest of the MENA region was only 10 percent (Astrup and Dessus, 2001). These authors also report that total transport costs for imports and exports were 30 percent higher for the Palestinians than for the Israelis.

[168] These restrictions, which first included only chemicals and fertilizers, have been gradually expanded since the Second Intifada. The original law describing these restrictions is "Import and Export Ordinance 5739-1979." However, we were unable to track down the original specific language as this law has been replaced by the newer restrictions. In 2002, 2008, and 2012, the list of restricted items was expanded to include increased restrictions on fertilizers (the territories are now allowed to import only low-concentration liquid fertilizers, which are produced only in a single factory located in Israel), chemicals, raw materials for industry, and a variety of machinery types (ARIJ, 2011, p. 5). Gaza faces an expanded list of dual-use goods that includes a range of construction materials and other imports, effectively restricting Gazan imports to only a few items. Import restrictions were eased somewhat following the fateful attempt of a flotilla to break Israel's blockade of Gaza. These "few items" include food, animal fodder, hygiene products, clothing, wood, and glass (OCHA 2011a, p. 4). The quote is from the Coordinator of Government Activities in the Territories report (Civil Administration of Judea and Samaria, 2012).

and Palestinian GDP by as much as $2 billion per annum.[169] While other reports have produced lower estimates, the relative magnitude of these constraints is still large.[170]

A variety of import restrictions—namely, "border controls that raise costs and cause delays, and restrictions on imports of 'dual use' goods"—are estimated to have an additional opportunity cost of between $260 million and $500 million.[171] The impact on the West Bank is likely shared about evenly between industry and agriculture.[172] The impact of the more comprehensive suite of import restrictions on Gaza is likely significantly larger than that for the West Bank. OCHA reports that Gaza-specific import restrictions have (1) stifled the manufacturing industry, reducing the utilization of existing capacity by more than 50 percent; (2) prevented the expansion of housing, as noted above, which has led to a significant shortage in the housing stock; and (3) limited the effectiveness of desalination and other water treatment capacity.[173]

---

[169] Eltalla and Hens, 2009, found that a 50-percent reduction in import, export, and domestic transaction costs, which it reports as a return to the pre–Second Intifada levels, would increase GDP by approximately $2 billion. These authors use a small-country CGE model to estimate the effect of a reduction in overall transaction costs for both imports and exports using data from 2007 (their data on transaction costs indicate that nearly $1 billion was spent in 2007 on transaction costs for the import and export of agricultural and manufacturing goods). They model the effect of this reduction, which they report as a return to the level in 2000 before the effects of the Second Intifada. They found that GDP, imports, and exports would increase by 21, 29, and 55 percent, respectively.

[170] Astrup and Dessus, 2001, which also uses a CGE approach to model the removal of security barriers as a 15-percent reduction in transaction costs, found that GDP would increase by approximately 3 percent (which is smaller in proportional terms). However, Astrup and Dessus, 2001, highlights that the GDP could increase by as much as 5.7 percent if Palestinians had control over their own borders. Bannister and Erickson von Allmen, 2001, which uses a gravity model approach, report that trade with the world excluding Israel is 80 percent below where it should be as a result of nontariff barriers.

[171] The smaller number is from ARIJ, 2011—see following footnote—while the larger number is from the U.S. Agency for International Development (USAID), 2010. Our $500 million figure is derived based on the following statement, as reported in Department for International Development (DFID), 2014, that references USAID, 2010: "Border controls: trade between the West Bank and other countries suffers from border controls that raise costs and cause delays, and restrictions on imports of 'dual use' goods that cost at least 5 percent GDP per year."

[172] ARIJ, 2011, reports a total cost of $260 million per annum, which includes a cost of $120 million for industry and $142 million for agriculture. ARIJ, 2011, attributes the analysis to the Trade Facilitation Project, though it does not provide a reference. It reports that the Trade Facilitation Project estimated that the "industry" effect is equally shared across manufacturing and information and communication technology (ICT). Its estimate of the impact on agriculture is based on the assumption that access to higher-quality fertilizer would increase the yield from vegetable crops and fruit trees by at least 20 percent.

[173] OCHA, 2011a, p. 5, reports that the 40-percent utilization in 2011 was less than half the utilization before the blockade. Further, as capacity utilization increased from 34 to 40 percent following Israeli's easing of import restrictions, there is some evidence that these import restrictions do play a substantive role in the low utilization.

Palestinian Opportunity Cost 4: Licensing Restrictions

Three major types of licensing restrictions imposed by the Israelis create significant impediments to doing business for the Palestinians. First, there are direct restrictions on economic activity, primarily affecting telecommunications, private banking, quarrying, and mining sectors in the West Bank.[174] In addition, there are licensing-like restrictions, which include most prominently the Israeli requirement of "security first," that have been applied to foreign aid projects.[175] Finally, in addition to the licensing restrictions in Area C, discussed above, Palestinians often have difficulty in acquiring requisite licenses for construction in both East Jerusalem and Area B.[176]

The overall magnitude of the direct effects of these restrictions on economic activity is likely modest. For example, the current licensing restrictions on telecommunications, which have impeded the development of the Palestinian telecommunication industry, are estimated to have a net effect of approximately $50 million.[177] While restrictions placed on the ability of Palestinian and Jordanian banks seeking to open automated teller machines in Area C create inefficiencies in the banking system, the effects are likely to be modest overall.

The indirect effect of these restrictions, however, is quite high and affects all areas of economic activity. The impact on the effectiveness of foreign aid is instructive, particularly given increasing Palestinian reliance on foreign aid in recent years. Chief among the restrictions placed on the type of foreign aid projects selected were the requirement for approval from Israeli military authorities[178] and the concentration of foreign aid flows through the PA with the aim of "combating unemployment and stabilizing the regime" in support of the peace process.[179] Though specific estimates of the impacts are not available, these restrictions are believed to have had effects. Importantly, during the 1990s and 2000s, they are thought to have encouraged the PA to

---

[174] These types of restrictions have been around since the pre–Oslo Accords period, when quotas and a variety of other licensing-like restrictions influenced the types of agricultural and manufacturing products that the Palestinians were allowed to build. The net impact of restrictions on quarrying and mining was discussed under "Palestinian Opportunity Cost 1: Restricted Control of Territory."

[175] Khan, Giacaman, and Amundsen, 2004.

[176] For East Jerusalem, see Institute for Middle East Understanding, 2005, and, for Area B, see Balls and Cunliffe, 2007. Unlike the estimates for Area C restrictions, discussed in "Opportunity Cost 1: Restricted Control of Territory," estimates of the magnitude of these restrictions are not available.

[177] World Bank, 2013b.

[178] Mansour, 1988, reports, referring to U.S.-funded projects, that "[p]rojects have to be approved by the US Agency for International Development (USAID) and thereafter the Israeli military authorities" (p. 83).

[179] Le More, 2005, p. 992.

create monopolies in order to channel development funding.[180] The restrictions may also have reduced the effectiveness of foreign aid.[181]

Palestinian Opportunity Cost 5: Restricted Tourism and Travel

A variety of barriers make it difficult for foreign nationals, both non-Israeli and Israeli, to travel in the WBG.[182] These restrictions have clear implications for tourism, with existing empirical evidence suggesting that the challenging entry and exit process for tourists likely reduces tourism by 20 to 60 percent.[183] The importance for tourism is demonstrated by the efforts of the PA to encourage Israel to allow Israeli visitors into Area A as a way of jump-starting both trade and tourism following the Second Intifada.[184]

The restrictions on travel also attenuate the level of trade and FDI in the Palestinian economy.[185] Though no specific estimates exist for the Palestinian economy,[186]

---

[180] Nasr, 2004. He reports that, in some cases, there was no "realistic alternative to the operation of Palestinian monopolies" (p. 169). These monopolies plus a centralized architecture for the PA, which was required to meet the Israel requirement of "security first," created a system that was susceptible to accusations of corruption. Though these monopolies were certainly not decisive, they may have contributed to the perception of corruption within the PA that is believed to have played an important role in Hamas's victory. More than 50 percent of Palestinians viewed the PA as corrupt from 1998 to 2009 (Sobovitz, 2010), and polling data from 2011–2013 indicate that more than 70 percent of Palestinians view the PA as corrupt (Palestinian Center for Policy and Survey Research, undated).

[181] During the early period of aid, Mansour, 1988, reports, Israeli restrictions redirected foreign aid from projects that would enhance Palestinian economic productivity to basic infrastructure that Israel would otherwise have needed to build. Le More, 2005, reports that this challenge continued through the beginning of the most recent period. However, while Brynen, 1996b, reports that funds were not being used as effectively as they could be—specifically that USAID efforts were being diverted away from projects that would be useful for economic development—he argues that this "restriction" can be attributed to the Israelis only in the sense that they created the complicated political environment in which these development donors are trying to function.

[182] Following the Second Intifada, there was an increase in Israeli visa rejections for foreigners working in the humanitarian aid and education sectors; further, though the Oslo Accords specified that permanent residency visas would be permitted in order to encourage investment in Palestine and many were issued before 2000, as of 2010, none had been issued since the Second Intifada (PalTrade, 2010). Israelis, with the exception of the Israeli Arabs post-2007, are restricted from physically entering Area A of the West Bank and are entirely restricted from entering Gaza (Harel, 2010; U.S. Department of State, 2013).

[183] Neumayer, 2010, shows, using global data, that the existence of visa restrictions reduces tourism by 50 to 60 percent. Artal-Tur, Pallardó-López, and Requena-Silvente, 2012, reports a significantly lower value of 20 percent.

[184] *Haaretz* (Harel, 2010) reports that "[t]he Palestinian Authority is interested in having Israelis visit Palestinian-controlled West Bank cities and their environs, designated as Area A, because it could signal the resumption of trade and tourism."

[185] Visa and entry issues were the fourth-most important constraint for exporters in the West Bank and the third-most important constraint for exporters in Gaza (World Bank Technical Team, 2007a). This is caused by the arbitrariness of visa renewals, restrictions faced by Arab citizens, and limited freedom of movement for Israelis within the West Bank and Gaza.

[186] ARIJ, 2011, did not calculate this but suggested that it could calculate the number of visas rejected and multiply it by the average amount invested.

evidence suggests that the restriction on non-Israeli visitors could reduce trade and FDI by as much as 19 percent and 25 percent, respectively.[187] Additionally, these restrictions affect Palestinian access to foreign experts.[188]

Restrictions on the travel of Jewish Israelis to the WBG are likely equally, if not more, important, curbing both Israeli and non-Israeli trade with, and investment in, Palestinian areas. The impact of such restrictions on Israeli investment in the Palestinian economy is clear.[189] Intermediaries play an important role in supporting the entry of foreign investors into local markets; Israeli intermediaries would be ideal given their experience, well-developed financial markets, and understanding of the politics and security challenges of working with and through Israel.[190] Further, in technology, there is a dramatic gap between the Israelis and Palestinians in basic, relatively low-tech industries that can be eliminated with sufficient peer-to-peer coordination.[191]

Palestinian Opportunity Cost 6: Political Instability and Investment

The World Bank considers private investment in Palestine overwhelmingly constrained by the political instability induced by "decades of military presence, violence, restrictions on the movement of people and goods, restricted access to economic space and resources, governmental crises, internal Palestinian political division, and relative isola-

---

[187] Neumayer, 2011.

[188] This affects primarily government institutions or large firms that often must respect national travel warnings. PalTrade, 2010, gives the example of the difficulty that Palestinian pharmaceutical firms have faced in getting EU certifiers to visit their facilities—only one firm was able to access Palestine and only after significant effort. This restriction on foreign experts has affected power generation in Gaza (Centre on Housing Rights and Evictions, 2008), the effectiveness of aid provision (Diwan and Shaban, 1999, p. 145), and universities (Rahman, 2009; Nemes, 2014), among others.

[189] World Bank, 2004, assesses, in discussing Israeli investment in the Gaza industrial estates, that if the government of Israel "persists with its ban on Israelis entering Gaza . . . it is unlikely that any Israeli investment will remain." However, there are significant amounts of Israeli private resources invested abroad—more than $50 billion in 2012 (OECD, 2012).

[190] The success of Rawabi (the first planned city built by and for Palestinians) exemplifies the role that Israeli partners could play (Abunimah, 2011). But given the proximity of Israel to Palestine in both geographic and cultural terms, Israelis, along with the Jordanians, should have the largest amount of private investment in Palestine. While Jordan contributes nearly 80 percent of Palestine's inward FDI, Israel contributes a negligible amount. Kinda, 2012, summarizes the importance of financial intermediaries in overcoming distance-related informational asymmetries.

[191] A dramatic example is in agriculture. Helpman, 2003, reports that agriculture accounted for 12 percent of Israel's GDP in 1953 and 4.5 percent in the 1990s. The Penn-World Tables reports that GDP was $5.4 billion in 1953 and $80 billion in the 1990s (in $US 2005). This implies that total production in Israeli agriculture roughly quadrupled during this time frame. Importantly, though the value of Israeli agriculture approximately quadrupled between the 1950s and the 1990s, without any significant increase in water utilization, total value added in Palestinian agriculture fell by nearly one-third. World Bank, 2013b, also mentions the decrease in Palestinian productivity.

tion from the global economy."[192] Limited investment in Palestine is, in this view, not a cause but instead a consequence of the constraints of present trends reflecting the limited opportunities for profit, rather than any financial constraints.[193]

Four types of evidence have been offered in support of this conclusion. First, Palestinian businesspeople may be investing primarily in Israel and not in Palestine.[194] Second, despite large and rapidly growing private savings and regulations stating that at least 40 percent of savings should be provided as credit to the WBG economy, total lending to the public and private sectors rarely exceeds 30 percent of GDP and is one of the lowest in the region.[195] Third, despite a large Palestinian diaspora, wealthy Arab nations that have expressed a direct interest in Palestinian development, and well-wishing donor nations, very little investment has flowed to sectors producing tradable goods. It has instead gone to internal trade, real estate, or other parts of the economy that produce nontradable goods and services.[196] Moreover, despite the advantageous

---

[192] Assaf, 2014, p. xiv. For additional discussions, see Botta and Vaggi, 2012; World Bank, 2007a, p. 23; and Fleischer and Buccola, 2002.

[193] Gal, Nashashibi, and Rock, 2015, provides a different interpretation of investment into Palestine. Rather than treat investment as requirement for the Palestinian economy to realize the benefits of various constraints on the economy being removed, as we have done here, those authors used the investment rate from a period that experienced rapid economic growth (1997–1999) and assumed that that investment rate would be maintained for ten years. The GDP growth estimates they obtained therefore rely on the assumption that there would be new economic opportunities to productively use that new investment in a two-state solution. Ours is a more conservative assumption, as we first describe the types of new economic opportunities that could occur and then calculate the amount of investment required. Thus, though their reported ten-year growth trajectory for the Palestinian economy is more rapid than what we report for the two-state solution, the difference is a direct consequence of our different assumptions.

[194] Hass, 2011, reports on a highly disputed study by Issa Smeirat that found that total private Palestinian investment in the West Bank was only $1.5 billion in 2011, while private Palestinian investment in Israel was between $2.5 billion and $5.8 billion. The PA had previously estimated total Palestinian investment in Israel at closer to $1 billion (Hass, 2011). Of the Palestinian businesspeople interviewed by Smeirat, one-third said that they had no interest in investing in the West Bank, and the other two-thirds said that they would move investment into the West Bank if the PA managed the economy better and conditions improved (e.g., infrastructure, availability of loans). Importantly, that one-third of the sample reported that the PA was not managing the economy well suggests that the Fayyad reforms may not have been benefiting all private-sector businesspeople equally. See Dunya al-Watan, 2011, for a response from the Ministry of National Economy.

[195] Avishai, 2009, reports that Palestinian banks have lent only $1.5 billion of the more than $6 billion in local savings and the more than $9 billion in additional savings in the diaspora. World Bank, 2008, provides a further discussion. However, there was a 30-percent increase in lending to the private sector between 2004 and 2007 that suggests that things may be improving (World Bank, 2008).

[196] Gillespie, Sayre, and Riddle, 2001.

position of Israelis who may wish to invest in the Palestinian market,[197] there is limited private Israeli capital invested in the WBG.[198]

As a consequence, though overall investment since the 1960s averaged over 25 percent of GDP, which is close to global averages, total investment in productive assets has been very low (Figure 2.4). Investment in productive capital has been consistently less than 5 to 10 percent of annual GDP, with investments being channeled into either residential construction or buildings.[199] The limited levels of FDI, shown in Figure 2.5, following the Oslo Accords highlight these challenges.

Reduced political instability associated with reduced Israeli-imposed restrictions on the Palestinian economy is anticipated to increase future private investment in Palestine—specifically, investment in productive capital. This private investment is likely to come from Palestinians, both domestic and in the diaspora, and individuals and private organizations throughout the international community.

New private investment will be required to realize the benefits associated with the removal of other opportunity costs, discussed above. Thus, rather than trying to estimate the independent effect that new investment could have on the Palestinian economy, we calculate the total new investment that would be required to realize these benefits. However, as calculating the total required private investment is beyond the scope of this analysis, we develop back-of-the-envelope estimates of the total magnitude of investment, including public and private, that is likely to be required.

---

[197] That investors prefer investing locally is well established (e.g., Portes and Rey, 2005). Ragozzino, 2007, describes three mechanisms that could drive this effect: (1) information asymmetries grow with distance; (2) distance exacerbates the risk of "ex-post opportunism" by foreign partners (note: this probably partially explains the very limited quantities of FDI in the West Bank and Gaza); and (3) distance increases cultural distance and political risk.

[198] World Bank, 2007a, p. 2, reports that "almost no Israeli or foreign capital was forthcoming" when referencing the period of 1967–2007. Following the war in 1967, there were no significant Israeli investments in the West Bank and Gaza, reflecting the fact that investment was neither encouraged nor allowed (Gross, 2000, p. 1544, citing Gazit, 1985). The first Israeli factory in the West Bank was built in 1985 as part of a settlement near Tulkarem (Othman, undated). Currently, despite several efforts to build economic partnerships, there is little evidence of meaningful Israeli investment in Palestine. The PCBS's *Foreign Investment Survey* (PCBS and PMA, 2013) indicates that Israel accounts for a very small amount of either FDI or portfolio investment. Israeli FDI data reported to the OECD indicate that the "Occupied Palestinian Territory" (OECD terminology) accounted for zero of the more than $52 billion in Israeli FDI in other countries. Economic partnerships include a reported $100 million in venture capital funds for the Palestinian information and ICT industry from "Israeli or Western sources" (Behar, 2013); $15 million of this alone seems to be from Cisco, which has a prosperous Israeli office (Cisco, undated). Other Israeli ICT companies subcontract work to Palestinians, though no obvious Israeli investments are made ("Israeli Companies Outsourcing to Palestinians," 2010).

[199] Arnon, Spivak, and Weinblatt, 1997, pp. 16–17, discusses this for the 1968–1990 period. Office of the UN Special Coordinator for the Middle East Peace Process, 2012, discusses this for more recent data.

Figure 2.4
Gross Capital Formation in the West Bank and Gaza

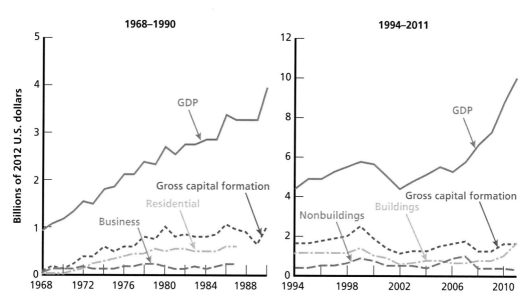

SOURCES: Data for the left panel (1968–1990) are from Arnon, Spivak, and Weinblatt, 1997, Table 2A.3.
Data for the right panel (1994–2011) are from PCBS, undated(a).
RAND RR740-2.4

Figure 2.5
Total Foreign Direct Investment in the West Bank and Gaza

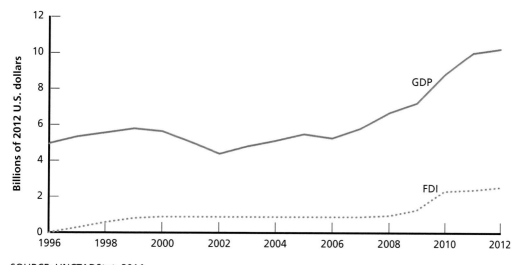

SOURCE: UNCTADStat, 2014.
RAND RR740-2.5

Potential Future Palestinian Opportunity: Dissolution of the Palestinian Authority

Dissolution of the PA, which could occur as either a Palestinian strategy to improve long-term conditions in the WBG[200] or as a side effect of ongoing conditions, would have drastic effects on the Palestinian economy as a whole. The PA's dissolution would impact the payment of public servants, affect rule of law and internal security, and have a variety of other deleterious effects. The PCBS estimates that the net impact of the dissolution of the PA would be approximately 15 percent of GDP.[201] These costs are not costs of the current impasse, but they have the potential to figure in future scenarios, and we include the costs in our analysis of the violent uprising trajectory discussed in Chapter Eight.

The collapse of the PA is also a possible outcome of nonviolent resistance, as Israel withholds tax revenue from the PA in response to the PA seeking membership in the International Criminal Court. As noted earlier, the present trends that existed when we began this project are changing complexion. The Gaza war in the summer of 2014, the subsequent recriminations, the aggressive Palestinian diplomatic moves, and the punitive responses from Israel seem more akin to nonviolent resistance.

2.3. Security Inputs

From an Israeli perspective, Middle East politics are becoming less predictable and thus potentially more threatening.[202] Israelis fear that a new Palestinian state would be vulnerable to the same regional trends that are shaking the foundations of the Arab world—including a growing cast of militant substate actors and an increasingly frustrated Arab polity. Thus, the "envelope" that Israel has established through its continued presence in the West Bank (and security control over Gaza's boundaries) seeks to keep out such militant substate actors and isolates those that are already inside it. Israel views its freedom of action and its military presence as impeding anti-Israeli violence and preventing the emergence of an anarchic and violence-prone West Bank.

Effectively mitigating security risks for both the Palestinians and for Israelis is a prerequisite to achieving a durable agreement between the two sides. Agreements will be negotiated and signed by political leaders. But assessments from their military and

---

[200] Shikaki, 2014, p. 4, reports that PA collapse or dissolution might force Israeli policymakers to confront three alternatives: maintain a modified version of the status quo by allowing Palestinians and donor countries to continue to manage service delivery, return to pre-1994 status in which Israel becomes directly responsible for the welfare of the Palestinian population under its occupation, or start a process of limited disengagement in which it consolidates its settlement enterprise in few large settlement blocs while maintaining a military presence throughout the West Bank.

[201] Abdel Karim, 2013.

[202] Rabinovich and Oren, 2014.

security advisers will shape the agreement and may ultimately be decisive as to whether an agreement is possible.

Inputs to Israeli Security

Most Israelis invoke security concerns as the primary and deciding factor in peace negotiations. Israeli opponents of negotiating with Palestinians most commonly argue that territorial concessions will threaten Israel on balance because Palestinians or other opponents of Israel will use a Palestinian state as a platform for attacking Israel and Israelis. They reference the history of Palestinian (and Arab) attacks on Israel and Israel's experience after withdrawing from Gaza and Lebanon. Israelis give the current and recent leadership of the PA some credit for the general cessation of attacks from the West Bank on Israelis in the past few years, at least until the kidnapping and murder of three Israeli teenagers in the West Bank in June 2014.

Israeli supporters of negotiations commonly argue that, on balance, a negotiated agreement will improve Israel's security, both directly—by helping to fulfill Palestinian national aspirations and redress Palestinian grievances and reducing Israeli exposure as the result of fewer Israeli soldiers and settlers being in the West Bank—and indirectly, via the benefits that could arise from wider Arab and Muslim recognition of Israel that Israelis expect to be part of a peace agreement.

In 2002, Israel started building a barrier separating Israel and the West Bank, to which Israelis generally refer as a "security fence" and to which Palestinians refer as "the wall." The route of the barrier lies entirely along or within the West Bank side of the Green Line; it generally follows the Green Line, but parts of it extend into—and sometimes far into—the West Bank to encompass some Israeli settlement areas.[203] Israelis generally regard the barrier as a legitimate and necessary response to Palestinian attacks on Israelis, particularly in the spring of 2002, but Israelis differ regarding the barrier's route.[204] The stated Israeli position is that the current barrier is not a political border.

Israel's security posture includes using a range of different proactive and reactive mechanisms designed to deter the emergence of security risks, which are described in detail below, as they affect the economic costs on security and influence the perceived amount of security risk. Israel has created structures designed to prevent an attack emanating from within its territory; from within Gaza and the West Bank; and from abroad, including the Arab states and Iran.

Strategic Warning

Strategic warning refers to Israel's capability to detect and prepare appropriate responses to an attack emanating in the longer term, most likely from other states, in order to

---

[203] Israel Ministry of Defense, 2005; "The Separation Barrier," 2011.

[204] Tirza, 2012.

provide sufficient time to react to and neutralize the threat. Strategic warning, which is designed both to mitigate the likelihood of an external attack and to attenuate the likely impact of such an attack, is currently secured through the continued presence of the IDF in the West Bank and a series of proactive intelligence early warning stations throughout the West Bank and in the Negev.[205]

The historical conventional threat that preoccupied Israeli strategic military thinking for decades has changed. Arab tank formations are highly unlikely to approach Israel from the east as they did generations ago. Iraq's army was devastated during Operation Desert Storm. Syria is consumed by civil war. Jordan's army was never a real conventional armored threat and is less so today. But as shown by the unexpected changes currently occurring in the Arab world, the ability to peer into its once- (and perhaps future) hostile neighbors is essential from Israel's view of its long-term security.

Tactical Warning

Tactical warning in this context refers to Israel's capability to detect an attack in the short term, emanating from nearby, mostly from the WBG, but also from Hezbollah in Lebanon and from newly emerging substate actors across what once were predictably stable borders, such as al Qaeda and ISIS elements in the Sinai Peninsula and across the Golan Heights in Syria. Good tactical warning provides sufficient time to react and to neutralize these threats.

Israel's current tactical warning strategy depends on a forward-deployed posture. This includes constant scrutiny of its borders and the development, maintenance, and protection of a network of informants within Palestinian cities.[206] Israel creates uncertainty among militants through periodic ground incursions.[207] These incursions are supplemented by a repertoire of other proactive tactics designed to degrade potential terrorism infrastructure, including house-to-house searches by internal security service operatives and IDF task forces and control of civilian infrastructure.[208] The adminis-

---

[205] Sharp, 2014, reports that the X-Band radar system has been deployed in the Negev to detect incoming missile launches. A series of signal intelligence platforms are common throughout the West Bank.

[206] This has been facilitated by the creation of an IDF intelligence corps detachment within Israeli Central Command and through close cooperation between the IDF and the internal security service. The creation and "care and feeding" of a network of informants within Palestinian cities (ICG, 2008, and Harris, 2014) has been vital to Israeli efforts to prevent attacks. (Human intelligence acquired in this way is augmented by a comprehensive technical surveillance and communication intercept.)

[207] According to a senior Israeli commander interviewed by *The New York Times*, the units under his command carry out six raids per night, on average, in Area A. He explained, "For intelligence dominance and freedom of action, this is the minimum number of entries we have to make per night." This tempo, however, represented a 50-percent reduction over the previous year. Elaborating on this drop in the number of raids, he said that he would endorse further reductions but that this "would require a political decision that would involve a security risk" (Bronner, 2011). Thus far, such a decision has not been made, despite U.S. encouragement through diplomatic channels.

[208] Byman, 2011, p. 28.

trative control exercised by Israeli authorities, especially selective granting of permits, also enhances security while reducing the need for large-scale use of force; Israeli intelligence is in a position to exploit the need for permits to gain information, while the system as a whole constrains the movement of individual Palestinians, as well as goods and services.[209]

Buffer Zone

Maintaining geographical separation between the populated areas of Israel and the Arab states is a key component of Israel's strategy for reducing external threats. Israel currently has a robust military presence in the Jordan Valley. This is complemented by a four-brigade Jordanian force deployed to the east bank of the river, sealing the envelope that prevents penetration of militants from other Arab states into Israel while keeping militants already based in the West Bank from getting into Israel or Jordan.

Strategic Depth

Israel's strategic depth reflects a combination of the buffer zone and strategic warning capability, providing both a better intelligence picture of the security environment and more physical space (crucially, away from Israeli population centers) in which to deal with threats. While the buffer zone typically includes only the narrow Jordan Valley, strategic depth includes the West Bank in this case, as this is the territory over which the Israelis are likely to have to respond in any type of cross-border incursion. The importance of strategic depth is reflected in the concern shown by Israeli planners and policymakers about the notion of the withdrawal of Israeli forces from the West Bank and the consequent dismantling of the security practices there that rely on the IDF presence.

A separate concern is exemplified by Israeli Defense Minister Moshe Ya'alon's fears that Hamas would be in a position to overthrow the current leadership of the PA and that the West Bank thereby would become a platform for attacks on Israel. As an example, a senior defense official, elaborating on this concern, is reported as saying,

> Thanks to the IDF's freedom of action [throughout Judea and Samaria], Hamas, Islamic Jihad and extremist Salafist groups can not even raise their heads in the West Bank [Judea and Samaria]. Just last month we saw what Special Forces had to do [to prevent terrorist attacks against Israel] in the village of Yatta in the South Hebron Hills, Jenin, Qalqiliya, Nablus and elsewhere. U.S. drones cannot stop suicide bombers in Jenin nor uncover bomb factories. . . . If we compromise the IDF's freedom of action and hand over security responsibilities to the Palestinians, we will see missiles being launched from Nablus onto Kfar Saba and Ben Gurion

---

[209] The leverage afforded by administrative control is quite considerable because Palestinians need Israeli permits to build anything, work, study, travel, or receive medical care. There are few activities that do not require some interaction with Israeli authorities and necessarily confer on these authorities a usable advantage over the supplicant.

Airport. Currently, the IDF and Shin Bet are doing the hard work of fighting Hamas. The Palestinian Authority has not been able to successfully combat terrorist activity.[210]

Freedom of Movement

Freedom of movement reflects Israel's ability to move forces rapidly to respond to imminent threats or to effectively pre-position forces to deter a threat. Since 1967, Israel has constructed a network of bypass roads that allows Israeli settlers and the IDF to move quickly through the West Bank and to minimize Palestinian contact, and hence minimize tactical risk, in doing so. Substantial resources have been allocated to this purpose. Although no precise figures are publicly available, the total length of these bypass roads is estimated to be between 700 and 800 km.[211] The threat of ground incursions—in the wake of the Second Intifada the Israelis were mounting an average of six per night—helps the IDF maintain its freedom-of-action capability within the West Bank.[212]

Israel has also used its freedom of action as a proactive means of disrupting would-be terrorist activity within the West Bank. The use of checkpoints began in a makeshift way during Operation Defensive Shield but proved so useful from an Israeli perspective that it became institutionalized. In addition, the military erects hundreds of surprise "flying checkpoints"—temporary roadblocks that can be installed quickly and with no notice in response to emerging threat information, to apprehend specific individuals, or randomly to increase overall security along West Bank roads. In December 2013, OCHA counted 256 flying checkpoints, as compared with approximately 340 in March 2012. OCHA counted a monthly average of roughly 495 flying checkpoints from January 2011 through September 2011, as compared with a monthly average of 351 flying checkpoints for the years 2009–2011 and 65 flying checkpoints from September 2008 through March 2009.[213]

Despite the value of checkpoints as a counterterrorism tool, intensive use of checkpoints quickly became a source of abuse and frustration, aggravating the Pales-

---

[210] January 2014 interview with Ya'alon (Ben-zvi, 2014).

[211] A completely reliable figure on total bypass road distance and construction appears to be unavailable. It seems that no precise figures are published; OCHA, the Department of State Human Rights Report, and the Congressional Research Service do not specify figures. There is some secondary evidence: "No exact figures exist for the total length of bypass roads in the West Bank" (Pullan et al., 2007); "There are no exact figures regarding how many kilometers of bypass roads there are in the West Bank" (Etkes, 2005); and "[Israel] has seized about 112km (2 percent) of the West Bank land for the construction of bypass road networks (about 800km)" (ARIJ, 2010); "The total length of bypass roads constructed on confiscated Palestinian territory to link between existing Israeli settlements, those under construction and Israel itself is approximately 700 kilometres" (Ramahi, 2012); "As of August 2008, there were 794 kilometers of bypass roads in the West Bank. All bypass roads have a 50–75m buffer zone on each side, where no construction is allowed" (Council for European Palestinian Relations, 2011).

[212] ICG, 2008, and Bronner, 2011.

[213] "Restriction of Movement," 2014.

tinian population and impeding economic and other activity essential to life on the West Bank.[214] These counterproductive effects were not unnoticed by the Israeli government, which, in recent years, has dismantled many checkpoints, a change made possible in part by the overall reduction in anti-Israeli violence emanating from Palestinian population centers and the increased effectiveness of the Palestinian national security forces.

Border Security

Effective control of the border with the West Bank, Gaza, and Jordan is necessary to prevent both internal and external attacks.

A key component of border security has been construction of the separation barrier, which is believed to have played a major role in mitigating the threat of attack. By segregating Israeli and Palestinian populations and controlling entry of Palestinians into Israel—except, of course, Palestinians residing in East Jerusalem—the barrier reduces opportunities for attacks within the Green Line or against settlements encompassed by the barrier. Most observers concede that the significant reduction of such attacks is, to a considerable extent, attributable to the impediment the barrier poses to the movement of terrorists. According to a former senior Israeli officer,

> The explanation is simple: before the barrier was built, if there was a warning about a suicide bomber approaching the Green Line from Jenin, there was no way to prevent it except by an offensive action in Jenin, which would presumably cause casualties. Once the fence was built, it was possible to alternate between offensive actions and defensive actions, and to deploy forces on the line of the fence.[215]

Inputs to Palestinian Security

Developing an effective Palestinian security apparatus is key to both parties and has featured prominently in all attempts to negotiate between the two sides. The Palestinians must be able to provide security to their own population: from internal factions, from external threats, and from Israeli settlers and the like. These policing functions are critically important to establishing stability in the WBG and to controlling disruptive groups that would make a viable Palestinian state impossible.[216] But, in terms of a lasting agreement with Israel, Palestinian security must also contribute to ensuring Israeli security, protecting Israel not just from possible threats within the future Palestinian state but from external threats, since Palestinian protection of its own borders also leads indirectly to protection of Israeli borders.

---

[214] Byman, 2011, p. 156.

[215] Eiland, 2010, p. 33.

[216] See *Building a Successful Palestinian State* for a full discussion of issues related to internal security (RAND Palestinian State Study Team, 2007, Chapter Three).

Two factors have shaped Palestinian security performance and development more than any others. First is its lack of experience and short history. Before the PA was established, Yasser Arafat's security organizations had no formal mechanisms for authority. They had structure and hierarchy, but they operated more like militias than state security forces. The concepts of operating under strict controls, under public scrutiny, and according to accepted norms were new ones for Palestinian security forces. In contrast, Israel has had more than 60 years to develop these structures and behaviors under a pluralistic and relatively open society.

The second factor influencing the development of Palestinian security is the subordination of these forces to Israeli priorities. At any moment, without warning and certainly without consultation, Israel can (and has) entered Palestinian areas, overruled the Palestinian leadership, and circumvented or ignored and thus undermined Palestinian security services to address what it perceives as threats to Israel and Israelis. Under these constraints, development of a capable security structure has been extremely difficult, uneven, and limited.

Strategic warning, a buffer zone, and strategic depth do not play a role in Palestinian security risks; funding, the requirements for a justice system, and the importance of chain of command are central. Developing responsible internal and external security structures, building basic capabilities, acquiring the essential tools of security, and negotiating authorities within the constrained Israeli framework are among the major challenges to effective Palestinian security.

What follows are the essential elements needed to develop Palestinian security forces. Some are required under any scenario, and some would apply only in the context of statehood. A few of these factors are entirely internal and can be developed by the Palestinians themselves. But the imbalance in security between Israelis and Palestinians is enormous—Israel controls virtually all aspects of security and can impose its will on the Palestinians, supporting the security services or attacking them as the IDF sees fit. The Palestinians have few independent options.

Chain of Command

Palestinian services have struggled in their first two decades under vacillating leadership; competing local and subnational interests (both between Gaza and the West Bank and within both regions); and an unclear, autocratic, and dysfunctional initial formation under the tutelage of Arafat. Remnants of Arafat's leadership's effects on his security services remain—loyalty is divided between local commanders and a central leadership. Lines of authority are rarely clear, and patronage remains an important factor in hiring, promotion, and performance.[217] Formed under a system that was based entirely on personal loyalty, the services have struggled to adjust to answering to a central authority. Developing a recognized chain of command is necessary for a

---

[217] Marten, 2013.

professional security service. Obstacles are both internal—the Palestinians lack a unified civilian authority—and external, as Israel limits mobility between key regions (not just between Gaza and the West Bank but within the West Bank as well). Palestinian security services have grown out of a much less centralized and less transparent tradition than in Israel.

Freedom of Movement

Like the Israelis, the Palestinians require mobility within their areas of responsibility to maintain security, but, unlike the Israelis, the Palestinians currently have little freedom of movement within the West Bank. The inability of Palestinian security forces to move freely among their constituencies as a result of Israeli restrictions is a fundamental obstacle to developing a professional, effective apparatus. Each service has purview over only its local areas, its loyalty often is determined more by the local commander rather than by the central chain of command, and its authorities are constricted by the boundaries of occupation. These restrictions limit the ability of the security services to provide security to their own population. Services are both victims of and reliant on Israeli action to preempt violence spilling over into Israel. Limited mobility within the West Bank raises any number of challenges, including the emergence of local leadership hierarchies that are less responsive to a central authority.

Border Security

The issue of border security would come into play with the emergence of a Palestinian state. Currently, Israel is responsible for all aspects of Palestinian border security. Manning the official border crossings between the new state and its neighbors, with all the bureaucracy, passport control, and additional responsibilities required, would be largely uncharted territory for a new Palestinian border service. The transfer of authority, if and when it takes place, would be gradual, but, on a few issues, the sides would be far apart. The Palestinians have repeatedly stressed that security along borders or a new Palestinian state must eventually be in the hands of Palestinians. Israel, on the other hand, has been willing to discuss passing along control over the strategic Jordan Valley, but, at a minimum, it has also insisted on a trial period much longer than the Palestinians have been willing to accept before the Palestinians are handed full control. In early 2014, the Israelis rejected the security arrangements for the Jordan Valley proposed by the United States, reportedly insisting in the John Kerry–led talks that security in the valley must remain in their hands.[218] How to handle the Rafah crossing between Gaza and Egypt is yet to be determined. Israel's tacit reliance on Egypt to maintain border security between Gaza and Sinai collapsed with Hosni Mubarak's fall and the Muslim Brotherhood's election, which eroded security mechanisms that controlled the flow of people and goods across the border. The new government of Abdul Fattah al Sisi has reestablished Mubarak-era levels of control.

---

[218] Tait, 2014.

Funding

As with the rest of their economy, Palestinians rely heavily on foreign donors, including the United States, to operate their security apparatus. Ensuring a consistent, responsive security apparatus requires a predictable, reliable source of funding, a constant challenge for the Palestinians. Some scenarios we consider entail expanded or entirely new Palestinian security missions that would stretch Palestinian personnel and financial resources. As long as the Palestinian budget is so dependent on external sources, development of the security services will be an irregular and unpredictable process.

In any scenario, the Palestinian security apparatus will face challenges that require it to make more investments for better security. With the prospect of a two-state solution, the Palestinians will absorb new missions that will require new technology, more manpower, and additional equipment—all things they cannot easily afford and for which sponsors are not readily identifiable. Israel's unilateral withdrawal from territory it currently occupies would also entail additional challenges.

Justice

Israel has an established legal system that is responsible for maintaining public order, arresting and prosecuting those who violate public order on the many dimensions defined by Israeli law, and maintaining prisons. Access to justice and the rule of law in the WBG are complicated both by the Israeli occupation and by the split between Fatah and Hamas and their competing visions of a judicial system. Separation between the two Palestinian entities has resulted in two parallel but very different legal foundations, while repeated clashes between Israel and Gaza have further weakened the rule of law in Gaza. The PA has made progress developing a justice sector, but the overall system is immature and requires further assistance and development. Other factors, such as the lack of freedom of movement, curtail the Palestinians' ability to pursue and investigate criminal activity. The inexact chain of command contributes to a muddled sense of who is in charge—local authorities, the PA, or Israel.

Liaison Services

Palestinian services have good visibility internally, even if bifurcated between the Gaza and the West Bank. Their capabilities to observe and disrupt threats have proven quite good, albeit with significant Israeli and U.S. cooperation. But, for external threats, the Palestinians rely wholly on liaison services to assess threats and take preemptive action. Without the assistance of Arab partners, such as Jordan and Egypt, or without the regular flow of information from the United States and Israel, the Palestinian services would have little peripheral vision outside the territories they control. Most external security responsibilities (i.e., detecting and preempting al Qaeda or ISIS penetration of Palestinian areas) are held by or in partnership with the Israeli authorities. While liaisons with other services contribute importantly to Israeli strategic and tactical warning, the Palestinians depend on these relationships for basic information.

2.4. Other Intangible Factors

In formal and informal conversations conducted as part of this endeavor, the research team repeatedly heard that among the most important factors delaying resolution to the Israeli-Palestinian conflict are cultural, religious, and emotional barriers. This theme is consistent with the literature.[219] Such barriers make concessions on either side extremely difficult, especially on the final status issues—i.e., borders, refugee right of return, security, and Jerusalem. Because we have no way to measure these factors, we do not include them in our formal analytical analysis. However, in Chapters Eleven and Twelve, we consider how the perceived cost of these factors might affect the conflict's resolution.

---

[219] See, for example, Bar-Tal, Halperin, and Oren, 2010.

CHAPTER THREE

Defining Present Trends

The political impasse significantly affects Israelis and Palestinians in almost all aspects of their lives but in two areas in particular: economics and security. The impact on economics stems from missed opportunities for greater economic productivity (opportunity costs) and from unproductive expenditures directly attributable to the impasse (direct costs). For security, the political impasse is associated with direct economic expenditure and on increased risk from both terrorists and conventional enemies. In addition, the mental, psychological, and emotional well-being of both Israelis and Palestinians is affected by and affects the sustained political, social, and psychological upheaval caused by the impasse.

In this chapter, we examine these critical components and explore how their characteristics are anticipated to evolve over the next ten years (through 2024) if existing trends do not change. This perpetuation of political impasse, which we term *present trends*, will be the reference case for our analysis in subsequent chapters.

The present trends base case assumes that economic and security outcomes continue along their current trajectories—i.e., the "final status accord" issues defined in the Oslo Accords remain unresolved, and there are no significant shocks or changes to economic, demographic, and security conditions. We assume that the impasse remains dynamic, as it has always been, and that conditions, including periodic business disruptions, flare-ups of military engagement, and continued construction of Israeli settlements, continue to evolve along current trajectories.

We describe present trends as a straight-line projection through 2024 based on developments in the past decade. That is, we assume that the key components we are considering evolve along the same trajectory. However, it is important to recognize that there can be significant uncertainty and instability even over a ten-year period. In the final section of this chapter, we focus on the uncertainties surrounding our straight-line projection by exploring the possible economic and security consequences of key events that have taken place over the past decade.

3.1. Economics

The economic performance of a country has important implications for the well-being of its citizens. Economic performance plays a major role in determining the quality of a country's political (e.g., justice, democratic elections) and social (e.g., health care, education) institutions, both of which are important for individual quality of life. There is now substantial evidence that a country's economic performance has a direct relationship to self-reported happiness.[1]

GDP Per Capita

A widely used measure of performance is GDP per capita. GDP is the value of all goods and services produced within a country; dividing GDP by the country's population yields a rough proxy for the average annual income of each individual in society.[2] As an example, in a country with a per capita GDP of $3,650, each individual would live on roughly $10 per day.

Despite the political impasse, and some associated disturbances along the way, the GDPs of the Israeli and Palestinian economies grew fairly rapidly in the post-1967 period through 2013, as shown in Figure 3.1. Israel's per capita GDP expanded by two and a half times during this period, from $13,000 to more than $35,000, while the per capita GDP of Gaza more than doubled ($800 to $1,800) and the per capita GDP of the West Bank more than quintupled ($650 to $3,500). These numbers do not reflect the impact of the 2014 conflict between Israel and Gaza, as discussed in Section 3.4.[3]

The growth of the Israeli economy in the post-1967 period to 2010 was accompanied by major sectoral shifts. Agricultural output, which accounted for more than 30 percent of GDP in the 1960s, accounted for barely 3 percent of GDP in 2010. Reported expenditures on defense fell from a peak of around 30 percent of GDP in the 1970s to less than 7 percent in 2012.[4] The Palestinian economy also experienced major shifts across this period—most importantly, reduced dependency on Israel's economy and increased dependency on foreign aid in the post–Oslo Accords period. In the past five years, GDP per capita in Gaza has been stagnant at best, while the West Bank and East Jerusalem continued to enjoy fairly rapidly rising GDP per capita.

---

[1] For example, Frey and Stutzer, 2002; McMahon, 2006; and Clark, Frijters, and Shields, 2008.

[2] An analogous measure is GNP, which includes the value of all goods and services produced by the citizens of a country. We focus on GDP because these data are more easily available.

[3] Some recent forecasts estimate that the GDP growth rate in Israel may be slowing. In its December 2014 forecast, the Bank of Israel stated, "According to the staff forecast, gross domestic product (GDP) is projected to increase by 2.5 percent in 2014, and by 3.2 percent in 2015, and 3.0 percent in 2016" (Bank of Israel, 2014b).

[4] Based on Bank of Israel, undated.

Figure 3.1
GDP Per Capita Growth in the Israeli and Palestinian Economies

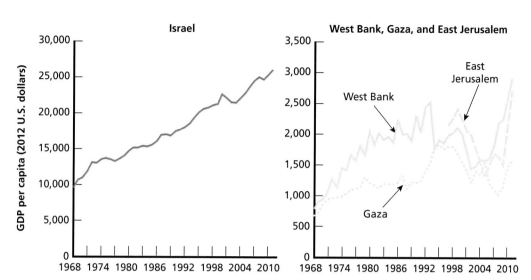

SOURCES: Data for Israel are from World Bank, 2015b. For the Palestinians, data on the West Bank and Gaza are from the PCBS, undated(b), and data on East Jerusalem are from UNCTAD, 2013a (which includes data from 1994–2000 based on PCBS, 2003a) and various other PCBS publications for later years (PCBS, 2009b; PCBS, 2012a; and PCBS, 2013). GDP data for East Jerusalem were not available for 2003–2007 but were estimated using various supplementary PCBS publications (PCBS, 2006, and PCBS, 2007) that provide data on economic activities but not overall GDP. Data for 2003 and 2006 were interpolated, as no economic data were available for those years.
RAND *RR740-3.1*

We use historical GDP growth rates to project how the economy is likely to evolve over the next ten years in present trends. One approach would be to assume that the GDP growth rates of both the Israeli and Palestinian economies will continue on their post-1967 long-term trajectories. From 1968 to 2013, the Israeli economy grew at an average annual rate of 4.6 percent, and the Palestinian economy grew at an annual rate of 6.1 percent.[5]

However, as we believe that more recent growth rates are more likely to provide accurate estimates, we use growth rates from 1999 through 2013 to estimate growth rates in present trends. This period includes the economic downturn of the Second Intifada (2000–2005), the economic recovery following the Second Intifada, and the economic side effects of Hamas's rise to power in Gaza and several Israeli military operations.

---

[5]   Authors' estimates based on data used for Figure 3.1. Estimates for the Palestinian economy are for the WBG only, as consistent data from East Jerusalem before 1994 were not available.

From 1999 to 2013, the compounded average growth rates for the Israeli and Palestinian economies were, respectively, 4.1 percent and 3.6 percent per annum. If we assume that Israel's economy will continue to grow at the same rate, it should expand from an estimated $295 billion (2013 dollars) in 2014 to $439 billion (2013 dollars) by 2024.[6] Analogously, the total Palestinian economy would expand from an estimated $13.9 billion (2013 dollars) in 2014 to $19.9 billion (2013 dollars) by 2024.[7] These values, as well as the corresponding per capita estimates adjusted for expected population growth, are summarized in Table 3.1.

Table 3.1
Ten-Year Projections of GDP and GDP Per Capita Under Present Trends: Israel Compared with West Bank, Gaza, and East Jerusalem

	Israel			West Bank, Gaza, and East Jerusalem		
	Average Growth Rate (1999–2013)	2014	2024	Average Growth Rate (1999–2013)	2014	2024
GDP (U.S.$ billion)	4.1%	$295	$439	3.6%	$13.9	$19.9
GDP per capita	1.9%	$35,900	$43,300	0.6%	$2,890	$3,080

SOURCES: See Figure 3.1 for source of historical data used in calculating 2003–2013 average growth rates. As the most recent data available were for 2013, the 2003–2013 average growth rate was used to estimate GDP for both 2014 and 2024.

NOTE: Data have been rounded.

---

[6]   GDP data are from the Israel Central Bureau of Statistics, undated(a), undated(b). The most recent GDP data available for Israel at the time of publication were for 2013, with an estimated NIS 965 billion in 2010. The shekel-to-dollar ratio in 2010 was approximately 3.85:1. Given that $1 in 2010 shekels was worth approximately $1.09 in 2014, this implies a 2013 GDP (in 2014 U.S. dollars) of 965 ÷ 3.85 × 1.09 = $273 million. If we assume that Israeli GDP growth follows the 1973–2013 trend of 4.1 percent growth, then Israeli GDP would be $284 billion (in 2014 U.S. dollars) in 2014. Extrapolating from 2014 to 2024 using this same 4.1-percent growth rate implies a 2024 GDP of $424 billion (2014 U.S. dollars). Note that, though it is likely that the BDS movement may pick up some momentum between 2014 and 2024, the total impact of this movement is likely to be modest. Estimates of total Israeli exports from the West Bank to the EU are approximately $300 million, out of $16.6 billion in total exports to the region (1.8 percent). However, this number rises to $5.53 billion if we assume that one-third of all exports to Europe are at least partially produced in the settlements (Horowitz, 2014).

[7]   GDP data are available from 1995 to 2013 from PCBS, undated(c). The most recent GDP data available for the Palestinians are for 2013 at $12.5 billion in US$2013. As these data do not include East Jerusalem, we used the fact that East Jerusalem GDP in 2012 was an estimated $930 million (authors' estimates based on data in PCBS, 2014, and previous versions of PCBS's *Jerusalem Statistical Yearbook*). If we assume that Palestinian GDP growth follows the 1999–2013 trend of 3.6-percent growth, then the Palestinian GDP for 2014 is estimated to be $13.9 billion (2013 U.S. dollars). Extrapolating from 2014 to 2024 using this same 3.6-percent growth rate gives us a 2024 GDP of $19.9 billion (2013 U.S. dollars).

Under present trends, we estimate that the capital stock will expand from $22 billion to $30 billion. This is based on the estimated $20.2 billion (2012 U.S. dollars) in capital stock as of 2002[8]; the destruction of $1.3 billion of capital during what Israel refers to as Operation Cast Lead in 2008–2009; and a net growth rate of the capital stock by 3.3 percent based on (1) average investment of 8.3 percent of capital stock[9] and (2) a depreciation rate of 5 percent for the Palestinian economy.[10]

Public and Private Expenditures

The second major economic consideration is expenditures, both by governments and by households. Governments have finite resources to allocate across a diverse set of public services. As an example, at the national level, increased economic expenditures on defense must coincide with reduced expenditures on public investment (e.g., transportation), welfare (e.g., poverty alleviation), or other public expenditures. Analogously, at the household level, unplanned economic expenditures (or reduced income) restrict the ability to spend on other household goods (e.g., education, health).

In Israel, current government expenditures are roughly 40 to 45 percent of GDP, which is similar to government expenditures rates in some other OECD countries.[11] The past 30 years have seen an increased public policy focus on welfare, social security, education, health, housing, and community services. All told, these social sectors account for nearly 70 percent of total public expenditures; the proportional and absolute increases have come at the expense of percentage reductions in military expenditures and spending on economic services (e.g., direct subsidies, capital account transfer payments and credit benefits, investments in transportation infrastructure), as shown in Figure 3.2. Total Israeli defense expenditures in 2012 were 6.3 percent of GDP, or just over $17 billion.

Amid other expenses, specialized resources are dedicated to supporting settlements of Israelis living in the West Bank on the non-Israeli side of the 1949 armistice lines established between Israel and its Arab neighbors (the Green Line); though the estimated total expenditures for the settlements as a percentage of GDP have fallen from levels as high as 6 percent in 2003, they still account for more than 2 percent of government expenditures.[12]

For the PA, the past 20 years have seen a rapid increase in expenditures. Government expenditures nearly tripled from 1996 to 2012, accounting for 56 percent of GDP

---

[8]   World Bank (2003, p. 20) reports a total of $11.2 billion as of 2002 in 1998 U.S. dollars. This is approximately $20.2 billion in 2014 U.S. dollars using the CPI provided by the PCBS.

[9]   PCBS, undated(a).

[10]   World Bank, 2003.

[11]   Dewan and Ettlinger, 2009. Government expenditures as a share of GDP were as high as 70 percent in the mid-1980s (OECD, 2011).

[12]   Amsterdamski, 2012 (quoted in L. Friedman, 2012), based on reports to the U.S. government and author calculations.

Figure 3.2
Economic Expenditures of Israel

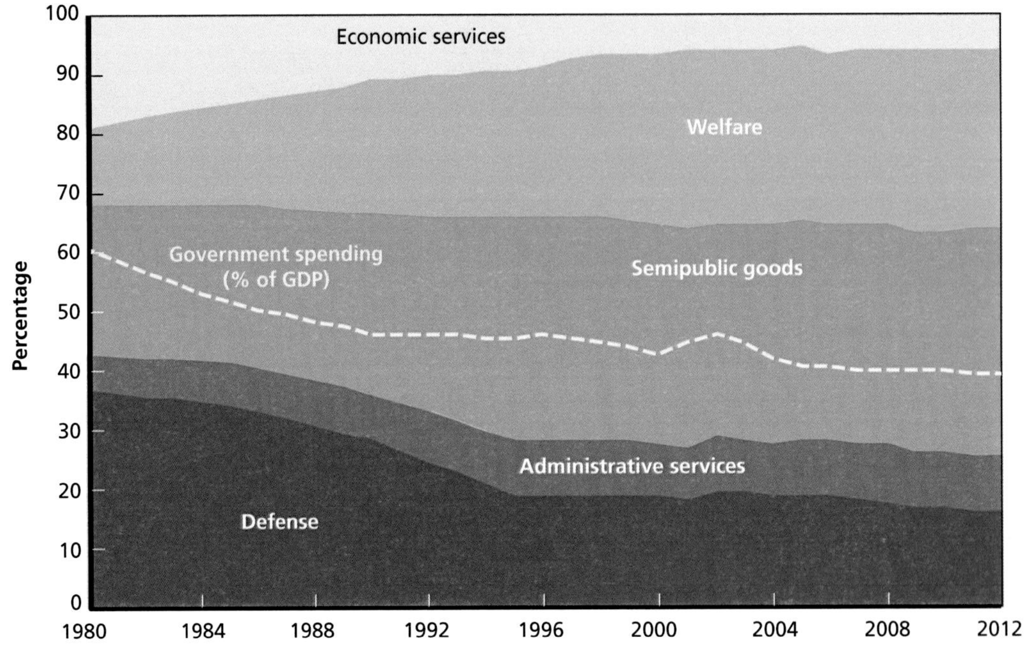

SOURCES: Bank of Israel, undated, and authors' calculations. Categories of spending defined by Bank of Israel.
RAND RR740-3.2

during 2007–2008. This rapid growth is illustrated in Figure 3.3, which also illustrates a slight reduction in expenditures since 2012, as nongovernmental sectors expanded. More than 50 percent of the PA's spending is on defense and administration; Israel's spending on defense and administration is just over 20 percent. As a result, the PA has more limited resources for economic and welfare support programs.

External support continues to be essential for the PA to function. In recent years, there have been modest increases in PA revenues and modest decreases in overall public expenditures, as illustrated in Figure 3.3. However, the PA ran a fiscal deficit from 2009 through 2012, despite more than $1 billion of external support; it ran a surplus only in 2013 because of a surge in external support.

Although the PA was able to maintain its financial viability and constrain the growth of government debt following the Second Intifada (2005–2013) so that debt fell as a share of GDP, the fiscal sustainability of the PA will become an increasing concern with contractions in GDP, Israeli withholding of Palestinian tax receipts for a long period of time, and any significant reduction in international assistance. If there is a significant reduction in government expenditures, the PA will be hard pressed to keep the large government workforce, including the 30,000-plus security workforce, paid and on the job. If the PA is unable to maintain its security force, Israel would

Figure 3.3
Government Spending for the Palestinian Authority

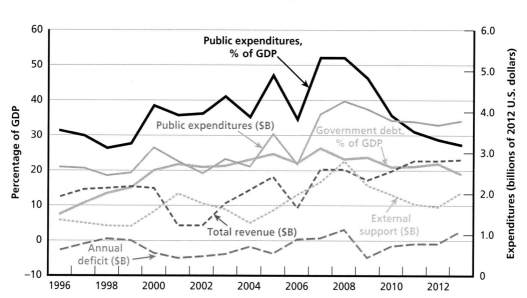

SOURCE: PMA, 2015.
RAND *RR740-3.3*

face a considerable direct cost to replace the role the Palestinian National Security Forces (PNSF) plays today. Reductions in expenditures will also likely disproportionately impact public investment.

Israel, on the other hand, will face steadily increasing expenditures for social welfare as the relative size of the Haredi and Israeli Arab populations continue to grow.[13] However, though the settler population may continue to grow at an average rate of approximately 5 percent per year, the cost of the settlers is unlikely to expand significantly as a share of the total Israeli budget. Despite an average annual growth rate in domestic expenditures of around 2 percent,[14] the total cost for the settlements during 2004–2012 was almost constant in total dollars (see Section 2.2.1 for more details).[15]

---

[13] The share of non-Haredi Jewish population is expected to decrease from 70 percent to 50 percent by mid-century, placing a growing burden on the social welfare system (D. Ben-David, 2013).

[14] Authors' estimates based on Bank of Israel data (Bank of Israel, 2014a).

[15] L. Friedman, 2012.

3.2. Security

Providing security for their citizens is a key challenge facing both the Israeli and the Palestinian governments. Effective security requires implementing and enforcing policies that reduce both the likelihood and the severity of potential attacks. A successful resolution to the current conflict will require mechanisms that keep overall security risks at a politically acceptable level for both populations.[16]

Israel simultaneously faces security threats from five different fronts. These include threats from three different terrorist organizations: (1) Palestinian rejectionists (e.g., Hamas, Palestine Islamic Jihad, and even some associated with the Palestine Liberation Organization [PLO], such as the Tanzim) who possess a limited rocket and mortar attack capability, in addition to the possibility of further "lone wolf" attacks;[17] (2) state-supported external forces (e.g., Hezbollah) that are acquiring greater rocket and ground precision weapons; and (3) nonstate actors (e.g., al Qaeda, the Islamic State of Iraq and Syria [ISIS]). The fourth type of security threat is from Israel's neighbors, including Syria's recently degraded conventional and chemical capabilities and a perceived growing closeness between Hamas and Turkey. Decreased stability within Israel's Arab neighbors could also result in state collapse. A fifth risk, which is the first and foremost risk in the minds of the Israelis but is only tangentially related to the conflict, is the threat posed by the Iranians and their potential nuclear weapon capability.

The Palestinians also face both internal and external security threats. Internally, the PA faces threats from political and ideological rivals (e.g., Hamas), from groups that categorically reject the possibility of political engagement with Israel, and from the possibility of systemic civilian disobedience like that experienced throughout the region in 2010–2012. Palestinians also face a security threat posed by Israel—incursions into Area A (where the PA is fully in charge of security, as negotiated in the Oslo Accords) and other disruptive security measures, such as roadblocks and long lines at crossing points—and by private Israelis, such as militant settlers, who destroy Palestinian agriculture and try to create a climate of fear.

Externally, the threats faced by the Palestinians are analogous to those Israel faces—namely, from extremist elements, such as al Qaeda, that would either seek to destabilize the Palestinian government or use Palestinian territory to engage in offensive operations

---

[16]   Most Israelis invoke security concerns as the primary and decisive factor in peace negotiations. Israeli opponents of negotiating with Palestinians most commonly argue that territorial concessions will threaten Israel on balance, because Palestinians or other opponents of Israel will use a Palestinian state as a platform for attacking Israel and Israelis. Israeli supporters of negotiations most commonly argue that, on balance, a negotiated agreement will improve Israel's security, both directly by helping to fulfill Palestinian national aspirations and redressing Palestinian grievances and by reducing Israeli exposure in the form of fewer Israeli soldiers and settlers in the West Bank; and indirectly via the benefits that could arise from wider Arab and Muslim recognition of Israel that Israelis expect to be part of a peace agreement.

[17]   The rocket capability of Hamas remained robust as of the summer of 2014, when 3,360 rockets were fired at Israel. Of these, 2,303 hit Israel, and 115 hit populated areas (IDF, 2014).

against Israel. The most immediate threats include violence and vandalism from settlers and Israeli security actions and military incursions (e.g., combat operations in Gaza in 2014), which have been very costly, particularly the latter, in terms of lives lost and infrastructure destroyed—for example, although estimates vary, the recent war in Gaza is estimated to have caused at least 1,400 Palestinian deaths, of which hundreds were children; damaged or destroyed over 100,000 homes; and caused perhaps as much as $4 billion in damage.[18]

Israeli security experts expect that Israel will face increasing threats over the next ten years, given an increasingly unstable Arab world and Iran's persistent hostility toward Israel and its nuclear ambitions.[19, 20] The type of violence experienced before and during the 2014 Gaza conflict is likely to continue. The separation barrier minimizes daily interaction between Israelis and Palestinians. However, the mixture of (1) rising regional tensions; (2) the lack of political progress or, indeed, any type of legitimate political process; and (3) growing internal dissent and dissatisfaction among Palestinians means that the relative stability of the post–Oslo Accords period is unlikely to continue indefinitely.[21]

The next decade may include further lone-wolf attacks against Israelis; rocket attacks on Israel emanating primarily from the Gaza Strip; and other violence from Hamas, Palestinian Islamic Jihad, and other groups, to which Israel responds with military offensives similar in scope to the 2008–2009 Gaza War and the more recent Gaza incursion in summer 2014.[22] However, we assume that the security environment faced by the Israelis over the next ten years will fall short of the sustained violent resistance experienced during the Second Intifada between 2000 and 2005 and that baseline IDF expenditures will not increase markedly in real terms.

Over this same ten-year period, two challenges facing the PA will likely become increasingly problematic:

- First, without signs of diplomatic progress toward statehood and with possibly stagnating or worsening economic conditions, rejectionists, such as Hamas and Islamic Jihad in the West Bank, may gain strength in the West Bank, as will more militant factions within Fatah, akin to the Fatah Tanzim.

---

[18] The UN reports estimates of the damage at $4 billion to $8 billion (UN News Centre, 2014). See also OCHA, 2014, 2015.

[19] Fishman, 2014.

[20] Rabinovich and Oren, 2014.

[21] The global jihadist movement, once based almost exclusively in Southwest Asia, is diversifying and spreading, with more affiliates based in Arab countries and with groups motivated by similar Salafist ideology. These groups are growing in strength in Syria but also in other areas on Israel's borders, such as the Sinai Peninsula, Lebanon, and even within the Palestinian territories.

[22] Instability and militancy in the Arab world—especially spawned by the civil war in Syria and the failure of the Muslim Brotherhood to hold power in Egypt—may encourage local actors to increasingly target Israel.

- Second, lacking a strong security partnership and facing budget shortages, the Palestinian security apparatus will be hard pressed to contain these increasing threats. The burden on the Palestinian security apparatus is likely to grow, and demands for training, equipment, and infrastructure will expand significantly. Efforts to reduce the overall size of the security workforce will continue. These efforts will improve efficiency and reform a confusing and overlapping bureaucracy, but they will also stretch the remaining manpower.

Available resources may also shrink, if foreign mentors and foreign sources of funding dry up. Palestinian requests for assistance will also compete with other pressing security crises, such as the effort to combat ISIS. This threat posed by Sunni militants is likely to divert attention away from the once-center-stage Palestinian issue and will demand more resources, which, to some extent, are likely to come at the expense of the Palestinians.

Given a continued stalemate on the negotiating front, coupled with the measures Israel takes to maintain security, including raids, an obvious military presence, and checkpoints (primarily on the West Bank), it seems likely that repeated bouts of violence in Gaza (e.g., Operation Protective Edge, Operation Cast Lead) will continue and perhaps become more violent and more corrosive. This violence may be driven by internal forces—from dissatisfied youth, such as those who launched the Second Intifada, in response to increasing settler violence against Palestinians, or as a reaction to the destruction in Gaza from the most recent Israeli incursion—or by external forces, from the increasing array of extremists, jihadists, and radicalized youth in the Arab world.

3.3. Sociopsychological Well-Being

The human dimensions of the conflict—which include national identity, safety, faith, dignity, freedom, and individual happiness—are difficult to measure but essential components of present trends and thus are critical to understanding the political impasse. These human dimensions affect the mental, psychological, social, and emotional well-being of both Israelis and Palestinians. No single term adequately captures the critical interaction of these social and psychological factors; for ease of exposition, we refer to this area collectively as *sociopsychological well-being*.

Sociopsychological well-being cannot be assessed along a single dimension, as is possible for economic or security costs. We reviewed published research on a wide spectrum of psychological outcomes, including diagnosable clinical disorders (e.g., posttraumatic stress disorder [PTSD], depression); psychological and emotional problems (e.g., distress, fear, shame, guilt); behavior issues (e.g., risk-taking, aggression, sleep disturbances); and cognition, identity, and attitude problems (e.g., hopefulness, religiosity, political extremism). In light of this review, we have examined sociopsychological well-being in the context of three nested categories:

1. **Clinical disorders:** The narrowest domain, clinical disorders, includes all diagnosable mental disorders (e.g., depression, anxiety, PTSD, alcohol or drug abuse). At the level of the individual, *clinical disorder* refers to whether a person meets the diagnostic criteria for specific mental disorders.[23] At a population level, levels of mental disorders are measured quantitatively via the incidence and prevalence rates of specific disorders.[24]

2. **Psychological problems:** The second category includes such psychological symptoms as distress, hopelessness, fear, guilt, and humiliation. Individuals may experience such symptoms but not meet all the criteria for a clinical disorder. However, the symptoms cause substantial suffering in their own right, and they influence people's attitudes, actions, and relationships, such as their orientation toward the future, tolerance of risk, help-seeking behavior, and ability to work and learn.

3. **Emotional priorities and well-being:** The broadest category includes aspects of sociopsychological well-being by which people and/or communities may define their place in the world—such as their feelings of safety and security, identity and belonging, faith, dignity, justice, and legitimacy—and that can affect a range of behaviors. This category links directly to how people experience and interpret the contours of their environment, status, and history, including—in the context of this report—fear, religious and ideological values, a sense of isolation, and other emotions that may contribute to parties' difficulties in making concessions necessary to achieve resolution of the Israeli-Palestinian conflict.

There is little evidence that the impasse itself has had a deleterious effect on overall measures of life satisfaction and psychological well-being of Israel's population. Indeed, Israelis tends to rank very high across a wide variety of existing measures of sociopsychological well-being.[25] Increased incidence of mental disorders (categories one

---

[23] American Psychiatric Association, 2013; World Health Organization, 2010, Section V, Mental and Behavioral Disorders.

[24] National Institute of Mental Health, undated.

[25] This includes the UN Human Development Index, in which Israel ranks 16th out of 186 countries (UN Development Programme [UNDP], 2013); OECD's Better Life Index, in which Israel ranks 9th out of the 36 OECD countries overall (OECD, 2015); the Happy Planet Index, in which Israel ranks 15th out of 151 countries overall and 8th out of 151 on well-being (Happy Planet Index, 2015; Wright and Pasquali, 2014); the Satisfaction with Life Index, in which Israel ranks 50th out of 178 rated countries (A. White, 2007); and the World Happiness Report, for which Israel ranks 11th out of 156 countries rated (Helliwell, Layard, and Sachs, 2014). These ranking are consistent with Israel's high level of economic development and ranking on a range of population health indicators. However, these rankings have been met with skepticism both domestically and internationally. For a discussion of this on the domestic side, see Weissberg, Bousso, and Linder-Ganz, 2013. On the international side, see Wen, 2013.

and two above) appears to be focused on individuals who have the most direct exposure to intense levels of violence.[26] As an important example, in the wake of the Second Intifada, during which Israeli life was demonstratively disrupted by widespread suicide attacks in buses and cafés, the incidence of mental disorders was no higher in Israel that in comparable countries.[27]

Similarly, mental disorders in Palestinians are most significantly associated with direct exposure to significant violence. However, Palestinians rank worse than their Israeli counterparts on overall measures of life satisfaction and well-being.[28] Effects of the conflict have been documented at the individual level, through impacts on mental and psychological well-being,[29] and the community level, through impacts on psychological well-being (e.g., social cohesion).[30, 31]

The indexes of general societal well-being and studies of specific impacts on mental and psychological health share important limitations, and the available evidence is fragmented and incomplete for Israelis and Palestinians alike. Collectively, the studies establish and reinforce each party's self-identification as victims at the hands of the other.

---

[26] See, for example, Hamama-Raz et al., 2008, and Lavi and Solomon, 2005. In terms of clinical disorders, researchers have found elevated levels of mental disorders as a consequence of experiencing political violence among children, adolescents, adults, soldiers, veterans, and emergency responders. There is also evidence of psychological problems with symptoms, including elevated levels of psychological distress, impaired coping, reduced hope and optimism, increased extremism, increased religiosity, and increased risk-taking behaviors (e.g., substance abuse) for those affected by political violence associated with Gaza; political violence associated with Lebanon, e.g., for the Second Lebanon War, the impact has been studied for adults and adolescents; for settlers who were evacuated from Gaza, this effect has been shown for mothers and children, adults, and the IDF involved. Indirect exposure via media outlets may also have effects. The effects may be particularly pronounced for some groups, such as the Arab Israelis and Bedouin. Discussions of the specific effect for Arab Israelis include analyses of university students, adults, adolescents, and the elderly.

[27] Israel's component of the World Health Organization's World Mental Health Survey Initiative conducted in 2003–2004—i.e., during the Second Intifada—found that levels of mental disorders in Israel were generally comparable to those in countries with no similar history of (recent) conflict (Kessler and Ustun, 2008).

[28] The Palestinian territories ranked 100th out of 150 countries in terms of "Overall Life Satisfaction" (as compared to 10th for the Israelis) in the 2013 UN Human Development Index (UNDP, 2013); 128th out of 178 on the Satisfaction with Life Index (A. White, 2007); and 113th out of 156 in the *World Happiness Report 2013* (Helliwell, Layard, and Sachs, 2013). However, a counterexample is the Happy Planet Index, for which the Palestinians rank 30th out of 151 countries (Happy Planet Index, 2015).

[29] Researchers found elevated levels of mental disorders, psychological distress, and impaired coping in relation to exposure to political violence among adults (Sousa et al., 2013; Gelkopf et al., 2012; Hobfoll, Canetti-Nisim, and Johnson, 2006; Lavi et al., 2014; Lavi and Solomon, 2005; Shalev et al., 2006; and Punamaki, 1990), adolescents (Henrich and Shahar, 2013; Qouta, Punamaki, and El Sarraj, 2003; Cohen and Eid, 2007; Muldoon, 2013; Dubow, Huesmann, and Boxer, 2009; Elbedour et al., 2007; Hamama-Raz et al., 2008; Pat-Horenczyk et al., 2007; Solomon and Lavi, 2005; Qouta et al., 2007; Al-Krenawi, Graham, and Sehwail, 2007; and Sagy and Braun-Lewensohn, 2009), and ex-prisoners (Punamaki et al., 2008). This includes individual and community exposures to political violence and humiliation (Giacaman et al., 2007a). In addition to the direct effects of political violence, the continuation of the impasse seems to be having an independent effect, provoked by the persistent presence of the IDF.

[30] The Palestinian territories ranked 124th out of 129 on the UN Human Development Index/Gallup World Poll measure of "Trust in People" (UNDP, 2013, p. 175). Israelis, in contrast, ranked among the top one-third of rated countries.

[31] There are not yet any studies on the mental health consequences of the war in Gaza in the summer of 2014, so they are not included here.

In terms of the present trends, history suggests that, over the next ten years, political violence and the threat of political violence are likely to persist; however, the intensity and duration of violence-related mental health conditions among either population are impossible to anticipate. With respect to sociopsychological priorities and well-being, some of the key final status accord issues embodied in the scenarios we consider will be viewed differently by subgroups within the Palestinian and Israeli populations. These political issues will often be zero sum (or very close to zero sum) so that some groups will be positively affected and others negatively affected by any change from the current impasse.

3.4. Present Trends Reflecting Key Events of the Past Ten Years

Ten-year projections are inherently uncertain, quintessentially so in the Israeli-Palestinian conflict. This uncertainty is highlighted in Figure 3.4, which displays significant events from the ten years following the end of the Second Intifada (2005–2015). Amid a variety of other significant political events, this period included the Israeli withdrawal from Gaza (2005); the Israel-Lebanon War (2006); Hamas's rise to power in Gaza (2007); Operation Cast Lead (2008–2009), Operation Pillar of Defense (2012), and Operation Protective Edge (2014); several efforts by the Palestinians to gain limited or full membership to the UN (2011, 2012, 2014); and failed peace initiatives involving both Republican and Democratic U.S. presidents. The ten years before that (1995–2005) were equally tumultuous, containing both the optimism of the post–Oslo Accords period and the instability of the Second Intifada.

The uncertainty and instability of the past ten years have had clear economic implications. While economic growth of Israel, the West Bank, and East Jerusalem were robust from 2005 to 2013, the Gazan economy stagnated amid the near-total isolation of its economy following the Israeli withdrawal. According to the World Bank, WBG growth appears to have slowed to 1.9 percent in 2013, and it is estimated to contract 3.7 percent in 2014 before growing again at a forecasted 4.4 percent in 2015.[32] Preliminary estimates of the economic consequences of the 2014 conflict between Israel and Gaza, though not yet comprehensive, suggest that Israel lost 0.4 to 0.5 percent of its GDP and that the Palestinian economy may have lost as much as 15 percent of its GDP.[33] Finally, although the international BDS movement has not reached a participation threshold that imposes a significant cost on the Israeli economy, one assessment of Israel's exposure to the BDS movement from Europe by Israeli finance minister Yair Lapid estimated that a "middle-range scenario" of a 20-percent drop in

---

[32]   World Bank, 2015a.

[33]   Filut, 2014; "Palestinian Economy to Shrink in 2014," 2014.

Figure 3.4
Ten-Year History of Key Events in the Israeli-Palestinian Impasse

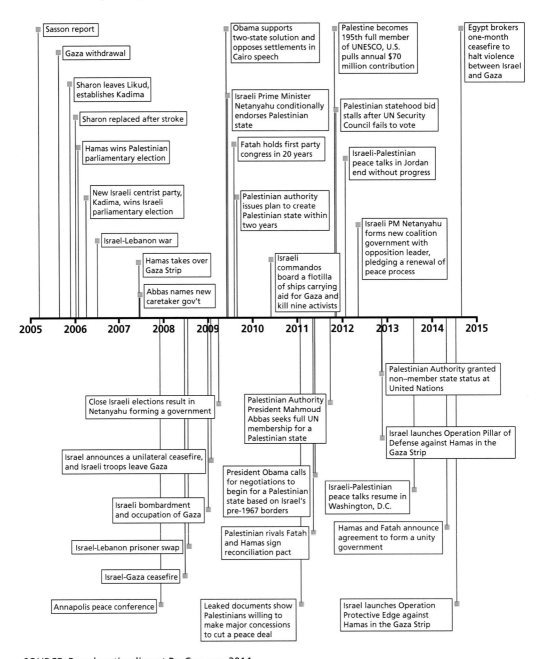

SOURCE: Based on timeline at ProCon.org, 2014.
NOTE: UNESCO = United Nations Educational, Scientific and Cultural Organization.
RAND RR740-3.4

European imports of Israeli goods and a halt in European FDI to Israel would lead to a U.S.$3.2 billion drop in Israeli GDP.[34]

The security costs over the past ten years have been high. Internally, the strife of the Israeli-Palestinian conflict from 2005 to 2015 caused an estimated 5,909 Palestinian and 250 Israeli fatalities, in addition to many thousands of casualties.[35] And recent events suggest that stability could worsen before it improves. Attacks by Israeli settlers against Palestinians in the West Bank, an important trigger of Palestinian retribution, quadrupled from 2006 to 2014;[36] rocket fire from Gaza, an analogous trigger of Israeli retribution, has become increasingly frequent and accurate in recent years.[37] Externally, both Palestine and Israel find themselves under pressure from a growing number of different types of Palestinian rejectionists; such state-supported external forces as Hezbollah; and, perhaps in the future, such nonstate actors as al Qaeda and ISIS.

The security concerns of both parties will remain a very high priority over the next ten years, for different reasons. Not only do internal issues persist, but the unrest and chaotic nature of the states surrounding Israel and the WBG, including ISIS, only heighten the situation.

---

[34] Bassok, 2014. Lapid's statements generated some skepticism within Israel, but his assessment underscores the concern some in Israel have with the possible political, economic, and financial impacts of BDS, if any, to the Israeli economy.

[35] Casualty numbers are from If Americans Knew, undated(a), which aggregates the data reported by B'Tselem, undated. Palestinian fatalities are reported as 190 (2005), 665 (2006), 385 (2007), 887 (2008), 1,034 (2009), 82 (2010), 112 (2011), 254 (2012), 38 (2013), and 2262 (2014). Israeli fatalities are reported as 51 (2005), 23 (2006), 13 (2007), 35 (2008), nine (2009), nine (2010), 11 (2011), seven (2012), six (2013), and 86 (2014).

[36] Levinson, Cohen, and Khoury, 2014.

[37] IDF, undated.

CHAPTER FOUR

Five Alternative Scenarios

We estimate the costs and benefits of a continuation of the present trends in the Israeli-Palestinian conflict as compared with five alternative futures: (1) a future with a sovereign Palestinian state living in peace side by side with Israel (the two-state solution); (2 and 3) two different futures involving unilateral withdrawal by Israel from the West Bank, one with and the other without coordination from Palestine and the internal community; (4) nonviolent Palestinian popular resistance; and (5) a violent uprising by the Palestinians. We posit these alternative future trajectories solely for the purpose of analysis and contrast; they are not predictions of future events.

In designing each of these scenarios, we derive economic and security assumptions based on historical precedent, a review of the existing literature, and conversations with subject matter experts. The assumptions for each scenario are clearly specified in the text. Appendix B provides specifics on how the various estimates, based on our assumptions, are calculated. In addition, the project website (www.rand.org/costsofconflict) houses a costing tool, which allows individuals to change key assumptions and explore how the change affects outcomes of interest.

The scenarios themselves were designed with four core criteria in mind:

- They should be credible.
- They must be sufficiently distinct from other scenarios to warrant analysis.
- They must be feasible in the ten-year analysis time frame.
- The counterfactual approach that we use must be appropriate for them.

We do not consider a "one-state" outcome as a potential sixth scenario because our counterfactual methodology requires comparison of distinct Israeli and Palestinian polities over a ten-year time period, and we do not think that achieving a one-state solution is feasible within ten years.

4.1. Two-State Solution

The basic contours of a negotiated two-state solution are well known; the RAND research team does not seek to provide an alternative formula to such existing models as the Clinton Parameters, the Geneva Initiative, the 2008 Olmert proposal, or the Arab Peace Initiative. Those models share several important characteristics. At their core, they are all predicated on an exchange of "land for peace."

The formulas do differ on several important issues (see Table 4.1). For example, the Clinton Parameters and the Olmert proposal allow Israel to annex a greater share of settlements than the Geneva Initiative or the Arab Peace Initiative does. Whereas Israel would annex between 4 and 6 percent of the West Bank under the Clinton Parameters and just over 6 percent of the West Bank under the Olmert plan,[1] Israel's annexation would be limited to 2 percent under the terms of the Geneva Initiative, while the original Arab Peace Initiative is based on acceptance of the 1967 borders. Another important difference is that not every plan mandates a one-to-one land swap for the territories annexed. Several of the proposals are silent on important details, such as how the issue of Palestinian refugees would be resolved or what the IDF's residual security presence or the introduction of a multinational force in the Jordan Valley would look like. (For a more detailed comparison of the various peace initiatives as they relate to final status accord issues, see Appendix A.) For a detailed description of the assumptions we make for each scenario, see Tables 4.2–4.4 at the end of this chapter.

These differences aside, the proposals generally agree on the issues that will most significantly affect the peace dividend we seek to calculate in Chapter Five. It matters little in overall terms for economics and security on the exact agreed-upon land swap; rather, what matters is that, under these proposals, Palestinians will receive most of the land of the West Bank and all of the land of the Gaza Strip.

Within the territory that would comprise a future Palestinian state, we assume that Palestinians will not face present restrictions on mobility except for some amount of territory in the Jordan Valley that will be monitored by either an international force or an enduring security presence by the IDF. Palestinians will be able to cultivate lands in Area C currently under Israel's control. Palestinians will have the right to establish a seaport in Gaza. Some number of Palestinian laborers would still be able to work in

---

[1]   The Olmert plan is not included in Table 4.1 because the only public information from it relates to borders. There are leaked maps proposing that Israel annex 6.3 percent of the West Bank to be compensated by the transfer of Israeli territory equivalent to 5.8 percent of the West Bank. In addition, the map depicts a safe passage between the West Bank and Gaza. The ratios depicted in the map—6.3 percent annexation of the West Bank for a transfer of Israeli territory equivalent to 5.8 percent of the West Bank—are not disputed, although the exact specifications of the map are. The map can be accessed at "Olmert's Peace Plan," undated.

Table 4.1
Comparison of Existing Proposals for a Two-State Solution

	Geneva Initiative	Clinton Parameters	Arab Peace Initiative
Jerusalem	• "Jewish neighborhoods of Jerusalem will be under Israeli sovereignty, and the Arab neighborhoods of Jerusalem will be under Palestinian sovereignty" • Jerusalem would be the capital of both states	• "Arab areas are Palestinian and Jewish ones are Israeli" • Jerusalem would be the capital of both states	• East Jerusalem would be the capital of the future Palestinian state
Refugees	• Resettlement options focus on Palestinian refugees returning to a new Palestinian state or remaining in a third country, although some limited return to Green Line Israel is possible • Refugees would be compensated	• Resettlement options focus on Palestinian refugees returning to a new Palestinian state or remaining in a third country, although some limited return to Green Line Israel is possible • Refugees would be compensated	• Calls for a "just and agreed solution" based on UN General Assembly Resolution 194 (1948). This is generally interpreted by Palestinians as an unconditional right of return
End of conflict borders	• Palestinian state would contain nearly 98 percent of the West Bank, and lost territory would be offset by 1:1 land swaps • Safe passage between the West Bank and Gaza	• Palestinian state would contain 94 to 96 percent of the West Bank with land swaps to compensate Palestinians for lost territory • Israel would retain the large settlement blocs along the Green Line, thereby keeping 80 percent of its settler population	• The original 2002 proposal was based on 1967 borders; in 2013, the Arab League opened the door to small land swaps without specifying a percentage
Security	• Multinational force in the Jordan Valley • Israel would retain two early warning stations	• Multinational force in the Jordan Valley • Israel would retain three early warning stations	• Establishment of full relations between the Arab states and Israel

SOURCES: Geneva Initiative, undated; United States Institute of Peace, 2000; BBC News, 2005.

Israel, and Palestinians would control their borders for the purposes of international trade.[2]

Under the two-state solution, we assume that 600,000 Palestinian refugees will return from abroad to the newly formed Palestinian state. Estimates of the number who are likely to return vary significantly, and we select 600,000—equivalent to an

---

[2] Israel would likely maintain some role in customs and immigration but under a Palestinian-run process.

approximate 10-percent increase in the size of the population of the Palestinian state—as an "average" value.[3]

As for Israel, the negotiated two-state solution scenario assumes that it will retain the large settlement blocs that are situated behind the security barrier or wall; that it will not experience large flows of Palestinian refugees returning to Green Line Israel; that Israel would be recognized by the Arab world; and that there would be opportunities to increase trade with such markets as Indonesia, Malaysia, and Saudi Arabia. It also assumes that the withdrawal of all settlers east of the security barrier would entail a significant transition cost in the form of compensation to the estimated 100,000 settlers who would have to be evacuated.[4] This transition cost would likely be offset, to a large extent, by aid from Western countries. Extrapolating from the post–Oslo Accords period, we assume that security benefits to Israel would be realized only after an initial lag in which rejectionist actors try to spoil the agreement.

In a two-state solution—assuming that peace holds and parties are in compliance—Israel's strategic warning capacity would remain intact. Tactical warning of threats could be reduced. The buffer value that the West Bank has served would also be reduced, as would Israel's strategic depth, once the option of forward-deploying forces ceased to be available. The transformation of the PA into a sovereign state would constrain Israel's mobility and freedom of action (although, given the assumption above that parties are in compliance with the terms of the agreement, one might then assume that the threat picture is more positive, and thus constrained mobility and freedom of action are less important).

Even as many key elements of Israeli security would be degraded in the short to medium term, others would be enhanced in a two-state solution scenario. Liaison relationships with the Palestinian state would certainly improve, as would those with European militaries. Liaison relationships with Jordan and Egypt are already sound but could be further improved if the issue of Palestinian independence were not a barrier to public tolerance for cooperation with Israel, although public opinion in these countries will likely remain fairly negative toward Israel. Relations with the United States would certainly be enhanced in ways that benefited Israel's security needs, in addition to ensuring continued U.S. diplomatic support for Israel in a wide variety of

---

[3]   This estimate is closest to that reported in Scenario I of Arnon, Bamya, et al., 2007. This estimate is higher than that implied by survey work conducted in 2003 (Palestinian Center for Policy and Survey Research, 2003) that reported that 10 percent of the approximately 2.6 million Palestinian refugees in Jordan and 21 percent of the approximately 400,000 Palestinian refugees in Lebanon would return to a newly formed Palestinian state. Note that estimates of the number of Palestinians living in the diaspora who may seek to return to the West Bank and Gaza but are prevented from doing so under the status quo range widely from 100,000 to 1,200,000. The estimate of 100,000 is from the U.S. Census Bureau, 2003a, 2003b, in RAND Palestinian State Study Team, 2007; the 500,000 is from the PCBS, 2003b, in RAND Palestinian State Study Team, 2007; and the 1.2 million is from RAND Palestinian State Study Team, 2007. The PA has used 760,000 in its own planning exercises (Brynen and El-Rifai, 2007). Dumper, 2010, provides more refined estimates, including characteristics of the returnees.

[4]   The estimate of the number of settlers east of the security barrier is from BWF, 2014.

settings. Relations with Europe and the Arab world would improve, increasing trade between countries.

Going forward, we will be specific about all assumptions and will clearly lay out how various security-related actions contribute to costs and benefits as they relate to both direct and opportunity costs. Presently, there are opportunities for benefits that are being missed—i.e., opportunity costs are incurred—but, to the degree that those lost opportunities are now taken advantage of, opportunity costs will fall.

Two-State Solution: Key Assumptions

Economic Assumptions

- **Israeli direct costs**
  - **Security:** No change in nonsettlement security costs; expenditures formerly for WBG activities reallocated to new security expenditures.[5]
  - **Settlements:** Resettlement of 100,000 settlers paid for by the international community.[6] Reduction in annual settlement expenditures proportional to number of settlers relocated—i.e., 16-percent reduction in annual costs as 100,000 of 600,000 settlers relocated.

- **Israeli opportunity costs**
  - **Investment:** Increase in rate of physical capital accumulation as result of increased stability, increasing to 15 percent above baseline investment.[7]
  - **Labor productivity:** Increase in labor productivity as a result of increased stability, increasing to 15 percent above baseline in years 3–6.
  - **Tourism:** 20-percent expansion in tourism.[8]
  - **Trade with the Arab world:** Trade with the greater Middle East triples.[9]

---

[5] We assume that any additional security costs are borne by the international community.

[6] The estimate of the number of settlers east of the security barrier is from BWF, 2014.

[7] Fielding, 2003, provides estimates of investment changes in the absence of violence used to formulate this assumption. That report estimates a maximum of a 28.5-percent increase in construction investment and 15.7-percent increase in machinery and equipment investment given a cessation of violence. In our estimation, we assume that ICT and non-ICT are both affected analogously. We assume that this positive shock to investment lasts for four years starting in the third year.

[8] Fleischer and Buccola, 2002, reports that tourism would expand by 20 percent, which implies a lower estimate of $1.2 billion (see footnote 104 in Chapter Two).

[9] Assumes a tripling in trade to the Arab world from $3 billion to $9 billion (Gilat, 1992; Fershtman and Gandal, 1998; Hufbauer and Schott, 1983; Sharaby, 2002; Arnon, Spivak, and Weinblatt, 1996; Hashai, 2004; Gal, 2012).

 – **Trade with Palestinians:** 150-percent increase in exports to Palestine realized.[10]
 – **Palestinian labor in Israel:** The number of Palestinians with work permits increases from 50,000 to 110,000. Illegal labor remains constant.[11]

- **Palestinian direct costs**
  – **Territorial waters:** Full access to territorial waters and ability to exploit mineral and other wealth (e.g., offshore Gaza gas).
  – **Labor in Israel:** The number of Palestinians with work permits increases from 50,000 to 110,000. Illegal labor remains constant.
  – **Internal transit costs:** All restrictions within the West Bank eliminated, reducing transport costs borne by the Palestinian economy. Travel through Israel (e.g., the Bethlehem–Ramallah route) remains restricted.
  – **Social services:** 25-percent reduction in costs as visas for medical services become more accessible.
  – **Banking regulations:** Release of all banking restrictions.
  – **Prisoners:** Release of all political prisoners, approximately 50 percent of prisoners. Total stipend payments reduced by half.

- **Palestinian opportunity costs**
  – **Territory:** Full control of Area B and most of Area C as a consequence of IDF redeployment and the removal of settlers.
  – **Water:** Unlimited water is made available to Palestinians at the prevailing market price.[12]
  – **Export and import restrictions:** 50-percent reduction in export and import costs.
  – **Licensing:** Elimination of licensing restrictions.

---

[10] PalTrade, 2006, p. 16, reports that Israeli exports to Palestine could increase by 150 percent (from $3 billion to $7.5 billion). The current level of Israeli exports to Palestine is $3.9 billion, without any changes in conditions—specifically, Palestine reported imports of $5.2 billion for 2013 (PCBS, undated[f]), and approximately three-fourths of Palestinian imports are from Israel. If the same ratio is true, then there is a possible $10 billion of exports.

[11] Assumes a gradual increase in legal labor by approximately 60,000 workers to reach pre–Second Intifada levels of 110,000 (Flaig et al., 2013, estimate from CGE model).

[12] Given Israeli insistence that water resources from the Mountain Aquifer are of "vital importance" (State of Israel Water Authority, 2009), the claimed historical use of the Mountain Aquifer by Israel prior to 1967 (Gvirtzman, 2012), and that there is (relatively) little potential for sustainable new freshwater supplies from natural sources, we make the assumption that, in a realistic two-state solution, the Palestinians will likely need to either (1) purchase water from potential sellers or (2) invest in costly infrastructure necessary to increase efficiency or treat wastewater. We assume the former as a first-order approximation, though it is likely that a combination of strategies for Palestinian water security would prevail in the event of peace. Given its experience with water reclamation and modern desalination technologies and past and current behaviors, Israel appears to be the most likely seller. The current price of water is around $0.45 per cubic meter (Bar-Eli, 2014).

  – **Tourism:** Elimination of visa restrictions for entry into the future Palestinian state.

  – **Investment:** Sufficient private and public investment to exploit 100 percent of viable new opportunities.

Security Assumptions

- **Israel**
  - **Strategic warning:** Dependent on infrastructure that replaces current physical presence; such technological measures as comprehensive imagery coverage (and the dramatic improvements in commercial and other imagery systems) and highly capable signals-intercept capabilities are likely sufficient to replicate current strategic warning apparatus.[13]
  - **Tactical warning:** Reduction in Israeli presence will reduce tactical warning of attack.
  - **Buffer zone:** Even with a small security presence in the Jordan Valley (an Israeli red line), the useful buffer between Israel and its eastern neighbors will decrease.
  - **Strategic depth:** Strategic depth will decrease, similarly to the buffer, with fewer Israeli forces between Israel and potential enemies to the east (notwithstanding that the lineup of enemies and their conventional threat to Israel has diminished).
  - **Mobility:** Israel's ability to inject its forces into the Palestinian areas will remain but will be more complicated, as an intervention would involve another sovereign state.

- **Palestinians**
  - **Force size:** The Palestinians will need substantially more manpower, facilities, and equipment to adequately assume responsibilities currently handled by the Israelis.
  - **Force structure:** The Palestinian security force will need to be restructured, reassigned to new areas, and subordinated to a new central command.
  - **Funding:** The expanded force size and structure will require infusions of money that is not currently available internally, which we assume is provided by the international community.
  - **Chain of command:** What is now a locally oriented, honest, and reliable force will have to answer to a single state authority.
  - **Liaison relationships:** The Palestinians will require more information, training, and partnering to absorb new duties.

---

[13] Based on RAND interview with former member of Dayton team.

- **Freedom of movement:** The withdrawal of Israeli forces from Palestinian areas and the removal of current obstacles to mobility should improve freedom of movement throughout the Palestinian areas.
- **Border security:** As Israel withdraws from the border areas, the Palestinians will have to assume responsibility for border crossings and border security and be transparent and reliable. This will happen gradually.
- **Justice:** The new Palestinian state would presumably assume responsibilities for investigations, trials, imprisonment, and rehabilitation of criminals—all areas that require significant development.

4.2. Unilateral Withdrawal from the West Bank: Uncoordinated and Coordinated

The international community, as represented by the Quartet (the UN, the United States, the EU, and Russia), favors the type of negotiated two-state solution described above.[14] However, some Israelis have proposed the establishment of two states through unilateral action. The concept of unilateral action has been criticized from both ends of the political spectrum; however, we found the idea widely discussed among Israeli opinion leaders.

Unilateral withdrawal, whether coordinated or uncoordinated, is not the preferred solution, even among its proponents. It is, rather, a least-bad option for those who assume that a two-state solution is no longer feasible and want to reduce Israeli exposure to Palestinians and violence.[15] Many of the changes to the status quo thus far have occurred through unilateral action, including Israel's disengagement from South Lebanon in 2000, Israel's withdrawal from Gaza in 2005, and Israel's earlier declared annexations of East Jerusalem and the Golan Heights. The shared underlying Israeli rationale for unilateral withdrawal, among the disparate groups supporting it, is that a peace agreement with the Palestinians might prove unachievable.[16] Israel, the

---

[14] See, for example, the Quartet's February 7, 2011, statement (UN, 2011), which reads,

> The Quartet reaffirmed that negotiations should lead to an outcome that ends the occupation that began in 1967 and resolves all permanent status issues in order to end the conflict and achieve a two-state solution. . . . The Quartet . . . reaffirms that unilateral actions by either party cannot prejudge the outcome of negotiations and will not be recognized by the international community.

[15] As an example, Gabi Ashkenazi (former chief of the IDF general staff) reports that unilateral withdrawal is a strategy to reduce the risk of violence without foreclosing the possibility of negotiations (Podolsky, 2012).

[16] A recent Israeli ambassador to the United States, Michael Oren, observed that Israelis should not "outsource our fundamental destiny to Palestinian decision making" (Ahren, 2014). Shlomo Brom, a respected strategic observer, endorses unilateral action as a crucial hedge, recommending "agreement and coordination with the Palestinians if and when possible, and unilaterally, based on an Israeli independent decision" (Israeli-Palestinian Research Group, 2012).

reasoning goes, should not be held hostage to a process that is potentially asymptotic and should therefore make decisions regarding borders, the settlement enterprise, and security concerns on its own.

The defining feature of these scenarios is that Israel would take a series of unilateral actions leading to the de facto emergence of two states. The most consequential would be the phased withdrawal of many Jewish settlers from the eastern side of the separation barrier, as well as the freezing of further settlement developments in these areas. Security forces would remain for an extended period of time after the evacuation of settlers who leave willingly, and Israel would maintain its security envelope, which would include maintaining troops in the Jordan Valley. The border between Israel and Palestine would be the present security barrier.

Conceptions of unilateral withdrawal vary widely. A prominent plan put forward by BWF, which it dubs *constructive unilateralism*, is a voluntary withdrawal of some 100,000 Jewish settlers to "prepare the ground" for peace.[17] BWF's plan calls for renouncing territorial claims to areas east of the security fence, a permanent halt to all settlement construction east of the fence, and a voluntary settlement evacuation and compensation law.[18] The evacuation of settlers, as envisioned by BWF, would be voluntary; settlers would receive compensation as an incentive to leave.[19] In BWF's assessment, negotiations are unlikely to produce a settlement that would be supported by a majority of Palestinians, let alone implemented by the PA: "We recognize that a comprehensive peace agreement is unattainable right now. We should strive, instead, to establish facts on the ground by beginning to create a two-state reality in the absence of an accord."[20] Moreover, "Israelis cannot continue to wait for the Palestinians. Israel must take charge of its future as a Jewish, democratic, secure, and legitimate state."[21]

Neither the BWF plan nor that of the INSS would entail the immediate withdrawal of Israeli security forces from the West Bank. BWF assumes that security forces would remain for an extended period of time after the evacuation of settlers who leave willingly: the Israeli Army would "remain in the West Bank until the conflict was offi-

---

[17] Rudoren, 2013.

[18] Yadlin and Sher, 2013.

[19] BWF's confidence in the feasibility of this approach is grounded in survey data that show that

> nearly 30 percent of these 100,000 settlers would prefer to accept compensation and quickly relocate within the Green Line, the pre-1967 boundary dividing Israel from the West Bank, or to adjacent settlement blocs that would likely become part of Israel in any land-swap agreement. . . . The numbers rise to 50 percent if a peace agreement is reached; 40 percent would refuse to leave (Ferziger, 2014a).

For a description of the BWF plan, see BWF, 2012.

[20] Ayalon, Petruschka, and Sher, 2012. BWF notes that there is still significant Israeli support for a peace agreement on a two-state basis. In the event that the Palestinians cannot accept an agreement reflecting the Clinton Parameters—in BWF's view, the closest to a reasonable compromise that has yet emerged—unilateral action by Israel would be, by default, the best course.

[21] Yadlin and Sher, 2013.

cially resolved with a final-status agreement."[22] Analogously, the INSS plan calls for Israel to maintain its security envelope, which would include maintaining troops in the Jordan Valley. Both plans state or imply that the border would be the present security barrier, or what some call "the wall."

Other notions of unilateral withdrawal vary significantly in the number of settlers who would move, though the security arrangements would be largely analogous. Plans advanced by more left-leaning politicians—for example, Omer Bar Lev, a Labor member of Knesset who had led Israel's elite commando unit—would maintain Israeli control of all of Jerusalem and the Jordan Valley while returning 60 percent of the West Bank to the Palestinians and removing 35,000 Jewish settlers.[23] Conversely, implementation by the right includes disparate plans ranging from the annexation of two-thirds of the West Bank (proposed by Naftali Bennett, head of the Jewish Home Party) to only 12 percent of the West Bank (proposed by Yoaz Hendel, a military historian and policy analyst who once served as chief of staff to Prime Minister Netanyahu). The latter plan would designate the Palestinian population centers a demilitarized state, leaving the status of the remainder, including 200,000 residents, split more or less evenly between Palestinians and Israelis, to be negotiated.

Unilateral withdrawal from the West Bank could take two different paths. The first path, which we call coordinated unilateral withdrawal, involves coordination by the Israelis with both the Palestinians and the international community. The second path, which we call uncoordinated unilateral withdrawal, takes place without such coordination as a result of either Israeli or Palestinian lack of cooperation or intransigence. These divergent paths are the two scenarios that we consider below.

Coordinated Unilateral Withdrawal: Key Assumptions

Among proponents of this approach, there is a perceived need for unilateral withdrawal to be carried out in coordination with Palestinian authorities and the United States. Both the BWF and INSS plans speak of coordinating Israeli unilateral moves with the Palestinians and the international community in order to achieve a smooth transfer and, perhaps, some international acceptance. They explain, "Israel should coordinate these moves—particularly those related to security—with the United States, the international community, and the PA, thereby lending legitimacy to the process."[24]

Advocates contend that Palestinian cooperation can be expected—despite a continuation of the status quo regarding Jerusalem, refugees, and final borders—because the prospect of the relocation of potentially large numbers of Israeli settlers and a much less intrusive security presence will prove to be compelling incentives.

---

[22] Ayalon, Petruschka, and Sher, 2012.

[23] Lev's plan is called "It's in Our Hands" (Rudoren, 2013).

[24] Yadlin and Sher, 2013. There is, of course, no guarantee that the PA would accept such a plan.

Our assumptions for coordinated unilateral withdrawal, provided below, are based on those of its proponents, who believe that mutual cooperation and coordination is feasible. We assume that the data collected by BWF on settler willingness to relocate are accurate (see footnote 19 in this chapter) and, therefore, that 60,000 of the 100,000 settlers east of the security barrier would be willing to move (with the right compensation package). We further assume that the PA subsequently agrees to receive control over all areas vacated by these 60,000 settlers. The IDF would maintain permanent control of the Jordan Valley, but the IDF's presence elsewhere in the West Bank would be temporary; at the end of the fifth year, the IDF would remove all forces and close all facilities in the West Bank outside of the Jordan Valley. Finally, we assume that the international community will support both Israel's efforts, by partially subsidizing the removal of settlers, and Palestine's efforts, by providing the necessary private and public investment to reap the limited benefits of this scenario.

Economic Assumptions

- **Israeli direct cost**
  - **Settlements:** Resettlement of 60,000 settlers with 75 percent of the cost of resettlement and compensation costs covered by the international community. Reduction in annual settlement expenditures proportional to number of settlers relocated—i.e., 10-percent reduction in annual costs as 60,000 of 600,000 settlers relocated.

- **Israeli opportunity costs**
  - **Tourism:** 5-percent expansion in tourism.[25]
  - **Trade with Palestinians:** 10 percent of potential $6 billion in exports to Palestine realized.[26]
  - **Palestinian labor in Israel:** Work permits for Palestinian laborers decrease by 30,000.[27]

- **Palestinian direct costs**
  - **Labor in Israel:** Work permits are reduced by 30,000.

---

[25] Fleischer and Buccola, 2002, reports that tourism would expand by 20 percent in a two-state solution. We therefore assume that 25 percent of this tourism benefit can be realized.

[26] PalTrade, 2006, p. 16, reports that Israeli exports to Palestine would expand from $3 billion to $7.5 billion. The current level of Israeli exports to Palestine is $3.9 billion, without any changes in conditions—specifically, Palestine reported imports of $5.2 billion for 2013 (PCBS, undated[f]), and approximately three-fourths of Palestinian imports are from Israel. Thus, we update this previous number with the same 2.5 ratio.

[27] We assume a symmetric response (different sign) as in the two-state solution using the Flaig et al., 2013, CGE approach, with an absolute magnitude of approximately half (about 30,000 workers restricted). Labor restrictions are assumed to be in response to Palestinian actions.

- **Internal transit costs:** All restrictions within the West Bank eliminated, reducing transport costs borne by the Palestinian economy. Travel through Israel (e.g., the Bethlehem–Ramallah route) remains restricted.

- **Palestinian opportunity costs**
  - **Territory:** Control of areas evacuated during the withdrawal process, including all of Area B and 60 percent of Area C. Excludes settlement blocks and 2-km buffer around the Jordan River.
  - **Water:** Unlimited water made available to Palestinians at prevailing market price.[28]
  - **Imports and exports:** 10-percent reduction in transaction costs.
  - **Investment:** Sufficient private and public investment to exploit all viable new opportunities.

Security Assumptions

- **Israel**
  - **Tactical warning:** Withdrawal from significant portion of Areas B and C will decrease Israel's warning of attack from and through those areas. Decrease in tactical warning becomes even more significant in the sixth year as IDF presence is reduced substantially.
  - **Mobility:** Reduced as Palestinians assume control of Areas B and C. Israel retains ability to inject its forces into the Palestinian areas, though operations will face greater risk given reduced forward-deployed assets.

- **Palestinian**
  - **Force size and structure:** Palestinian security forces will assume many tasks formerly performed by the departed Israeli forces.
  - **Funding:** The international community will provide requisite funding for any expansion of force size and structure.
  - **Freedom of movement:** In the absence of Israeli forces and roadblocks, Palestinian mobility should be enhanced.
  - **Justice:** In the absence of Israeli civil authorities, Palestinian court systems will be expected to take on a larger role, prison systems will incarcerate more criminals, and police will be responsible for investigating more crimes.

---

[28] We make the assumption that, in a realistic two-state solution, the Palestinians will likely need to either (1) purchase water from potential sellers or (2) invest in costly infrastructure necessary to increase efficiency or treat wastewater. We assume the former as a first-order approximation, though it is likely that a combination of strategies for Palestinian water security would prevail in the event of peace. Given its experience with water reclamation and modern desalination technologies and past and current behaviors, Israel appears to be the most likely seller (Gvirtzman, 2012). The current price of water is around $0.45 per cubic meter.

Uncoordinated Unilateral Withdrawal: Key Assumptions

The uncoordinated unilateral withdrawal scenario involves a situation in which Israel decides to take a number of unilateral moves, such as withdrawing some settlers from the West Bank and/or taking unilateral actions affecting the status of East Jerusalem. In this scenario, the Palestinians are assumed to accept the removal of some settlers as desirable but not to cooperate with a policy that is primarily designed to consolidate Israel's "facts on the ground" without addressing the core final status accord agreements. Lack of cooperation with the process could also come from some Israelis—e.g., settlers who refuse to cooperate. As a consequence of this situation, the international community is assumed to be unsupportive and to be unwilling to shoulder all but a relatively small percentage (25 percent) of the costs of moving settlers from the West Bank.

The skeptics of unilateral withdrawal warn that a lack of preparation and coordination, as a result of either Israeli or Palestinian intransigence, would lead to chaotic outcomes, as illustrated by Israel's previous forays into unilateralism. The uncoordinated unilateral withdrawals from both Gaza and Southern Lebanon created security vacuums that were eventually filled with hostile forces—by Hamas in Gaza and by Hezbollah in Lebanon. And, as illustrated by the total cost of the Gazan withdrawal to Israeli taxpayers, there are also likely to be important economic consequences. The potential cost of an uncoordinated West Bank withdrawal would likely be much larger than that incurred in the withdrawals from Gaza or Southern Lebanon, as the number of settlers being removed is much larger.

Yet, the PA leadership is not likely to endorse such unilateral moves as anything more than Israel's continued "occupation" of the WBG on its terms. Thus, though the PA might accept the new status of Areas B and C, politically, it will not support a mutually coordinated withdrawal. It has already made it clear that it will not accept Israel maintaining a presence on the Jordan River (in a two-state solution) other than for a few years for transition, and it is not likely in the context of unilateral withdrawal that it would back away from recent diplomatic moves at the UN or efforts to encourage European restrictions on trade.

On the rightward part of the political spectrum within Israel, the need for such coordination is discounted, in part because there is less of a perceived need for U.S. and European support and in part because it is believed that the residual settler population and heavy security presence would make Palestinian cooperation unlikely. From this perspective, uncoordinated unilateral withdrawal is less of an expedient that keeps the door open to a two-state solution than it is a downsizing designed to render the existing arrangements more permanent without requiring ideologically unacceptable territorial concessions.

Our assumptions for the uncoordinated unilateral withdrawal scenario are that the Palestinians and the PA will not coordinate with the Israelis and that the international community will condemn Israeli moves and refuse to pay for such a move.

We assume that the PA will refuse to cooperate with Israeli withdrawal and in no way will accept these half-measures as a solution to the long-term problems. Again using the BWF data, which report that only 30 percent of the settlers would be willing to withdraw without a peace agreement, we assume that only 30,000 of the 100,000 settlers east of the security barrier will be willing to move. All of Area B and those parts of Area C abandoned by the settlers will be returned to the PA, but a robust IDF presence will maintain restrictions on mobility within the West Bank, in addition to permanently controlling the Jordan Valley. Because part of the reason given by proponents of unilateral withdrawal is to separate Israel from the WBG economies, we assume that Palestinian permits to work in Israel and the settlements will fall by 30,000. Finally, we assume that the international community will be unwilling to provide any financial support to either Israel or Palestine. As the Palestinians will have limited access to water for agriculture and limited international investment, their ability to exploit any new economic opportunities from the land transferred to them will be limited.

Economic Assumptions

- **Israeli direct costs**
  - **Security:** Defense expenditures increase by 2 percent.[29]
  - **Settlements:** Resettlement of 30,000 settlers with 100 percent of the cost of resettlement and compensation costs covered by Israel. Reduction in annual settlement expenditures proportional to number of settlers relocated—i.e., 5-percent reduction in annual costs as 30,000 settlers relocate.

- **Israeli opportunity costs**
  - **Investment:** Decrease in rate of physical capital accumulation as result of decreased stability, falling to 5 percent below baseline investment during years 3–6.[30]
  - **Tourism:** 5-percent contraction in tourism.[31]
  - **Palestinian labor in Israel:** Work permits are decreased by 30,000.[32]

---

[29] There are no data available to estimate defense expenses from uncoordinated unilateral withdrawal, but defense expenditures increase by 9 percent during years of conflict (authors' estimates by comparing defense spending during 2001–2003 and 2000 using Bank of Israel, undated).

[30] There are no data available to estimate investment response from uncoordinated unilateral withdrawal, but the assumptions made here are within the bounds provided by Fielding, 2003. Note that the contribution of ICT and non-ICT investment was 20 percent lower from 2001 to 2004 during the Second Intifada—0.51 and 1.01, respectively, as compared with 0.61 and 1.23, respectively, during 1999–2013 (Conference Board, 2014).

[31] PalTrade, 2006, p. 67, reports that tourism hit a low of 70 percent below pre–First Intifada tourism levels during the Second Intifada.

[32] We assume a symmetric response (different sign) as in the two-state solution using the Flaig et al., 2013, CGE approach, with an absolute magnitude of approximately half (about 30,000 workers restricted). Labor restrictions

- **Palestinian direct cost**
  - **Labor in Israel:** Work permits are reduced to 30,000.

- **Palestinian opportunity costs**
  - **Territory:** Control of areas evacuated during the withdrawal process, including all of Area B and 30 percent of Area C. Excludes settlement blocks and 2-km buffer around the Jordan River.
  - **Investment:** Sufficient private and public investment to exploit 50 percent of viable new opportunities.

Security Assumptions

- **Israel**
  - **Tactical warning:** Withdrawing from a significant part of the Palestinian areas will decrease Israel's warning of attack from and through those areas.

- **Palestinians**
  - **Force size:** Palestinian security forces will assume many tasks formerly performed by the departed Israeli forces.
  - **Force structure:** Same assumptions as for force size: Palestinian security forces will assume many tasks formerly performed by the departed Israeli forces.
  - **Funding:** More funding will be needed, but it will not be available to support this increased force structure.
  - **Justice:** In the absence of Israeli civil authorities, Palestinian court systems will be expected to take on a larger role, prison systems will incarcerate more criminals, and police will be responsible for investigating more crimes. However, ability to pursue these criminals will be limited by continued restrictions on mobility imposed by Israel.

4.3. Nonviolent Resistance

In one variant of a future uprising, Palestinians may eschew violence for nonviolent tactics. Palestinians could adopt the tactics of mass demonstrations and street politics employed in late 2010 and early 2011 in Egypt and Tunisia, where Arab Spring protests in large urban centers, organized in part through social media, were used to agitate for political change. Comparing conditions in the Palestinian territories to their Arab Spring counterparts, Palestinians enjoy roughly equivalent rates of Internet penetration and Facebook use as in Tunisia and Egypt. In addition, the catalytic event in Tunisia

---

are assumed to be in response to Palestinian actions.

was the self-immolation of a fruit vendor, and Palestinians have had no shortage of people killed by Israelis who could be used to galvanize demonstrations.

There are several limitations on the portability of this model to the WBG. The first is that the Palestinian population is divided between two isolated territories (the West Bank and Gaza), and, even within the West Bank, the population is dispersed among several medium-sized cities.[33] The absence of a megacity stands in sharp contrast to Egypt and Tunisia, where Cairo and Tunis house more than one-fifth of each country's population, increasing the regimes' vulnerability to mass protests. In the West Bank, no single city surpasses even the 10-percent threshold as a proportion of the territory's total population.

The second limitation is that, in Egypt and Tunisia, protestors had direct access to the audiences they were seeking to pressure. That is to say, Egyptians and Tunisians could bring demonstrations right to the seat of government. Citizens were protesting against their own governments. But Palestinians are protesting against an occupying power. If the power to be pressured is Israel, Palestinians lack access to public space in Israel's political capital equivalent to Tahrir Square in Cairo.

One variant of a nonviolent uprising, and the one on which we focus, includes legal efforts at the UN and other world bodies; continued support for trade restrictions on Israel, including general support for the BDS movement; and nonviolent demonstrations. This approach is consistent with the PA's recent efforts, such as its successful bid to gain non–member state observer status in the UN General Assembly.[34]

Having achieved this partial recognition, a second avenue available to the PA is to become a full member of the International Criminal Court and pursue charges there against Israel over settlement policy or targeted assassinations.[35] Such efforts may fail, given the legal complexities governing International Criminal Court jurisdiction,[36] but even an unsuccessful attempt at bringing charges in the International Criminal Court could create a platform for increased Palestinian activism. The Hague is just one possible venue for initiatives aimed at isolating Israel in the international community. Israel is thought to be committed to a harshly punitive response to such a strategy; an

---

[33]   For a breakdown of Palestinian population by city, see City Population, 2014.

[34]   Palestinians have explored several nonviolent concepts for compelling Israel to negotiate a final status accord on Palestinian terms. None has yet been implemented except for occasional general strikes, but even these have not been a feature of recent Palestinian pressure on Israel. Other approaches, including, for example, civil disobedience, have not figured prominently, if at all, in the actual Palestinian response to occupation.

[35]   Currently, the most discussed nonviolent approach to internationalization of the conflict and coercion of Israel entails Palestinian membership in the International Criminal Court on the strength of the PA's November 2012 accession to non–member state status in the UN. Whether this is a legally available option is currently open to question (e.g., Bisharat, 2013). On April 1, 2015, the Palestinians became an official member of the International Criminal Court.

[36]   Keller, 2013.

initial response in January 2015 has been to freeze $127 million in tax revenues that it has collected for the PA, severely hampering the PA's ability to meet salaries.[37]

Another effort would be for the Palestinian leadership to continue pressing the EU to tighten its trade policies with Israel.[38] Rather than assuming an economic boycott on the scale of the divestment and sanctions experienced by South Africa in the 1980s, we look at the cost of a more limited scenario that includes a consumer-organized boycott of Israeli products that would somewhat restrict trade with Europe, Israel's largest trading partner. In 2013, the EU ruled that it could not provide funding to Israeli organizations operating in West Bank settlements or in territory annexed by Israel after 1967 (i.e., East Jerusalem and the Golan Heights).[39] The significance of that ruling is not in its immediate economic effect—the affected exports and funds are small—but in the potential that the move could translate into further restrictions.

The Israeli government regards these threats seriously. Taking Israel to the International Criminal Court is a serious threat because it could lead to restrictions on travel of senior Israeli officials and perhaps other actions. Some Israelis consider Palestinian recourse to the International Criminal Court a form of "lawfare" deployed to criminalize necessary acts of self-defense undertaken by Israel.[40] Some Israelis are beginning to take the economic boycott seriously, which may be indicative of a broader trend; as noted by former Israeli Justice Minister Tzipi Livni, "Europe is boycotting goods. True, it starts with settlement [goods], but their problem is with Israel, which is seen as a colonialist country. Therefore, it won't stop at the settlements, but [will spread] to all of Israel."[41]

Most Israeli policymakers disagree with Livni's formulation. However, European countries are showing greater propensity to oppose Israeli policies in international fora. For example, in the UN General Assembly vote for Palestine to be accorded observer status, 14 of the EU's 28 member states voted for the resolution, while 13 abstained and only one (the Czech Republic) opposed.[42]

---

[37] On March 26, 2015, Israel announced that it would be ending the freeze on these tax receipts.

[38] Once movements, such as BDS, begin, they are no longer controlled by any one group or individual; many local groups will splinter and define what BDS means to them. So the Palestinians will likely support the BDS movement, but they will not control it.

[39] To be clear, these restrictions apply to EU funding and not the funding provided by individual member states.

[40] The court is seen by the Palestinians as a powerful tool because, experts say, Israel risks prosecution there for its policy of settlement building in the West Bank and East Jerusalem, territories Israel seized in the 1967 war and that, along with Gaza, the Palestinians claim for their state. Israel has warned both the United States and the PA that a move toward International Criminal Court membership would be regarded as a serious escalation of the Israeli-Palestinian dispute and warrant retaliatory action (B. White, 2014).

[41] Keinon, 2013a.

[42] More recently, the Israeli incursion into Gaza in July and August 2014 has generated mass protests in numerous European countries. In some cases, these rallies have become anti-Semitic to the great concern of many Israelis. Note that the votes from the UN General Assembly 11317 are available at UN, 2012.

The Israeli government is likely to respond to economic pressure with moves of its own, including withholding tax revenue, as has already occurred on various occasions.

Nonviolent Resistance: Key Assumptions

Economic Assumptions

- **Israeli direct costs**
  - None.

- **Israeli opportunity costs**
  - **Investment:** Decrease in rate of physical capital accumulation as result of decreased stability, falling to 10 percent below baseline investment during years 3–6.[43]
  - **BDS:** GDP falls by 2 percent as result of financial sanctions and limited restrictions on exports to Israel.[44]
  - **Tourism:** 10-percent contraction in tourism.
  - **Palestinian labor in Israel:** Work permits are decreased by 30,000.

- **Palestinian direct costs**
  - **Labor in Israel:** Work permits are reduced by 30,000.
  - **Internal transit costs:** 25-percent increase in internal transit costs as a result of punitive restrictions.
  - **Social services:** 25-percent increase in value of Israeli-related medical and water direct costs.
  - **Prisoners:** 10-percent increase in number of prisoners held in Israel.

- **Palestinian opportunity cost**
  - **Imports and exports:** 25-percent increase in transaction costs for both exports and imports.

---

[43] There are no data available to estimate investment response from unilateral withdrawal but the assumptions made here are within the bounds provided by Fielding (2003). Note that the contribution of ICT and non-ICT investment was 20 percent lower from 2001 to 2004 during the Second Intifada—0.51 and 1.01, respectively, as compared with 0.61 and 1.23, respectively, during 1999–2013 (Conference Board, 2014).

[44] The Israeli finance minister estimated the potential cost of BDS at 1 percent of GDP (see footnote 34 in Chapter Three). Financial sanctions (common between countries with close relations) reduce GDP by 1.7 percent, on average; trade-only sanctions (either export or import) reduce GDP by 0.7 percent, on average; and combined financial and trade sanctions have effects of nearly 3 percent of GDP (Hufbauer et al., 2008).

Security Assumptions

- **Israel**
  - **Liaison:** In the wake of successful nonviolent actions, the Israelis could lose important partners that no longer want to bear the political cost of maintaining close liaison relationships with Israel.

- **Palestinians**
  - **Liaison:** Some partners, including the Egyptians and possibly the Jordanians, might be leery of taking sides in a politically sensitive arena.

4.4. Violent Uprising

Perhaps the most challenging scenario to define is the form of a violent uprising or "Third Intifada." This is because neither of the previous two intifadas is likely to serve as an exact blueprint for a third, though both help to inform the broad outlines of uprisings and provided decent precedents to use in our analysis. Some of the conditions that shaped previous uprisings—e.g., the absence of the separation barrier—no longer apply. Palestinians have also internalized the costs from those previous uprisings, just as they have closely observed developments in nearby countries that have led to political change (e.g., Egypt and Tunisia) and where nonviolent uprisings have morphed into armed conflict (e.g., Syria), and also Israel's changing tactics as exhibited in the summer of 2014 in Gaza. A Third Intifada would take place under the heavy shadow cast by other regional actors, including nonstate actors, such as al Qaeda and ISIS.

A violent uprising nonetheless could be sparked by several developments: a nonviolent demonstration that turns violent against Israeli soldiers or settlers, a routine Israeli incursion into Area A that inflicts serious casualties, intensive operations against Gaza-based forces that inspire violent protests on the West Bank, a terrorist attack—similar to the one that led to the Israeli decision to launch Operation Defensive Shield—carried out without the knowledge of Palestinian leaders, deliberate provocation by the Palestinian leadership (or aspirants to such leadership) in a bid to shake up the frozen peace process and internationalize the conflict, Israelis occupying the Al-Aqsa Mosque, or a series or Palestinians raids into Israel resulting in the capture of some Israeli troops. (But, given good Israeli security cooperation with Jordan, if a violent uprising occurs, it is not likely to involve a cross-border rocket or terrorist infiltration elements from the east.) Although there are events suggesting that a new uprising is a distinct possibility,[45] both

---

[45] As an example, in early 2011, Palestinian activists created a Facebook page called "Third Intifada," which gained nearly 390,000 fans before it was shut down at the request of Israel. After Facebook administrators removed the page, a replacement was created, which continues to exist at the time of this writing (spring 2015). In our interviews with Israeli and Palestinian opinion leaders, many cited the possibility of a Third Intifada—at least

Palestinians and Israelis learned important lessons from the Second Intifada, making a reoccurrence less likely.[46]

However, the passage of time has had an effect; the children of the Intifada are now young adults for whom memories of ten to 12 years ago exert less restraint on today's actions. When growing frustration among the Palestinian public about the lack of process toward a final status accord agreement is added to the equation, a change in trend appears more plausible. The relative increase in "populist" terrorist attacks—not initiated by a formal known terrorist organization—may signal this change of atmosphere. Such an outbreak would differ in nature and scope from the riots in the Palestinian territories during the First Intifada in the late 1980s and from the Second Intifada in the early part of the 2000s. Israel's responses to outbreaks of violence may also accelerate existing efforts to disparage Israel's reputation in the Western world.[47]

In the violent uprising scenario that we postulate, violence erupts—perhaps beginning in Gaza but spreading to the West Bank and possibly involving foreign actors, such as Hezbollah in South Lebanon or jihadists operating in the Levant.[48] Hamas and its fellow travelers among extremist groups have a different cost-benefit calculation from that of the Fatah-led Palestinian leadership in the West Bank. Extremist groups, whose strongest base is in Gaza, could conclude that violence was in their interest as a way of mobilizing supporters or reinforcing their claim to the mantle of leader of the resistance. In comparison to the geographic limitations of Gaza-based violence,[49] an uprising joined by Palestinians from the West Bank with perhaps other groups operating from outside Israel's northern border would be significantly more threatening than

---

one interviewee believing that it had already begun. Similarly, U.S. leaders, including Secretary of State Kerry, noted the possibility of a Third Intifada should the peace initiative ultimately fail.

[46] The Palestinian economy has only just recovered from the severe contraction it experienced during that uprising, when per capita GDP fell by one-third. This memory may make Palestinians, and in particular the leadership of the PA, reluctant to take that road a second time. For their part, many Israelis note that the construction of the separation barrier was in direct response to the tactics employed in the Second Intifada and believe that the barrier has succeeded in mitigating Israel's risk to that type of campaign. On the other hand, a return to violence cannot be dismissed even if the lessons internalized by Palestinians and Israelis suggest that its form is likely to differ from previous iterations.

[47] Brom and Kurz, 2014.

[48] Although Hezbollah and Hamas are separated by sect and do not see eye to eye on many issues, they do share a common patron in Iran. Hezbollah could seek to use a Third Intifada as a platform for burnishing its resistance credentials. Hezbollah's involvement in the Syrian conflict on the side of the Assad regime has left it vulnerable to the charge that it is pursuing a sectarian agenda, so such a move would hold the added appeal of helping to restore its brand among Sunni Arabs. Hezbollah may also feel tempted to renew its confrontation with Israel based on its reading of the 2006 war, in which it outperformed expectations and received a short-term bounce in popularity.

[49] As demonstrated by the periodic flare-ups of violence since the Second Intifada, the capabilities of Palestinian militant groups are quite limited. Their ability to receive outside assistance is constrained by Israeli control over most access points into Gaza with the exception of the tunnels that traverse the "Philadelphia corridor" separating Gaza from Egyptian territory, but over which the current Egyptian government has shown some commitment to limit weapon flows.

a scenario with violence limited to Gaza alone.[50] Perhaps the big difference is the threat of more effective indirect attack posed by Hezbollah rockets (with Hezbollah's being more effective than Hamas's, with greater range and larger warheads) and the prospect of suicide attacks against settlers living in the West Bank and outside the security barrier.

Both Hamas and Hezbollah also put a premium on capturing Israeli soldiers and subsequently holding them in exchange for the freedom of their own captured fighters. While rockets and indirect fire have become the most common and seemingly preferred tactics, the extensive tunneling Israel uncovered across the Gaza-Israeli border and previous attempts by Hezbollah to breach the northern border underscore its interest in conducting attacks in Israel proper. Indeed, the terrorist attacks by Palestinians who infiltrated the Green Line during previous intifadas were the most lethal methods they used. Both Gazans and Hezbollah have attempted a wide variety of largely unsuccessful tactics to attack Israel in the past, including using small aircraft and attempting seaborne attacks.

Although the Israelis have not disclosed their plans for countering a violent uprising, Israel's response to the outbreak and subsequent intensification of the Second Intifada and more recent violence can be used to infer the likely response.[51] Israel's more recent tactics have included reoccupying urban areas in order to force Palestinians into high-intensity engagements;[52] new tactics combining the efforts of infantry, engineer, armor, and air units in ways to limit the potential for engagements characterized by constant close-quarters combat and direct assaults on civilians; rapid expansion of intelligence collection and dissemination, including the deployment of undercover

---

[50] This could take the form of Hezbollah launching rockets against Israeli population centers as a show of solidarity with the Palestinian resistance. Should Hezbollah, Hamas, or al Qaeda decide to piggyback on a West Bank conflict to enhance perceptions of its relevance or effectiveness while complicating Israel's counterinsurgency efforts, the regional costs of renewed violence would rise. In 2006, damage to Lebanon's infrastructure, particularly its power grid, was extensive. Infrastructural damage inflicted on Gaza in Cast Lead and Pillar of Defense was equally profound. There is little doubt that al Qaeda involvement would trigger attacks on its infrastructure in Syria. There would be reciprocal effects, of course, if Hamas and Hezbollah unleashed either collectively or separately their ballistic missile inventories on Israeli population centers. Both the very limited Iraqi bombardment of 1991 and the Hezbollah attacks in 2006 precipitated population movements and degraded economic performance.

[51] Some sense of Israel's response options can also be gleaned from Operation Cast Lead, a three-week combined arms assault that was launched in late December 2008 against Palestinian forces in Gaza, and Operation Pillar of Defense, a sharp Israeli eight-day air campaign against targets also in Gaza that took place in November 2012. Both of these Gaza campaigns were intended to disarm Gazan forces to the extent possible and establish deterrence by demonstrating to Hamas Israel's determination to destroy its military capabilities.

[52] Jones, 2007. Additionally, the IDF seized the headquarters of several Palestinian security forces in order to weaken these forces (Byman, 2011).

units;[53] mass arrests;[54] and increasingly precise air strikes using the Israeli equivalent of Hellfire missiles coupled with "roof knocking," in which buildings would be struck by nonlethal munitions to allow civilians time to evacuate the structure in advance of a lethal strike.[55]

While Operation Defensive Shield succeeded in achieving its objectives vis-à-vis violent resistance in the West Bank, it carried heavy costs for both the Israelis and the Palestinians, and similar costs are anticipated as a consequence of any additional violence. On the Israeli side, there was a significant negative economic impact, with calls for economic boycott among Europeans[56] and a growing sense of unease for Europeans about doing business in Israel.[57] There were diplomatic and military consequences as well,[58] although, from an Israeli perspective, these costs were outweighed by the benefit of pressure exerted by these governments—all of which were worried about the effect of satellite television images of Operation Defensive Shield on their populations—on President Abbas to curtail Palestinian violence. The potential for a UN inquiry and possible war-crime prosecution was an additional cost.[59] The operations may have had more intangible effects, including a global growth in anti-Israeli, or perhaps even anti-

---

[53] A robust forward-deployed intelligence-gathering effort, including Arabic-speaking plainclothes security teams (*mistaravim*), allowed the IDF to interrogate fighters or civilians in the field and then rapidly disseminate the intelligence to operational forces (Byman, 2011).

[54] This tactic was not new, but it was used more aggressively during Defensive Shield (Cordesman, 2006).

[55] The IDF went to great efforts in Gaza to warn civilians and avoid collateral damage, largely because it knew that, if it did not, it would lose domestic support and face international sanction.

[56] There were, for example, European calls for a boycott of Israeli goods (Goodman, 2002).

[57] Dan Propper, chair of Osem Group, reported that the "lack of confidence results from a perceived lack of stability and is fueled by unclear media messages" and that, although Israeli companies have found some solutions, the "overall economic damage incurred, however, is significant and will be long-term" (as reported in Goodman, 2002, p. 29).

[58] Diplomatic consequences included the withdrawal of the Egyptian and Jordanian ambassadors, economic consequences included the cancellation of fledgling economic arrangements with Gulf States and Morocco, and military consequences included the halt of military imports from Germany (Goodman, 2002).

[59] Goodman, 2002.

Semitic, feelings.[60] These problems would presumably reemerge in a violent uprising, given the virtual impossibility of controlling the flow of images from embattled areas.[61]

Should the same approach be used in a new violent uprising, the deleterious consequences for Israel might be somewhat less extensive than during the Second Intifada. Depending on how Israel prosecuted these interwoven conflicts, it could gain a measure of international sympathy as it did in 2006 and November 2012, when Hezbollah and Hamas, respectively, were perceived as the aggressors. On the other hand, instant video and the Internet showing the results of the actions Israel takes that affect civilians could have the opposite effect, much as they did in Gaza in the summer of 2014, where Israel was widely criticized.

On the Palestinian side, the Israeli response to the Second Intifada caused heavy damage in terms of lost lives and damage to infrastructure. On the economic infrastructure side, the Israelis inflicted an estimated $1.7 billion in damage during Operation Defensive Shield.[62] Similar impacts on Palestinian life and infrastructure are

---

[60] Ephraim Kam, a retired but very experienced IDF intelligence officer, noted that,

> In the Palestinian mindset, Jenin is now associated with massacre, despite those reports having been partially corrected in the West. Even informed Palestinians express no doubt that there was indeed a massacre, just as there is a collective memory of 10,000 Palestinians massacred in "Black September" 1970, though the real number was closer to 1,000. (quoted in Goodman, 2002, p. 28)

Kam added that, even though "the rumors of a massacre were largely dismissed as baseless in Europe, they provided grounds there for allegations of war crimes and justifications of Palestinian terror. They also contributed to the rise of anti-Semitism in Europe." Goodman notes that "[i]n France 56 synagogues and Jewish institutions were attacked in a month" (2002, p. 28). Israeli Minister of Foreign Affairs Gideon Meir conceded that "[t]he images broadcast from Jenin had an enormous impact on international public opinion" (quoted in Goodman, 2002, p. 30).

[61] Catignani, 2008, writes,

> Despite subsequent IDF and UN reports negating the Palestinians' claims of an IDF massacre the media was able to damage temporarily the IDF's image and legitimacy. Even though the IDF attempted thereafter to prepare its soldiers and commanders to understand the important role of the media in counter-insurgency campaigns and to deal with the media in general, other media setbacks occurred throughout the conflict due to the IDF's overall inability to manage more carefully the media's portrayal of its operations throughout the current Intifada.

[62] Cordesman, 2006, p. 11, writes,

> During this operation, the IDF also began major efforts to destroy civilian facilities of the Palestinian Authority in addition to its security institutions, targeting not only Arafat's compound and Palestinian police offices but the Legislative Council offices, the Chambers of Commerce, and the Ministries of Agriculture, Education, Trade and Industry as well. Moreover, the Palestinian headquarters for Preventative Security was targeted for the first time by the IDF.

Jones, 2007, p. 291, writes,

> Even infantry tactics could inflict infrastructural damage. "Streets were far too dangerous to use, except with the protection of armored personnel carriers and tanks, and buildings and houses needed to be entered by breaching the walls. In order to avoid passing through narrow streets that might include prepositioned explosive devices or snipers, small squads of dismounted infantry conducted "hot breeching" operations by breaking through walls.

Structures that might appear outwardly to be untouched could be wrecked inside.

anticipated in the context of a violent uprising. Given the perception that the relatively measured response to the start of the Second Intifada provided Palestinian militants with the space and time to step up their operations, a response similar to Israel's responses in the context of Gaza in 2008 and 2012–2014 is anticipated.

That said, Hamas, Hezbollah, and radical jihadists in Gaza and the West Bank are not likely to change except to seek new ways to inflict harm on Israel and Israelis. Rockets will likely be fired from Gaza in large numbers, and rockets with longer ranges and better guidance systems could be fired from southern Lebanon or Syria. Any new tunnels from Gaza to Israel will be used, as before, to attempt to capture IDF soldiers to be held as hostages and/or to launch terrorist attacks on Israel. As technology evolves, one could also imagine the use of drones or other terrorist actions not presently contemplated.

Weak public support for the PA, combined with a possible leadership turnover, given President Abbas's advanced age, have spurred considerable anxiety over a possible collapse of the PA.[63] This collapse would entail Israel's taking on more of the burden of providing public services in the West Bank. The PA is far from an efficient provider of these services, but, with the support of international donors, it is currently responsible for civil services in Areas A and B and security in Area A. The PA is also the largest employer in the West Bank, by far. So a collapse of the PA would transfer these responsibilities to Israel, imposing significant costs on Israel above and beyond the cost of a reoccupation of the territory. Further, that development and the fear of foreign jihadi elements taking root in the West Bank would almost certainly lead to a large-scale Israeli reoccupation of the territory.

In order to model this scenario, we assume that the violence begins three years in the future and lasts for three years, after which the economy regains its original growth rate. This is, in a sense, a discrete event, but it will have lasting consequences, as the GDP growth line trend will always then be below what it might have been, had the violence not occurred.

Violent Uprising: Key Assumptions

Economic Assumptions

- **Israeli direct costs**
  - **Security:** Defense expenditures increase by 9 percent during three years of conflict.[64]

---

[63] For a series of papers analyzing the consequences of a PA collapse, see Palestinian Center for Policy and Survey Research, 2014a.

[64] Expenditures increase by 9 percent during years of conflict (authors' estimates by comparing defense spending during 2001–2003 and 2000 using Bank of Israel, undated).

- **Spending on Palestinian services:** Israel assumes 100 percent of cost of Palestinian ministries of education, health, and social affairs as the PA collapses and the international community is unwilling to pay.[65]

- **Israeli opportunity costs**
  - **Investment:** Decrease in the rate of physical accumulation of capital matching analogous to that experienced during the Second Intifada.[66]
  - **Labor force:** Decrease in Israeli labor force growth matching the Second Intifada (2000–2005) for four years.[67]
  - **Total factor productivity (TFP):** Decrease in the rate of TFP development matching Second Intifada (2000–2005) for four years.[68]
  - **Tourism:** 25-percent contraction in tourism.[69]
  - **Trade with Palestinians:** 15-percent contraction as Palestinian GDP contracts.[70]
  - **Palestinian labor in Israel:** Palestinian labor in Israel assumed to match levels during Second Intifada (2000–2005), implying virtually no Palestinian labor during the peak of violence.[71]

---

[65] It is assumed that Israel maintains real social spending at the same level as a share of Palestinian GDP as in 2012 (World Bank, 2013a). We assume that the PA dissolves immediately ,and Israel assumes the costs for the Palestinian ministries of social affairs, health, and education, which make expenditures equivalent to 12 percent of Palestinian GDP. Data for 2012 indicate a total of 41.7 percent of budget spent on these three ministries (World Bank, 2013a). The estimate assumes a PA budget of 30 percent of GDP, as reported in Figure 3.3 in Chapter Three.

[66] Contribution of ICT and non-ICT investment was 20 percent lower from 2001 to 2004 during the Second Intifada—0.51 and 1.01, respectively, as compared with 0.61 and 1.23, respectively, during 1999–2013 (Conference Board, 2014). The choice of four years of effects is based on the Second Intifada, which saw three years of active conflict but at least four years of economic effects.

[67] Contribution of employment growth to GDP growth was 1.46 from 1999 to 2013 but 60 percent lower (0.59) during 2001–2004 (Conference Board, 2014). The choice of four years of effects is based on the Second Intifada, which saw three years of active conflict but at least four years of economic effects.

[68] Contribution of TFP growth to GDP growth was 0.36 from 1999–2013 but was negative during 2001–2004 (Conference Board, 2014). We assume that it zeroes out during the years of conflict. Four years of effect is based on the Second Intifada, which saw three years of active conflict but at least four years of economic effects.

[69] PalTrade, 2006, p. 67, reports that tourism hit a low of 70 percent below pre–First Intifada tourism levels during the Second Intifada.

[70] PalTrade, 2006, p. 11, reports a strong negative correlation between conflict and Israeli exports to Palestine, though Palestine will remain a captive market during this time.

[71] This assumption is implicit in the historical data used to represent the violent uprising. Estimated salary based on 2013 PMA data. They report a total of 127,000 Palestinians working in "Israel & Settlements" = 4,420 (population) × 0.59 (population over 15) × 0.436 (labor force participation) × 0.112 (employed in Israel and settlements). Data available at PMA, undated.

- **Palestinian direct costs**
  - **Physical destruction:** IDF operations cause $1.5 billion in damage to physical capital—both private and public infrastructure.[72]
  - **Labor in Israel:** All Palestinian labor to Israel ceases.[73]
  - **Internal transit costs:** 100-percent increase in internal transit costs as a result of severely increased restrictions.
  - **Social services:** 25-percent increase in value of Israeli-related medical and water direct costs.
  - **Banking regulations:** 50-percent increase in costs.
  - **Prisoners:** 100-percent increase in number of prisoners as result of violence.[74]

- **Palestinian opportunity costs**
  - **Imports and exports:** 50-percent increase in transaction costs.
  - **Palestinian Authority:** The PA collapses.

Security Assumptions

- **Israel**
  - **Tactical warning:** Reoccupation of Palestinian areas will improve Israel's visibility into possible terrorist cells and enhance warning.
  - **Strategic depth:** Resumed violence with the Palestinians will undermine Israel's relationship with friendly Arab regimes and those "on the fence" and will increase the longer-term threat.
  - **Mobility:** Israel's reoccupation of Palestinian areas will remove barriers to mobility.
  - **Border security:** Prolonged closures of Palestinian areas and security clampdowns will reduce the immediate threat (but could create longer-term problems).
  - **Liaison:** The return to violence will constrict partners' willingness to share information with Israel.

- **Palestinians**
  - **Force size:** As happened in the post–Second Intifada period, the Israelis are likely to target Palestinian security forces.

---

[72] World Bank, 2003, p. xi, reports the replacement cost of damage to infrastructure from Operation Defensive Shield at $1.7 billion. UNCTAD, 2010, p. 8, reports damage of $1.3 billion for Operation Cast Lead. PECDAR ("Scale of Gaza Destruction Unprecedented," 2014) reports $1.7 billion in damage from Operation Protective Edge.

[73] This is a very restrictive assumption as employment in Israel has accounted for at least 10 percent of total employment by residents of the West Bank.

[74] The number of prisoners increased by 200 percent during the Second Intifada ("Statistics on Palestinians in the Custody of the Israeli Security Forces," 2015).

- **Force structure:** Renewed violence is likely to destroy much of the rebuilt security infrastructure.
- **Funding:** Funding, particularly if Palestinian security is seen as complicit in the violence, will plummet.
- **Chain of command:** Loyalty and authority will revert to the lowest common denominator: the local level.
- **Liaison relationships:** Israel and the United States are likely to loosen ties, at least temporarily; others may do the same.
- **Freedom of movement:** Israeli reoccupation forces will severely restrict, if not eliminate, Palestinian security force mobility.
- **Border security:** The Israelis will clamp down on border security.
- **Justice:** All civil and criminal matters will revert to Israeli authority.

4.5. Comparison of Key Assumptions

The following three tables compare the assumptions made across the four scenarios. Tables 4.2 and 4.3 describe the economic assumptions made for Israel and the Palestinians, respectively. Table 4.4 describes the combined security assumptions for Israel and the Palestinians.

4.6. General Considerations About the Assumptions

There are several additional assumptions that we hold constant across the five scenarios.

First, we assume unlimited access to public and private investment to fund new economic opportunities. This assumption has salience for the Palestinians in the scenarios that come with new economic opportunities—the two-state solution scenario, coordinated unilateral withdrawal, and uncoordinated unilateral withdrawal. We anticipate that this investment would come from at least two sources: (1) Gulf countries and (2) Western donors. Though calculating the total public investment required is beyond the scope of this analysis, we develop back-of-the-envelope estimates of the total magnitude of investment, including public and private, that is likely to be required.

Second, we assume that the international community will provide financial support to repatriate the refugees in a two-state solution. Specifically, we assume that the international community will provide sufficient public and private capital investment so that any influx of labor will not lower per capita GDP. The total cost of this repatriation is modest, as discussed in detail below. A second, related assumption is that the return of refugees will have no significant effect on Palestinian labor markets. Though the rapid influx of Palestinian migrants elsewhere has been a boon for local

Table 4.2
Economic Assumptions for Israelis

	Scenario	Two-State Solution	Unilateral Withdrawal		Nonviolent Resistance	Violent Uprising
			Coordinated	Uncoordinated		
Direct costs	1. Security	No change	No change	Defense expenditures increase by 1%	No change	Defense expenditures increase by 3%
	2. Settlement	100,000 settlers leave West Bank with proportional (16%) reduction in annual costs; relocation costs paid for by international community	60,000 settlers leave West Bank with proportional (10%) reduction in annual costs; 75% of relocation costs paid for by international community	30,000 settlers leave West Bank with proportional (5%) reduction in annual costs; 0% of relocation costs paid for by international community	No change	No change
	3. Palestinian services	No change	No change	No change	No change	Israel pays for Palestinian health, education, and social welfare
Opportunity costs	1. Instability and uncertainty	15% increase in investment and labor productivity for 4 years	No change	5% decrease in investment rate for 4 years	10% decrease in investment rate for 4 years	20% decrease in investment, 100% reduction in total factor productivity, 50% reduction in labor market growth for 4 years
	2. BDS	No change	No change	No change	2% reduction in GDP	No change
	3. Tourism	20% increase	5% increase	5% decrease	10% decrease	25% decrease
	4. Arab world trade	Trade with the greater Middle East triples	No change	No change	No change	No change
	5. Palestinian trade	150% increase	10% increase	No change	No change	15% decrease
	6. Palestinian labor in Israel	Permits increase by 60,000	Permits reduced by 30,000	Permits reduced by 30,000	Permits reduced by 30,000	Palestinian labor in Israel stopped

Table 4.3
Economic Assumptions for Palestinians

| | | Unilateral Withdrawal | | | |
Scenario	Two-State Solution	Coordinated	Uncoordinated	Nonviolent Resistance	Violent Uprising
Direct costs					
1. Destruction of property	No change	No change	No change	No change	$1.5 billion in damage to capital stock
2. Territorial waters	Access for resource extraction	No change	No change	No change	No change
3. Palestinian labor in Israel	Permits increase by 60,000	Permits reduced by 30,000	Permits reduced by 30,000	Permits reduced by 30,000	No Palestinian labor in Israel
4. Freedom of movement	All costs removed	All costs removed	No change	25% increase	100% increase
5. Access to social services	25% reduction in costs	No change	No change	25% increase in costs	50% increase in costs
6. Banking regulations	50% reduction in costs	No change	No change	No change	50% increase in costs
7. Prisoners in Israel	All political prisoners released	No change	No change	10% increase in number of prisoners	100% increase in number of prisoners
Opportunity costs					
1. Control of territory	Full control of land vacated by IDF and 100,000 settlers	Full control of land vacated by IDF and 60,000 settlers	Full control of land vacated by 30,000 settlers	No change	No change
2. Access to water	Unlimited access at market price	Unlimited access at market price	No change	No change	No change
3. Barriers to trade	50% reduction in transaction costs	10% reduction in transaction costs	No change	25% increase in transaction costs	50% increase in transaction costs
4. Licensing	Elimination of licensing restrictions	No change	No change	No change	No change
5. Tourism and travel	Visa restrictions lifted	No change	No change	No change	No change
6. Dissolution of PA	No change	No change	No change	No change	PA collapses
7. Investment in public and private infrastructure	Sufficient for all new economic opportunities	Sufficient for all new economic opportunities	Sufficient for 50% of new economic opportunities	No change	No change

Table 4.4
Security Assumptions

	Scenario	Two-State Solution	Unilateral Withdrawal		Nonviolent Resistance	Violent Uprising
			Coordinated	Uncoordinated		
Israeli	1. Strategic warning	No change	No change	No change	No change	No change
	2. Tactical warning	Reduced	Reduced	Reduced	No change	Increased
	3. Buffer zone	Reduced	No change	No change	No change	No change
	4. Strategic depth	Reduced	No change	No change	No change	Reduced
	5. Mobility	Reduced	Reduced	No change	No change	Increased
	6. Border security	No change	No change	No change	No change	Increased
	7. Liaison	Increased	No change	No change	Decreased	Reduced
Palestinian	1. Force size	Significant expansion in new mission areas	Increased	Need increased	No change	Significant decrease and/or destruction
	2. Force structure	Significant growth	Increased	Need increased	No change	Reduced
	3. Funding	Increased	Increased	No change	No change	Reduced
	4. Chain of command	Increased	No change	No change	No change	Dispersal of authority; local militias dominate
	5. Liaison relationships	Increased	No change	No change	Reduced	Cut off
	6. Freedom of movement	Increased	Increased	No change	No change	Decreased
	7. Border security	Increased	No change	No change	No change	Decreased
	8. Justice	Increased	Increased	Somewhat increased	No change	No change

economies in some circumstances,[75] there is a notion that a rapid infusion of unskilled workers could have negative effects.[76] However, the only empirical study of the impact of returning migrants on domestic labor market outcomes in the WBG reported no significant effect. There is little systematic evidence in the econometric literature for a large negative impact of migration on domestic wages and employment.[77]

Third, most of our assumptions for direct costs and opportunity costs do not have a dynamic component—the only exception is the opportunity cost of instability for the Israelis. All of our assumptions, and their associated opportunity costs or direct costs, should be interpreted to be as of year 10 of our counterfactual exercise. As an example, in our violent uprising scenario (Chapter Nine), we report the economic impact for the Israelis of a loss of 127,000 Palestinian laborers as nearly $3 billion; this is true only for 2024. In calculating the dynamic growth path of the economies for each scenario (reported in Chapter Twelve), we assume that the opportunity costs and direct costs for each of the scenarios are realized gradually over the ten-year period. As an example, for the violent uprising scenario, the number of Palestinian laborers working in Israel is assumed to fall by approximately 13,000 each year until all 127,000 are eliminated by the tenth year. The growth path for each scenario is assumed to follow the trajectory implied by our assumptions for the Israeli instability opportunity cost.

Fourth, we assume that there will be no change in Palestinian institutions (e.g., land titling) within the ten-year window that is the focus of this study. Though the dysfunctionality of some Palestinian institutions is at least partially attributable to the conflict, we assume that these institutions will not change appreciably within the ten-year window.

The economic assumptions used in this analysis have two important characteristics. First, the assumptions focus on changes in economic characteristics of the conflict—either direct costs or opportunity costs—rather than on sectors of the economy. Further, we do not make specific assumptions about economic characteristics that are too small to have a significant impact on either of the economies (e.g., equivalent land swaps are anticipated to have only a marginal impact on either economy).

In addition, we specify only a single set of assumptions for each scenario and therefore do not allow for any uncertainty in these assumptions. This is a direct consequence of our intentionally simplified approach; our goal is to describe paradigmatic scenarios of what could happen rather than what might happen.

---

[75] Van Hear, 1995, reports that the forced migration of Palestinians into Jordan during Operation Desert Storm was a boon to the Jordanian economy and may have contributed to Jordan's economic recovery.

[76] Dumper, 2006, indicates that returning refugees would bring an influx of low-skilled migrants to the Palestinian economy. RAND Palestinian State Study Team, 2007, p. 18, reports similar concerns.

[77] Sayre, 2003, presents this evidence for the West Bank and Gaza. For a more general treatment in the literature, see Card, 1990.

We monetize our estimates in terms of the impact on government spending and GDP, which is a measure of new economic activity in a region during each year. These measures are indicators of economic well-being across a society; however, they do not account for distributional issues.

CHAPTER FIVE

Two-State Solution

In this chapter, we use our counterfactual approach to estimate the forgone opportunities and additional costs of the Israelis and Palestinians *not* agreeing to a two-state solution. The results presented in this chapter are derived from Chapters Two and Four, which reviewed, respectively, (1) the factors that influence economic and security outcomes and (2) the specific assumptions about those factors for the two-state solution. Appendix B provides additional specifics on how the various estimates reported in this chapter are calculated.

The overall cost of not agreeing to the two-state solution includes a mixture of economic and security costs for both the Israelis and the Palestinians. On the economic side, as shown in Table 5.1, by not agreeing to a two-state solution, Israel forgoes nearly $23 billion in additional economic output in 2024 and the Palestinians forgo approximately $7 billion in economic output in 2024.

On the security front, both the Israelis and Palestinians will face new threats. Although these threats will differ, both Israel and the Palestinians will require significant resources to address these threats. From a security perspective, a successful two-state agreement requires both states to feel safe. The security equation for Israel includes the immediate environment—that is, the Palestinians and their ability to keep those borders quiet—and potential cross-border trouble from other Arab neighbors, principally Syria and Lebanon, but, increasingly, Egypt's Sinai as well. The Israelis will expect enhanced cooperation on those fronts to ensure that those cross-border variables are managed. And, of course, Israel's biggest long-term and over-the-horizon threat is Iran—principally, the nuclear threat that Israel perceives. We can expect, in the context of a long-term agreement that creates a Palestinian state, for the Israelis to be even more insistent that their interests are taken into consideration with regard to any deal that is struck with Iran.

The success of the two-state solution will depend on significant input from the international community. For Israel, the settlement-related ten-year total costs of the two-state solution alone are estimated to be a minimum of approximately $30 billion, and security-related costs, including security guarantees, are anticipated to cost billions more. We assume that the international community, and the United States in particular, will bear this cost. We also assume that the international community will

Table 5.1
Itemized Changes in GDP in 2024 in the Two-State Solution Relative to Present Trends (in millions of U.S. dollars)

Israel		Palestine	
Change in GDP from All Costs (Direct and Opportunity)			
Total Change in GDP	**$22,800**		**$7,180**
Change in GDP from Direct Costs[a]			
Security	$0	Destruction of property	$0
Settlement	$90	Territorial waters	$280
Palestinian services	$0	Palestinian labor in Israel	$360
		Freedom of movement	$80
		Access to services	$10
		Banking regulations	$4
		Prisoners in Israel	$90
Total change in GDP from direct costs	**$90**		**$820**
Change in GDP from Opportunity Costs			
Instability and uncertainty	$9,100	Control of territory	$480
BDS	$0	Access to water	$780
Tourism	$1,120	Barriers to trade	$4,300
Arab world trade	$5,580	Licensing	$30
Palestinian trade	$5,580	Tourism and travel	$770
Palestinian labor in Israel	$1,320	Dissolution of PA	$0
Total change in GDP from opportunity costs	**$22,700**		**$6,360**

[a] In order to translate changes in direct costs into changes in GDP, we assume (1) a fiscal multiplier of 0.5, (2) an export-to-GDP multiplier of 0.93, and (3) that any changes in direct costs are reflected by a 1:1 change in government expenditures.

help the Palestinians meet and fund their security challenges. The potential economic benefits of the two-state solution for the Palestinians will require large, external public and private investment from both the international community and Palestinians, both domestically and from the diaspora. Our estimate of the total new private and public investment required for both new economic opportunities and the absorption of refugees, without a reduction in per capita GDP, is $58 billion.

5.1. Israelis

The only direct cost of the two-state solution for Israel as compared to present trends in 2024 is a reduction in government expenditures for the settlements. As there are an estimated 600,000 settlers in the West Bank, not counting the settlers living in Jerusalem, the removal of 100,000 settlers is equivalent to an approximate reduction in the number of settlers by one-sixth. We assume that the annual expenditures in the settlements are reduced by a similar amount, for a total savings of approximately $180 million, which increases Israeli GDP by $90 million.

While the overall change in security costs for Israel is insignificant, this is because we assume that the United States will offset any additional security costs. The technological and organizational substitutes necessary to replace Israeli assets on the West Bank and in the Jordan Valley are likely to be substantial. The price range for the sensors, data analytic packages, physical barriers, communication links, and other components of an overall solution is quite wide but may well be in the (low) billions of dollars. While the United States is assumed to bear most of this burden, Israel is anticipated to contribute to the cost of these additional capabilities, with any direct reductions in expenditures from a reduced posture in the West Bank and Jordan Valley reallocated to funding these requirements.[1] In the longer term, Israel may be able to phase out select capabilities in tandem with increases in the competence and reliability of Palestinian security forces, but this is assumed to be beyond the scope of our ten-year focus.

There are five major types of opportunity cost changes for Israel in the two-state solution, as compared to present trends:

---

[1]   Excluding the cost of troops, the estimated variable costs for security in the settlements are $425 million to $449 million. Though it is expected that there will be a reduction of approximately $60 million in coordination activities and $80 million to $90 million in emergency security expenses, these will be repurposed for other security-related activities. The Israelis will continue to pay for the operation and maintenance of the separation barrier, at least for the time frame considered. In the much longer run, it is possible that a portion of these costs will be saved.

- The first is the economic expansion associated with increased investment in physical capital, with the total impact of this expanded capital base equivalent to a rise of just over 2.1 percent of 2024 GDP, or just over $9 billion.[2]
- Second, a 20-percent expansion in tourism would result in a GDP increase of approximately $1.1 billion.[3]
- Third, the assumed tripling in exports to the Arab world, equivalent to a $6 billion increase in the dollar value of exports, is estimated to increase GDP by $5.6 billion.[4]
- Fourth, the 150-percent expansion in trade with Palestinians would lead to an additional $6 billion increase in exports and a $5.6 billion expansion in GDP.
- Fifth, the expansion of Palestinian labor in Israel by 60,000 legal workers, in addition to existing legal and illegal workers, will expand GDP by 0.3 percent, or $1.3 billion.[5]

On the security front, the risk from an external threat will increase slightly. Though Israel will lose some of its early warning capability, the additional capabilities discussed above will mostly compensate for this loss, and the resolution of the conflict will reduce the value of Israel as a target to many external players. The one major loss for responding to these threats will be the freedom of maneuver, as Israelis will be able to respond to an imminent external threat only in coordination with the PNSF.

While the external threat will increase only slightly, the internal threat may grow significantly. This will include Israeli spoilers who will target either other Israeli or Palestinian targets, and Palestinians who will target Israeli interests. A particularly dangerous threat, given the growing prominence of religious extremists in the region, is the spillover of an ISIS-like ideology to Palestinians with resident status in Israel.[6]

---

[2]   We assume that the investment rate increases by 5 percent over its historical (1990–2013) average during the first three years, by 10 percent during years 4–7, and by 15 percent during years 8–10. We operationalize using the Israeli growth decomposition data from Conference Board, 2014, by assuming that the contribution of capital to growth increases by 5, 10, and 15 percent during the three periods, respectively. The net impact of this increased capital investment is an increase in the GDP by 2.2 percent (authors' estimates), which is equivalent to $9.3 billion (U.S.$2014). A counterfactual GDP forecast with augmented investment uses identical parameterization except for the assumed changes in the rate of investment.

[3]   PalTrade, 2006, p. 14, provides a significantly larger estimate of $6 billion ($5 billion for 2006—inflated to 2012 dollars using GDP deflator in World Bank, 2015b).

[4]   The export-to-GDP multiplier is assumed to be 0.93 (A. Friedman and Hercowitz, 2010), based on a general equilibrium model of the Israeli economy.

[5]   Based on Flaig et al., 2013.

[6]   In January 2014, Israel revealed that it had arrested three Palestinians recently, two of whom are residents of Jerusalem, who were recruited by a group of Salafists in Sinai (Harel, 2014).

5.2. Palestinians

There are six types of direct cost changes associated with a two-state solution for the Palestinians relative to present trends in 2024; in each case, there is a net *reduction* in direct costs:

- The first direct cost change is the budgetary savings that the Palestinians would gain from being able to extract natural gas from Palestinian territorial waters: Though we project that the benefit would last only ten years, the annual savings would increase GDP by $280 million per year.
- The largest direct economic benefit would be the new opportunities for Palestinians to work in Israel; given the assumed expansion in the number of legal Palestinian workers by 60,000 and the current average salary of $12,000 per Palestinian worker in Israel, this effect is equivalent to an additional $360 million added to GDP by 2024.[7]
- Third, the reduced restrictions on Palestinian freedom of movement are worth approximately $150 million per annum, which increase GDP by $80 million.[8]
- Fourth, for social services, the Palestinians are assumed to benefit from a 25-percent decrease in the costs of both medical services and water, for a total increase in GDP of approximately $10 million.[9]
- The assumed 50-percent reduction in restrictions on banking, the fifth direct cost, is valued at an estimated $7.5 million per annum.[10]
- Sixth is the expected decrease in stipends for families of prisoners, as we assume that political prisoners held by Israel—who are roughly 50 percent of the total held—are released, for a total reduction in direct costs that results in a $90 million increase in GDP.

The Palestinians have five major types of opportunity cost gains in the two-state solution:

- The first is via territorial control, including new opportunities for mining and construction. The value of the missed mining opportunities under present trends

---

[7] The estimated salary is based on the data reported by the PMA, undated. It reports, for 2012, an average of 20.5 workdays and an average daily wage of NIS 164.

[8] This estimate is from ARIJ, 2011, and includes time and resources spent in transit as a result of restrictions on freedom of movement in the status quo. This is based on p. 28 in ARIJ, 2011, and includes only those costs included in the Bethlehem-Ramallah and Jericho-90 sections, as we do not assume that there will be increased access for the Palestinians to Jerusalem.

[9] This includes both the health impacts and water tanker costs associated with the current artificial restriction on water access of, respectively, $20 million and $50 million (World Bank, 2009).

[10] The estimated total cost of this restriction is $15 million (2013 interview with representative from the PMA).

(but available in a two-state solution) has been estimated at $240 million per annum, and the construction opportunity cost is an additional $240 million.[11]

- The second is associated with current restrictions on access to water for agriculture: In a two-state solution, GDP would expand by approximately $780 million with unlimited access to water, even if purchased at market prices, and enhanced control of the West Bank would allow significantly increased irrigation of agricultural land.[12]

- Third, a 50-percent reduction in the barriers to trade would increase GDP by 21 percent as a result of increased exports and expand GDP as a result of more limited dual-use restrictions for a total of $4.3 billion.[13]

- Fourth, we assume that a 50-percent reduction in licensing restrictions, which now impede the development of the Palestinian telecommunication industry, would be equivalent to a $30 million per annum increase in GDP.[14]

- Finally, the expansion of tourism that would follow if the visa restrictions on foreigners were eliminated would expand tourism by 150 percent, stimulating a $760 million increase in GDP.[15]

The new Palestinian state will face two immediate security risks as a result of the shift to the two-state solution. Threats from outside Palestine, such as al Qaeda, ISIS, and other extremists who will continue to target Israel for attack, will likely seek to do so from Palestinian territory. Whether the extremists misread Palestinian capabilities or intent, they will likely test the new borders. Although reporting on extremist penetrations in the Palestinian areas is scarce and often unreliable, Syria and portions of Iraq under ISIS have become the fulcrum of the Sunni Jihadist movement, with global jihadist propaganda mixing with familiar anti-Israeli rhetoric about Jerusalem and Israel.

The second security issue demanding attention from the new Palestinian state would be the increased likelihood of destabilizing internal threats. Palestinian rejectionists and some right-wing Israelis will look to opportunities to overturn the agreement by destabilizing the new Palestinian government. As the Palestinian services grapple with more territory to control and new missions, they may well face a worsened terrorism threat. With statehood, it seems likely that Palestinian security services will

---

[11]   See World Bank, 2013b, pp. 15, 20.

[12]   We estimate that this would allow increased production worth $865 million and the additional water would cost $90 million (see Appendix B). Note that this is actually likely a lower bound for the effect on agriculture in this scenario as we are assuming no new technological transfer from the Israelis to the Palestinians. If the Palestinians could achieve Israeli-level agricultural productivity, the net benefit would be significantly higher.

[13]   Eltalla and Hens, 2009, Table 2, reports that a 50-percent reduction in transaction costs would increase GDP by 21 percent. Border controls and dual-use restrictions cost $260 million annually (ARIJ, 2011, pp. 7–9).

[14]   World Bank, 2013b.

[15]   Artal-Tur, Pallardó-López, and Requena-Silvente, 2012.

be more focused on this internal challenge and will redouble their efforts to prevent threats both to the new state and to Israel.

While the Israelis will play the dominant role in providing security between the states, addressing these threats will require the Palestinian security apparatus to safeguard Palestine's external borders and maintain sufficient internal security. Statehood will therefore not only expand territorial responsibility but also bring significant new security missions.

Though the United States and the EU are assumed to be willing to fund the increased Palestinian security cost from these missions, the PNSF will need to be reinforced, retrained, and refocused in four ways in order to handle the expanded responsibilities and the new mission areas:

- It will need to develop a reinforced internal capability to eventually take over all the tasks that the Palestinians accomplish now with Israeli assistance or that the Israelis do themselves. In addition to an approximate doubling in manpower, the Palestinians will need all the support and administrative aspects of national police and intelligence forces, including information technology, vehicle fleets, arms, and an expanded and improved physical infrastructure.
- In addition, the Palestinians will need to develop a capability to provide coastal water security and airspace security or, at a minimum, monitoring, though these responsibilities will be transitioned only gradually and are likely outside the ten-year window being considered.
- Border control—manning the official border crossings between the new state and its neighbors—with all the bureaucracy, passport control, and additional responsibilities required, will be largely uncharted territory for the new Palestinian border service.[16]
- Finally, establishing a comprehensive justice infrastructure, with the emphasis not only on the law enforcement tasks but also on expanded courts and prisons, will be an immediate requirement.[17] The new Palestinian state's security will depend on liaison relationships with Israel, the United States, the EU, Jordan, and Egypt to help facilitate the requisite development; however, developing these capabilities

---

[16] Among the most urgent, challenging, and likely expensive responsibilities of the new Palestinian state will be regulating the new state's borders with Israel, Jordan, and Egypt, monitoring, detecting, and preventing infiltration. Access to Jerusalem and the West Bank is now controlled by the government of Israel. Current border crossings into and out of the Palestinian areas—at the Allenby–King Hussein Bridge, the Jordan River–Sheikh Hussein crossing, the Arava border crossing and the crossings at Eilat/Aqaba and Taba, would eventually come under the control of a new Palestinian border guard.

[17] The current U.S. effort to bolster the PA's judicial capabilities has made important strides, but more progress and larger staffs, including more judges, will be needed. Israel currently holds nearly 9,000 Palestinian prisoners—many, if not most, of whom will likely be transferred to the future Palestinian state.

to ensure the near-term survival and success of the future State of Palestine will fall on the Palestinians themselves.[18]

5.3. Requirements of the International Community

Realizing these benefits of a two-state solution will require significant support from the international community, and the United States in particular. For Israel, the primary support from the international community will be the financing of the relocation of 100,000 settlers, which is estimated to cost $30 billion. The international community will also provide additional technology and funding to implement the variety of requisite warning systems discussed earlier and any agreed-to security guarantees. Though the price tag for this cost is unknown, it could easily run into the billions of dollars.

For Palestine, the greatest support required will be significant inflows of public and private investment to realize the economic potential associated with the two-state solution. In addition to these new economic opportunities, we also assume that the return of refugees would not reduce the per capita GDP of the Palestinian economy. Thus, the 10-percent expansion in the population (600,000 refugees) will be accompanied by a 10-percent expansion in the size of the entire economy, or roughly $2.7 billion. Realizing all these opportunities would yield a potential $9.7 billion increase in GDP, equivalent to a 49-percent increase over present trends in 2024 GDP. The $6.4 billion in opportunity costs for this scenario, following a general rule, would require an approximate 152-percent increase in the size of the present trends 2024 capital stock.[19] As the capital stock under present trends would reach $39 billion in 2024,

---

[18]   The United States, EU, and even Russia, as a member of the Quartet, will see it in their interests to ensure that the Palestinians have the wherewithal to penetrate, detect, and preempt potential threats, both internal and external. The Israelis will aggressively monitor Palestinian willingness and capability to keep Palestinian borders safe so that Israel does not have to intervene militarily.

[19]   We assume a Cobb-Douglas function with $\alpha = 1/3$. This implies that

$$\frac{Y^{TSS}}{Y^{PT}} = \frac{A_{TSS} * \left(K_{TSS}\right)^{1/3} * \left(L_{TSS}\right)^{2/3}}{A_{PT} * \left(K_{PT}\right)^{1/3} * \left(L_{PT}\right)^{2/3}} = 1.35$$

Assuming that technology and labor would be the same in the present trends ($A_{PT} = A_{TSS}$, $L_{PT} = L_{TSS}$), it follows that

$$\frac{\left(K_{TSS}\right)^{1/3}}{\left(K_{PT}\right)^{1/3}} = 1.35$$

It follows directly that the amount of capital stock would have to expand by approximately 144 percent.

this implies that roughly $58 billion in additional public and private investment will be required to achieve this expansion of the economy.

We also assume that the return of refugees would not reduce the per capita GDP of the Palestinian economy. Thus, the 10-percent expansion in the population (600,000 refugees) will be accompanied by a 10-percent expansion in the size of the entire economy, or roughly $2.7 billion. This will require an estimated $9 billion in additional public and private investment.[20] Therefore, a total of $65 billion in additional public and private investment would be required for the two-state solution.[21]

---

[20] Note that this additional investment is equivalent to $2,500 per individual, which is somewhat lower than existing estimates. Arnon, Spivak, and Weinblatt (1997) estimates that an additional $5,000 in investment per person would be required to maintain a constant per capita GDP. This difference is driven by the fact that the new investment required for the overall expansion of the economy covers part of these costs.

This $2.7 billion expansion of GDP in addition to the $6.9 billion from the change in opportunity costs would entail a net change in GDP of $9.6 billion, which is equivalent to a 48-percent expansion of the economy. If we again assume a Cobb-Douglas function with $\alpha = 1/3$. This implies that

$$\frac{Y^{TSS}}{Y^{PT}} = \frac{A_{TSS} * \left(K_{TSS}\right)^{1/3} * \left(L_{TSS}\right)^{2/3}}{A_{PT} * \left(K_{PT}\right)^{1/3} * \left(L_{PT}\right)^{2/3}} = 1.48$$

As technology would be the same in the present trends ($A_{PT} = A_{TSS}$) and the labor force will expand by 10 percent as a result of the return of refugees

$$\left(L_{TSS} = 1.1 * L_{PT}\right)$$

it follows that

$$\frac{\left(K_{TSS}\right)^{1/3} * \left(1.1\right)^{2/3}}{\left(K_{PT}\right)^{1/3}} = 1.48$$

It follows directly that the capital stock would have to expand by approximately 168 percent, which is 24 percent more than without these refugees. This is equivalent to $9 billion in 2024.

[21] These estimates do not include any potential refugee claims for restitution (e.g., lost property).

CHAPTER SIX

Coordinated Unilateral Withdrawal

In this chapter, we use our counterfactual approach to explore the costs of a coordinated unilateral withdrawal by Israel from the West Bank. Appendix B provides specifics on how the various estimates reported in this chapter are calculated.

The overall cost of coordinated unilateral withdrawal will be primarily economic for both the Israelis and the Palestinians. On the economic side, as shown in Table 6.1, the Israelis gain both economic output and reduced security and settlement costs by withdrawing. However, the situation for the Palestinians is reversed. They stand to benefit economically from new economic opportunities resulting from the increased territorial control associated with Israeli withdrawal, but these increased economic opportunities will be partially offset by the modest reduction in employment opportunities for Palestinians in Israel.

In particular, as we assume that the Israelis will internalize the lessons learned from the previous two unilateral withdrawals, the net impact on Israeli security will be negligible, and Palestinians will have only a limited expansion in internal threats that they will need to manage as a consequence of the increased territory that they need to monitor.

The success of coordinated unilateral withdrawal will also depend on significant input from the international community. For Israel, the net settlement-related costs of the coordinated unilateral withdrawal are estimated to be approximately $1.8 billion per year for ten years, for a total of $18 billion. In this case, we assume that the international community, and the United States in particular, will pay 75 percent of these costs, for a total ten-year cost of $13.5 billion.[1] Security-related costs are likely to cost billions more. The potential economic benefits of coordinated unilateral withdrawal for the Palestinians will also require substantial public and private investment from the international community and Palestinians, both domestically and from the diaspora. We estimate that $10 billion of new investment ($1.0 billion per year) will be required over the ten-year period of analysis to take full advantage of the new economic opportunities provided to the Palestinians in this scenario.

---

[1] The international community is assumed to take on 75 percent of the cost of relocating the 60,000 settlers moved in this scenario.

Table 6.1
Itemized Changes in GDP in 2024 in Coordinated Unilateral Withdrawal Relative to Present Trends (in millions of U.S. dollars)

	Israel	Palestine	
Change in GDP from All Costs (Direct and Opportunity)			
Total Change in GDP	**–$180**		**$1,510**
Change in GDP from Direct Costs[a]			
Security	$0	Destruction of property	$0
Settlement	–$170	Territorial waters	$0
Palestinian services	$0	Palestinian labor in Israel	–$180
		Freedom of movement	$80
		Access to services	$0
		Banking regulations	$0
		Prisoners in Israel	$0
Total change in GDP from direct costs	**–$170**		**–$110**
Change in GDP from Opportunity Costs			
Instability and uncertainty	$0	Control of territory	$290
BDS	$0	Access to water	$470
Tourism	$280	Barriers to trade	$860
Arab world trade	$0	Licensing	$0
Palestinian trade	$370	Tourism and travel	$0
Palestinian labor in Israel	–$660	Dissolution of PA	$0
Total change in GDP from opportunity costs	**–$8**		**$1,610**

[a] In order to translate changes in direct costs into changes in GDP, we assume (1) a fiscal multiplier of 0.5, (2) an export-to-GDP multiplier of 0.93, and (3) that any changes in direct costs are reflected by a 1:1 change in government expenditures.

6.1. Israelis

By unilaterally withdrawing (with coordination) from the West Bank, the only direct cost that Israel will face is the cost of moving settlers. We assume that 60,000 settlers will be relocated in this scenario and that Israel will be required to cover 25 percent of the $300,000 required to move each settler. Thus, the total relocation cost faced by Israel is $4.5 billion—or $450 million for each of the ten years. However, as the movement of 60,000 settlers is equivalent to a 10-percent reduction in the number of settlers, we assume that the annual direct costs of the settlements fall by an equivalent 10 percent. This is equivalent to a savings of $110 million per year, so the total annual cost of moving the settlers is $340 million, which will cause GDP to rise by $170 million by 2024.

There are several major decreases in opportunity costs for Israel in the coordinated unilateral withdrawal scenario. First, a 5-percent expansion in tourism would bring in a net GDP increase of approximately $280 million.

In addition, the 10-percent expansion in trade with Palestinians would lead to an additional $400 million annual increase in exports, and a $370 million expansion in GDP. However, the net change in GDP is slightly negative, as the impact on GDP of the reduction in the number of Palestinian laborers in Israel by 30,000, at $660 million, is slightly larger than the combined benefit from expanded trade and tourism.

The implications of coordinated unilateral withdrawal for security, both in terms of internal and external threats, depend crucially on how it is carried out and how the Palestinians react. Two uncoordinated precedents, withdrawals from southern Lebanon in 2000[2] and from Gaza in 2005,[3] clearly showed Israel what not to do. In both cases, the Israelis left behind a security vacuum, and, in both cases, that vacuum was filled by a hostile force: by Hamas (eventually) in Gaza and by Hezbollah in Lebanon.

Thus, the coordination will specifically seek to avoid creating these types of security vacuums. Israel will coordinate its withdrawal with the PNSF, to ensure that the PNSF fills the security void left by departing Israeli forces, and with both the United States and the EU. PA support might be forthcoming for the same reason that many in

---

[2]   After Israel's withdrawal from Lebanon in 2000, its primary adversary, Hezbollah, promptly filled the void, maintained that Israel continued to occupy some territory across the border, rallied local support against Israel, refused to accept Israel's withdrawal, and ratcheted up both violence and rhetoric, culminating in the 2006 Israel-Hezbollah war, killing more than 1,000 Hezbollah fighters, 165 Israelis, and large numbers of Lebanese.

[3]   Israel's unilateral withdrawal from Gaza resulted in a number of unintended, and mostly negative, consequences. After winning the 2006 elections in Gaza, Hamas fought a quick and bloody civil war with Fatah, which Hamas won. Israel's withdrawal from Gaza was complete—it removed all vestiges of its presence in Gaza— including settlements and security outposts, hoping to rid itself of the security problems their presence entailed. Instead, it became embroiled in a cycle of tit-for-tat violence with the new Hamas-led leadership in Gaza, culminating in large and costly military engagements, including Cast Lead in 2008, Protective Edge in 2014, and repeated volleys of rocket fire into southern Israel.

Israel would oppose it: The withdrawal would remove Israelis from much of the West Bank without reciprocal concessions by the Palestinians.

Overall, Israel's security costs would be unlikely to change very much. Though Israel would lose some of its territorial buffer and, to a lesser extent, its early warning capability, the additional capabilities discussed above (under the two-state solution scenario) would mostly compensate for such a loss, and the resolution of the conflict would reduce the value of Israel as a target to many external players. The one major loss for responding to these threats will be the freedom of maneuver, as Israelis would be able to respond to an imminent external threat only in coordination with the PNSF.

As indicated earlier, while the external threat will increase only somewhat, internal threats will grow significantly. Threats would include Israelis or Palestinians who reject such a policy (e.g., radical settlers or Hamas), who will target either other Israeli or Palestinian targets or Palestinians who would target Israeli interests. A particularly dangerous threat, given the growing prominence of religious extremists in the region, is the spillover of ISIS-like ideology to the Palestinians in Israel—and elsewhere, including Syria, Lebanon, and Egypt—and their potential for spilling into the Palestinian areas.

6.2. Palestinians

The economic cost implications of coordinated unilateral withdrawal for the Palestinians relative to present trends by 2024 are limited and come from the change in territorial access, as we have assumed that the PA accepts the withdrawal reluctantly. On the direct cost side, the Palestinians will benefit from increased freedom of movement, with an estimated effect of increasing GDP by $80 million per year.[4] However, the assumed net reduction of 30,000 laborers as Israel seeks to separate its economy from the WBG, using an estimated average salary of $12,000 per Palestinian worker in Israel, would cost the Palestinians $180 million in lost GDP.

In terms of opportunity costs, the first change is in territorial control, including new opportunities for mining and construction. We assume that the Palestinians would be returned 60 percent of Areas B and C and thus that they would be able to exploit 60 percent of the $480 million in missed mining and construction opportunities, for a total value of $290 million per annum to GDP.[5] In terms of agriculture, the Palestinians would again reap 60 percent of the total benefit of the two-state solution as a result of the more limited transfer of land; this is worth an estimated $470 million annually. Finally, the assumed 10-percent reduction in the barriers to trade would

---

[4]   See ARIJ, 2011.

[5]   See World Bank, 2013b, pp. 15, 20.

increase GDP by 4.2 percent as a result of increased exports and expand GDP by an additional $26 million as a result of more limited dual-use restrictions.[6]

The impact of coordinated unilateral withdrawal on the Palestinians will hinge on several factors: the extent to which the withdrawal is coordinated, local reaction to the move, the number of Palestinians allowed to work in Israel afterward, and the impact on foreign assistance to the PA's security structure. Even in the best case, it is likely that some resistance to Israel's unilateral but coordinated move may result in increased violence, may heighten attempts to conduct cross-border attacks, and may possibly attract other groups and individuals who will seek to exploit the controversy. Such events may unfold just as Palestinians will be attempting to fill the security void left by departing Israeli military and security troops.

The burden on Palestinian security forces with a coordinated Israeli unilateral withdrawal will grow, as they will have more area to protect and more responsibilities.

Palestinian liaison relationships will also suffer; certainly Palestine's cooperation with Israel would suffer in light of the unilateral pullout. The United States and the EU will likely assist, as will the neighboring states, but while Israel will have departed from much of the Palestinian areas, it will still control the air, land, and sea around the territories, including borders and border crossings and the Jordan Valley. That may invite attack from both internal rejectionists and external militants, who will see these Israeli outposts as attractive targets. Any Israeli preventive measures, such as continued raids or airstrikes into Palestinian areas, would exacerbate tensions and increase the likelihood of violence.

6.3. Requirements of the International Community

Coordinated unilateral withdrawal will require significant support from the international community, and the United States in particular. For Israel, the primary support from the international community will be the 75-percent financing of the relocation of 60,000 settlers, which is estimated to cost the international community a total of $13.5 billion. The international community will also provide additional technology and funding to implement the variety of requisite warning systems discussed earlier. Though the price tag for this cost is unknown, it could easily run into the billions of dollars in addition to the $13.5 billion.

For Palestine, the greatest support required will be significant inflows of public and private investment to realize the economic potential associated with coordinated unilateral withdrawal. In total, realizing all these opportunities would yield a potential $1.5 billion increase in GDP, equivalent to an 8-percent increase over present trends

---

[6] Eltalla and Hens, 2009, Table 2, reports that a 50-percent reduction in transaction costs would increase GDP by 21 percent. Border controls and dual-use restrictions cost $260 million annually (ARIJ, 2011, pp. 7–9).

in 2024 GDP. Following our approach to estimating these changes explained in Section 5.3 and Appendix B, this would require an approximate 26-percent increase in the size of the present trends 2024 capital stock. As the capital stock under present trends would reach $39 billion in 2024, this implies that roughly $10 billion in additional public and private investment will be required to achieve this expansion of the economy.

CHAPTER SEVEN

Uncoordinated Unilateral Withdrawal

In this chapter, we assume that the Palestinians do not cooperate with Israel's unilateral moves; politically, Israel continues to control the West Bank, and none of the final status accord issues is resolved. The international community, particularly European countries, also does not cooperate. Appendix B provides specifics on how our various estimates are calculated.

Uncoordinated unilateral withdrawal will have negative economic and security costs for the Israelis. On the economic side, as shown in Table 7.1, the Israelis both forgo economic output and incur increased security and settlement costs by withdrawing unilaterally. And while we assume that the Israelis will internalize the lessons learned from the previous two unilateral withdrawals, minimizing the internal and external threats from an uncoordinated withdrawal will likely require additional security costs.

The Palestinians will similarly be worse off economically. Though they will benefit economically, albeit in a very limited way, from a slight increase in territorial control associated with Israeli withdrawal, their political resistance to these moves will preclude access to either the financing or freedom of movement that they require to benefit from these economic opportunities. Further, reductions in employment opportunities for Palestinians in Israel will exceed any possible economic benefit. And we assume that the Palestinians may only have a limited expansion in internal threats that they will need to manage as a consequence of the increased territory that they need to monitor.

We assume that the role of the international community in realizing these outcomes is likely to be much more limited than its role in the two-state solution. Since the international community is unlikely to enthusiastically support such a course of action, we assume that Israel will have to self-finance most of its withdrawal and consolidation activities. Given the instability in this scenario and as the new economic opportunities for the Palestinians will be more limited than in a two-state solution, only limited external public and private investment will be required.

Table 7.1
Itemized Changes in GDP in 2024 in Uncoordinated Unilateral Withdrawal Relative to Present Trends (in millions of U.S. dollars)

Israel		Palestine	
Change in GDP from All Costs (Direct and Opportunity)			
Total Change in GDP	**−$4,010**		**−$110**
Change in GDP from Direct Costs[a]			
Security	−$130	Destruction of property	$0
Settlement	−$420	Territorial waters	$0
Palestinian services	$0	Palestinian labor in Israel	−$180
		Freedom of movement	$0
		Access to services	$0
		Banking regulations	$0
		Prisoners in Israel	$0
Total change in GDP from direct costs	**−$550**		**−$180**
Change in GDP from Opportunity Costs			
Instability and uncertainty	−$2,530	Control of territory	$70
BDS	$0	Access to water	$0
Tourism	−$280	Barriers to trade	$0
Arab world trade	$0	Licensing	$0
Palestinian trade	$0	Tourism and travel	$0
Palestinian labor in Israel	−$660	Dissolution of PA	$0
Total change in GDP from opportunity costs	**−$3,460**		**$70**

[a] In order to translate changes in direct costs into changes in GDP, we assume (1) a fiscal multiplier of 0.5, (2) an export-to-GDP multiplier of 0.93, and (3) that any changes in direct costs are reflected by a 1:1 change in government expenditures.

7.1. Israelis

In an uncoordinated unilateral withdrawal from the West Bank, the Israelis experience two types of direct costs relative to present trends in 2024:

- For security, there is a 1-percent increase in defense expenditures, which causes GDP to fall by $130 million.
- For settlements, we assume that Israel will cover the entire cost of relocating 30,000 settlers at a total cost of $9 billion, or $900 million for each of the ten years. However, as the movement of 30,000 settlers is equivalent to a 5-percent reduction in the number of settlers, we assume that the annual direct costs of the settlements fall by an equivalent 5 percent. This is equivalent to a savings of $55 million per year, so the total annual cost of moving the settlers is $845 million, which reduces Israeli GDP by $420 million.

In an uncoordinated unilateral withdrawal from the West Bank, the Israelis experience three types of opportunity costs:

- Despite the lack of violence, the political instability associated with this scenario is assumed to reduce the contribution of investment to growth by 5 percent during years 3–6. The net effect due to this instability is approximately a $2.5 billion reduction in GDP.[1]
- The loss from a 5-percent reduction in tourism is estimated at just under $300 million in lost GDP.
- A reduction of 30,000 Palestinian laborers in Israel would reduce GDP by an additional $660 million.

The implications of uncoordinated unilateral withdrawal for security, both in terms of internal and external threats, depend crucially on how the withdrawal is carried out and how the Palestinians react. As noted above, two precedents, withdrawals from southern Lebanon in 2000 and from Gaza in 2005, clearly showed Israel what not to do. In both cases, the Israelis left behind a security vacuum, and, in both cases, that vacuum was filled by hostile forces—by Hamas (eventually) in Gaza and by Hezbollah in Lebanon. If the withdrawal is implemented along the lines of the 2005 Gaza withdrawal, Israel's security environment might deteriorate internally, as settler opponents of withdrawal may also resort to violence.

Having studied both precedents carefully, we believe that it is unlikely that Israel will make the same mistakes again. But, as we assume that no coordination occurs, the risk of degradation in security conditions is a significant concern.[2]

---

[1]   Based on the Israeli growth decomposition data from Conference Board, 2014.

[2]   Defense Minister Moshe Ya'alon has argued that unilateral withdrawal, in effect, weakens Israel's credibility and reputation for resolute action. Thus, from his perspective, "Unilateral steps are a disincentive to President

7.2. Palestinians

The economic cost implications of uncoordinated unilateral withdrawal for the Palestinians are limited; they stem from the change in territorial access (which is positive) and the loss of opportunities for Palestinians to work in Israel. On the direct cost side, the assumed net reduction of 30,000 laborers, using an estimated average salary of $12,000 per Palestinian worker in Israel, will cost the Palestinians $180 million in lost GDP.[3] In terms of opportunity costs, the only benefit is a slight increase in access to land, with the Palestinians able to access 30 percent of the lands that they might have accessed in a two-state solution. However, given the uncoordinated nature of the withdrawal, to include Palestinian intransigence, we assume that the Israelis do not make unlimited water available at market prices and that investors are wary about investing in the new territory. Under these assumptions, the opportunity cost of this scenario's modest access to land is only a $70 million reduction in GDP.

The impact of uncoordinated unilateral withdrawal on the Palestinians will also hinge on the extent of Israeli withdrawal from Area C, the local reaction to the move, the resulting effect on foreign assistance to the PA's security structure, and the degree to which Israel reacts to resistance by the Palestinians by such actions as withholding tax revenues that it collects for the Palestinians. In this scenario, it is very likely that resistance to Israel's unilateral move will result in increased violence—perhaps even heightened attempts by foreign terrorists to exploit the situation. Therefore, the burden on Palestinian security with an uncoordinated Israeli unilateral withdrawal will grow: Palestinian security forces will have more area to protect, but they will also be faced with a public that, at the very least, will protest the moves by Israelis. In short, such a scenario offers Palestinians little economic advantage, grave security risks, and no solution to their long-term national aspirations.

7.3. Requirements of the International Community

Though the Palestinian economy will shrink slightly as a result of uncoordinated unilateral withdrawal, some modest investment will be required to realize the limited new opportunities in agriculture and mining. We estimate total value of this new investment, using our general rule, at $400 million.

Mahmoud Abbas of the Palestinian Authority 'to come to the table. . . . We as a government say O.K., we have a strategy, we're ready to sit to the table if there's a partner. . . . When we retreat or withdraw, we show weakness" (quoted in Rudoren, 2012).

[3]   The estimated salary is based on the data reported by PMA, undated. It reports, for 2012, an average of 20.5 workdays and an average daily wage of NIS 164.

CHAPTER EIGHT

Nonviolent Resistance

We now use our counterfactual approach to explore the costs of Palestinian-led nonviolent resistance.

The overall cost of nonviolent resistance, as compared to the status quo, is derived from its effects on the economy. The scenario is based on the assumption that there is no violence or damage to infrastructure; rather, the scenario unfolds through diplomatic and other international pressure levied against Israel, instigated by the Palestinians. However, the estimated economic effects to both economies are serious, as reported in Table 8.1. We calculate that Israel would experience a loss over present trends of nearly $15 billion in GDP by the tenth year; the Palestinians would lose over $2 billion in GDP, of which $230 million is in direct costs.

8.1. Israelis

While there are no significant changes in direct costs for Israel in this scenario, four categories of opportunity costs are incurred relative to present trends in 2024:

- The first is that, despite the lack of violence, the political instability associated with nonviolent resistance is assumed to reduce the contribution of investment to growth by 10 percent during years 3–6, when the nonviolent resistance is at its strongest. This net effect due to instability is an estimated 1.2-percent reduction in GDP by the tenth year, at an estimated annual value of over $5 billion.[1]
- The second cost is the impact of the BDS movement, primarily through financial investment flows, which is estimated to reduce GDP by an additional 2 percent, or just under $9 billion annually.[2]

---

[1] Based on the Israeli growth decomposition data from Conference Board (2014).

[2] The Israeli finance minister estimated the potential cost at 1 percent of GDP (see footnote 34 in Chapter Three). Financial sanctions (common between countries with "close relations") reduce GDP by 1.7 percent, on average; trade-only sanctions (either export or import) reduce GDP by 0.7 percent, on average; and combined financial and trade sanctions have combined effects of nearly 3 percent of GDP (Hufbauer et al., 2008).

Table 8.1
Itemized Changes in GDP in 2024 in Nonviolent Resistance Relative to Present Trends (in millions of U.S. dollars)

Israel		Palestine	
Change in GDP from All Costs (Direct and Opportunity)			
Total Change in GDP	–$15,000		–$2,380
Change in GDP from Direct Costs[a]			
Security	$0	Destruction of property	$0
Settlement	$0	Territorial waters	$0
Palestinian services	$0	Palestinian labor in Israel	–$180
		Freedom of movement	–$20
		Access to services	–$10
		Banking regulations	$0
		Prisoners in Israel	–$20
Total change in GDP from direct costs	**$0**		**–$230**
Change in GDP from Opportunity Costs			
Instability and uncertainty	–$5,050	Control of territory	$0
BDS	–$8,780	Access to water	$0
Tourism	–$560	Barriers to trade	–$2,150
Arab world trade	$0	Licensing	$0
Palestinian trade	$0	Tourism and travel	$0
Palestinian labor in Israel	–$660	Dissolution of PA	$0
Total change in GDP from opportunity costs	**–$15,000**		**–$2,150**

[a] In order to translate changes in direct costs into changes in GDP, we assume (1) a fiscal multiplier of 0.5, (2) an export-to-GDP multiplier of 0.93, and (3) that any changes in direct costs are reflected by a 1:1 change in government expenditures.

- The assumed 10-percent reduction in tourism in Israel is worth just over $560 million per annum.
- Finally, the loss of 30,000 Palestinian laborers would lead to a contraction in GDP of 0.15 percent, or nearly $660 million.[3]

8.2. Palestinians

There are four types of direct costs for the Palestinians associated with the nonviolent resistance scenario relative to present trends:

- The first is the assumed reduction in Palestinian labor employed in Israel. The assumed net reduction of 30,000 laborers, using an estimated average salary of $12,000 per Palestinian worker in Israel, is equivalent to a $180 million reduction in GDP.[4]
- The second is the increased time and resources spent in internal transit as a result of likely new restrictions on freedom of movement; we assume that these costs will increase by 25 percent, or reduce GDP by $20 million.[5]
- Third, for social services, the Palestinians are assumed to have to expend 25 percent more for Israeli medical care and water. Medical costs will therefore increase by over $10 million, and water-related costs will increase by approximately $20 million, for a total of approximately $30 million.[6]
- Finally, the 10-percent increase in the number of prisoners will increase total expenditures on prisoners by 10 percent—i.e., from 6 to 6.6 percent of the Palestinian budget—for a total increase in costs that results in a fall of $20 billion in GDP per annum.

There is only one major opportunity cost of nonviolent resistance for the Palestinians, though the magnitude is large. We assume that trade transaction costs increase by 25 percent, which we estimate will reduce GDP by 10.5 percent, at a total per annum value of almost $2.2 billion by 2024.[7]

---

[3]   Flaig et al., 2013, reports that an increase in labor from 50,000 to 114,000 would increase Israeli GDP by 0.3 percent. Therefore, if we assume linearity in this effect, a 30,000-worker reduction would entail a reduction in GDP of approximately 0.15 percent, or $600 million.

[4]   The estimated salary is based on the data reported by PMA, undated. It reports, for 2012, an average of 20.5 workdays and an average daily wage of NIS 164.

[5]   See ARIJ, 2011.

[6]   This is 25 percent of the estimated annual cost of reliance on Israel for electricity production—ARIJ, 2011, estimates the total cost at $440 million.

[7]   This follows Eltalla and Hens, 2009, who estimate the effect of a 50-percent reduction in costs. We assume that a 50-percent reduction and a 50-percent increase in costs have the same impact on GDP, in percentage terms.

If, as it has done periodically since 2006, Israel decides to withhold tax revenues that it collects for the PA, it could directly undermine the effectiveness of the security personnel coordinating with Israel's own security forces. Under this situation, the PA's estimated 165,000 employees, including its security forces, would not receive their monthly paychecks. In the heavily government-dependent Palestinian economy, these employees and the money they spend form the economic backbone of the West Bank. Thus, the impact of tax revenue withholdings has wider impacts on the Palestinian condition than its effect on PA government employees alone.[8] Yoram Cohen, chief of the Shin Bet, Israel's domestic intelligence agency, warned in 2012 that Palestinian security cooperation in the West Bank was "highly affected by the atmosphere on the street, public opinion and state of the economy."[9] We did not include those effects in our model.[10]

8.3. Requirements of the International Community

We assume that the international community imposes a mixture of sanctions on Israel as part of nonviolent resistance. This will include financial sanctions—e.g., "delaying or denying credits or grants"—which are the type of sanction used primarily against countries with close relations to the sanctioning countries. However, it will also include restrictions on exports to Israel—the most common form of trade sanctions.[11] Note that the current BDS movement has focused on restrictions on imports from Israel, which are a much less common form of sanctions. Together, these two types of sanctions are assumed to reduce Israeli GDP by at least 2 percent.[12]

---

[8] Lynfield, 2013.

[9] Azulay, 2012.

[10] We also considered the possibility that, if tax revenues were withheld, the PA might be forced to dissolve. We did not include that in our modeling of this scenario, but it remains a real possibility. We did model PA dissolution in the violent uprising scenario.

[11] A third type of economic sanction is asset freezes, though these are unlikely, given the close relationship between Israel and the international community (e.g., Hufbauer et al., 2008).

[12] This is a modest assumption as the average effect of combined financial and trade sanctions, historically, is nearly 3 percent of GNP (Hufbauer et al., 2008).

CHAPTER NINE

Violent Uprising

We now describe the direct costs and the opportunity costs that Israelis and Palestinians would experience in a violent uprising scenario.

The violent uprising scenario would impose huge economic and security costs on both Israel and the Palestinians. On the economic side, as reported in Table 9.1, the cost for Israel is estimated to be some $45 billion in lost economic output *per year*, and the corresponding estimate for the Palestinians is approximately $9.1 billion. On the security side, violent uprising is expected to bring expanded external and internal threats for both parties.

9.1. Israelis

Two types of direct costs for the Israelis are highlighted in Table 9.1 relative to present trends:

- First, we assume that the defense expenditures will increase by 9 percent during the three years of the conflict, for a total additional cost of nearly $7 billion,[1] which is just under $700 million per year in additional costs across the ten years of our analysis, resulting in a fall in GDP in 2024 of $340 billion.
- The second is that, as the PA collapses, the Israelis assume all costs for the Palestinian ministries of social affairs, health, and education, equivalent to 12 percent of 2014 Palestinian GDP, at $1.7 billion per annum, which reduces Israeli GDP by $830 million in 2024.[2]

The opportunity costs for the Israelis from violent uprising are driven by reductions in investment, a slowdown in labor force and productivity growth, lost tourism,

---

[1] Defense expenditures increase by 9 percent during years of conflict. Authors' estimates by comparing defense spending during 2001–2003 and 2000 using Bank of Israel, undated.

[2] Data for 2012 indicate a total of 41.7 percent of budget spent on these three ministries (World Bank, 2013a). The estimate assumes a PA budget of 30 percent of GDP, as reported in Figure 3.3 in Chapter Three.

Table 9.1
Itemized Changes in GDP in 2024 in Violent Uprising Relative to Present Trends (in millions of U.S. dollars)

Israel		Palestine	
Change in GDP from All Costs (Direct and Opportunity)			
Total Change in GDP	–$45,100		–$9,080
Change in GDP from Direct Costs[a]			
Security	–$340	Destruction of property	–$750
Settlement	$0	Territorial waters	$0
Palestinian services	–$830	Palestinian labor in Israel	–$760
		Freedom of movement	–$80
		Access to services	–$30
		Banking regulations	–$4
		Prisoners in Israel	–$180
Total change in GDP from direct costs	–$1,170		–$1,800
Change in GDP from Opportunity Costs			
Instability and uncertainty	–$39,200	Control of territory	$0
BDS	$0	Access to water	$0
Tourism	–$1,400	Barriers to trade	–$4,300
Arab world trade	$0	Licensing	$0
Palestinian trade	–$560	Tourism and travel	$0
Palestinian labor in Israel	–$2,790	Dissolution of PA	–$2,980
Total change in GDP from opportunity costs	–$43,900		–$7,280

[a] In order to translate changes in direct costs into changes in GDP, we assume (1) a fiscal multiplier of 0.5, (2) an export-to-GDP multiplier of 0.93, and (3) that any changes in direct costs are reflected by a 1:1 change in government expenditures.

and increased restrictions on the Palestinian economy. As a result of the instability associated with the violence, we assume that the contributions of investment, total factor productivity, and labor force growth to GDP growth will fall by, respectively, 20 percent, 100 percent, and 50 percent.[3] The net effect of these changes for years 3–6 is just under $40 billion per year. Additionally, our conservative assumption of a 25-percent reduction in tourism translates into an additional fall in GDP of $1.4 billion. Increased restrictions on the Palestinian economy, including a 15-percent reduction in trade and the loss of an estimated 127,000 Palestinian laborers, will reduce Israeli GDP by an additional $3.2 billion.[4]

The rise of violence will have direct effects on the scale of the internal security threats that Israel faces on a recurring basis. As an example, as a result of the collapse of the PA in the West Bank, this violent uprising would likely create new types of internal WBG threats because Hamas and jihadi groups operating in the Levant might try to fill that vacuum. Combating foreign jihadists holed up in densely populated camps, akin to Fatah al-Islam's campaign against the Lebanese Armed Forces in 2007, would require significant Israeli reserve call-ups to deal with the potential for fighting to extend for several months.

Israel's reoccupation of the West Bank and the collapse of the recognized representative of the Palestinian people—the PA—will invite new threats and accelerated attacks against the reoccupation forces and probably against Israel itself. Existing extremist groups looking to bolster their credentials, including Sunni Jihadists in Syria, new ISIS-aligned terrorists in the Sinai (Ansar Bayt al Maqdis), possibly radicalized Jordanian extremists, and others, will likely vent their anger against Israel and Israelis.

9.2. Palestinians

For the Palestinians, relative to present trends, the first direct cost of a violent uprising, which is based on historical precedent, is our assumed $1.5 billion in damage to the capital stock, and a resulting $750 million fall in GDP.[5] We also assume that a violent uprising will lead to a complete cessation of labor working in Israel or the settlements, for a total direct cost of more than $750 million to GDP, as 127,000 Palestinian labor-

---

[3]   Assumptions based on analysis of Conference Board, 2014, from 2001 to 2004 during the Second Intifada.

[4]   As discussed in Section 4.6 in Chapter Four, we assume that the restrictions on Palestinian labor increase gradually across the ten-year period and are in full effect as of the tenth year.

[5]   World Bank, 2003, p. xi, reports the replacement cost of damage to infrastructure from Operation Defensive Shield at $1.7 billion. UNCTAD, 2010, p. 8, reports damage of $1.3 billion for Operation Cast Lead. PECDAR ("Scale of Gaza Destruction Unprecedented," 2014) reports $1.7 billion in damage from Operation Protective Edge.

ers working in Israel lose their jobs.[6] We make the following additional assumptions: The resources lost as a result of internal restrictions will double, at a total cost of $150 million per annum.[7] Palestinians will have to spend 50 percent more for medical care in Israel and for water. Medical costs will therefore increase by at least $20 million, and water-related costs will increase by approximately $40 million, for a total of $60 million.[8] The regulations placed on Palestinian banks will tighten, increasing the net value of this cost by 50 percent, for a total value of $7.5 million. A doubling of the number of prisoners will double the number of stipends paid to their families, expanding this amount from 6 to 12 percent of the Palestinian budget, for a total cost of just over $350 million to GDP in 2024.

There are two major opportunity costs for the Palestinians in violent uprising. We estimate that the 50-percent increase in the nontariff barriers imposed by Israel on imports and exports will lead to a contraction in GDP by $4.3 billion.[9] The second is the collapse of the PA; existing estimates indicate that this collapse would decrease GDP by approximately 15 percent as a result of the PA's importance as an employer and a player in internal financial systems.[10] The total value of this drop is just under $3 billion.

The violent uprising would have direct deleterious impacts on the internal and external threats facing the Palestinians, as it would cripple the PNSF. Another violent intifada would also almost certainly have devastating consequences for the Palestinian security apparatus.[11] Palestinian security forces would find themselves in a no-win situation—accused of participating in the violence by Israel and of complicity with Israel by the Palestinian public. In the Second Intifada, Israel viewed any Palestinian with a weapon as a threat. Israeli security forces would likely take a similar approach if violence resurged. Palestinian police and intelligence officers would be unable to move freely for fear of becoming targets, and many would also fear becoming targets of the Palestinian public, having earned a reputation as being too close to Israel.

---

[6]   Estimated salary is based on 2013 PMA data. It reports a total of 127,000 Palestinians working in "Israel & Settlements" = 4,420 (population) × 0.59 (population over 15) × 0.436 (labor force participation) × 0.112 (employed in Israel and settlements). It reports an average annual salary of $12,000 = 12 (months) × 19.8 (days per month) × 175.4 (daily wage in NIS) ÷ 3.5 (NIS-to-dollar conversion). Data are available at PMA, undated.

[7]   See ARIJ, 2011.

[8]   This is 25 percent of the estimated annual cost of reliance on Israel for electricity production—ARIJ, 2011, estimates the total cost at $440 million.

[9]   This includes a 50-percent increase in restrictions on imports and exports.

[10]   Abdel Karim, 2013.

[11]   The nascent Palestinian security infrastructure—and the PA itself—nearly did not survive the aftermath of the last major uprising more than a decade ago; another similar experience would again threaten its viability. Very extensive damage was done to the Palestinian security infrastructure in the wake of the Second Intifada. Most buildings, including prisons, headquarters, barracks, and communication facilities, were destroyed. Hundreds of security officers were killed. The PA, after the attacks, was virtually without a security apparatus.

External resources available to the Palestinian security apparatus would almost certainly evaporate.[12] Critical liaison relationships would end with another intifada—not just with the Israelis, who would cut contact with Palestinian counterparts, but also with key patrons and mentors, such as the United States, Europeans, and Saudis. The Jordanians and even the Egyptians may be unlikely to risk relations with either Israel or the United States and may hold the Palestinians at arm's length. The Palestinians would be isolated.

Recent improvements in force structure to streamline the organization, to make authorities and jurisdictions clearer, and to prevent the emergence of local warlords likely would collapse in the aftermath of violence. Local Palestinian youths would band together, loyal to local and not national leaders, undermining any discipline established in recent training. This internal fractionalization would be amplified by the reoccupation of significant portions of the West Bank by the IDF.

9.3. Requirements of the International Community

The role of the international community in this scenario is limited. Europeans would likely wish to be seen as not approving of Israeli policy. This will likely mean increased calls for sanctions and divestitures and other actions, such as requiring Israelis to obtain visas prior to EU country visits. Relationships will be further strained, and Europe will be likely to support movements by the PA in the UN. The United States would likely be highly concerned but would not actively oppose Israel while it faced such a serious internal threat of violence. U.S. military and other assistance to both parties would likely continue.

---

12   The PNSF is almost entirely dependent on foreign assistance for its security budget. It is unlikely that any major donor would be willing to continue to contribute to a security force engaged in another violent uprising—major donors, such as the Europeans and the Gulf Arabs, would be loath to be seen as contributing to the violence. Unable to make its payroll, much less continue to equip its forces or replace and repair damaged infrastructure, authority and the chain of command of the national organization would crumble.

CHAPTER TEN

Costs for the International Community

The five scenarios that we analyzed in the preceding chapters have cost implications for the United States and Europe. The Americans and Europeans have provided financial and political support to both Israel and the Palestinians since World War II. In addition to the investment specifically required for the Palestinian economy to reap the benefits of the two-state solution and unilateral withdrawal scenarios (discussed in Chapters Five, Six, and Seven), each of these scenarios would be likely to affect the types of ongoing support provided to both Israel and the Palestinians.

This chapter begins by summarizing the type of economic support that has been provided to Israel and the Palestinians since World War II. While continued support to both economies is anticipated across all scenarios, the anticipated types and total value of this support will vary across the scenarios; thus, we use a counterfactual approach analogous to that used in Chapters Five through Nine to estimate the costs to the international community for each of the five scenarios.

As an example, we take a closer look at the two-state solution scenario. In this case, we calculate a total ten-year additional cost to the international community of $88 billion: $30 billion for Israel and $58 billion for the WBG. Though the specific breakdowns of the costs in each of the scenarios are provided in Section 10.3, in this case, "Israel's cost" of $30 billion to the international community is the burden that the international community would assume for relocating settlers in the context of a two-state solution. The analogous "Palestinian cost" of $58 billion is the total size of private and public investment that the international community would need to make so that the Palestinian economy can reap the full benefit of the two-state solution, in addition to the estimated cost of supporting approximately 600,000 refugees returning from abroad to the newly formed Palestinian state ($8 billion).

It should be pointed out that Israel will also need significant investment to fund the economic opportunities that peace would bring. These investment funds will come from a combination of international and domestic sources. We do not try to calculate the amount that would be international in origin because Israel has well-developed capital markets that will enable these funds to flow smoothly at market-clearing prices.

As the Israeli economy is so much larger than the Palestinian economy, these funds will likely be substantial in absolute amounts.

One somewhat counterintuitive scenario is violent uprising, in which we see a "negative" Palestinian cost. This result indicates that the costs to the international community would decline by some $24 billion if the violent uprising scenario should occur. This result follows from our assumption (see Chapter Four) that Israel would be forced by the PA's collapse to assume responsibility for Palestinian security functions and for Palestinian education and health care systems and that the international community would reduce its contributions by a corresponding amount. This is discussed in greater detail in Section 10.3.

10.1. Historical Support to Israel

The support of the U.S. government has played an important role in Israel's successful economic development. Israel is the largest recipient of U.S. government official foreign aid since World War II, having received $118 billion to date. In recent years, the nation has received approximately $2.6 billion per year (Figure 10.1). Aid includes defense assistance and a variety of nondefense support, including grants,[1] emergency assistance during various economic slowdowns and other geopolitical events,[2] and loan guarantees,[3] in addition to other programs since 1948.[4] Israel also benefits from U.S. budget appropriations related to joint U.S.-Israeli missile defense programs, the deployment of the X-Band radar system, and various technology and development transfer programs in the defense and high-technology sectors.[5]

---

[1]   Such as Migration and Refugee Assistance grants beginning in 1973. Funding levels have declined since 2000.

[2]   An important example of this is during the Israeli-Palestinian peace process (Sharp, 2014).

[3]   These allow Israel to borrow from commercial sources through bond issues at rates lower than market rates (Sharp, 2014). Backed by the government of the United States, these subsidies are a percentage of the total loan amounts, amounting to 4.1 percent in the 1990s. Legally, Israel is prohibited from using proceeds from guaranteed loans for military purposes or to support activities in the West Bank and Gaza; however, in FY 2003 and FY 2005, the U.S. Department of State reduced the amount available for loans for continuation of construction of settlements outside of the 1967 borders. In FY 2003, the reduction was $289.5 million out of $3 billion. In FY 2005, the amount was reduced by $795.8 million. Israel has not borrowed under the program since FY 2004, instead raising funds on international capital markets. Nevertheless, the loan guarantee program provides benefits in the market for capital as a "safety net" that reduces risk for lenders. The amount available to borrow under the program has increased from $1.1 billion in FY 2003 to $3.8 billion in FY 2013. Under current U.S. law, the loan guarantee authority extends until September 30, 2015, though the authority has been extended many times.

[4]   The United States also funds the American Schools and Hospitals Abroad program and, from time to time, funds programs that aid joint Israeli-U.S. cooperation in business, science, and energy (Sharp, 2014).

[5]   Sharp, 2014.

Figure 10.1
Official U.S. Aid to Israel

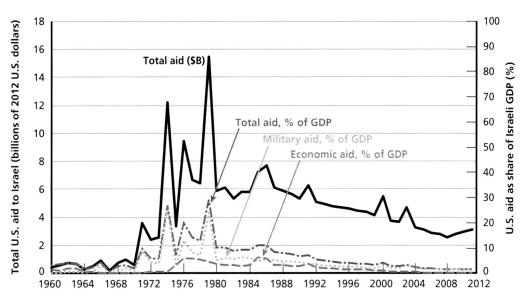

SOURCE: Authors' calculations based on Sharp, 2014.
RAND RR740-10.1

U.S. military aid has contributed to the Israeli domestic defense industry, which is a major supplier of arms worldwide.[6] Annual U.S. Foreign Military Financing accounts for 20 to 25 percent of the Israeli defense budget; roughly one-fourth of these Foreign Military Financing funds can be used for domestic military procurement.[7] The United States also provides funding in defense appropriations for joint U.S.-Israeli missile defense programs, including $486 million in aid for the Iron Dome missile defense system[8] and half of the funding for the Arrow antimissile system.[9] Other assistance is not reported publicly.

Israel has received nondefense Migration and Refugee Assistance grants from the United States since 1973, though funding levels have declined since 2000.[10] The United States has also consistently provided emergency assistance during various eco-

---

[6] Sharp, 2014. Between 2004 and 2011, the value of arms exports from Israel was $12.9 billion.

[7] Sharp, 2014; Schmid et al., 2006.

[8] Sharp, 2014. Iron Dome was developed by Israel, and it retains proprietary technology rights to it.

[9] Schmid et al., 2006.

[10] Sharp, 2014.

nomic slowdowns and other geopolitical events, including the Israeli-Palestinian peace process.[11]

Since 1972, the United States has provided loan guarantees, which allow Israel to borrow from commercial sources through bond issues at rates lower than those offered by the market. Backed by the government of the United States, these subsidies are a percentage of the total loan amounts, amounting to 4.1 percent in the 1990s. Legally, Israel is prohibited from using proceeds from guaranteed loans for military purposes or to support activities in the WBG, but, because funds are fungible, the guaranteed loans would increase Israel's budgetary flexibility. In FY 2003 and FY 2005, the U.S. Department of State reduced the amount available for loan guarantees because of continuation of construction of settlements outside of the 1967 borders. Israel has not borrowed under the program since FY 2004, instead raising funds on the open international capital markets. Nevertheless, the loan guarantee program provides benefits in the market for capital as a "safety net" that reduces risk for lenders. The United States also funds the American Schools and Hospitals Abroad program and, from time to time, funds programs that aid joint Israeli-U.S. cooperation in business, science, and energy.

Donations from private U.S. organizations have also been a major source of financial support to Israel;[12] such support has been encouraged by U.S. government policy that has made most of these donations tax deductible.[13] Recent data suggest that private contributions are upward of $1.65 billion annually, including approximately $500 million for historically Zionist organizations, $390 million for social welfare, and $370 million for secular education.[14] American private giving to Israel comprises approximately 16 percent of all U.S. international donations and constitutes just over 9 percent of nonprofit- and NGO-sector revenues in Israel.[15] Trends in this support

---

[11] Sharp, 2014.

[12] There are four types of funding organizations that donate funds through these rules: (1) federations, which either donate directly to Israeli NGOs or transfer funds to United Israel Appeal (an American nonprofit) that transfers funds to the Jewish Agency for Israel; (2) American Friends organizations that support specific Israeli organizations; (3) pass-through organizations that function as umbrella charities; and (4) ideological umbrella funds, which support organizations with ideological or political missions. The primary source of giving has been the United Jewish Appeal and successor organizations (e.g., United Jewish Communities, Jewish Federations of North America). These organizations raise money from over 150 federations and transfer a portion to the United Israel Appeal, which, in turn, transfers funds to the Jewish Agency for Israel (Fleisch and Sasson, 2012).

[13] Fleisch and Sasson, 2012. Conditions for tax deductibility include that (1) donations must be made through a domestic nonprofit with a board consisting of mostly American citizens, (2) the foreign NGO must be judged equivalent to a U.S. nonprofit, and (3) the American nonprofit must exercise oversight over foreign grants.

[14] Within the ideological categories, $46 million was deemed to be in the progressive (politically left) category, while $40 million was donated to organizations supporting Israeli settlement activity (politically right) (Fleisch and Sasson, 2012).

[15] Fleisch and Sasson, 2012. Overall philanthropic support comprised 19 percent of revenue in this sector, implying that U.S. donations comprise one-half of all philanthropic support for the nonprofit and NGO sector.

have not been well documented, but existing research suggests an approximate 50-percent rise in donations from 1998 through 2007, followed by an approximate drop of 35 percent from peak giving in the following two years (corresponding to the recession in the United States).

The U.S. government has used official aid, along with additional foreign assistance to other regional actors, "to encourage and reward Israeli and Arab leaders for choosing diplomacy over war."[16] While the EU has consistently called for the withdrawal of Israel from the West Bank, it supports the Israelis through a variety of bilateral and multilateral initiatives and exchanges, including a trade treaty that eliminated customs duties, accepted Israel into its Research and Development Framework Programmes, and provides a framework for political dialogue aimed "to strengthen mutual understanding and solidarity."[17]

10.2. Historical Support to the Palestinians

During the first stage of the conflict, from 1967 until the Oslo Accords, the total flow of American donor resources to Palestinians was relatively limited, as shown in Figure 10.2.[18] During this stage, U.S. support to Palestinians flowed primarily through the UN, with the United States providing an average of $40 million per year in support for the UN Relief and Works Agency for Palestine Refugees in the Near East (UNRWA) between 1950 and 1991, for a total of $1.6 billion (nominal dollars).[19] Jordan, the PLO, and other Arab states were the primary sources of support for municipalities, cooperatives, universities, and charitable societies during this stage.[20] Though their total support was relatively modest initially, the flow of resources from these states increased dramatically, to approximately $100 million per annum with Arab League support in 1979.[21]

---

[16]   Lasensky, 2004, p. 215.

[17]   Schmid et al., 2006, p. 14; Gilat, 1992.

[18]   We have not been able to identify a reliable source on the history of European aid flows during this period. However, Schmid et al., 2006, reports that the Europeans did not become major players in the provision of aid until after the Oslo Accords. Mansour, 1988, reports that the Europeans contributed $2 million starting in 1981 and that the UNDP contributed $12 million from 1982 to 1986.

[19]   The United States contributed $16 million in bilateral aid between 1977 and 1983 (Mansour, 1988).

[20]   Jordan provided foreign aid by maintaining the payroll of its former employees (Brynen, 2000). The PLO, which raised money with the Palestine National Fund through a 5-percent tax on Palestinian labor throughout the Gulf, had a significant windfall during the 1970s and 1980s from Arab nations following increases in oil prices (Brynen, 2000; Challand, 2008 [cited in DeVoir and Tartir, 2009]). Until 1990, Arab countries did not contribute to the UNRWA because they thought that Israel should be responsible for the plight of the Palestinians (Zanotti, 2013).

[21]   Total support provided from 1967 to 1979 by the PLO and other Arab states is not well documented. However, as Brynen, 2000, reports that aid "increased sharply" in 1979, we assume that total support from the Arab states was less than 50 percent of the levels achieved in 1979. We have two primary sources in estimating support

Figure 10.2
Estimated Foreign Aid Provided to Palestinians

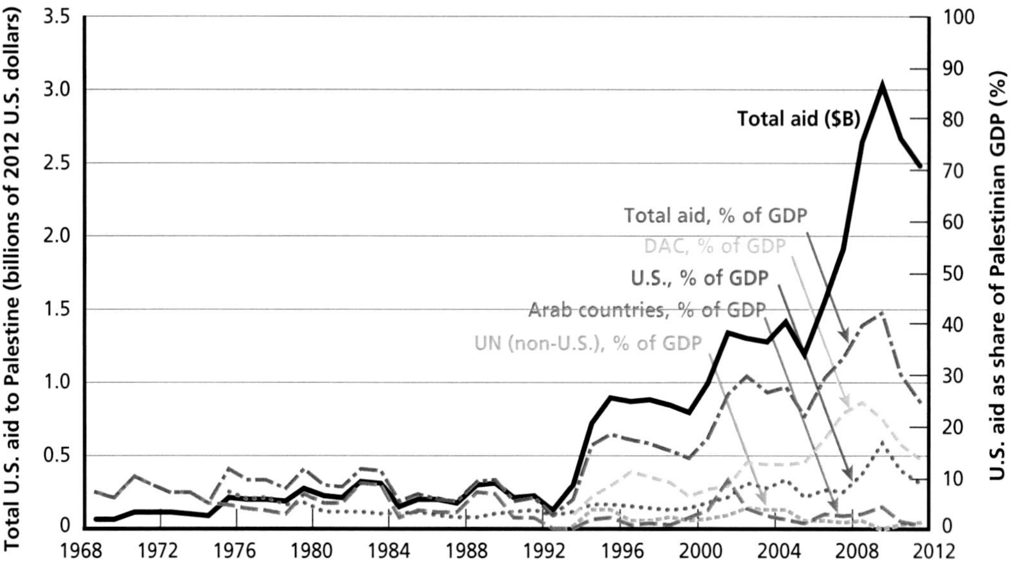

SOURCES: Data for the United States are from Mark, 2005, which include U.S. bilateral contributions from 1975 to 2004; Zanotti, 2013, which provides U.S. support to UNRWA from 1950 to 2013; and the WDI, which reports U.S. bilateral contributions from 1993 to 2011 (the data from the WDI and Mark disagree, so we prefer Mark in all years but 2004). The data from the DAC countries (*DAC countries* are Australia, Austria, Belgium, Canada, Czech Republic, Denmark, Finland, France, Germany, Greece, Iceland, Ireland, Italy, Japan, Republic of Korea, Luxembourg, Netherlands, New Zealand, Norway, Portugal, Spain, Sweden, Switzerland, United Kingdom, United States, and EU institutions—note that we exclude the United States) reflect bilateral contributions as reported in the WDI. Note also that we exclude U.S. contributions to UNRWA from the total UN contributions. Chapter Ten, which summarizes economic costs to international partners, describes our estimates of foreign aid from the Arab states during 1979 to 1991. Data from 1993 to 2011 for the Arab countries are estimated by calculating the difference of total official development assistance and the amount contributed by DAC nations.
RAND RR740-10.2

However, aid from Arab states fell dramatically before the Oslo Accords and eventually fell to zero after the PLO sided with Iraq in the 1990–1991 Gulf War.[22]

The conclusion of the Oslo Accords marked the beginning of a second stage in U.S. assistance policy. Aid to the Palestinians was seen as critical to the success of the

---

provided from 1979 until the Oslo Accords. Mansour, 1988, reports that support from the Joint Jordanian-Palestinian Committee for the Steadfastness of the Palestinian People in the Occupied Homeland (henceforth, "Joint Committee") "reached a peak of $101 million in 1982" and then fell significantly in 1984 and 1985. Brynen, 2000, p. 47, reports that the support of the Arab League was secured following a Baghdad summit in 1979. Brynen reports several estimates indicating that (1) total support from 1979 to 1987 was $500 million, (2) $110 million was provided annually during the early 1980s, (3) $50 million to $60 million was provided in 1988, and (4) $120 million annually was provided in 1988 and 1989.

[22] Brynen, 2000, p. 47, reports that aid from the Joint Committee fell to about $30 million per annum after 1989.

peace process, helping to ensure a "peace dividend" to the Palestinians.[23] This stage, which saw a dramatic increase in the total flows of foreign aid, was characterized by a reduction in support for Palestinian NGOs, while support for the PA and direct programming expanded. The international community started providing budget support to the PA, which assumed responsibility for many of the social services that had previously been administered by NGOs.[24] In addition, foreign donors shifted their support to a coordinated donor-led effort to support long-term development through public and private investment.[25]

In the third stage, in the wake of the Second Intifada, the Palestinian economy became heavily reliant on the direct support of the international community.[26] Though President Bill Clinton's offer of $35 billion at Camp David to stop the Oslo Accords process from collapsing was not realized,[27] there was dramatic growth in foreign aid dependence following the Second Intifada: By 2008, aid disbursements accounted for more than 60 percent of Palestinian GNI.[28] This stage also saw a significant change in the form of U.S. support, which began to include direct support to the PA.[29] Though there was growing evidence of donor disillusionment in 2005,[30] international aid

---

[23] These authors have not identified any specific estimates of a peace dividend before the Oslo Accords. However, both the Israelis and the Palestinians believed that large-scale international aid would bring a peace dividend that would help maintain the momentum of the peace process (Lasensky, 2004). Polling data from this period indicated that Palestinians did view international aid as important (Saïd, 2005, cited by Schmid et al., 2006, p. 28). Lasensky reports a senior Palestinian negotiator as saying that the aid component "was critical to this process" (p. 220). Interestingly, Lasensky reports that Israel was more focused on making sure that Palestine received the funds that it needed to succeed than in trying to raise more funds for itself.

[24] This support was provided through the Holst Fund, which was "chronically short of funds" (Brynen, 1996a). The Holst Fund, which was administered through the World Bank, provided roughly $250 million to support recurrent and start-up costs for the PA between 1994 and 1997 (Khadr, 1999). Other countries also provided direct support to the PA—e.g., the U.S. government provided $36 million in direct support to the PA in 1994 (Mark, 2005).

[25] Lasensky, 2004, reports that, initially, a "good deal of interest was expressed, particularly in the tourism field" by private investors.

[26] UNCTAD, 2005. Reported in 2012 dollars. Specifically, UNCTAD estimates the total opportunity cost from 2000 to 2004 as $6.4 billion in 1997 dollars. We were unable to find any specifics on how these results were derived.

[27] The offer was made up of $10 billion for refugees, $10 billion for water desalination, $15 billion for the IDF.

[28] Calì, 2011. Overall aid increased dramatically in the aftermath of the Second Intifada, and there was again a shift by donors to the provision of emergency assistance instead of development projects. This shift was to deal with the consequences of the closures associated with the Second Intifada (DeVoir and Tartir, 2009).

[29] The United States provided limited support to the PA in FY 2003 and FY 2005—respectively, $36 million and $20 million (Mark, 2005). However, support increased dramatically following the departure of Hamas, with the United States providing $300 million in 2008, $275 million in 2009, $225 million in 2010, $50 million in 2011, and $350 million in 2013 (Zanotti, 2013).

[30] Schmid et al., 2006, p. 22, provides a discussion of this donor fatigue, which was articulated by both the World Bank and the Ad Hoc Liaison Committee.

surged once again in 2007 following the departure of Hamas from the West Bank and the arrival of Prime Minister Salam Fayyad's caretaker government.[31]

Significant challenges limited the effectiveness of aid in bringing about the promised peace dividend. During the early period of aid, Mansour argues,[32] Israeli restrictions redirected foreign aid from projects that would enhance Palestinian economic productivity to basic infrastructure that Israel would otherwise have needed to build; this substitution effect continued after the Oslo Accords.[33] In addition, there was limited capacity within the PA and aid community to effectively exploit the increased resources available in the wake of the Oslo Accords.[34] The PA also resisted the requirements for transparency and other regulations associated with Western aid.[35] As a result of Israeli closures following a wave of suicide attacks in 1994, aid destined for long-term investment and technical assistance programs was shifted to emergency efforts, and many investment and infrastructure programs were delayed.[36] Despite the fact that aid faced significant challenges, it has been attributed with creating incentives for potential Palestinian spoilers to participate in the peace process.[37]

10.3. Costs of the Five Scenarios

Each of the scenarios we consider has cost implications for the international community. In each of the following subsections, we first describe the assumptions implicit for the international community from our assumptions in Chapter Four and then describe the cost implications for both the United States and the Europeans.

---

[31] World Bank, 2012.

[32] Mansour, 1988.

[33] Brynen, 1996b, reports that USAID efforts were being diverted away from projects that would be useful for economic development and that there was, overall, a significant mismatch between Palestinian goals and the willingness of the international community to fund programs to achieve those goals. However, this "restriction" can be attributed to the Israelis only in the sense that they created the complicated political environment in which these development donors have been trying to function.

[34] Brynen, 1996b; Khadr, 1999. Lasensky, 2004, argues that "the US did not provide Palestinians with sufficient political and security inducements to maximize aid effectiveness" (p. 211).

[35] Lasensky, 2004, reports that disbursement was "hampered by 'intra-PLO politics, the Palestinian leadership's resistance to donors' standards of accountability and inexperienced [Palestinian] middle management'" (p. 221). Further, "Arafat wanted walking-around money . . . to use for PA and PLO political purposes" (p. 223).

[36] Khadr, 1999; Le More, 2005.

[37] Lasensky, 2004, reports that aid created incentives for PA and PLO personnel, especially security personnel, to support the Oslo Accords process (p. 229).

Two-State Solution

The cost implications for the international community of the assumptions specified in Chapter Four are as follows:

- **Israeli settlers:** Resettlement of 100,000 Israeli settlers is paid for by the United States.
- **Warning systems:** The United States would enhance the early warning capability of the Israelis through access to new systems, new technologies, and increased funding streams.
- **Investment for Palestinians:** The international community would coordinate the provision of the public and private investment requisite for the Palestinian economy to reap the benefits of a two-state solution and to maintain a constant per capita GDP despite the return of refugees.

There are, therefore, a total of three different costs that the international community will face in the two-state solution:

- The first is the direct costs of moving the settlers back to Israel. As in costing the unilateral withdrawal scenarios for Israel, we assume that the cost per settler will be similar to those in previous resettlements—approximately $300,000 per settler—so that the total cost of resettlement will be $30 billion.[38]
- Getting Israel to agree to the two-state solution is assumed to require that the United States (or Europe) provide additional technology and funding to implement the variety of requisite warning systems associated with Israel's reduced presence in the West Bank. Though the price tag for this cost is unknown, it could easily run into the billions of dollars.
- The final cost that the international community will face is either providing or coordinating the provision of an estimated $58 billion in public and private investment required over the ten years of analysis for the Palestinian economy to reap the benefits of the two-state solution and to successfully integrate returning Palestinian refugees from the diaspora. Though the private sector may support some of this investment, it is likely that a significant amount of investment will need to come directly from the international community. We also anticipate that humanitarian assistance from the UN High Commissioner for Refugees will continue.

Coordinated Unilateral Withdrawal

The cost implications for the international community of the assumptions specified in Chapter Four are as follows:

---

[38] Estimated resettlement costs are from U.S. Senate Committee on Foreign Relations, 2005, and based on estimated per-settler costs incurred from Gaza withdrawal.

- **Israeli settlers:** 75 percent of the cost of resettling 60,000 Israeli settlers is paid for by the United States.
- **Warning systems:** The United States would enhance the early warning capability of the Israelis through access to new systems, new technologies, and increased funding streams.
- **Investment for Palestinians:** The international community would coordinate the provision of the public and private investment requisite for the Palestinian economy to reap the benefits of access to Areas B and C but will not approve or assist the Israelis in paying to move settlers, as the unilateral actions of the Israelis do not solve the need for a final status accord agreement.

The cost of relocating the settlers is slightly lower, at $13.5 billion, as the international community will cover only 75 percent of the costs and a slightly lower number of settlers—60,000—will be relocated. As in the two-state solution, this scenario assumes that the United States (or Europe) would provide additional technology and funding to implement the variety of requisite warning systems associated with Israel's reduced presence in the West Bank. Though the price tag for this cost is unknown, it could easily run into the billions of dollars.

Realizing the limited economic benefits of coordinated unilateral withdrawal for the Palestinians will require limited new investment that the international community will likely need to help facilitate. Our estimates suggest that some $10 billion in public and private investment will be required to achieve this expansion of the economy.

Uncoordinated Unilateral Withdrawal
There are no net cost changes to the international community.

Nonviolent Resistance
There are no net cost changes to the international community.

Violent Uprising
In Chapter Four, we assume that, under the violent uprising scenario, direct U.S. support to the Palestinians stops as the PA collapses and Israel assumes the cost of maintaining basic services for the Palestinians.

Our analysis suggests that the most pronounced "cost" for the international community would be the elimination of U.S. support to the Palestinians following the resumption of violence. Thus, the total impact would be reduced expenditures of approximately $1.7 billion per year, for a total savings of an estimated $17 billion.

CHAPTER ELEVEN

Noneconomic Factors Surrounding the Conflict

Multiple studies, including our own, clearly demonstrate that a peaceful resolution of the conflict is the best option economically for both Palestinians and Israelis, while a return to violence is very costly to both sides.[1, 2] Yet the conflict persists. Perhaps the parties do not properly recognize the economic benefits of an agreement, or the economic benefits of an agreement have not been and may not be high enough to outweigh the imputed costs of intangible factors, such as distrust, religion, and fear of relinquishing some degree of security. In this chapter, we suggest what some of those factors might be.

11.1. Power Imbalance and Economic Incentives

From both an economic and a security perspective, Israel is by far the dominant player. For example, the difference in outcomes between present trends and any of the scenarios is dramatic if looked at in terms of changes in GDP per capita versus absolute changes in GDP. To illustrate: In the two-state solution, we estimate that Israel would benefit by $22.8 billion in 2024, compared to only $9.7 billion for the WBG; however, income for the average Israeli would rise by only about 5 percent, as compared to 36 percent for the average Palestinian. In every comparison, this dramatic difference presents itself because the Israeli economy is more than 20 times larger than the economy of the WBG, including Jerusalem. As a result of this basic imbalance, Israelis have a smaller financial incentive and the Palestinians a larger incentive to reach an accord.

In addition, Israel's economic costs for maintaining the status quo are not relatively that large. As we have shown, Israel maintains security in the West Bank cost-

---

[1]   Nonviolent resistance will reduce GDP in both areas (–$15.1 billion in Israel versus –$2.2 billion in the WBG) but would cause GDP per capita to decrease about three times as much in the WBG as in Israel (–10.8 percent versus –3.4 percent), although the effects were significant for particular groups within each population.

[2]   Kaufmann, 2014; a 2014 study by a group of 300 businesspeople called Breaking the Impasse found significant benefits for both Israelis and Palestinians from peace (Elis, 2014b). Finance Minister Lapid estimated that peace would benefit Israel by as much as NIS 20 billion per year.

effectively and has essentially walled off Gaza. The summer 2014 war in Gaza was far more expensive than Israel may have originally anticipated, but most of the physical damage and loss of life occurred in Gaza.

Thus, Israel, the party with the greater power, has learned how to maintain the status quo at minimal cost and has a smaller economic incentive to resolve the impasse than the Palestinians have.

11.2. Perceived Security Risk

Direct economic costs associated with security are unlikely to fall for either party in the short run under any scenario. On the other hand, Israel sees unchanged or increased security risks under any of the scenarios we examined. Even unilateral withdrawal increases security risk from the perspective of many Israelis. As evidence, they cite Israel's unilateral (uncoordinated) withdrawals from Lebanon in 2000 and from Gaza in 2005; in those cases, radical groups (Hezbollah and Hamas, respectively) took control of the areas from which Israel withdrew and have posed significant security threats to Israel ever since.

Palestinians would presumably be eager to assume the new security responsibilities it would encounter under a two-state solution or coordinated unilateral withdrawal, but it lacks the experience, manpower, and resources to fulfill all of them quickly. Externally, the PNSF would have to secure the borders against the same threats Israel faces currently, including ISIS, Hezbollah, multiple threats emanating in Syria, elements in Jordan, and terrorists and bandits in the Sinai, to name but a few. Internally, the PNSF would face sharply increased responsibilities in a two-state solution, taking over functions currently handled by the IDF, as well as maintaining peace in Gaza. In the other scenarios, it would be even more challenged.

From a security perspective, movement away from the present trends entails significant uncertainty and risk that clearly influences both parties as they consider final status accord issues.

11.3. Lack of Political Consensus

Both Jewish Israelis and Palestinians living in the WBG are deeply divided politically. This lack of political consensus constitutes a barrier to an accord. Neither party currently appears able to muster the political support needed to achieve a final political settlement.

Political Divisions in Palestinian Society

Fatah, which controls the PA and the West Bank, and Hamas, which controls Gaza, are the two primary political actors among the Palestinians. Paradoxically, each party has significant support in the area it does not control. For example, in a June 2014 representative poll conducted before the 2014 war in Gaza, 40 percent of those polled indicated that they would support Fatah[3] and 39 percent would support Hamas if the same parties ran in the next election. Disaggregated figures reveal that Fatah was more popular in Gaza than in the West Bank (support from 42 percent of Gazans and 39 percent of West Bank residents). Hamas would have received 30 percent of the vote in the West Bank and 35 percent in Gaza.[4] Thus each party was *less popular* in the area it controlled than in the area controlled by the other.

A poll conducted immediately after the summer 2014 Gaza war[5] asked the same questions. Hamas had enhanced its popularity by "standing up to Israel," receiving support of 46 percent of the population, compared with 31 percent for Fatah. More recent polls have found that support for Hamas has fallen from this high level.[6]

Although both major parties have support within both the West Bank and Gaza, they have very different views about Israel and the Israeli-Palestinian conflict. Fatah has recognized Israel's right to exist and seeks a negotiated settlement with Israel. Fatah has also disavowed terrorism, and the PNSF actively cooperates with Israel's IDF to combat terrorism and maintain peace. Led by President Abbas, the PA has, for years, engaged in sporadic negotiations with Israel in an attempt to reach a final status accord. Secretary Kerry's peace initiative is only the most recent in a list of such efforts. Fatah also supports and insists on upholding agreements made with Israel in the past.

In contrast, the charter of Hamas calls for the elimination of the State of Israel and establishment of an Islamic state in the land that is now Israel. In the past, Hamas, and particularly its military wing, the Izz ad-Din al-Qassam Brigades, has supported violence, including firing rockets at Israel and other forms of terror, as acceptable tactics for achieving its objectives.[7] Hamas has also refused to recognize or be bound by any past PA agreements with Israel.

As one would expect, these deep political divides reflect various subgroups in Palestinian society, including those defined by geography, refugee status, and reli-

---

[3]   The slate on the ballot was the "Change and Reform" list, which was dominated by Hamas but did include several other smaller groups.

[4]   Palestinian Center for Policy and Survey Research, 2014b.

[5]   Palestinian Center for Policy and Survey Research, 2014c.

[6]   Lieber, 2014.

[7]   Many countries, including the United States, Canada, and Egypt, classify Hamas as a terrorist organization; many others, such as the United Kingdom and Australia, classify only the military wing as a terrorist organization.

gion. More than 95 percent of Palestinians are Muslim.[8] However, as among Israelis, the degree (and form) of religious observance varies substantially along the spectrum from more secular to more fundamentalist.[9] Religion and political affiliation are often strongly correlated. In general, fundamentalists more often support Hamas, which emphasizes Islamic values; secular Muslims are more likely to be better off economically and more nationally than religiously oriented. They are usually better educated and more likely to live in urban areas of the West Bank.

Although both Fatah and Hamas have significant levels of support, they have profoundly different attitudes about Israel and divergent approaches to resolving the conflict, making cooperation between them and agreement on a final status accord agreement very difficult.

Political Divisions in Israeli Society

Israel also has deep, complex political divisions. For example, in the 2013 Israeli elections, 13 political parties received more than the required 3.5 percent of the vote and won representation in the 120-seat Israeli Knesset. No single party won more than 19 seats, and only six had ten or more. These divisions meant that the Netanyahu government of 2015 was based on a coalition of five parties in order to assemble the 61 members of the Knesset needed to form a government. But in that coalition, there were deep divisions on how to deal with the Israeli-Palestinian impasse—which eventually became one of the reasons leading to a call in late 2014 for new elections.

In the elections held March 17, 2015, ten parties received the necessary percentage vote to be included in the Knesset. The Likud party won 30 seats. In a political speech immediately before the election, Likud's head, Netanyahu, vowed that there would be no Palestinian state as long as he was prime minister of Israel.[10] The second-largest vote total (24 seats) went to the Zionist Union party; this party favored a two-state solution. The third-largest party (13 seats) was the Joint List, composed mostly of Israeli Palestinians, who comprise about 20 percent of the Israeli population.[11] The remaining seven parties won from five to 11 seats.

As in Palestinian society, political divides reflect various subgroups in Israeli society. A major distinguishing feature is religiosity. Notwithstanding variations in the degree of observance, Jewish society in Israel generally assumes one of three religious identities: secular, Orthodox (including National Religious camps and, within them, ideological settlers), and ultra-Orthodox (Haredi). The latter two groups tend to favor

---

[8]   Central Intelligence Agency, 2015a, 2015b.

[9]   Brown, 2010. This split is sometimes characterized as a split between those Palestinians who are more secular and those who are more religious.

[10]   Booth, 2015.

[11]   Kaplan, undated.

the political right and hold beliefs that oppose making concessions toward resolving the Israeli-Palestinian conflict; secular Israelis see themselves as generally more liberal and vote across the moderate right-center-left spectrum. They tend to support a two-state solution and urge flexibility in resolving the conflict.

Deep political divisions make it more difficult for Palestinians, Israelis, and the leaders of both groups to garner popular support for accepting the compromises required to break the impasse. Furthermore, subgroups in each population are powerful enough to make change difficult. There is little on the horizon to suggest that these configurations will change any time soon.

11.4. Leadership

Leadership has been called "the capacity to translate vision into reality."[12] Strong leadership requires courage, the ability to think beyond the near term, and the power to convince others to follow one's lead. As relates to Israeli-Arab affairs, at least two individuals stand out as meeting those criteria: Anwar Sadat and Yitzhak Rabin. Both men fundamentally changed the course of history with their vision, and both paid for their courage with their lives.

A common refrain in Israel is that there is no partner with whom to make peace. In his election-eve campaign speech, Prime Minister Netanyahu repeated what he has often articulated: "There are no forces for peace, no partner for peace."[13] Many Israelis feel that there is no partner for peace as long as there is a Palestinian coalition government that includes Hamas.

Palestinians have similar feelings. Saeb Erekat mirrored Prime Minister Netanyahu when he said that Palestinians have "no partner for peace in Israel."[14] After Prime Minister Netanyahu's declaration about a Palestinian state, Palestinians have little expectation that Israel under Netanyahu will negotiate a final status accord agreement.

To date, neither Palestinians nor Israelis have had a leader with a vision to transcend the conflict and the power to sell that vision to the people. Lacking such leadership, neither side views the other as a potential partner in establishing a lasting peace.

---

[12] Booher, 1992, p. 34.

[13] Booth, 2015.

[14] "Saeb Erekat: 'No Partner for Peace in Israel,'" 2014.

11.5. A Dangerous Neighborhood

Since the beginning of the Arab Spring, the Middle East has been a cauldron of political change, instability, and violence. The dynamic regional context of the Israeli-Palestinian issue has affected the parties' views of the costs and benefits of the current stalemate compared with alternative trajectories in a number of ways. What matters for the purposes of this study is that regional instability has altered the context in which the Israeli-Palestinian impasse continues and has amplified the uncertainty and perceived security risk for Israelis and, to a lesser extent, for Palestinians.

The Political Terrain Has Shifted

Egypt, which has shared a stable, peaceful border with Israel for decades, has seen in rapid succession the sudden overthrow of Hosni Mubarak, the election of Mohamed Morsi, a military takeover and imprisonment of Morsi, and the election of Abdul Fattah al Sisi. Elsewhere in the region, the rise of ISIS (including in the Sinai), revolution and repression in Syria, continued Hezbollah power in Lebanon, near chaos in Iraq, uncertainty about Turkey, unrest in Bahrain, revolution in Yemen, and Iranian nuclear ambitions have left Israelis and Palestinians alike with considerable concern about their need for secure borders and doubts over their future in what many refer to as "a dangerous neighborhood."

Today, it is hard to find a place in the Middle East that is more stable and less risky than it was ten years ago. These risks and uncertainties constitute significant intangible costs in the minds of both the Israelis and Palestinians, but particularly Israelis, as they weigh the costs and benefits of movement away from the status quo.

The Importance of the Israeli-Palestinian Conflict Appears to Be Receding

Many today question whether the Israeli-Palestinian issue holds the same significance it once did.[15] With Jordan and Egypt having concluded peace treaties with Israel, and Saddam Hussein's Iraq removed as a regional power, Israel no longer faces a serious conventional military threat. The other Arab states lack either the capability or the intent to challenge Israel militarily.

Many other issues in the region and elsewhere have taken center stage. The ISIS invasion of Iraq, the metastasizing Syrian civil war, Shi'a-Sunni tensions, Egyptian and Gulf State hostility to the Muslim Brotherhood, Russia's seizure of Crimea and incursion into Ukraine, and Iran nuclear and regional ambitions continue to distract the world's attention away from the Israeli-Palestinian conflict.

---

[15]   See, for example, Assistant Secretary for Near Eastern Affairs Anne Patterson's remark that the Israeli-Palestinian conflict "is certainly not the most urgent problem that we face now in the Middle East" (quoted in Groll, 2013).

Commenting on this situation,[16] Prime Minister Netanyahu noted, "If we have peace with the Palestinians, the centrifuges will not stop spinning in Iran, the turmoil will not stop in Syria, the instability in North Africa will not cease."[17] For political reasons, such topics are often prioritized over the Palestinian issue as matters of concern in Jerusalem.

Within the Arab world, publics still report caring a great deal about the Palestinian cause,[18] but governments are clearly investing greater energies and resources in coping with other regional challenges. Indeed, the threat of a nuclear-armed Iran has served to reinforce the mutual interests—and at times, tacit cooperation—between Israel and the Sunni Arab states. The advance of ISIS into Syria and Iraq led Israel to publicly declare its readiness to militarily support Jordan, should ISIS set its sights on the Hashemite Kingdom. The ISIS threat has taken center stage (along with Iran and nuclear negotiations) for the U.S. government, most of Europe, and leading Arab nations, such as Saudi Arabia.

Absent some dramatic shift, regional instability and the erosion of the centrality of the Israeli-Palestinian conflict seem likely to persist. Only a violent uprising or a Third Intifada has the potential for upsetting the stasis. Given the enormous costs that the Second Intifada imposed on the Palestinians, they are unlikely to take that road again.

The Middle East is plagued with upheaval and instability, but there is little on the region's ten-year horizon that seems likely to change the progression of present trends.

11.6. Conflicting Societal Narratives and Perspectives

The conflicting narratives[19] and perceptions of the Israelis and Palestinians are fundamental to understanding why the impasse has endured.[20] These narratives and perceptions have spawned distrust and generated sociopsychological barriers that make reaching any enduring agreement very challenging.[21]

---

[16] Bronner, 2012.

[17] Keinon, 2013b.

[18] Telhami, 2008.

[19] Rotberg, 2006; Laqueur and Rubin, 2008.

[20] See, for example, Bar-Tal, Halperin, and Oren, 2010.

[21] Others have told both the Palestinian and Israel "stories" in detail. For example, Flick, 2002.

Sociopsychological Issues in Israeli Society

Over the past few years, the priorities of the Israeli public have shifted.[22] Current polls indicate that the primary concern among Israelis is growing inequality and the high cost of living.[23] In an April 2014 survey on the desired national order of priorities, the Jewish public gave top ranking to reducing socioeconomic gaps (47 percent) and second place to creating housing solutions at affordable prices (21 percent).[24] Only about one-quarter of those surveyed highlighted issues in the security-political arena. [25]

Underlying these issues, however, is a range of sociopsychological issues that influence Israelis' perspectives on the Israeli-Palestinian conflict. Israelis are aware of the psychological toll of direct exposure to violent and traumatic events, whether seen in IDF service members or in victims of terrorism. Such experiences can cause serious psychiatric disorders and substantial distress and impairment among those exposed, whether they are Israeli children near Gaza exposed to constant rocket attacks[26] or Israeli soldiers experiencing PTSD.[27] Our interviews suggest, however, that many Israelis are also aware of the less severe but more insidious sociopsychological effects of the conflict. Effects include greater levels of general distress and higher health care utilization,[28] support for political violence and authoritarianism,[29] an increased sense of insecurity,[30] greater risk-taking behaviors,[31] and aggressive behaviors.[32]

In times of open conflict, Israeli-Palestinian issues dominate the agenda. At other times, they blend with powerful sociopsychological factors that compose part of the Israeli narrative. Among those are the following.

Fear

Partly rooted in the Holocaust, fear dominates Jewish Israeli society.[33] Surveys in the 1960s first captured high rates of fear among Israeli Jews who had experienced both

---

[22]   Yaar and Hermann, 2013.

[23]   Yaar and Hermann, 2014c.

[24]   Yaar and Hermann, 2013, 2014c.

[25]   The need for affordable housing does affect prospects for a peace settlement, as it is one factor underlying the political constituency for settlement expansion.

[26]   Berger, Pat-Horenczyk, and Gelkopf, 2007.

[27]   Bleich et al., 2008.

[28]   Gelkopf et al., 2012.

[29]   Hobfoll, Canetti-Nisim, and Johnson, 2006.

[30]   Korn and Zukerman, 2011.

[31]   Pat-Horenczyk et al., 2007.

[32]   Boxer et al., 2013.

[33]   Kurtzer, 2015.

wars and terrorism;[34] subsequent surveys have shown rising fear levels, primarily due to terrorism. Fear levels reached their peak after the Second Intifada, when 92 percent of Israelis said that they feared that they or their family members would be victims of terrorism.[35] Israeli Jews reported a similar level of fear throughout 2009, even when acts of terrorism dropped dramatically.[36]

The shift in public priorities from national security to socioeconomic issues[37] implies that immediate fear levels may have declined. However, the surveys were conducted before Operation Protective Edge in the summer of 2014. Thus, the survey results do not reflect fear levels resulting from the most recent round of fighting in Gaza, which may have had a profound impact on Israelis living in the main urban areas, such as Tel Aviv and Jerusalem.

Different groups in Jewish society[38] may experience fear in different ways, but movement away from the status quo involves change, uncertainty, and perceived security risk. Israelis are risk averse, and any scenario that reduces security or introduces uncertainty is a trajectory that invokes fear.

National Religious Ideology

A vocal minority in Israeli Jewish society—represented primarily by the National Religious group and its supporters—rejects any compromise about the division of the land between the Jordan River and the Mediterranean Sea. This rejection directly pertains to at least two of the final status accord issues—borders and settlements and the status of Jerusalem.

Some groups in Israeli Jewish society oppose compromise on security grounds. But the resistance of the National Religious group to any concession embodies its ideological view. In addition, unlike the majority of the Jewish and certainly the Arab populations, this group acknowledges neither the existence of the Palestinian people nor their claim for statehood.[39] That does not mean that the majority of the Israeli population accepts the Palestinian narrative.[40] Nevertheless, a majority of Israelis—Jewish and Arab—accept the concept of a two-state solution.

---

[34] Antonovsky and Arian, 1972.

[35] Arian, 2002.

[36] Ben-Dor, and Canetti, 2009.

[37] Yaar and Hermann, 2013.

[38] According to the Jewish Agency, Israeli society is made up of many different groups. Most crudely, there are the Jewish and Arab subgroups. There are several ways to classify the Jewish population into groups, including by ethnic subgroups, referred to in Israel as *edot*, or by religious identity, which, notwithstanding variations in general, assumes one of three forms: secular, Orthodox (including National Religious camps and, within them, ideological settlers), and ultra-Orthodox (Haredi). See Kaplan, undated.

[39] Yaar and Hermann, 2008, 2009.

[40] Harry S. Truman Institute for the Advancement of Peace, undated.

The ultra-Orthodox Jewish (known as Haredim) have similar religious ideology but, depending on the subgroup, may or may not have similar nationalistic views. For example, this camp includes non-Zionist ultra-Orthodox Jews, who oppose the idea of a Jewish state altogether and are thus nonnationalistic. The Shas party—which represents traditionally Mizrahi and Sephardi Jews—initially followed a moderate policy line on the Israeli-Palestinian conflict[41] but, over its 30 years of existence, has moved to the right. Nevertheless, in contrast to the National Religious camp, its leaders are more concerned about the issue of conscription of the Haredi into national service,[42] affordable housing, and other non–conflict-related dimensions.

Most subgroups would prefer peace over preservation of the whole "Land of Israel."[43] But for the Zionist-religious camp, including the settlement movement, the effects of an accord would be profoundly negative.

Siege Mentality

Jewish Israelis believe that most countries, and people, in the world are against them. In an August 2014 survey,[44] two-thirds of the Jewish public agreed with the statement "The whole world is against us."

Recently, the rise in anti-Semitism in Paris, London, Brussels, and other European cities[45] has reinforced perceptions of bias among Israelis and undermined legitimate internal and external criticism of Israel's actions. Jewish Israeli society at large does not trust the Arab world. In 2007, over 80 percent of the Jewish Israeli population agreed with the statement "[d]espite Israel's desire for peace, the Arabs have repeatedly imposed war."[46] A growing number of Israeli Jews also fear that the ultimate goal of the Arabs is to eradicate the State of Israel.[47]

An increase in the extent to which Israel feels accepted—and even liked—in the world could have a positive effect on its willingness to come to an agreement with the Palestinians. On the other hand, a deterioration of Israel's global position, rising criticism of Israeli settlement expansions and other policies, rising anti-Israel sentiment, and active anti-Israel boycotts could lead to the opposite outcome and generate resistance to any movement toward peace. In such a scenario, Israel might see no reason to compromise, and fear of the risks of concessions might overwhelm its thinking.

---

[41] Berenbaum and Skolnik, 2007, pp. 419–420.

[42] Yaakov, 2013.

[43] This area is also referred to by the biblical names of Judea and Samaria, usually by Orthodox Jewish groups. Israelis refer to the WBG as the "territories," while a more neutral designation would be "British Mandate Palestine."

[44] Rosner, 2014.

[45] Yardley, 2014.

[46] Halperin et al., 2008.

[47] Bar-Tal, Halperin, and Oren, 2010.

Mistrust and Skepticism

Polls indicate that a majority of Israelis, ranging from 50 to 70 percent, support a comprehensive two-state agreement. Support for such an agreement reaches high into the 80th percentile when additional Israeli requirements—such as a strong security fence or a mutual defense treaty with the United States—are included.[48]

However, most of the Israeli public does not believe that such a peace is possible. Jewish Israelis were unprecedentedly skeptical that the peace talks facilitated by Secretary Kerry would succeed. Over 90 percent of the population, in all political camps, said that such chances were very or moderately low. About two-thirds of the Arab public also saw scant likelihood that the talks would be successful.[49]

In addition, most of the public does not think that such an agreement, even if reached, would bring an end to the conflict.[50] Through in-depth studies, Raviv, Bar-Tal, and Arviv-Abromovich showed that even Israelis who identify themselves as doves—i.e., who recognize the rights of Palestinians to the same land and are willing to make territorial concessions—do not believe that peace will be achieved because they believe that Palestinians and Arabs cannot be trusted.[51]

It is important to note that the National Religious group, wishing to preserve Israel's control over all the lands west of the Jordan River, including the West Bank and Gaza (what they refer to as "the Land of Israel"), finds the present trends quite comfortable and has no motivation to depart from them.

Fear, isolation, and mistrust have led Israel to approach the peace process with great caution. Studies show that Israelis do not trust the Europeans or the international community to stand behind them, and they are very reluctant to trust Palestinians or other Arab states. All of these feelings have made accommodation with the Palestinians extremely difficult.

Sociopsychological Issues in Palestinian Society

Since the Oslo Accords, the majority of Palestinians have expressed support for resolving the Israeli-Palestinian conflict through a negotiated two-state solution. Even after the most recent Gaza war, a poll taken in November 2014 shows that a majority of Palestinians support an accord.[52] But, like those of the Israelis, the narratives, fears, and mistrust of Palestinians have presented significant barriers to agreement. Although

---

[48] S. Daniel Abraham Center for Middle East Peace, 2014.

[49] Yaar and Hermann, 2014b.

[50] Bar-Tal, Halperin, and Oren, 2010.

[51] Raviv, Bar-Tal, and Arviv-Abromovich, forthcoming.

[52] Lieber, 2014. A poll, conducted by Zogby Research Services and taken before the recent war in Gaza, "showed that barely one-third of Israelis (34 percent) and Palestinians (36 percent) still believe that a two-state solution is feasible. And, while the two-state solution remains the most popular option among both peoples, that support is much stronger among Israelis (74 percent) than among Palestinians (47 percent)" (Plitnick, 2014).

Palestinians have, at times, focused on other economic and governance issues, central to their narrative is victimization, occupation, humiliation, and oppression by Israelis. Here are some of the key themes in that narrative.

Justice

The desire and demand for historical justice is central to Palestinian perspectives regarding the conflict, as suggested by the Palestinian term that describes both the establishment of Israel and the resulting Palestinian experience: *nakba* (catastrophe).[53] In this context, Israeli occupation (West Bank) and control (Gaza) over this territory perpetuate historical injustice, are illegal under international law, and prevent Palestinians from exercising their sovereign rights.

Palestinians view East Jerusalem as intrinsically Palestinian territory that should be under sovereign Palestinian control. They view Israeli settlement activity in East Jerusalem since 1967 as illegitimate and specifically intended to undermine Palestinian sovereignty. Israeli settlements elsewhere in the West Bank are also viewed as an a priori violation of legitimate Palestinian sovereignty and of established international law.

The issue of Palestinian refugees is also centrally tied to seeking historical justice: Palestinians generally feel that they were illegally displaced from Israel in 1948 and are entitled to return and to reclaim their property. Anything short of this betrays the inalienable rights of Palestinians to be secure in their persons and property under international law.[54]

Secular Nationalism

Palestinians also seek fulfillment of their long-standing aspirations to national independence and sovereignty. They have been neither independent nor fully self-governing at any point since the area became part of the Ottoman empire in the 16th century. Since the end of that empire, political control over Palestinians has been exercised by Britain, Jordan, Egypt, and now Israel.

Islamism and Religious Nationalism

As among Israelis, an important segment of Palestinians frame their national struggle and the Israeli-Palestinian conflict in religious, as well as nationalist, terms. These groups include Hamas, most notably, as well as Palestinian Islamic Jihad and others. This religious framing typically manifests itself through categorical rejection of recognizing or accepting Israel as a permanent entity and, in many cases, of rejecting any kind of political compromise with Israel, except for near-term strategic reasons, such as the ceasefire agreements negotiated (indirectly) between Hamas and Israel after the

---

[53] Israel, for its part, has sought to restrict recognition of the nakba, particularly by Israeli Arabs (Schocken, 2012).

[54] Qafisheh, 2012.

2008 and 2014 Israel-Gaza wars. While secular Palestinian political leaders formally support a permanent resolution of the Israeli-Palestinian conflict on the basis of a negotiated two-state solution, Islamist Palestinians generally allow for, at most, a long-term truce or ceasefire, albeit without specifying its duration or the circumstances under which they would no longer feel bound by it.

Physical and Psychological Security

Palestinians identify many different forms of insecurity attributable to Israeli occupation and control (or, put another way, to the absence of Palestinian sovereignty and self-determination), including threats to physical safety from Israeli soldiers and police, from Israeli settlers, and from drones and other military technology; threats of damage to and loss (including seizure and forfeiture) of personal, commercial, and community property, including land, by both public and private Israeli actions; intrusion into public and private spaces by Israeli soldiers and police; and the risk of being detained or imprisoned.

A substantial number of Palestinians who directly experience violent and traumatic events will go on to develop psychiatric disorders or impairing psychological distress, whether they are children and adolescents[55] or adults.[56] Similar to Israelis, however, there is a broader range of sociopsychological issues related to the Israeli-Palestinian conflict that affect Palestinians without such direct exposure. These effects can include a general decrement in health-related quality of life[57] and increased physical health issues;[58] family functioning;[59] the ability to forgive others;[60] support for political violence and authoritarianism;[61] worsening attitudes toward peace and hopefulness toward the future;[62] increased perceptions of threats, fear, and hatred toward Israelis;[63] and increased behavioral problems among children.[64]

Essentially all Palestinians have had direct experience with Israel's security regime, in the forms of checkpoints, surveillance, detention, search, or seizure; and all have personal, familial, or community experience of physical injury and death related to the ongoing conflict. Most Palestinians view Israeli actions as collective punishment

---

[55] Elbedour et al., 2007; Giacaman et al., 2007b; Khamis, 2005; Thabet and Vostanis, 2000.

[56] Giacaman et al., 2004; Heath et al., 2012.

[57] Abu-Rmeileh et al., 2012.

[58] Giacaman et al., 2007a; Punamaki et al., 2008.

[59] Al-Krenawi, Graham, and Sehwail, 2007.

[60] Hamama-Raz et al., 2008.

[61] Hobfoll, Canetti-Nisim, and Johnson, 2006.

[62] Lavi and Solomon, 2005.

[63] Lavi and Solomon, 2005.

[64] T. Miller et al., 1999; Thabet and Vostanis, 2000; Boxer et al., 2013; Punamaki and Puhakka, 1997.

or humiliation and subjugation intended to penalize and suppress Palestinians' legitimate national aspirations and instill docility.[65] The Palestinian government viewed the summer 2014 war in Gaza as criminal and is now pursuing a case against Israel in the International Criminal Court.[66, 67] Palestinians point to the way in which Prime Minister Netanyahu withheld information about the kidnapping and murder of three students in order to use the episode as an opportunity to degrade Hamas. The subsequent bombing, destruction of large parts of Gaza, and the deaths of thousands—many of whom were children or civilians—have left many Palestinians[68] angry at Israel and more supportive of Hamas, which a majority of Palestinians believe "won" the war.[69]

Mistrust and Skepticism

A majority of Palestinians, like Israelis, express support for a comprehensive two-state agreement. However, Palestinians are deeply pessimistic about whether Israel is negotiating in good faith. Analogous to Israeli narratives about how Israel's withdrawal from Gaza demonstrates the futility of land for peace, Palestinians point to their experiences after the Oslo Accords as evidence that Israel is insincere in pursuing a negotiated agreement.

For example, Palestinians point to the fact that the scope and scale of Israeli settlement beyond the Green Line expanded faster after the Oslo Accords than before[70] and to the widespread sense among Palestinians that travel between Gaza and the West Bank became more difficult after the Oslo Accords than before. Palestinians view both factors as major contributors to the Second Intifada.

Most recently, polls suggest that Palestinians feel that the PA's nonviolent efforts to improve conditions for the population of Gaza were materially less successful than the strategy of violence pursued by Hamas through the 2014 Gaza-Israel war.[71]

Nurturing an environment of mistrust is the fact that Palestinians and Israelis now have little or no direct contact with each other except in the specific context of conflict. As we have described elsewhere, the number of Palestinians working in Israel, and of Israelis visiting Palestinian areas in the West Bank, began to fall during the First Intifada and has never really rebounded. These changes, reinforced by Israeli policy

---

[65] "Israel's Assault on Gaza Is 'Collective Punishment of the Palestinian People,'" 2014; Khalidi, 2014; Bannoura, 2014; Schechter, 2014.

[66] Melhem, 2015.

[67] Toameh, Keinon, and Lazaroff, 2015.

[68] R. Cohen, 2014.

[69] In a recent poll, 79 percent (83.9 percent in Gaza and 70.0 percent in West Bank) thought that Hamas had won the last Gaza war, whereas only 2.6 percent thought that Israel won (Palestinian Center for Policy and Survey Research, 2014b, 2014c).

[70] Lazareva and Foster, 2014; Ahren, 2012; "2013 Was Record Year in New Settlement Construction," 2014.

[71] Palestinian Center for Policy and Survey Research, 2014c.

that forbids Israeli citizens from traveling to the WBG (except to and from settlements) and the high fraction of Palestinians who were born or came of age during or after the First Intifada, mean not only that a large majority of Palestinians have lived principally or solely under Israeli occupation, but also that increasing fractions have never experienced periods of that occupation during which there was regular and routine contact between Israelis and Palestinians. Similarly, an increasing fraction of Israelis has never had any personal contact with Palestinians except through military service.

The historical narratives of Israelis and Palestinians, although parallel in many ways, are fundamentally in conflict with each other. As a consequence, the parties have approached final status accord issues from such different perspectives that achieving empathy, understanding, and trust has been very difficult, let alone reaching agreement on the issues themselves. The clash of these narratives significantly increases the probability that the impasse will continue.

11.7. International Donor Enabling of the Impasse

Since 1947, and especially since the Oslo Accords in 1993, the international community has contributed billions of dollars to both Israel and the Palestinians in official aid and private donations (see Chapter Ten). In spite of the continuing impasse, the international aid and military assistance coming primarily from the United States, the EU, and the UN have continued.

The cost of the status quo to both Israelis and Palestinians would be significantly higher were it not for the large amount of donor aid provided to both parties in various ways and at various times. These donations have, to some extent, insulated both Israelis and Palestinians from the total cost of the impasse.

11.8. No Change in Sight

The economic benefits of peace and negative consequences of violence are clear. But many other less tangible considerations, including the ones discussed above, create a complex web of factors and imputed costs, making it exceedingly difficult for the parties to reach an understanding—even internally among various groups in each society, let alone externally to bridge the divide that the final status accord issues have always posed.

None of the scenarios we examined seems likely to change this situation in the short run.

CHAPTER TWELVE

Conclusions

In this study, we examined the net costs of a continuing impasse between Israelis and Palestinians over the next ten years versus movement along one of five alternative trajectories (a two-state solution, coordinated unilateral withdrawal, uncoordinated unilateral withdrawal, nonviolent resistance, and violent uprising). We focused on the economic costs related to the conflict, including the economic costs of security. In addition, we calculated the costs of each scenario to the international community. We also highlighted perceived security risks and the broader sociopsychological dimensions that, while intangible, influence the parties' views on final status accord issues.

In this concluding chapter, we summarize our key findings and briefly consider the policy environment that decisionmakers—Israeli, Palestinian, American, and European—will face over the longer term if the seemingly path-dependent impasse endures.

12.1. Comparing the Five Scenarios

Economic Outcomes

Our economic analysis showed that the two-state solution would be clearly the best option financially for both Palestinians and Israelis, while violent uprising was very costly to both sides. Although the effects were significant for particular groups within each population, pursuing either unilateral withdrawal (coordinated or uncoordinated) or nonviolent resistance did not result in positive economic outcomes and/or was not dramatically different from those under present trends over the next ten years.

Both direct and opportunity costs are important. Recall that direct costs measure outlays that must be made as a result of the impasse in real dollars, while opportunity costs measure opportunities missed or benefits achieved. Also recall that, in calculating the aggregate "economic outcome" for each scenario, a $100 change in direct costs is equivalent to only $50 in opportunity costs. This is based on our assumption that any direct costs are reflected by a corresponding change in government spending and that the fiscal multiplier for each country is a conservative 0.5.[1]

Two-state solution: If a mutually agreeable two-state solution were achieved, both parties would benefit significantly in both absolute and GDP per capita terms (see Figures 12.1–12.3). Israel would benefit far more than the WBG in absolute terms— $22.8 billion versus $9.7 billion. In contrast, while income for the average Israeli in year 10 would have increased by about $2,250 (about 5 percent), the average Palestinian's income would rise by about $1,100 (about 36 percent). A similar pattern emerges when one looks at the effects of a two-state solution on changes in GDP relative to the size of the economy in 2024 (Figure 12.3).

From the perspective of an individual Israeli, the benefits of a two-state solution may not seem overwhelming. Although almost every sector of both economies is affected by the ongoing conflict, individuals may not fully appreciate the benefits of peace: Most of the benefits come from opportunity costs that will not have to be "paid," rather than direct costs that people experience more directly.

Seen from the Palestinian point of view, the opposite is true. Their absolute gains may be one-fourth those of Israel, but, on a percentage basis, peace makes a very large difference in per capita income growth.

Figure 12.1
Change in Combined Economic Costs in 2024 for the Five Scenarios (in billions of U.S. dollars)

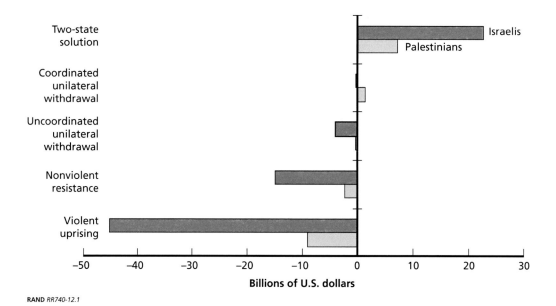

---

[1]   Existing estimates from the Bank of Israel suggest that the number is higher, at 0.7, but we assume a conservative 0.5 and for the export-to-GDP multiplier a conservative 0.93 for both economies (Bank of Israel, 2013).

Figure 12.2
Change in GDP Per Capita for the Five Scenarios Studied Relative to Present Trends in 2024

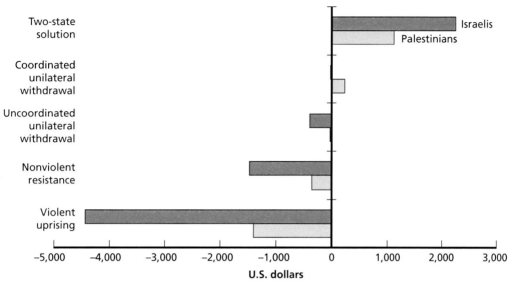

RAND RR740-12.2

Figure 12.3
Change in Economic Costs in 2024 for the Five Scenarios Studied Relative to Present Trends as a Percentage of GDP

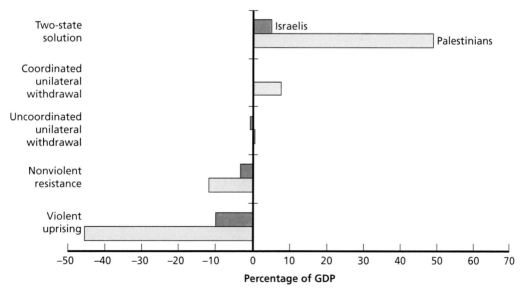

RAND RR740-12.3

It is useful to consider the benefits to the parties in terms that may be easier to relate to. For example, at today's housing prices, the increase in GDP in 2024 in a two-state solution versus present trends would have allowed Israelis to purchase over 15,000 apartments priced at $400,000 (about NIS 1.5 million).[2]

For Palestinians, what the benefits of a two-state solution will buy is also dramatic. The gain in GDP in 2024 of a two-state solution versus present trends would fund over 100,000 apartment units priced at the lowest level in the new city of Rawabi,[3] which only a small percentage of the population can afford. Alternatively, by the year 2024, these funds would enable the PA to build 3,450 new UNRWA environmentally friendly, zero-emission "green schools" in Gaza, each of which can serve 800 students.[4]

Violent uprising: Our analysis also demonstrates that a return to violence would have strong negative effects on both parties. GDP would fall $9.1 billion in the WBG and $45 billion in Israel. Israeli per capita GDP would fall by $4,400 (10 percent), while Palestinian GDP per capita would fall by $1,400 (46 percent). The decline in Israel's GDP stems primarily from the effects of an unstable environment on investment and tourism and the productivity loss as a result of Palestinians not being able to work in Israel. Palestinians suffer primarily because of increased Israeli barriers to trade and economic activity and because of our assumption that the PA would dissolve in the case of a violent uprising. Dissolution of the PA will reduce GDP by almost $3 billion, most of which will be in the areas of security, health, and education that Israel will most likely have to bear.[5] The Palestinians will experience significant direct costs, which are not included in the figures above, to cover destruction of infrastructure and the inability of Palestinians to work in Israel.

The other three alternative trajectories have less dramatic but, in some cases, important economic effects on the economies of both Israel and the WBG.

Coordinated unilateral withdrawal assumes withdrawal coordinated with the Palestinians and the international community and implemented in stages over the next ten years. Sixty thousand settlers would be withdrawn, and the lands they occupied would come under full Palestinian control and be available for full economic use. Seventy-five percent of the cost of settler evacuation would be covered by the international community and 25 percent by Israel. West Bank checkpoints and other barriers to trade would be greatly reduced, and other transaction costs to international trade would fall by 10 percent. Investment needed to exploit the new economic opportunities would need to be forthcoming from a combination of the diaspora, international direct investment, and/or donor aid.

---

[2]   Most Israelis live in apartments, which vary widely in price by location and size. NIS 1.5 million is enough to purchase an average multiroom apartment in most places in Israel (Maor, 2014). Also see Numbeo, 2015; Israel Central Bureau of Statistics, 2015. Note that housing prices have been rising rapidly in recent years (Bousso, 2014); also see Ferziger, 2014b, and C. Ben-David, 2014.

[3]   Kershner, 2014.

[4]   "UN Constructing Green Schools in Gaza," 2011.

[5]   We modeled collapse of the PA only in the violent uprising scenario. But collapse could occur under other conditions—for example, if tax revenue were withheld.

Israel's security footprint and costs would change little, while Palestinian security cost would increase significantly to cover expanded responsibilities. Labor permits for Palestinians to work in Israel would be decreased by 30,000.

Israel experiences little if any economic effect because the various positive and negative factors cancel each other out; in the future, Palestinian GDP would be 8 percent higher than in the present trends scenario, and per capita GDP would be 4.45 percent more. Growth results from the potential opened up in Area C, reduction in internal and external barriers, and transaction costs to economic activity and trade.

Uncoordinated unilateral withdrawal is consistent with a widespread belief that neither the Palestinians nor the international community is likely to agree to a policy that does not address any of the Palestinians' long-standing aspirations. In this scenario, we assume that only 30,000 settlers will willingly leave Area C and that Israel will have to pay approximately $845 million to cover 75 percent of their relocation costs. Although there will be a reduction in some direct Israeli security costs related to the settlements, we expect little overall change in security costs, as the IDF will have more or less the same responsibilities, coupled with increased unrest from both settlers and Palestinians. Overall, per capita GDP in Israel would be about 1 percent less in 2024 than under present trends, and GDP would be $4 billion less. Similarly, Palestinians will see a slight 0.5-percent fall in GDP. Both economies will be negatively impacted by the reductions of Palestinian labor working in Israel, and the Israeli economy will be particularly negatively impacted by reduced investment resulting from instability.

The **nonviolent resistance** scenario assumes that the Palestinians take actions to put economic and international pressure on the Israelis. This includes efforts in the UN and the International Criminal Court and boycotts of Israeli products in the WBG. We also assumed growth of the BDS movement around the world but primarily in Europe. We assume that Israel will respond with a number of measures, including reducing the number of work permits by 30,000, increasing internal and external barriers to trade and movement, and withholding payment of Palestinian taxes that it collects for the Palestinians. In this scenario, security costs for both Palestinians and Israelis are likely to rise. Many feel that the present trends baseline we have defined has already evolved into nonviolent resistance.

Nonviolent resistance will cause Israeli GDP to fall by $15 billion, a reduction of 3.4 percent per capita (about $1,500). Palestinians experience a reduction in GDP of $2.4 billion, or 12 percent per capita (−$370). The decrease in Israeli GDP primarily results from reduced international investment and tourism because of perceived instability in the region and the effects of an increased BDS movement in Europe. Palestinians suffer as a result of Israeli retaliation, which increases barriers and transaction costs to trade, and from decreased income resulting from fewer Palestinian workers being in Israel.

Tables 12.1 and 12.2 summarize all of the changes in 2024 in GDP, GDP per capita, and percentage change in GDP.

Table 12.1
Summary of the Economic Change of Present Trends for Israel in the Five Scenarios in 2024

| | 2014 | 2024 Extrapolation | 2024 Scenarios | | | | |
| | | | Two-State Solution | Unilateral Withdrawal | | Nonviolent Resistance | Violent Uprising |
				Coordinated	Uncoordinated		
Population (millions)[a]	8.2	10.2	10.2	10.2	10.2	10.2	10.2
Total GDP (U.S.$, billions)	$295	$439	$462	$439	$436	$424	$395
Change in GDP (U.S.$, billions)	–	–	$22.7	$0.0	–$3.5	–$15.0	–$43.9
Change in GDP (%)	–	–	5.2%	0.0%	–0.8%	–3.4%	–10.0%
GDP growth rate (average)	–	4.1%	4.6%	4.1%	4.0%	3.70%	3.0%
GDP per capita (U.S.$)	$35,900	$43,300	$45,500	$43,300	$42,900	$41,800	$39,000
Change in GDP per capita (U.S.$)	–	–	$2,240	–$1	–$340	–$1,480	–$4,330
Change in GDP per capita (%)	–	–	5.2%	0.0%	–0.8%	–3.4%	–10.0%
GDP per capita growth rate	–	1.9%	2.4%	1.9%	1.8%	1.5%	0.8%
Physical capital (U.S.$, billions)	–	–	–	–	–	–	–
Change in physical capital (U.S.$, billions)	–	–	–	–	–	–	–
Change in physical capital (%)	–	–	–	–	–	–	–
Physical capital growth rate (average)	–	–	–	–	–	–	–

Opportunity costs only

Table 12.1—Continued

		2014	2024 Extrapolation	2024 Scenarios: Two-State Solution	Unilateral Withdrawal: Coordinated	Unilateral Withdrawal: Uncoordinated	Nonviolent Resistance	Violent Uprising
Combined economic costs	Total GDP (U.S.$, billions)	$295	$439	$462	$439	$435	$424	$394
	Change in GDP (U.S.$, billions)	–	–	$22.8	–$0.2	–$4.0	–$15.0	–$45.1
	Change in GDP (%)	–	–	5.2%	0.0%	–0.9%	–3.4%	–10.3%
	GDP growth rate (average)	–	4.1%	4.6%	4.1%	4.0%	3.70%	2.90%
	GDP per capita (U.S.$)	$35,900	$43,300	$45,500	$43,300	$42,900	$41,800	$38,800
	Change in GDP per capita (U.S.$)	–	–	$2,250	–$20	–$400	–$1,480	–$4,440
	Change in GDP per capita (%)	–	–	5.2%	0.0%	–0.9%	–3.4%	–10.3%
	GDP per capita growth rate	–	1.9%	2.4%	1.9%	1.8%	1.5%	0.8%
	Total ten-year difference in GDP (U.S.$, billions)	–	–	$123	–$1	–$22	–$80	–$250
	Total support required from international community (U.S.$, billions)[b]	–	–	$30.0	$13.5	$0.0	$0.0	$0.0

NOTE: Data may not match total because of rounding.

[a] All scenarios assume that any nonsecular increase in Palestinian GDP (e.g., return of refugees) is met with increased investment such that GDP per capita remains constant.

[b] For the Israelis, this includes the total ten-year costs required for supporting the removal of settlers. For the Palestinians, this includes the level of investment that will be required to satisfy the change in opportunity costs, as well as any reductions if the Israelis take over payments for PA functionality.

Table 12.2
Summary of the Economic Change of Present Trends for Palestine in the Five Scenarios in 2024

| | 2014 | 2024 Extrapolation | Two-State Solution | 2024 Scenarios | | | |
| | | | | Unilateral Withdrawal | | Nonviolent Resistance | Violent Uprising |
				Coordinated	Uncoordinated		
Population (millions)[a]	4.8	6.5	7.1	6.5	6.5	6.5	6.5
Total GDP (U.S.$, billions)	$13.9	$19.9	$28.7	$21.5	$19.9	$17.7	$12.6
Change in GDP (U.S.$, billions)	–	–	$8.8	$1.6	$0.1	–$2.2	–$7.3
Change in GDP (%)	–	–	44.3%	8.1%	0.4%	–10.8%	–36.7%
GDP growth rate (average)	–	3.6%	7.5%	4.5%	3.7%	2.5%	–1.0%
GDP per capita (U.S.$)	$2,890	$3,080	$4,060	$3,330	$3,090	$2,740	$1,950
Change in GDP per capita (U.S.$)	–	–	$980	$250	$10	–$330	–$1,130
Change in GDP per capita (%)	–	–	32.0%	8.1%	0.4%	–10.8%	–36.7%
GDP per capita growth rate	–	0.6%	3.5%	1.4%	0.7%	–0.5%	–3.9%
Physical capital (U.S.$, billions)	$27.9	$38.6	$97.0	$48.8	$39.0	$38.6	$38.6
Change in physical capital (U.S.$, billions)	–	–	$58.4	$10.2	$0.4	$0.0	$0.0
Change in physical capital (%)	–	–	151.3%	26.4%	1.1%	0.0%	0.0%
Physical capital growth rate (average)	–	3.3%	13.3%	5.7%	3.4%	3.3%	3.3%

Opportunity costs only

Table 12.2—Continued

	2014	2024 Extrapolation	Two-State Solution	Unilateral Withdrawal		Nonviolent Resistance	Violent Uprising
				Coordinated	Uncoordinated		
Combined economic costs							
Total GDP (U.S.$, billions)	$13.9	$19.9	$29.6	$21.4	$19.8	$17.5	$10.8
Change in GDP (U.S.$, billions)	—	—	$9.7	$1.5	-$0.1	-$2.4	-$9.1
Change in GDP (%)	—	—	48.8%	7.6%	-0.5%	-12.0%	-45.7%
GDP growth rate (average)	—	3.6%	6.9%	4.4%	3.6%	2.3%	-2.5%
GDP per capita (U.S.$)	$2,890	$3,080	$4,190	$3,310	$3,060	$2,710	$1,670
Change in GDP per capita (U.S.$)	—	—	$1,110	$230	-$20	-$370	-$1,410
Change in GDP per capita (%)	—	—	36.1%	7.6%	-0.5%	-12.0%	-45.7%
GDP per capita growth rate	—	0.6%	3.8%	1.4%	0.6%	-0.6%	-5.3%
Total ten-year difference in GDP (U.S.$, billions)	—	—	$50	$8	-$1	-$12	-$46
Required investment in public and private infrastructure by international community (U.S.$, billions)[b]	—	—	$58.4	$10.2	$0.4	$0.0	-$16.7

NOTE: Data may not match total because of rounding.

[a] All scenarios assume that any nonsecular increase in Palestinian GDP (e.g., return of refugees) is met with increased investment such that GDP per capita remains constant.

[b] For the Israelis, this includes the total ten-year costs required for supporting the removal of settlers. For the Palestinians, this includes the level of investment that will be required to satisfy the change in opportunity costs, as well as any reductions if the Israelis take over payments for PA functionality.

Ten-Year Trajectories

In this section, we explore the dynamic path of the Israeli and Palestinian economies over the ten-year horizon for each of the scenarios. The results for the Israeli economy are reported in Figure 12.4, which combines the dynamics of the impacts of instability in each of the scenarios with a phased roll-in of each of the other costs. We assume that the costs of each of the scenarios are realized gradually and follow the growth path implied by the assumptions for the opportunity cost of instability for Israel.[6]

The results for the Palestinian economy are reported in Figure 12.5. In this case, the projection of present trends assumes a 3.6-percent annual GDP growth rate. Again, we assume that the costs of each of the scenarios are realized gradually and follow the growth path implied by the assumptions for the opportunity cost of instability for Israel.

Ten-Year Aggregate Costs and/or Benefits

The difference between the economies after ten years in each of the five scenarios, reported in Figure 12.1, captures only the difference in the final year of our ten-year counterfactual analysis. However, as illustrated in Figures 12.4 and 12.5, these economies will either be richer or poorer across each of the ten years for each of the scenarios.

Figure 12.4
Ten-Year Trajectories for the Israeli Economy

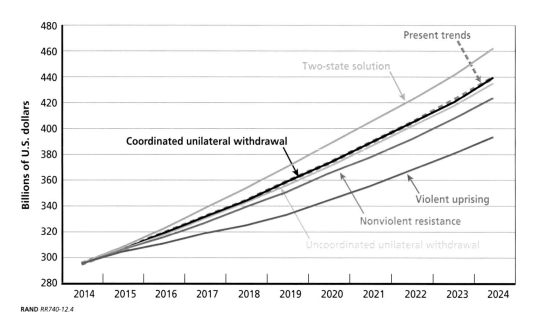

RAND RR740-12.4

---

6   See discussion in Section 4.6 in Chapter Four for more details.

Figure 12.5
Ten-Year Trajectories for the Palestinian Economy

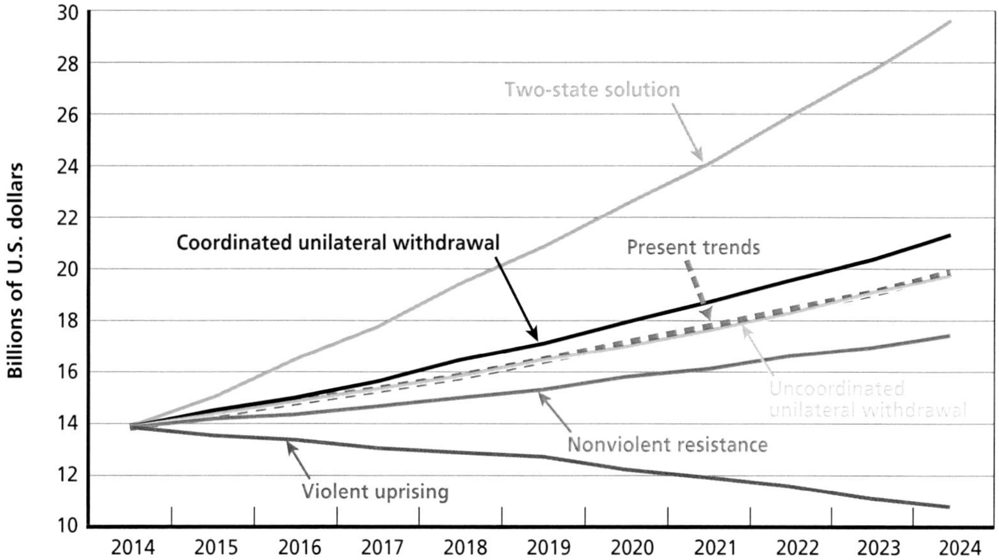

RAND RR740-12.5

We used the data from the ten-year extrapolations reported in Figures 12.4 and 12.5 to calculate the aggregate, ten-year difference across each of the scenarios. Figure 12.6 reports the difference in aggregate costs and benefits of each of the five scenarios compared with those if present trends continue.

Cost Implications of Each Scenario for the International Community

Each of the five scenarios we considered also has cost implications for the United States and Europe, which have provided financial and political support to both Israel and Palestinians since World War II. It is, of course, an open question—beyond the scope of this study—as to whether the United States and Europe have the capacity to sharply increase support, given requirements in other areas of the world (e.g., Ukraine, Iraq, Afghanistan).

Support to Israel

Israel is the largest recipient of U.S. government official foreign aid since World War II. Official U.S. aid includes billions of dollars in defense assistance and a variety of non-defense support, including grants, emergency assistance, and technology and development transfer programs. Donations from private U.S. organizations, usually tax deductible, have also been a major source of financial support. Recent data suggest that private contributions are upward of $1.65 billion yearly, compared with official annual U.S. support of $2.6 billion.

Figure 12.6
Ten-Year Total Combined Changes in GDP for the Five Scenarios Studied Relative to Present Trends

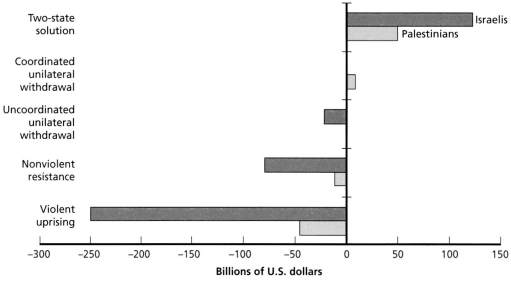

RAND RR740-12.6

Support to Palestine

Until the Oslo Accords, limited U.S. support to Palestine flowed primarily through the UNRWA. After the Oslo Accords, foreign aid increased dramatically, with expanded support for the PA, which assumed responsibility for many of the social services formerly administered by NGOs. After the Second Intifada, the Palestinian economy became heavily reliant on the direct support of the international community. Indeed, international aid is the lifeline of the PA. By 2008, aid disbursements accounted for more than 60 percent of Palestinian GNI. Support has come primarily from the United States, other Arab countries, European countries, and the UN, including such UN agencies as the UN Refugee Agency.

For the *two-state solution*, costs to the international community for Israel include the assumed cost of moving settlers and additional funding and technology for warning systems. The international community will also have to supply approximately $58 billion in public and private investment in order for the Palestinian economy to reap the benefits of the two-state solution and is assumed to continue to provide humanitarian assistance.

The *coordinated unilateral withdrawal* scenario assumes that the international community will pay 75 percent of the costs of relocating 60,000 settlers. It also assumes that the international community will likely contribute either directly or indirectly to the parties to guarantee that security capabilities are not degraded. In this case, public and private investment would need to be forthcoming to enable the Palestinians to take advantage of the economic opportunities created in vacated Area C land.

In the case of *uncoordinated unilateral withdrawal*, we assume that Israel will be forced to pay for the costs of relocating 30,000 settlers, but the international community, through private and public donations, is assumed to pay 25 percent of those costs. Palestinians will need less public and private funding because the investment opportunities in Area C will be reduced by half.

In the *nonviolent resistance* scenario, the international community will impose a mixture of financial and trade sanctions on the Israeli economy. The financial sanctions will be limited and focused on those typically used when sanctioning countries with close relations. The trade sanctions will be primarily on exports flowing to Israel, rather than on imports from Israel, as is the current focus of the BDS movement.

In the case of *violent uprising*, the international community will have reduced expenditures. Private investment in both Israel and the WBG is assumed to fall because of the economic and political instability. The United States is likely to stop all direct support to the Palestinians; the European community is also likely to reduce support to some degree. We would expect humanitarian assistance through the UN to continue.

Security Outcomes

We examined direct security costs and risks for Palestinians and Israelis, as well as their security needs and frameworks. We also examined the increase or reduction in perceived security risk resulting from each scenario. In the short run, security costs are unlikely to fall significantly for either party under any scenario.

Palestinian Security Costs and Risks

Under a two-state solution, Palestinian security expenditures would likely rise rapidly as the role of the PNSF expands greatly both internally and externally. In uncoordinated withdrawal, nonviolent resistance, and violent uprising, we expect both Israeli and Palestinian security costs to rise.

In a two-state solution, the PNSF would have to assume responsibility for internal policing and security issues formerly handled by Israel. It would also likely face rejectionist actors within Palestine (Hamas and others) that would be focused on scuttling any peace effort. There would be significant policing concerns about maintaining order and enforcing peace accords. In our scenario of a two-state solution, the Palestinians would have total control of the West Bank, so they would be responsible for protecting anyone living in the West Bank, including Israeli settlers who stay behind. This is likely to be a small group, but they might require a significant security investment from the Palestinians or the international community.

Externally, the PNSF would have to assume the border security responsibilities now handled by Israel, as well as face many of the same threats that others in the region encounter—e.g., expansion of ISIS, jihadists seeking to infiltrate across the border,

Hezbollah in Lebanon, and radicals in Syria, to name only a few. Making the challenge even more daunting is the fact that Palestinians are likely to confront these increased responsibilities without a matching increase in necessary funds, unless the international community steps in to help.

Israeli Security Costs and Risks

Many Israelis believe that security risks will be unchanged or increased in any of the scenarios we examined. Although its role may change in a two-state solution, the IDF is likely to see the need for increased security spending, not less. The Israelis do not trust the Palestinians to maintain the degree of security the IDF currently provides or to protect the borders against foreign jihadists. Overall, Israeli military officials see a two-state solution as degrading their strategic and tactical warning capability, shrinking the buffer zone, diminishing strategic depth, reducing border security and the IDF's freedom of movement within the WBG, and diminishing their ability to gather intelligence from their present extensive system of informants. The summer 2014 war in Gaza and the discovery of an expansive network of tunnels have only hardened this attitude.

In the short term, such concerns would likely increase Israel's security expenditures. However, if a peaceful relationship with a new Palestinian state were sustained over an extended period, one would expect to see conflict-related security expenditures in both the WBG and Israel falling over time. Total security expenditures may rise or fall for other reasons, but those related to the conflict are likely to increase somewhat in the initial years of a two-state solution and fall after that if peace is sustained.

Sociopsychological Dimensions of the Impasse

In this report, we have identified two types of sociopsychological dimensions of the conflict: (1) psychological conditions with symptoms, some of which are clinically classified as mental health diseases, and (2) broader sociopsychological factors.

Psychological Conditions

In an extensive literature review, we identified a range of psychological conditions that have resulted from the long, uncertain, and occasionally violent Israeli-Palestinian conflict. The degree and intensity of exposure to violence and trauma were key factors associated with the development of mental health disorders and often with trauma-related psychological distress in individuals. However, intense exposure to violence is often localized; as a result, the Israeli and Palestinian populations as a whole appear quite resilient with respect to mental health disorders, even after wars and the Second Intifada.

Given the close association between the degree and intensity of exposure to violence and trauma and the incidence of mental health issues, one would expect fewer mental health conditions if violence is reduced in a two-state solution; the converse would be true in a violent uprising. There is not enough information to support speculation about the incidence of mental health disorders in the other three scenarios (coordinated unilateral withdrawal, uncoordinated unilateral withdrawal, and nonviolent resistance).

However, our review of the literature also identified a range of other psychological effects among individuals with less direct exposure to traumatic or violent events. While this literature is not as extensive, it documents a wide range of reactions. A number of studies found effects on the behavior of individuals, their perceived health, and their interactions with family members; physical health complaints; risk-taking and sense of safety; and increased feelings of insecurity. Additional studies found changes in perspectives on the conflict that would make future reconciliation more challenging, including increased support for political violence and authoritarianism; glorification of war; perceived threat, fear, and hatred of others; decreased ability to forgive; and more pessimistic attitudes toward peace and future orientation.

Broader Sociopsychological Issues

We also highlighted larger sociopsychological forces that are important in determining how people regard final status accord issues. People we interviewed almost universally told us that historical and emotional barriers were critical to understanding the conflict and resistance to compromises needed to achieve peace. But outside the literature that articulates each party's "narrative," there is little research from which to draw solid conclusions about the role that the broader sociopsychological forces play in the impasse.

The historical narratives of Israelis and Palestinians, although parallel, are in fundamental conflict with each other. Key aspects of the Israeli narrative include fear for personal and national safety and perceived security risk, religious identity, siege mentality, mistrust of other countries, and skepticism about their support. The Palestinian narrative focuses on historical injustice, occupation, unfulfilled national aspirations, religion, safety, and mistrust. All of these broader issues influence individual and ultimately collective societal attitudes toward the final status accord issues—borders, settlements, refugees, security, and Jerusalem.

12.2. Where Do We Go from Here?

Many analyses, including our own, have documented some of the economic and other benefits to peace and the very negative consequences of slipping back into violent confrontation. But, despite these apparent motivations, many factors have made it exceedingly difficult for the various groups within Israeli and Palestinian society to reach an understanding internally, let alone externally to bridge the divide that the final status accord issues have always posed.

None of the scenarios we examined seems likely to change this situation in the short run. Indeed, barring some major change in policy that disrupts the trends we have described, the impasse seems likely to persist over the next decade. Below, we turn our attention briefly to the more distant future and consider where these trends might lead.

The Destructive Cycle

Key characteristics of Israeli, Palestinian, and international policymaking, strategic thinking, political dynamics, and demographic and social trends will shape Israeli and Palestinian relations in the coming years. These trends will be part of a sustained feedback loop, influencing the responses of all parties in ways that reinforce these characteristics. These trends will, in turn, reinforce, perpetuate, and intensify the cycle of action and reaction.

Each cycle will progressively close off options that the parties might have had to break the cycle in potentially favorable ways. As options fade, parties become trapped in circumstances that may be quite far from the outcomes they had imagined at earlier stages of the larger cycle.

Outcomes projected in our scenarios may already be appearing. The cycle of tit-for-tat moves to pressure the other side has begun in earnest. The PA's UN and International Criminal Court bids were among the assumptions of our nonviolent resistance scenario. In response, as anticipated, Israel withheld Palestinian tax receipts. For their part, Palestinians have responded by boycotting Israeli goods and services. The Israelis may, in turn, respond by boycotting Palestinian goods and services. The United States is reassessing its aid to the PA, and some members of Congress have introduced legislation to cut off aid completely.

The cycle, which locks parties into positions that they might not have chosen, continues to evolve.[7]

Looking 20 Years Out

At least five broad trends will exert powerful influences on this cycle of action and reaction.[8] Given their nature, the trends are likely to persist. In contrast to the ten-year horizon we observed in the rest of our analysis, the following discussion takes a 20-year perspective to consider how the trends might affect the cycle of action and reaction just described.

Settlement expansion: Today, there are about 600,000 settlers living in the West Bank and East Jerusalem.[9] This number is growing at a rate of about 5 percent per year; the amount of land they are occupying is also expanding, although at a slower rate. If the pace of settlements continues at the present rate over 20 years, the area in

---

[7] Bar'el, 2015.

[8] We exclude trends that are already embedded in the status quo, such as continued economic growth in Israel at the present rate.

[9] About 190,000 of the settlers live in East Jerusalem.

the West Bank and East Jerusalem available for creating a Palestinian state would be substantially smaller and composed of noncontiguous areas. The difficulty and cost of moving such a large number of settlers would be dramatically larger than the resources required to move today's settlers, and, thus, the ability to create a successful Palestinian state would be greatly eroded.

Open media environment: An increasingly open media environment allows instant communication and worldwide exposure to news. Widespread Internet access makes real-time information readily accessible nearly everywhere. The diverse coverage and vivid images from the Gaza war in the summer of 2014 illustrate the power of this information flow, which makes it problematic for parties to disseminate their own interpretations of events. It also gives terrorists an easy way to communicate and recruit that cannot be easily tracked.

Technology: The technology of war will continue to evolve rapidly. With external state actor support, range and guidance systems for terrorist rockets will improve and will be pitted against Israeli improvements in antimissile technology and Israel's Iron Dome system. Drones will continue to improve and become readily available, posing many significant security challenges.

American public opinion: America's favorable public opinion of Israel is likely to continue, but so is the trend that young American Jews will seem to feel much less affinity for Israel and its policies than previous generations.[10] Perhaps a case in point: Israel's actions in the 2014 Gaza war were viewed negatively by a majority of all Americans and negatively by a margin of two to one in the 18- to 29-year-old group. This trend may or may not continue.[11] This does not necessarily translate into support for Palestinians; the latter has remained constant at about 10 to 20 percent since 1993.[12] The U.S. public is likely to continue seeing Arabs as different from Americans and Israelis as more like Americans (because of assumptions based on pictures in the news, if nothing else). The increasingly open flow of information and immediacy of images facilitated by social media could potentially modify that perception.

European public opinion: European opinion of Israel has become increasingly critical. In a poll taken in 2013, over 60 percent of respondents in France and Germany viewed Israel "very or somewhat unfavorably."[13] Among British and French publics, strong pluralities report sympathizing more with Palestinians than with Israelis. Increasingly, European parliaments, including Sweden, Ireland, the UK, and France, are voting to recognize a Palestinian state.

---

[10]   Beinart, 2012.

[11]   Bruck, 2014; Wertheimer and Cohen, 2014. According to the Pew Survey, "Among seniors, support for Israel compared with support for the Palestinians is 6 to 1. Among youths, the ratio declines to 2 to 1. In other words, the support is still there, but the trend is clear" ("'Young Jewish Americans Are Less Supportive of Israel,'" 2014).

[12]   Gallup World Affairs Survey, 2013.

[13]   Some have claimed that this reflects increased anti-Semitism.

BDS movement: The BDS movement has not reached a point at which it has a significant negative effect on Israel. However, the movement is growing, particularly in Europe, Israel's largest trading partner. For instance, in July 2014, the EU issued guidelines that Israeli entities seeking funds from the EU must demonstrate that they were not operating in the Golan Heights, East Jerusalem, or the West Bank. Some Israelis point to rapidly increasing trade with China, India, and Africa as a countervailing trend to the BDS efforts in Europe.

Demography: Opinions can and do change dramatically, but demographic trends do not. The latter are highly stable and change slowly over time. Although the exact numbers are debated, the basic population trends in Israel, the West Bank, and Gaza have been clearly delineated for years.

Using the work of Professor Emeritus Sergio DellaPergola, a respected demographer at the Hebrew University of Jerusalem, Aaron David Miller has described what he called "Israel's Demographic Destiny." In brief, "Jews constitute 49.8 percent" (52 percent if their non-Jewish relatives are included) "of the total population that lives between the Mediterranean Sea and the Jordan River"[14] (what today is Israel and the WBG). The Jewish population is growing at a rate of 1.8 percent,[15] the population of Arabs living in Israel is growing at 2.2 percent, and the population in the WBG is growing at 2.7 percent. The share of Jews in the total population in the area including Israel, the West Bank, and Gaza is slowly shrinking. In Israel proper, the Jewish majority of 79 percent is expected to fall only slightly by 2030, but, when one includes the WBG, "the current roughly 50-50 division will change to a 56 percent Palestinian majority in 2030."[16] If one excludes Gaza from the calculation, Jews do not lose their majority for 30 years.

Clouds on the Horizon?

As policymakers have pointed out, Israel now faces a core policy choice: whether to be a Jewish state with a predominantly Jewish population living side by side with a Palestinian state, a democratic state with a diverse citizenry that is treated equally, or a Jewish state comprised of all the lands between the Jordan River and the Mediterranean Sea (Israel and the WBG) with preferential rights for Jews.[17, 18] Israelis cannot have all three. The Palestinians, although the weaker partner, also need to make fundamental decisions about peace.

---

[14]   Gallup World Affairs Survey, 2013.

[15]   The most rapidly growing population group in Israel is the strictly Orthodox group known as the Haredim, who have significantly lower labor market participation rates, productivity, and educational attainment than other Israeli Jews (A. Miller, 2013a).

[16]   A. Miller, 2013a.

[17]   A. Miller, 2013a.

[18]   DellaPergola, 2002, 2013.

All of these trends suggest clouds on the horizon 20 years out that cannot be easily ignored, just as those who ignore history are condemned to repeat it.[19] The Israeli-Palestinian conflict has now lasted for decades. If the trends we have just described endure for another 20 years, the option of a two-state solution becomes increasingly difficult and expensive. Some observers feel that it is already unattainable.[20]

Some scholars say that, given recent trends, the two sides are marching toward a one-state solution unless Israel opts for unilateral withdrawal, an alternative that also becomes increasingly problematic as settlements expand throughout the West Bank. Exactly what one-state options are and how a single state—even a federation—would operate has not been extensively examined. Research is needed on how a one-state solution could be structured in a way that preserves democratic principles.

A deviation from the trajectory could happen, but only if all the parties were to dramatically change the way they currently view the impasse and the policies they pursue.

We hope that our work can help Israelis, Palestinians, and the international community understand more clearly the realities of the status quo and the costs and benefits of alternatives to the current destructive cycle of action, reaction, and inaction so that they can collectively find a way to end the impasse.

---

[19] Paraphrase of "Those who cannot remember the past are condemned to repeat it" (Santayana, 1905).

[20] Lustick, 2013; Beauchamp, 2014; Dershowitz, 2014; Tharoor, 2014.

Key Assumptions of the Five Scenarios Compared with Present Trends

Table A.1
Key Assumptions of the Five Scenarios Compared with Present Trends

	Status Quo	Two-State Solution	Coordinated Unilateral Withdrawal	Uncoordinated Unilateral Withdrawal	Noviolent Resistance	Violent Uprising
Security	IDF controls Areas B and C IDF conducts operations in Area A Israel controls Palestinian airspace	Palestinians assume control in West Bank Palestinians remain demilitarized IDF controls Jordan Valley	Palestinians assume control of areas evacuated by settlers Palestinians remain demilitarized IDF controls Jordan Valley	Palestinians assume control of areas evacuated by settlers Palestinians remain demilitarized IDF controls Jordan Valley	No change	IDF assumes control of security in Area A
Jerusalem	East Jerusalem annexed by Israel	Jerusalem exists as a shared capital Holy sites under custodianship	Separation barrier divides Jerusalem Settlement construction stops in East Jerusalem	Separation barrier divides Jerusalem Settlement construction continues in East Jerusalem	No change	No change
Settlements	5% annual growth in number of settlers east of separation barrier	100,000 settlers east of separation barrier move to Israel or join future Palestinian state International community pays relocation costs	60,000 settlers east of separation barrier move to Israel Israel pays 75% of relocation costs	30,000 settlers east of separation barrier move to Israel Israel pays relocation costs	No change	No change
Right of return	None	Limited, symbolic return of refugees	No change	No change	No change	No change
Borders	No formal Palestinian state	Pre-1967 borders with some limited land swaps	Separation barrier becomes de facto border	Separation barrier becomes de facto border	No change	No change

Costing Tool

This appendix describes the specific assumptions made for calculating the opportunity costs and direct costs of each of the scenarios, as reported in Chapters Five through Nine. These assumptions are delineated in Tables B.1–B.4. The analysis that translates these assumptions into the results provided in Chapters Five through Nine is available at www.rand.org/cc-calculator.

For each opportunity or direct cost (note that each is described in greater detail in Section 3.2 in Chapter Three), we describe the types of economic assumptions that our analysis uses. In each case, we also provide the source for this assumption in a footnote. These assumptions specify an economic impact in one of two units: (1) percentage of GDP or (2) U.S. dollars. All of our results reported in Chapters Five through Nine are presented as of 2024, but in 2014 U.S. dollars. Thus, while the numbers reported in percentage of GDP are calculated as a share of present trends GDP (Chapter Three), the dollar numbers are not inflated in any way. A special case of this calculation is for the opportunity cost of instability for Israel; here, the scenario-specific assumption is converted into a percentage of GDP change using Conference Board data.[1] Each of the rows describes the units of the scenario-specific assumption that are required for that specific direct cost or opportunity cost. Chapter Four describes how specific values for these assumptions were selected for each of the five scenarios considered.

In addition to these specific assumptions, for the various Israeli and Palestinian direct and opportunity costs, we make some general assumptions (which are discussed throughout the rest of this document but summarized here). First, we assume that the population growth in present trends and each of the five scenarios is the same; the one exception to this assumption is that we assume the return of 600,000 Palestinian

---

[1] Conference Board, 2014.

refugees to a new Palestinian state in the two-state solution.[2] Second, we assume that a Cobb-Douglas production function is an appropriate back-of-the-envelope tool for calculating the amount of private and public investment that the Palestinians will need to realize any new economic opportunities.[3] Third, when reporting the overall economic differences between present trends and each scenario, we make two assumptions that allow us to compare the direct and opportunity costs: (1) any direct costs are reflected by a corresponding change in government spending and (2) the fiscal multiplier for each country is at least 0.5—that is, for each $100 in government spending, the GDP of the country increases by $50—and the export-to-GDP multiplier is 0.93.[4] Fourth, the economic costs (or benefits) for the international community for Israel include only the international community's contribution toward removing the settlers. However, for the Palestinians, this includes the level of investment required to satisfy the change in opportunity costs (discussed immediately above), in addition to any change in expenditures on Palestinian services. Note that we always report the total ten-year cost for the international community.

Fifth, most of our assumptions for direct costs and opportunity costs do not have a dynamic component—the only exception is the opportunity cost of instability for the Israelis. In calculating the dynamic growth path of the economies for each scenario

---

[2]　An implication of this assumption is that percentage changes for GDP and GDP per capita are the same:

$$\left(\frac{GDP^{Scenario}}{GDP^{Present\ Trends}} = \frac{GDP^{Scenario}\ /\ P}{GDP^{Present\ Trends}\ /\ P} \right)$$

except of course for the case of the new Palestinian state in the two-state solution.

[3]　The simplest Cobb-Douglas function posits that GDP (Y) can be represented as a function of technology (A), physical capital (K), and labor (L) as

$$\frac{\left(K_{TSS} \right)^{1/3}}{\left(K_{PT} \right)^{1/3}} = 1.35$$

Given our counterfactual approach, we can then estimate the amount of physical capital necessary for reach of the scenarios as

$$\frac{K^{S}}{K^{PT}} = \left[\frac{Y^{S}}{Y^{PT}} \left(\frac{L^{PT}}{L^{S}} \right)^{1-\alpha} \right]^{\frac{1}{\alpha}}$$

In this case, we assume that $\alpha = 1/3$. Note that this approach is used only for calculating new opportunities arising from opportunity costs.

[4]　This is a conservative assumption, as existing estimates from the Bank of Israel suggest that the number is higher, at 0.7, but we assume a conservative 0.5 for both economies (Bank of Israel, 2013).

(reported in the executive summary and Chapter Twelve), we assume that the opportunity costs and direct costs for each of the scenarios are realized gradually over the ten-year period. Thus, for the violent uprising scenario, the number of Palestinian laborers working in Israel (127,000) is assumed to fall by an additional 12,700 each year until no workers remain by the tenth year. In order to provide a plausible growth patch for each scenario, we assume that the trajectory implied by our assumptions for the Israeli instability opportunity cost is a reasonable approximation for both the Palestinian and Israeli economies.

Table B.1
Israeli Direct Costs—Costing Inputs

Type of Cost	Economic Assumption	Assumption Required
Security	• Defense expenditures are 5.7% of GDP.[a] • Defense expenditures increase by 9% during years of conflict.[b]	Annualized ten-year percentage change in defense expenditures
Settlement		
Relocation costs	• $300,000 per settler for compensation and resettlement[c]	Number of settlers relocated
Expenditures on settlement	• Annual expenditures in settlements around $1.1 billion[d] • Estimated 600,000 total settlers in West Bank and East Jerusalem[e] • Reduction in number of settlers reduces annual expenditures by equivalent amount.[f]	Number of settlers relocated
Palestinian services	• Palestinian ministries of social affairs, health, and education equivalent to 12% of Palestinian GDP[g]	Percentage of expenditures assumed by Israel

[a] Based on 2013 data provided in Bank of Israel, undated.

[b] Authors' estimates by comparing defense spending during 2001–2003 and 2000 using Bank of Israel, undated.

[c] "The average family evacuated from settlements in the Gaza Strip cost the state NIS 4.9 million in compensation and resettlement costs" (Shragai, 2009). Eighteen hundred families (number of families: Bannoura, 2007) were relocated, implying a total cost of $2.5 billion (assuming an exchange rate of 3.5). As the total number of settlers moved was 8,500 ("Israel Begins Forced Removal of Jewish Settlers from Gaza as Deadline Expires", 2005), this implies a per-settler cost of $300,000. Note that earlier reports indicate significantly lower numbers (e.g., Bannoura, 2007). BWF estimates indicate that per-family compensation for the West Bank would be only $300,000–$400,000 (Stewart, 2014).

[d] See "Israel Direct Cost 2: Settlements" in Chapter 2.2.1 for more details.

[e] The current estimates of the number of settlers in the West Bank is between 500,000 and 650,000 (UN, 2013, para. 10).

[f] Authors' assumption.

[g] Data for 2012 indicate a total of 41.7 percent of budget spent on these three ministries (World Bank, 2013a). The estimate assumes a PA budget of 30 percent of GDP, as reported in Figure 3.3.

Table B.2
Israeli Opportunity Costs—Costing Inputs

Type of Cost	Economic Assumption	Assumption Required
Instability		
Investment	• Instability restricts investment.[a] • Change lasts for four years.	Percentage change in contribution of capital to GDP growth
Total Factor Productivity (TFP)	• Instability restricts TFP growth.[b] • Change lasts for four years.	Percentage change in contribution of TFP to GDP growth
Labor force	• Instability restricts labor market growth.[c] • Change lasts for four years.	Percentage change in contribution of capital to GDP growth
BDS	• BDS could reduce GDP by 1–2%.[d]	Percentage reduction in GDP
Tourism	• Tourism industry is $6 billion.[e] • Could expand by 20%[f] • Export-to-GDP multiplier of 0.93[g]	Percentage of expansion realized
Trade with Arab world	• Israel's exports to non-Palestinian Middle Eastern markets at $3 billion[h] • Export-to-GDP multiplier of 0.93[i]	Percentage of expansion in Israeli trade with Arab world
Palestinian trade	• Israel's exports to Palestine could increase by 150%[j] • Export-to-GDP multiplier of 0.93[k]	Percentage of Palestinian trade benefit realized
Palestinian labor in Israel	• 60,000 change in Palestinian laborers equivalent to 0.3% change in GDP[l]	Change in number of laborers

[a] Contribution of ICT and non-ICT investment was 20 percent lower from 2001 to 2004 during the Second Intifada—0.51 and 1.01, respectively, as compared with 0.61 and 1.23, respectively, during 1999–2013 (Conference Board, 2014).

[b] Contribution of TFP growth to GDP growth was 0.36 from 1999 to 2013 but was negative during 2001–2004 (Conference Board, 2014).

[c] Contribution of employment growth to GDP growth was 1.46 from 1999 to 2013 but 60 percent lower (0.59) during 2001–2004 (Conference Board, 2014).

[d] The Israeli finance minister estimated the potential cost at 1 percent of GDP (see footnote 34 in Chapter Three). Financial sanctions (common between countries with close relations) reduce GDP by 1.7 percent, on average; trade-only sanctions (either export or import) reduce GDP by 0.7 percent, on average; and combined financial and trade sanctions have combined effects of nearly 3 percent of GDP (Hufbauer et al., 2008).

[e] The estimated $6 billion is based on data from the Israel Central Bureau of Statistics, which reports that tourism contributes about 2 percent to GDP (Israel Central Bureau of Statistics, 2014) and the overall GDP numbers of $295 billion.

[f] Fleischer and Buccola, 2002, reports that tourism would expand by 20 percent, which implies a lower estimate of $1.2 billion (see footnote 104 in Chapter Two).

[g] Based on results from A. Friedman and Hercowitz, 2010.

[h] Total trade estimates are from Israel Central Bureau of Statistics, undated(c), and based on 2014 non-diamond trade date. Estimates include only Jordan, Egypt, and Turkey, though Gal, 2012, reports some GCC trade.

[i] Based on results from A. Friedman and Hercowitz, 2010.

[j] PalTrade, 2006, p. 16, reports that Israeli exports to Palestine would expand by 150 percent, from $3 billion to $7.5 billion. The current level of Israeli exports to Palestine is $3.9 billion, without any changes in conditions—specifically, Palestine reports imports of $5.2 billion for 2013 (PCBS, undated[f]), and approximately three-fourths of Palestinian imports are from Israel.

[k] Based on results from A. Friedman and Hercowitz, 2010.

[l] Flaig et al., 2013, reports that a 64,000-laborer increase is equivalent to an 0.3-percent change in GDP.

Table B.3
Palestinian Direct Costs—Costing Inputs

Type of Cost	Economic Assumption	Assumption Required
Destruction of property	• Israeli operations cause significant damage to infrastructure.[a]	Dollar value of infrastructure damaged
Territorial waters	• Natural gas production will save "the Palestinian economy close to $560 million annually."[b]	Percentage change in natural gas extracted
Palestinian labor in Israel	• Average salary of Palestinian labor in Israel and settlements is $12,000.[c]	Change in number of laborers
Freedom of movement	• Deadweight loss of movement costs are estimated at $150 million per annum.[d]	Percentage change in restrictions
Access to services		
Medical	• At least $40 million per annum[e]	Percentage change in restrictions
Water	• Tanker-provided water costs $50 million per annum.[f] • Negative health outcomes cost $20 million.[g]	Percentage change in restrictions
Banking regulations	• Restrictions on Palestinian banks cost the Palestinian economy approximately $15 million per year.[h]	Percentage change in restrictions
Prisoners in Israel	• 6% budget spent supporting prisoner families.[i] • Budget at 30% of GDP[j]	Percentage change in number of Israelis

[a] World Bank, 2003, p. xi, reports the replacement cost of damage to infrastructure from Operation Defensive Shield at $1.7 billion. UNCTAD, 2010, p. 8, reports damage of $1.3 billion for Operation Cast Lead. PECDAR ("Scale of Gaza Destruction Unprecedented," 2014) reports $1.7 billion in damage from Operation Protective Edge.

[b] Palestine Investment Fund, 2010, p. 59. Note that ARIJ, 2011, p. 24, reports a slightly lower estimate of $440 million. However, inefficiencies in power distribution as a result of the restrictions in Area C (World Bank, 2007a, p. 1) suggest that the total effect may be slightly higher.

[c] Estimated salary based on 2013 PMA data. The PMA reports a total of 127,000 Palestinians working in "Israel & Settlements" = 4,420 (population) × 0.59 (population over 15) × 0.436 (labor force participation) × 0.112 (employed in Israel and settlements). It reports an average annual salary of $12,000 = 12 (months) × 19.8 (days per month) × 175.4 (daily wage in NIS) ÷ 3.5 (NIS-to-dollar conversion). Data available at PMA, undated.

[d] See ARIJ, 2011.

[e] Approximately $30 million is spent on Palestinian treatment in Israel per year—e.g., in 2012, NIS 58 million for 2,525 patients from the West Bank and NIS 46 million for 2,600 patients from Gaza. (Palestinian Ministry of Health, 2013, Annex 186, p. 213). However, the 210,000 health travel permits issued by the Civil Administration in 2012 (Adoni, 2013) entail additional costs.

[f] World Bank, 2009, p. 23. The World Bank cites Palestinian Economic Policy Research Institute—MAS, 2009, though we were unable to find this cited report.

[g] World Bank, 2009, p. 24. The World Bank reports $20 million for sickness in children alone, though reductions in adult productivity imply a larger estimate.

[h] RAND interview with representative from the PMA, 2013.

[i] The PA is reported to spend 6 percent of its budget on stipends for families of prisoners (Ben Zion, 2012).

[j] Based on Figure 3.3.

Table B.4
Palestinian Opportunity Costs—Costing Inputs

Type of Cost	Economic Assumption	Assumption Required
Control of Area C		
Mining	• Mining from Area C is worth $240 million.[a]	Percentage of Area C returned
Construction	• Construction from Area C access is worth $240 million.[b]	Percentage of Area C returned
Access to water	• Irrigation of all agricultural land is worth $865 million.[c] • Water for irrigation costs $90 million.[d]	Percentage of Area C returned Water available
Barriers to trade		
Export restrictions	• A 50% reduction in transaction costs would increase GDP by 21%.[e]	Percentage reduction in costs
Import restrictions	• Border controls and dual-use restrictions cost $260 million annually.[f]	Percentage reduction in costs
Licensing	• Licensing in ICT costs $50 million per annum.[g]	Percentage reduction
Tourism and travel	• A 60% reduction in tourism is caused by visa restrictions.[h] • Tourism contributes 2.6% to GDP.[i]	Visas eliminated (or not)
Dissolution of PA	• GDP contracts by 15%.[j]	PA collapses (or not)

[a] World Bank, 2013b, p. 15.

[b] World Bank, 2013b, p. 20.

[c] This estimate relies on (1) total irrigable land for the West Bank being 630,000 dunums (Glover and Hunter, 2010); half of settlement land under cultivation is already being used by the Israelis and will not be relinquished, and 93,000 dunums of irrigable land (one-half of the 187,000 dunums of land currently controlled by the Israelis) will not be available (World Bank, 2013b); (3) yields from irrigated land being approximately twenty-fold larger than nonirrigated land, a differential of $2,521 per dunum in 2011 dollars (World Bank, 2013b); and (4) there being currently 194,000 dunums under irrigation, including 67,000 for trees (Tables 10 and 11), 112,000 for vegetables (Table 17), and 15,000 for field crops (Table 19) (PCBS, 2012b). This leaves 343,000 dunums for potential new irrigation (= 630,000 [total irrigable land] – 93,000 [agricultural land in settlements] – 194,000 [current land irrigated]) worth an additional $865 million (2011 dollars). Note that Gal, Stern, and Greenapple, 2010, estimate the potential agricultural value of the Jordan Valley at $1 billion.

[d] Water is purchased at the same prices as Jordan—at $0.45 per cubic meter (Bar-Eli, 2014)—so that irrigating one dunum costs $260 (for a total benefit of irrigation at $2,261 per dunum).

[e] Eltalla and Hens, 2009, Table 2. Astrup and Dessus, 2001, and Bannister and Erickson von Allmen, 2001, report slightly lower estimates. We assume that a 50-percent increase and decrease have equivalent effects.

[f] ARIJ, 2011, reports a total cost of $260 million per annum, which includes a cost of $60 million for industry (p. 7), $60 million for ICT (p. 7), and $142 million for agriculture (p. 9). Another source provides a larger estimate of $500 million—DFID, 2014, which references USAID (2010): "Border controls: trade between the West Bank and other countries suffers from border controls that raise costs and cause delays, and restrictions on imports of 'dual use' goods that cost at least 5 percent GDP per year."

[g] World Bank, 2013b, p. 28. This is likely an understatement as licensing creates a variety of inefficiencies that have not been estimated in the past.

[h] Neumayer, 2010, reports that visa restrictions reduce tourism by 60 percent. Artal-Tur, Pallardó-López, and Requena-Silvente, 2012, reports lower estimates of 25 percent, though its panel identification focused on only new visa restrictions.

[i] The total contribution of tourism to GDP in 2010 was $250 million (PCBS, 2011c, Table 1). This is 2.6 percent of GDP based on our 2010 GDP data reported in Figure 3.1.

[j] Abdel Karim, 2013, p. 4, reports that GDP would contract by 14.5 percent with the collapse of the PA.

Abbreviations

ARIJ	Applied Research Institute—Jerusalem
BDS	boycott, divestment, and sanctions
BWF	Blue White Future
CGE	computable general equilibrium
DAC	OECD Development Assistance Committee: Australia, Austria, Belgium, Canada, Czech Republic, Denmark, Finland, France, Germany, Greece, Iceland, Ireland, Italy, Japan, Republic of Korea, Luxembourg, Netherlands, New Zealand, Norway, Portugal, Spain, Sweden, Switzerland, United Kingdom, United States, and EU institutions
DFID	Department for International Development
EU	European Union
FDI	foreign direct investment
FY	fiscal year
GCC	Gulf Cooperation Council
GDP	gross domestic product
GNI	gross national income
GNP	gross national product
GPP	Gaza Power Plant
ICT	information and communication technology
IDF	Israel Defense Forces
INSS	Institute for National Security Studies

ISIS	Islamic State of Iraq and Syria
MCM	million cubic meters
MENA	Middle East and North Africa
NGO	nongovernmental organization
NIS	new Israeli shekel
OCHA	United Nations Office for the Coordination of Humanitarian Affairs
OECD	Organisation for Economic Co-operation and Development
PA	Palestinian Authority
PalTrade	Palestine Trade Center
PCBS	Palestinian Central Bureau of Statistics
PECDAR	Palestinian Economic Council for Development and Reconstruction
PLO	Palestine Liberation Organization
PMA	Palestine Monetary Authority
PNSF	Palestinian National Security Forces
PTSD	posttraumatic stress disorder
TFP	total factor productivity
UK	United Kingdom
UN	United Nations
UNCTAD	United Nations Conference on Trade and Development
UNDP	United Nations Development Programme
UNRWA	United Nations Relief and Works Agency for Palestine Refugees in the Near East
USAID	U.S. Agency for International Development
WB	West Bank
WBG	West Bank and Gaza
WDI	World Development Indicators

Glossary

Areas A, B, and C	The three administrative areas into which the West Bank was divided by the Oslo II Accord: Area A corresponds to all major population centers, and the Palestinian Authority (PA) has responsibility for all civilian and security matters; Area B covers rural areas in which the PA has civilian control, but military matters are handled by Israel; and Area C is under the full control of Israel's military
Clinton Parameters	Guidelines proposed by former U.S. President Bill Clinton in 2000
coordinated unilateral withdrawal	A scenario in which Israel withdraws from a good portion of the West Bank and coordinates withdrawal with both the Palestinians and the international community
direct costs	Specific budgetary or financial expenditures related to the conflict
Fatah	A major Palestinian political party, originally known as the Palestinian National Liberation Movement
final status accord issues	Unresolved issues under the Oslo I Accord that both parties identified as needing resolution before a final agreement was signed—including borders, refugee right of return, security, settlements, and Jerusalem
Geneva Initiative	A 2003 track-two draft agreement for a two-state solution (also known as the Geneva Accord); an expanded 2009 version covered final status issues
Green Line	Demarcation lines between Israel and neighboring territories established by 1949 armistice agreements
Hamas	Radical Palestinian Islamic organization

Haredi	Strictly or ultra-Orthodox Jews characterized by rejection of modern secular culture
Hezbollah	Shi'a Islamist militant organization based in Lebanon
Iron Dome	Israel's missile defense system
Israel	Used in this report to refer to the State of Israel and to the territory defined by the Green Line
Israelis	Used in this report to designate Israel's inhabitants in general; *Jewish Israelis* and *Palestinian citizens and residents of Israel* are used when appropriate to distinguish between these groups
Judea and Samaria	The ancient names of the kingdoms of Judea and Samaria, including all of what today is the West Bank
nonviolent resistance	A scenario that considers nonviolent resistance by Palestinians in pursuit of their national aspirations, including Palestinian legal efforts at the United Nations and other world bodies, continued support for trade restrictions on Israel, and nonviolent demonstrations
Olmert-Abbas package	2008 negotiations between Israeli Prime Minister Ehud Olmert and Palestinian Authority President Mahmoud Abbas
opportunity costs	Lost opportunities for fruitful activity resulting from the conflict
Oslo Accords	1993 and 1995 agreements between the State of Israel and the Palestine Liberation Organization that created the Palestinian Authority and implied a future two-state solution
Palestine	Used in this report (along with *West Bank and Gaza*) to refer to the area of the West Bank and the Gaza Strip as defined by the Green Line
Palestinian Authority (PA)	Used in this report to refer to the entity set up after the Oslo Accords to administer parts of the West Bank and Gaza
Palestinians	Used in this report to refer to the inhabitants (except settlers) of the West Bank, Gaza, and East Jerusalem

present trends	Our base case, which assumes that economic and security outcomes continue along their current trajectories—i.e., the final status accord issues defined in the Oslo Accords remain unresolved, and there are no significant shocks or changes to economic, demographic, or security conditions. We assume that the impasse remains dynamic, as it has always been, and that conditions, including periodic business disruptions, flare-ups of military engagement, and continued construction of Israeli settlements, continue to evolve along current trajectories.
Quartet	The United Nations, the United States, the European Union, and Russia
Second Intifada	2000–2005 Palestinian uprising against Israeli occupation (the First Intifada began in 1987 and ended in 1993)
security barrier	Israel's term for a barrier it constructed to separate Israel and the West Bank (called *the wall* by Palestinians). The route of the barrier, construction of which started in 2002, lies entirely along or within the West Bank side of the Green Line; it generally follows the Green Line, but parts of it extend into the West Bank to encompass some Israeli settlement areas. Israel's stated position is that the current barrier is not a political border.
State of Palestine	Used in this report when appropriate to refer to such a prospective entity, especially with respect to the two-state solution scenario
track-two diplomacy	Informal conflict-resolution activities conducted by private citizens (*track one* refers to official negotiations between governmental representatives)
two-state solution	A scenario in which a sovereign Palestinian state is established alongside the State of Israel
uncoordinated unilateral withdrawal	A scenario in which Israel withdraws from part of the West Bank but does not coordinate with the Palestinians or the international community, and they do not support Israel's actions
violent uprising	A scenario that considers the effects of a violent Palestinian uprising, perhaps emanating from Gaza but also including the West Bank and possibly participation from foreign terrorists

the wall   Palestinian term for an Israeli barrier separating Israel and the West
           Bank (called a *security barrier* by Israel). The route of the barrier,
           construction of which started in 2002, lies entirely along or within
           the West Bank side of the Green Line; it generally follows the Green
           Line, but parts of it extend into the West Bank to encompass some
           Israeli settlement areas. Israel's stated position is that the current
           barrier is not a political border.

West Bank   Used in this report (along with *Palestine*) to refer to the area of the
and Gaza   West Bank and the Gaza Strip as defined by the Green Line
(WBG)

Bibliography

"2013 Was Record Year in New Settlement Construction, and 2014 Rate Is Already Higher," *Mondoweiss*, March 8, 2014. As of April 27, 2015:
http://mondoweiss.net/2014/03/settlement-construction-already

Abdel Karim, Nasser, *Economic Repercussions for the Dissolution or Collapse of the PA*, Ramallah, Palestine: Palestinian Center for Policy and Survey Research, The Day After: Paper #1, October 2013.

Abed, George T., "The Economic Viability of a Palestinian State," *Journal of Palestine Studies*, Vol. 19, No. 2, Winter 1990, pp. 3–28.

Abu-Rmeileh, N. M., W. Hammoudeh, A. Mataria, et al., "Health-Related Quality of Life of Gaza Palestinians in the Aftermath of the Winter 2008–09 Israeli Attack on the Strip," *European Journal of Public Health*, Vol. 22, No. 5, 2012, pp. 732–737.

Abunimah, Ali, "Rawabi Developer Masri Helps Deepen Israel's Grip on West Bank," *Electronic Intifada*, January 6, 2011. As of May 17, 2015:
http://electronicintifada.net/content/rawabi-developer-masri-helps-deepen-israels-grip-west-bank/9170

Adoni, Menachem, "The Coordination in the Health Field in the Judea and Samaria Region and in the Gaza Strip Goes On and Also Increases," Coordination of Government Activities in the Territories, Israel Defense Forces, January 23, 2013. As of April 28, 2015:
http://www.cogat.idf.il/901-10737-en/Cogat.aspx

Ahren, Raphael, "If Peace Talks Fail: Michael Oren's Plan B," *The Times of Israel*, February 26, 2014. As of April 27, 2015:
http://www.timesofisrael.com/if-peace-talks-fail-michael-orens-plan-b/

———, "Settlers Celebrate Passing 350,000 Mark; Peace Now Says Figures Are Inflated," *The Times of Israel*, July 26, 2012. As of April 27, 2015:
http://www.timesofisrael.com/
settlers-celebrate-passing-350000-mark-in-west-bank-settlers-celebrate-passing-350000-mark-peace-now-says-figures-are-inflated/

Akkaya, Sebnem, Norbert Fiess, Bartlomiej Kaminski, and Gael Raballand, *Economics of "Policy-Induced" Fragmentation: The Costs of Closures Regime to West Bank and Gaza*, World Bank, Middle East and North Africa Working Paper 50, January 2008.

Al-Krenawi, A., J. R. Graham, and M. A. Sehwail, "Tomorrow's Players Under Occupation: An Analysis of the Association of Political Violence with Psychological Functioning and Domestic Violence, Among Palestinian Youth," *American Journal of Orthopsychiatry*, Vol. 77, No. 3, July 2007, pp. 427–433.

Alpher, Yossi, "How Middle East Regional Dynamics Affect the Israeli-Palestinian Peace Process," Oslo, Norway: Norwegian Peacebuilding Resource Center (NOREF), December 2013.

American Psychiatric Association, *Diagnostic and Statistical Manual of Mental Disorders, Fifth Edition (DSM-5)*, 2013.

Americans for Peace Now, "Instead of Tax Hikes, Stop Indulging the Settlements: Peace Now's Proposal to Save NIS 1.6 Billions, July 2012," 2013. As of January 14, 2015: http://settlementwatcheastjerusalem.files.wordpress.com/2012/07/peacenowsavingsplan.pdf

Amsterdamski, Shaul, "[Exposure by *Calcalist* of Secret Document Nobody Wants You to See]" (in Hebrew), *Calcalist*, July 30, 2012. As of January 13, 2015: http://www.calcalist.co.il/local/articles/0,7340,L-3578591,00.html

Antonovsky, A., and A. Arian, *Hopes and Fears of Israelis: Consensus in a New Society*, Jerusalem, Israel: Jerusalem Academic Press, 1972.

Applied Research Institute—Jerusalem, *Jannatah Town Profile*, 2010. As of April 27, 2015: http://vprofile.arij.org/bethlehem/pdfs/VP/Jannatah_tp_en.pdf

"Arab Boycott Said to Cost Israel $45 Billion over the Past 40 Years," *JTA*, August 7, 1992. As of April 24, 2015: http://www.jta.org/1992/08/07/archive/arab-boycott-said-to-cost-israel-45-billion-over-the-past-40-years

Aranki, Ted Nabil, *The Effect of Israeli Closure Policy on Wage Earnings in the West Bank and Gaza Strip*, Örebro, Sweden: School of Business, Örebro University, Working Paper No. 4, 2004.

Arian, A., "Israeli Public Opinion on National Security 2002," Tel Aviv, Israel: Tel Aviv University, Jaffee Center for Strategic Studies, Memorandum No. 61, 2002.

Arieli, Shaul, Roby Nathanson, Ziv Rubin, and Hagar Tzameret-Kertcher, *Historical Political and Economic Impact of Jewish Settlements in the Occupied Territories*, Israeli European Policy Network, June 2009.

ARIJ—*see* Applied Research Institute—Jerusalem.

Arnon, Arie, and Saeb Bamya, eds., *Economics and Politics in the Israeli Palestinian Conflict*, AIX Group, March 2015.

Arnon, A., and J. Weinblatt, "Sovereignty and Economic Development: The Case of Israel and Palestine," *Economic Journal*, Vol. 111, No. 472, June 2001, pp. 291–308.

Arnon, Arie, *Israeli Policy Towards the Occupied Palestinian Territories: The Economic Dimension 1967–2007*, Beer Sheva, Israel: Monaster Center for Economic Research, Ben-Gurion University of the Negev, Discussion Paper No. 07-13, July 2007.

Arnon, Arie, Saeb Bamya, Tamar Hacker, Edith Sand, and Sharon Hadad (The Aix Group, Palestinian Refugees Team), "Palestinian Refugees," in Arie Arnon and Saeb Bamya, eds., *Economic Dimension of a Two-State Agreement Between Israel and Palestine*, Aix Group, 2007.

Arnon, Arie, A. Spivak, and J. Weinblatt, *The Palestinian Economy: Between Imposed Integration and Voluntary Separation*, Social, Economic and Political Studies of the Middle East and Asia (Book 60), Leiden, Netherlands: Brill Academic Publishers, August 1997.

———, "The Potential for Trade Between Israel, the Palestinians and Jordan," *The World Economy*, Vol. 19, No. 1, January 1996, pp. 113–134.

Artal-Tur, Andrés, Vicente J. Pallardó-López, and Francisco Requena-Silvente, "Examining the Impact of Visa Restrictions on International Tourist Flows Using Panel Data," 2012.

Assaf, Nabila, *West Bank and Gaza Investment Climate Assessment: Fragmentation and Uncertainty*, Washington, D.C.: World Bank Group, 2014.

Astrup, Claus, and Sébastien Dessus, *Trade Options for the Palestinian Economy: Some Orders of Magnitude*, Washington, D.C.: World Bank, Middle East and North Africa Working Paper Series, No. 21, March 2001.

Avishai, Bernard, "The Economics of Occupation," *Harper's Magazine*, October 2009, pp. 7–11.

Ayalon, Ami, Orni Petruschka, and Gilead Sher, "Peace Without Partners," *New York Times*, April 23, 2012. As of April 27, 2015:
http://www.nytimes.com/2012/04/24/opinion/peace-without-partners.html

Azulay, Moran, "Shin Bet Chief: We Thwarted Abduction at Last Minute," May 30, 2012. As of August 8, 2015:
http://www.ynetnews.com/articles/0,7340,L-4236158,00.html

Bahgat, Gawdat, "Israel's Energy Security: Regional Implications," *Middle East Policy*, Vol. 18, No. 3, Fall 2011. As of April 24, 2015:
http://www.mepc.org/journal/middle-east-policy-archives/
israels-energy-security-regional-implications?print

Balls, Ed, and Jon Cunliffe, "Economic Aspects of Peace in the Middle East," UK: HM Government, September 2007. As of April 24, 2015:
http://www.procon.org/sourcefiles/FCO.gov.uk.pdf

Bank of Israel, "Table 6.A.8: General Government Expenditure, by Type of Intervention, 1980–2013," undated. As of April 27, 2015:
http://www.boi.org.il/en/DataAndStatistics/Lists/BoiTablesAndGraphs/f_8_e.xls

Bank of Israel, "The Following Is a Summary of an Article That Will Appear in the Forthcoming Issue of Recent Economic Developments (No. 128), May–August 2010: Sales by Israel to the Palestinian Authority," April 10, 2010. As of August 6, 2015:
http://www.boi.org.il/en/NewsAndPublications/PressReleases/Pages/101004d.aspx

Bank of Israel, "The Fiscal Multiplier," March 20, 2013. As of April 27, 2015:
http://www.bankisrael.gov.il/en/NewsAndPublications/PressReleases/Pages/19032013.aspx

Bank of Israel, "Public Sector Activity > Government Expenditure," 2014a. As of January 5, 2015:
http://www.boi.org.il/en/DataAndStatistics/Pages/MainPage.aspx?Level=2&Sid=22&SubjectType=2

Bank of Israel, "Research Department Staff Forecast, December 2014," December 29, 2014b. As of May 15, 2015:
http://www.boi.org.il/en/NewsAndPublications/RegularPublications/Pages/
29-12-2014-StaffFore.aspx

Bannister, G., and U. Erickson von Allmen, "Palestinian Trade: Performance, Prospects and Policy," in R. Valdivieso, U. Erickson von Allmen, G. Bannister, H. Davoodi, F. Fischer, E. Jenkner, and M. Said, *West Bank and Gaza: Economic Performance, Prospects and Policies*, Washington, D.C.: International Monetary Fund, 2001.

Bannoura, Saed, "Settler Families Evacuated from Gaza to Receive 1.5–2 M Each in Compensation," International Middle East Media Center, February 22, 2007. As of April 27, 2015:
http://www.imemc.org/article/47137

Bannoura, Saed, "Palestine: Israeli 'Home Demolitions, Collective Punishment, Are a War Crime' Says Rights Group," *Muslim News*, November 23, 2014. As of April 27, 2015:
http://www.muslimnews.co.uk/news/palestine/
palestine-israeli-home-demolitions-collective-punishment-war-crime-says-rights-group

Bar'el, Zvi, "Freezing Palestinian Tax Money a Double-Edged Sword for Israel," *Haaretz*, January 5, 2015. As of January 16, 2015:
http://www.haaretz.com/news/diplomacy-defense/.premium-1.635420

Bar-Eli, Avi, "Jordan, Palestinians Seek to Buy Israel's Excess Desalinated Water," *Haaretz*, January 9, 2014. As of January 5, 2015:
http://www.haaretz.com/business/.premium-1.567667

Bar-Tal, Daniel, Eran Halperin, and Neta Oren, "Socio-Psychological Barriers to Peace Making: The Case of the Israeli Jewish Society," *Social Issues and Policy Review*, Vol. 4, No. 1, 2010, pp. 63–109.

Barbieri, Katherine, Omar M. G. Keshk, and Brian Pollins, "Trading Data: Evaluating Our Assumptions and Coding Rules," *Conflict Management and Peace Science*, Vol. 26, No. 5, 2009, pp. 471–491.

Bassok, Moti, "The Cost of the Settlements: The Extra Non-Military Price Tag: At Least NIS 2.5 Billion Per Year," *Haaretz*, September 23, 2003a. As of April 24, 2015:
http://www.haaretz.com/print-edition/news/
the-cost-of-the-settlements-the-extra-non-military-price-tag-at-least-nis-2-5-billion-per-year-1.100896

———, "The Extra Civilian Price Tag: At Least NIS 2.5 Billion a Year," *Haaretz*, September 25, 2003b. As of January 14, 2015:
http://www.haaretz.com/print-edition/business/
the-extra-civilian-price-tag-at-least-nis-2-5-billion-a-year-1.101241

———, "Lapid: If Talks with Palestinians Collapse, Economy Will Be Battered," *Haaretz*, January 30, 2014. As of April 24, 2015:
http://www.haaretz.com/news/diplomacy-defense/.premium-1.571334

BBC News, "Text: Arab Peace Plan of 2002," 2005. As of August 8, 2015:
http://news.bbc.co.uk/2/hi/middle_east/1844214.stm

———, "Donors Pledge $5.4bn for Palestinians at Cairo Summit," October 12, 2014. As of April 24, 2015:
http://www.bbc.com/news/world-middle-east-29586636

BBC World Service, "Poll: Views of Europe Slide Sharply in Global Poll, While Views of China Improve," May 10, 2012. As of January 14, 2015:
http://www.worldpublicopinion.org/pipa/pdf/may12/BBCEvals_May12_rpt.pdf

BDS Movement, "Timeline," undated. As of April 24, 2015:
http://www.bdsmovement.net/timeline

———, "Palestinian Civil Society Call for BDS," July 9, 2005. As of April 24, 2015:
http://www.bdsmovement.net/call

Beauchamp, Zack, "How America Lost the Middle East," *Vox*, August 13, 2014. As of January 14, 2015:
http://www.vox.com/2014/8/13/5991047/how-america-lost-the-middle-east

Behar, Richard, "Peace Through Profits? Inside The Secret Tech Ventures That Are Reshaping The Israeli-Arab-Palestinian World," *Forbes*, August 11, 2013. As of April 27, 2015:
http://www.forbes.com/sites/richardbehar/2013/07/24/
peace-through-profits-a-private-sector-detente-is-drawing-israelis-palestinians-closer/

Beinart, Peter, *The Crisis of Zionism*, Holt, 2012.

Ben-David, Calev, "Gaza War Could Push Slowing Israeli Economy into Contraction," BloombergBusiness, August 25, 2014. As of April 24, 2015:
http://www.bloomberg.com/news/articles/2014-08-24/
gaza-war-risks-pushing-slowing-israeli-economy-into-contraction

Ben-David, Dan, *Brain Drained*, CEPR Discussion Paper No. 6717, 2008.

———, *Public Spending in Israel Over the Long Run*, Taub Center for Social Policy Studies in Israel, Policy Paper No. 2011.04, 2011. As of April 24, 2015:
http://www.tau.ac.il/~danib/israel/SNR2010-PublicSpending%28Eng%29.pdf

———, "Labor Productivity in Israel," in Dan Ben-David, ed., *State of the Nation Report: Society, Economy and Policy in Israel*, Jerusalem, Israel: Taub Center for Social Policy Studies in Israel, November 2013. As of January 14, 2015:
http://taubcenter.org.il/wp-content/files_mf/stateofnation_013eng8.pdf

Ben-Dor, G., and D. Canetti, *The Social Aspect of National Security: Israeli Public Opinion After the Gaza War*, Haifa, Israel: National Security Studies Center, 2009.

Ben Shitrit, Lihi, and Mahmoud Jarabel, "Jihadism Rears Its Head in the West Bank," February 18, 2014. As of April 27, 2015:
http://www.dailystar.com.lb/Opinion/Commentary/2014/Feb-18/
247646-jihadism-rears-its-head-in-the-west-bank.ashx

Ben-zvi, Gidon, "Report: Israeli Defense Minister Says IDF Withdrawal From West Bank Could Lead to Hamas Conquest," The Algemeiner, January 5, 2014. As of April 27, 2015:
http://www.algemeiner.com/2014/01/05/
report-israeli-defense-minister-says-idf-withdrawal-from-west-bank-could-lead-to-hamas-conquest/

Ben Zion, Ilan, "PA Spends 6% of Its Budget Paying Palestinians in Israeli Jails, Families of Suicide Bombers," *The Times of Israel*, September 3, 2012. As of April 24, 2015:
http://www.timesofisrael.com/
cash-strapped-pa-spends-4-5-million-per-month-compensating-security-detainees/

Benvenisti, Meron, and S. Khayat, *The West Bank and Gaza Atlas*, Jerusalem, Israel: West Bank Data Base Project, 1988.

Berenbaum, Michael, and Fred Skolnik, eds., *Encyclopaedia Judaica*, 2nd ed., Vol. 18., Detroit, Mich.: Macmillan Reference USA, 2007.

Berger, R., R. Pat-Horenczyk, and M. Gelkopf, "School-Based Intervention for Prevention and Treatment of Elementary-Students' Terror-Related Distress in Israel: A Quasi-Randomized Controlled Trial," *Journal of Traumatic Stress*, Vol. 20, No. 4, 2007, pp. 541–551.

Biglaiser, Glen, and David Lektzian, "The Effect of Sanctions on US Foreign Direct Investment," *International Organization*, Vol. 65, 2011, pp. 531–551.

Bisharat, George, "Why Palestine Should Take Israel to Court in The Hague," *New York Times*, January 29, 2013.

BitterLemons.org, *Palestinian-Israeli Crossfire: Foreign Aid and the Conflict*, Edition 11, March 22, 2004. As of April 22, 2015:
http://www.bitterlemons.org/previous/bl220304ed11.html

Bleich, A., M. Gelkopf, R. Berger, et al., "The Psychological Toll of the Intifada: Symptoms of Distress and Coping in Israeli Soldiers," *Israel Medical Association Journal*, Vol. 10, No. 12, 2008, pp. 873–879.

Blue White Future, "White Paper—A New Paradigm for the Israeli-Palestinian Political Process: Promoting Two States for Two People via Constructive Unilateralism with International Support," January 6, 2012. As of January 14, 2015: http://bluewhitefuture.org/the-new-paradigm-2012/

Blue White Future, "30% of West Bank Settlers Would Evacuate Voluntarily Before an Agreement in Exchange for Compensation New Survey Finds," press release, March 17, 2014. As of April 24, 2015: http://bluewhitefuture.org/wp-content/uploads/2014/03/PressRelease-voluntary-evacuation-final.pdf

Booher, Dianna Daniels, *Executive's Portfolio of Model Speeches for All Occasions*, Prentice Hall, 1992.

Booth, William, "Israeli Leaders Cry Foul Over Kerry's Boycott Warning," *Washington Post*, February 2, 2014a. As of January 14, 2015: http://www.washingtonpost.com/world/israeli-leaders-cry-foul-over-kerrys-boycott-warning/2014/02/02/fcf097e0-8c41-11e3-9ed8-259977a48789_story.html

———, "Here's What Really Happened in the Gaza War (According to the Israelis)," *Washington Post*, September 3, 2014b. As of April 24, 2015: http://www.washingtonpost.com/blogs/worldviews/wp/2014/09/03/heres-what-really-happened-in-the-gaza-war-according-to-the-israelis/

———, "Netanyahu Says No Palestinian State If He Wins," *Washington Post*, March 16, 2015.

Botta, Alberto, and Gianni Vaggi, "A Post-Keynesian Model of the Palestinian Economy: The Economics of an Investment-Constrained Economy," *Review of Political Economy*, Vol. 24, No. 2, April 2012, pp. 203–226.

Bousso, Nimrod, "The 7-Year Glitch: Will Israeli Housing Prices Ever Stop Rising?" *Haaretz*, April 6, 2014. As of May 18, 2015: http://www.haaretz.com/business/real-estate/1.584086

Boxer, P., L. Rowell Huesmann, E. F. Dubow, et al., "Exposure to Violence Across the Social Ecosystem and the Development of Aggression: A Test of Ecological Theory in the Israeli-Palestinian Conflict," *Child Development*, Vol. 84, No. 1, 2013, pp. 163–177.

Brodet, David, *Report of the Defense Budget Examination Committee*, 2007.

Brom, Shlomo, and Anat Kurz, eds., *A Time for Decisions: Toward Agreements and Alternative Plans, in Strategic Survey for Israel 2013–2014*, Tel Aviv: Institute for National Security Studies, 2014.

Bronner, Ethan, "Israel Kills Two Palestinians as Raid in West Bank Refugee Camp Goes Awry," *New York Times*, August 1, 2011. As of August 31, 2015: http://www.nytimes.com/2011/08/02/world/middleeast/02mideast.html?_r=0

———, "Mideast Din Drowns Out Palestinians," *New York Times*, March 7, 2012.

Brown, Nathan J., "Religion and Politics in Palestine: Debates about Islam and the Hamas-Fatah Schism," Heinrich Böll Stiftung, March 9, 2010. As of April 27, 2015: http://www.boell.de/de/node/274086

Bruck, Connie, "Friends of Israel," *New Yorker*, September 1, 2014. As of January 14, 2015: http://www.newyorker.com/magazine/2014/09/01/friends-israel

Bryant, Christa Case, and Sarah Miller Llana, "European Boycotts Begin to Bite, Catching Israel's Attention," *Christian Science Monitor*, February 16, 2014. As of January 14, 2015: http://www.csmonitor.com/World/Middle-East/2014/0216/European-boycotts-begin-to-bite-catching-Israel-s-attention-video

Brynen, Rex, "International Aid to the West Bank and Gaza: A Primer," *Journal of Palestine Studies*, Vol. 25, No. 2, Winter 1996a, pp. 46–53.

———, "Buying Peace? A Critical Assessment of International Aid to the West Bank and Gaza," *Journal of Palestine Studies*, Vol. 25, No. 3, Spring 1996b, pp. 79–92.

———, *A Very Political Economy: Peacebuilding and Foreign Aid in the West Bank and Gaza*, Washington, D.C.: United States Institute of Peace Press, 2000.

Brynen, Rex, and Roula El-Rifai, eds., *Palestinian Refugees: Challenges of Repatriation and Development*, London; New York; and Ottawa, Canada: I.B. Tauris & Co. Ltd. and the International Development Research Centre, 2007. As of January 5, 2015:
http://web.idrc.ca/openebooks/231-0/

B'Tselem, "Statistics," website, undated. As of April 24, 2015:
http://www.btselem.org/statistics

———, *Acting the Landlord: Israel's Policy in Area C, the West Bank*, Jerusalem, Israel, June 2013.

Busbridge, Rachel, "Performing Colonial Sovereignty and the Israeli 'Separation' Wall," *Social Identities: Journal for the Study of Race, Nation and Culture*, Vol. 19, No. 5, September 16, 2013, pp. 653–669.

BWF—*see* Blue White Future.

Byman, Daniel, *A High Price: The Triumphs and Failures of Israeli Counterterrorism*, Saban Center at the Brookings Institution Books, Oxford University Press, 2011.

Cagaptay, S., and T. Evans, "The Unexpected Vitality of Turkish-Israeli Trade," Washington, D.C.: The Washington Institute for Near East Policy, Research Notes: Number 16, 2012.

Calì, Massimiliano, "Military Occupation, Foreign Aid and the Elusive Quest for a Viable Palestinian Economy," preliminary draft, April 2011.

———, *Economic Options for a Viable Palestinian State*, a study for UNDP Jerusalem, 2012.

Calì, Massimiliano, and Sami H. Miaari, *The Labor Market Impact of Mobility Restrictions: Evidence from the West Bank*, World Bank, Policy Research Working Paper 6457, May 2013.

Card, David, "The Impact of the Mariel Boatlift on the Miami Labor Market," *Industrial and Labor Relations Review*, Vol. 43, No. 2, January 1990, pp. 245–257. As of January 13, 2015:
http://www.jstor.org/stable/2523702

Caruso, Raul, "The Impact of International Economic Sanctions on Trade: An Empirical Analysis," *Journal of Peace Economics, Peace Science and Public Policy*, Vol. 9, No. 2, 2003.

Catignani, Sergio, "The Israel Defense Forces and the *al-Aqsa Intifada*: When Tactical Virtuosity Meets Strategic Disappointment," San Domenico di Fiesole, Italy: European University Institute, Max Weber Programme, EUI Working Paper MWP No. 2008/04, 2008. As of January 13, 2015:
http://cadmus.eui.eu/bitstream/handle/1814/8135/MWP-2008-04.pdf?sequence=1

Central Intelligence Agency, "Middle East: Gaza Strip," *World Factbook*, 2015a. As of April 27, 2015:
https://www.cia.gov/library/publications/the-world-factbook/geos/gz.html

Central Intelligence Agency, "Middle East: West Bank," *World Factbook*, 2015b. As of April 27, 2015:
https://www.cia.gov/library/publications/the-world-factbook/geos/we.html

Centre on Housing Rights and Evictions, *Hostage to Politics: The Impact of Sanctions and the Blockade on the Human Right to Water and Sanitation in Gaza*, Position Paper, Geneva, Switzerland, June, 2008.

Challand, Benoit, *Palestinian Civil Society: Foreign Donors and the Power to Promote and Exclude*, London: Routledge, 2008.

Cheslow, Daniella, "Business Boycott: Israelis Feeling the Pinch," *Deutsche Welle*, February 14, 2014. As of January 13, 2015:
http://www.dw.de/business-boycott-israelis-feeling-the-pinch/a-17430688

Churchill, Winston, "If Lee Had Not Won the Battle of Gettysburg," in J. C. Squire, ed., *If It Had Happened Otherwise*, London: Longmans, Green, 1931.

Cisco, "CSR Program: Palestinian Investment Commitment," undated. As of April 27, 2015:
http://csr.cisco.com/casestudy/commitment-for-palestine

City Population, "Palestinian Territories," 2014. As of April 27, 2015:
http://www.citypopulation.de/Palestine.html

Civil Administration of Judea and Samaria, *Inside the Trade and Industry Department*, May 2012. As of April 27, 2015:
http://www.cogat.idf.il/Sip_Storage/FILES/7/3367.pdf

Clark, Andrew E., Paul Frijters, and Michael A. Shields, "Relative Income, Happiness, and Utility: An Explanation for the Easterlin Paradox and Other Puzzles," *Journal of Economic Literature*, Vol. 46, No. 1, March 2008, pp. 95–144.

Cohen, Gili, "Top Israeli Think Tank: If Talks Fail, Israel Should Withdraw from 85% of West Bank," *Haaretz*, January 28, 2014. As of May 16, 2015:
http://www.haaretz.com/news/diplomacy-defense/.premium-1.570945

Cohen, M., and J. Eid, "The Effect of Constant Threat of Terror on Israeli Jewish and Arab Adolescents," *Anxiety, Stress, and Coping*, Vol. 20, No. 1, March 2007, pp. 47–60.

Cohen, Roger, "A War of Choice in Gaza," *New York Times*, September 8, 2014. As of April 27, 2015:
http://www.nytimes.com/2014/09/09/opinion/roger-cohen-a-war-of-choice-in-gaza.html?_r=1

Cohen, Steven M., and Ari Y. Kelman, *Beyond Distancing: Young Adult American Jews and Their Alienation from Israel*, The Jewish Identity Project of Reboot, 2007. As of January 13, 2015:
http://www.jewishdatabank.org/studies/downloadFile.cfm?FileID=2772

Cohen, Y., "Israeli-Born Emigrants: Size, Destinations and Selectivity," *International Journal of Comparative Sociology*, Vol. 52, Nos. 1–2, 2011, pp. 45–62.

Cordesman, Anthony H., *Arab-Israeli Military Forces in an Era of Asymmetric Wars*, Westport, Conn.: Praeger, September 30, 2006.

Conference Board, "Total Economy Database," January 2014. As of January 13, 2015:
http://www.conference-board.org/data/economydatabase/

Council for European Palestinian Relations, "Illegal Israeli Settlements," 2011. As of April 27, 2015:
http://thecepr.org/index.php?option=com_content&view=article&id=115:ille
gal-israeli-settlements&catid=6:memos&Itemid=34

Dajani, Souad, *The Untold Story: The Cost of Israel's Occupation to the Palestinians in the West Bank and Gaza Strip*, Washington, D.C.: The Palestine Center, Jerusalem Fund for Education and Community Development, February 2005.

DellaPergola, Sergio, *Demography in Israel/Palestine: Trends, Prospects, Policy Implications*, Jerusalem, Israel: Harman Institute of Contemporary Jewry, 2001.

———, "Demographic Shifts in the Jewish World—Forecasts and Implications: Task Force Report," Harman Institute of Contemporary Judaism, The Hebrew University of Jerusalem, presented at the Herzliya Conference, 2002.

———, "Demographic Trends, National Identities and Borders in Israel and the Palestinian Territory," in Andras Kovacs and Michael L. Miller, eds., *Jewish Studies at the Central European University*, Vol. VII, Central European University Press, 2013, pp. 37–62.

Department for International Development, *Business Case and Intervention Summary: Support to the Work of the Office of the Quartet Representative (OQR) in the Occupied Palestinian Territories*, London, 2014.

Dershowitz, Alan M., "Has Hamas Ended the Prospects for a Two-State Solution?" Gatestone Institute, July 22, 2014. As of January 13, 2015:
http://www.gatestoneinstitute.org/4467/hamas-israel-airport

DeVoir, Joseph, and Alaa Tartir, *Tracking External Donor Funding to Palestinian Non-Governmental Organizations in the West Bank and Gaza Strip 1999–2008*, Jerusalem, Israel: Palestine Economic Policy Research Institute (MAS), 2009.

Dewan, Sabina, and Michael Ettlinger, *Comparing Public Spending and Priorities Across OECD Countries*, Center for American Progress, October 2009. As of April 24, 2015:
https://www.americanprogress.org/issues/economy/report/2009/10/02/6746/comparing-public-spending-and-priorities-across-oecd-countries/

DFID—*see* Department for International Development.

Diwan, Ishac, and Radwan A. Shaban, eds., *Development Under Adversity: The Palestinian Economy in Transition*, Washington, D.C.: World Bank, March 1999.

Dubow, E. F., L. R. Huesmann, and P. Boxer, "A Social-Cognitive-Ecological Framework for Understanding the Impact of Exposure to Persistent Ethnic-Political Violence on Children's Psychosocial Adjustment," *Clinical Child and Family Psychology Review*, Vol. 12, No. 2, June 2009, pp. 113–126.

Dumper, M., ed., *Palestinian Refugee Repatriation: Global Perspectives*, London: Routledge, 2006.

Dumper, Mick, "Future Prospects for the Palestinian Refugees," *Refugee Survey Quarterly*, Vol. 28, Nos. 2–3, 2010, pp. 561–587.

Dunya al-Watan, ["A Statement Issued by the Ministry of National Economy Regarding `Issa Samirat's Study on Palestinian Investment in Israel and the Settlements"] (in Arabic), November 24, 2011. As of June 4, 2015:
http://www.alwatanvoice.com/arabic/content/print/219624.html

EcoPeace Middle East, "Shared Israeli-Palestinian Groundwater Is Threatened by Pollution," undated. As of April 24, 2015:
http://foeme.org/www/?module=projects&record_id=53

Eiland, Giora, "The IDF in the Second Intifada," *Strategic Assessment*, Vol. 13, No. 3, October 2010, pp. 27–37. As of June 4, 2015:
http://www.inss.org.il/uploadimages/Import/%28FILE%291289896504.pdf

Elbedour, S., A. J. Onwuegbuzie, J. Ghannam, J. A. Whitcome, and F. Abu Hein, "Post-Traumatic Stress Disorder, Depression, and Anxiety Among Gaza Strip Adolescents in the Wake of the Second Uprising (Intifada)," *Child Abuse and Neglect*, Vol. 31, No. 7, July 2007, pp. 719–729.

Elis, Niv, "Breaking Down the Economic Implications of Israeli-Palestinian Peace," *Jerusalem Post*, February 1, 2014a. As of April 27, 2015:
http://www.jpost.com/Features/Front-Lines/Playing-the-numbers-on-war-and-peace-339959

———, "Breaking the Impasse, at an Impasse?" *Jerusalem Post*, May 14, 2014b As of August 9, 2015:
http://www.jpost.com/Business/Business-Features/Breaking-the-Impasse-at-an-impasse-352207

————, "Israel's Shadow Economy Equal to 18.9% of GDP," *Jerusalem Post*, June 25, 2013. As of January 9, 2015:
http://www.jpost.com/Business/Business-News/
Israels-shadow-economy-equivalent-to-189-percent-of-GDP-317723

Elis, Niv, and Tovah Lazaroff, "Lapid: EU Considering Striking Central Treaty with Israel If Peace Talks Fail," *Jerusalem Post*, January 29, 2014. As of January 9, 2015:
http://www.jpost.com/Diplomacy-and-Politics/
WATCH-LIVE-Lapid-addresses-the-INSS-conference-339760

Eltalla, Hakeem, and Luc Hens, *The Impact of Trade Transaction Costs on Palestine*, 19th International Conference of the International Trade and Finance Association, Working Paper 4, Beijing, China, May 27–30, 2009. As of January 9, 2015:
http://services.bepress.com/cgi/viewcontent.cgi?article=1148&context=itfa

Eshet, Gideon, "Political Breakthrough and Peace Dividends: A Complex Reality," *Palestine-Israel Journal of Politics, Economics and Culture*, Vol. 6, No. 3, 1999. As of January 9, 2015:
http://www.pij.org/details.php?id=903

Etkes, Dror, "Bypass Roads in the West Bank," Peace Now, August 2005. As of April 27, 2015:
http://peacenow.org.il/eng/content/bypass-roads-west-bank

Farsakh, Leila, "Palestinian Labor Flows to the Israeli Economy: A Finished Story?" *Journal of Palestine Studies*, Vol. 32, No. 1, Autumn 2002, pp. 13–27.

Fershtman, C., and N. Gandal, "The Effect of the Arab Boycott on Israel: The Automobile Market," *RAND Journal of Economics*, Vol. 29, No. 1, Spring 1998, pp. 193–214.

Ferziger, Jonathan, "Third of Deep West Bank Settlers Would Leave for Pay: Survey," Bloomberg, March 17, 2014a. As of April 27, 2015:
http://www.bloomberg.com/news/articles/2014-03-17/
third-in-deep-west-bank-settlements-would-leave-for-pay-survey

————, "Israel Housing Boom Threatened as Netanyahu Seeks Caps," Bloomberg, March 25, 2014b. As of April 27, 2015:
http://www.bloomberg.com/news/articles/2014-03-25/
israel-housing-boom-threatened-as-netanyahu-seeks-caps

Fielding, David, "Modeling Political Instability and Economic Performance: Israeli Investment During the *Intifada*," *Economica*, Vol. 70, February 2003, pp. 159–186.

Filut, Adrian, "Operation Protective Edge to Cost NIS 8.5b," *Globes*, July 9, 2014. As of January 9, 2015:
http://www.globes.co.il/en/article-Operation-Protective-Edge-to-cost-NIS-85b-1000953306

Fischer, Stanley, Patricia Alonso-Gamo, and Ulric Erickson von Allmen, "Economic Developments in the West Bank and Gaza Since Oslo," *The Economic Journal*, Vol. 111, June 2001, pp. 254–275.

Fishman, Alex, "Military Intelligence Foresees Threats to Israel in 2015," ynetnews.com, December 28, 2014. As of April 24, 2015:
http://www.ynetnews.com/articles/0,7340,L-4608294,00.html

Fisk, Robert, "Robert Fisk's World: Arieli Is a Man with a Plan. The Trouble Is, It's a Map of Israel," *The Independent*, February 13, 2010. As of April 24, 2015:
http://www.independent.co.uk/voices/commentators/fisk/
robert-fiskrsquos-world-arieli-is-a-man-with-a-plan-the-trouble-is-its-a-map-of-israel-1898173.html

Fitch, Asa, and Nicholas Casey, "Donors Pledge $5.4 Billion to Rebuild Gaza: Gulf State Donates $1 Billion to Help Rebuild Gaza Strip," *Wall Street Journal*, October 12, 2014. As of April 24, 2015: http://www.wsj.com/articles/u-s-pledges-212-million-to-palestinians-1413107569

Fitch, Asa, Rory Jones, and Adam Entous, "Early Failure to Detect Gaza Tunnel Network Triggers Recriminations in Israel," *Wall Street Journal*, August 10, 2014. As of April 24, 2015: http://www.wsj.com/articles/gaza-tunnel-network-fuels-recriminations-in-israel-1407714903

Flaig, Dorothee, Khalid Siddig, Harald Grethe, Jonas Luckmann, and Scott McDonald, "Relaxing Israeli Restrictions on Palestinian Labour: Who Benefits?" *Economic Modelling*, Vol. 31, 2013, pp. 143–150.

Fleisch, Eric, and Theodore Sasson, *The New Philanthropy: American Jewish Giving to Israeli Organizations*, Waltham, Mass.: Brandeis University, Maurice and Marilyn Cohen Center for Modern Jewish Studies, April 2012. As of April 24, 2015: http://www.brandeis.edu/cmjs/pdfs/TheNewPhilanthropy.pdf

Fleischer, A., and S. Buccola, "War, Terror, and the Tourism Market in Israel," *Applied Economics*, Vol. 34, No. 11, 2002, pp. 1335–1343.

Flick, Deborah L., "Toward Understanding the Israeli-Palestinian Conflict," presentation summary, June 2002. As of January 9, 2015: http://traubman.igc.org/two-narr.htm

Fogel, Robert W., *Railroads and American Economic Growth: Essays in Econometric History*, Baltimore, Md.: Johns Hopkins Press, 1964.

"Former MI Chief: Israel Beat Terror, Can Now Afford Unilateral Withdrawal from West Bank," *Jerusalem Post*, June 29, 2014. As of May 16, 2015: http://www.jpost.com/Diplomacy-and-Politics/ Former-MI-chief-Israel-beat-terror-can-now-afford-unilateral-withdrawal-from-West-Bank-360927

Frey, Bruno S., and Alois Stutzer, "What Can Economists Learn from Happiness Research?" *Journal of Economic Literature*, Vol. 40, No. 2, June 2002, pp. 402–435.

Friedman, Amit, and Zvi Hercowitz, *A Real Model of the Israeli Economy*, Jerusalem, Israel: Research Department, Bank of Israel, Discussion Paper No. 2010.13, December 2010.

Friedman, Lara, "Must-Read: Major Report in Israeli Press on Government Spending on Settlements," *Americans for Peace Now*, July 30, 2012. As of January 12, 2015: http://archive.peacenow.org/entries/ must-_read_major_report_in_israeli_press_on_government_spending_on_settlements#more

Gabison, Yoram, "Israel Chemicals Puts Desalination Unit Up for Sale," *Haaretz*, December 11, 2014. As of April 24, 2015: http://www.haaretz.com/business/.premium-1.626157

Gal, Yitzhak, "Israeli Trade with Middle East Markets in 2011: Healthy Growth Despite Adverse Political Environment," *Middle East Economy*, Tel Aviv University and the Moshe Dayan Center for Middle Eastern and African Studies, Vol. 2, No. 1, January 2012.

Gal, Yitzhak, Karim Nashashibi, and Bader Rock, "Palestinian-Israeli Economic Relations: Trade and Economic Regime," Palestine International Business Forum Research Paper, March 2015.

Gal, Yitzhak, Yoav Stern, and Barak Greenapple, *The Employment of Palestinian Workers in Israel*, The Peres Center for Peace, Res 01-10/802, February 2010.

Gallup, "Latest Gallup Poll Shows Young Americans Overwhelmingly Support Palestine," *MintPress News*, August 4, 2014. As of January 12, 2015:
http://www.mintpressnews.com/
latest-gallup-poll-shows-young-americans-overwhelmingly-support-palestine/194856/

Gallup World Affairs Survey, "Final Topline Results," February 2013.

Gazit, Shlomo, *ha-Makel ve-ha-Gezer: ha-Mimshal ha-Yisraeli be-Yehuda ve-Shomron* [*The Stick and the Carrot: The Israeli Administration in Judea and Samaria*], Tel Aviv, Israel: Zmora-Bitan, 1985.

Gelkopf, M., R. Berger, A. Bleich, and R. C. Silver, "Protective Factors and Predictors of Vulnerability to Chronic Stress: A Comparative Study of 4 Communities After 7 Years of Continuous Rocket Fire," *Social Science and Medicine*, Vol. 74, No. 5, March 2012, pp. 757–766.

Geneva Initiative, "Summary," undated. As of August 8, 2015:
http://www.geneva-accord.org/mainmenu/summary

Gertstein, Josh, "Iran Talks Complicate U.S. Push on Israeli-Palestinian Negotiations," *Politico*, November 10, 2013. As of April 27, 2015:
http://www.politico.com/story/2013/11/iran-nuclear-negotiations-israel-palestine-99624.html

Getmansky, A., "Does Tourism Promote Peace? An Empirical Exploration," *Journal of Territorial and Maritime Studies*, Vol. 1, No. 1, January 2014. As of January 11, 2015:
https://files.nyu.edu/ag1796/public/Research_files/tourism_paper.pdf

Giacaman, R., N. M. Abu-Rmeileh, A. Husseini, H. Saab, and W. Boyce, "Humiliation: The Invisible Trauma of War for Palestinian Youth," *Public Health*, Vol. 121, No. 8, August 2007a, pp. 563–571.

Giacaman, R., A. Husseini, N. H. Gordon, and F. Awartani, "Imprints on the Consciousness: The Impact on Palestinian Civilians of the Israeli Army Invasion of West Bank Towns," *European Journal of Public Health*, Vol. 14, No. 3, September 2004, pp. 286–290.

Giacaman, R., H. S. Shannon, H. Saab, et al., "Individual and Collective Exposure to Political Violence: Palestinian Adolescents Coping with Conflict," *European Journal of Public Health*, Vol. 17, No. 4, August 2007b, pp. 361–368.

Gilat, Eliyau Zeev, *The Arab Boycott of Israel: Economic Political Warfare Against Israel*, Monterey, Calif.: Naval Postgraduate School, thesis, December 1992.
http://www.dtic.mil/dtic/tr/fulltext/u2/a257312.pdf

Gillespie, Kate, Edward Sayre, and Liesl Riddle, "Palestinian Interest in Homeland Investment," *Middle East Journal*, Vol. 55, No. 2, Spring 2001, pp. 237–255.

Ginsburg, Mitch, "IDF General: Israel Did Not Target Gaza's Power Plant," *The Times of Israel*, July 30, 2014. As of April 24, 2015:
http://www.timesofisrael.com/idf-general-israel-did-not-target-gazas-power-plant/

Global Water Intelligence, "Israel Assesses Impact of Reduced Desal Volumes," Vol. 14, No. 11, November 2013.

Glover, S., and A. Hunter, *Meeting Future Palestinian Water Needs*, Palestine Economic Policy Research Institute (MAS), 2010.

Goodman, Hirsh, "Defensive Shield: A Post-Mortem," *Insight: A Middle East Analysis*, Jaffee Center for Strategic Studies, June 5, 2002.

Goodstein, Laurie, "Poll Shows Major Shift in Identity of U.S. Jews," *New York Times*, October 1, 2013.

Gorenberg, Gershom, *The Unmaking of Israel*, Harper, 2011.

Gradstein, Linda, "Gaza Conflict Redraws Mideast Alliances," *MediaLine*, August 5, 2014. As of January 11, 2015:
http://www.ynetnews.com/articles/0,7340,L-4554469,00.html

Groll, Elias, "Israel-Palestine Isn't America's Top Mid-East Priority Anymore," *Foreign Policy*, December 11, 2013.

Gross, Oren, "Mending Walls: The Economic Aspects of Israeli-Palestinian Peace," *American University International Law Review*, Vol. 15, No. 6, 2000, pp. 1539–1626.

Gvirtzman, Haim, *The Israeli-Palestinian Water Conflict: An Israeli Perspective*, Ramat Gan, Israel: The Begin-Sadat Center for Strategic Studies, Bar-Ilan University, Mideast Security and Policy Studies No. 94, January 2012.

Haberman, Clyde, and Chris Hedges, "Key to Israel-PLO Pact Is Seen in Economic Ties," *New York Times*, September 18, 1993. As of January 11, 2015:
http://www.nytimes.com/1993/09/18/world/key-to-israel-plo-pact-is-seen-in-economic-ties.html

Halperin, E., D. Bar-Tal, R. Nets-Zehngut, and E. Almog, "Fear and Hope in Conflict: Some Determinants in the Israeli-Jewish Society," *Journal of Peace Psychology*, Vol. 14, 2008, pp. 1–26.

Hamama-Raz, Y., Z. Solomon, A. Cohen, and A. Laufer, "PTSD Symptoms, Forgiveness, and Revenge Among Israeli Palestinian and Jewish Adolescents," *Journal of Traumatic Stress*, Vol. 21, No. 6, December 2008, pp. 521–529.

Happy Planet Index, website, 2015. As of April 24, 2015:
http://www.happyplanetindex.org/

Harel, Amos, "IDF Mulls Lifting Ban on Israelis Entering Palestinian-Controlled West Bank," *Haaretz*, July 19, 2010. As of April 27, 2015:
http://www.haaretz.com/print-edition/news/
idf-mulls-lifting-ban-on-israelis-entering-palestinian-controlled-west-bank-1.302689

———, "Israel Arrests Al-Qaida Recruits Trying to Bomb U.S. Embassy in Tel Aviv," *Haaretz*, January 22, 2014. As of April 27, 2015:
http://www.haaretz.com/news/diplomacy-defense/.premium-1.569984

Harris, Emily, "A Palestinian Explains Why He Worked as an Israeli Informant," *NPR*, January 2014. As of August 31, 2015:
http://www.npr.org/sections/parallels/2014/01/28/267836867/
a-palestinian-explains-why-he-worked-as-an-israeli-informant

Harry S. Truman Institute for the Advancement of Peace, "Polls Archive," undated. As of April 27, 2015:
http://truman.huji.ac.il/?cmd=joint_polls.256

Hashai, N., "Forecasting Trade Potential Between Former Non-Trading Neighbours—The Israeli-Arab Case," *Journal of World Trade*, Vol. 38, No. 2, 2004, pp. 267–284.

Hass, Amira, "Study: Palestinians Invest Twice as Much in Israel as They Do in West Bank," *Haaretz*, November 22, 2011. As of April 27, 2015:
http://www.haaretz.com/print-edition/features/
study-palestinians-invest-twice-as-much-in-israel-as-they-do-in-west-bank-1.396979

Hawthorn, Geoffrey, *Plausible Worlds: Possibility and Understanding in History and the Social Sciences*, New York: Cambridge University Press, 1991.

Heath, N. M., B. J. Hall, E. U. Russ, et al., "Reciprocal Relationships Between Resource Loss and Psychological Distress Following Exposure to Political Violence: An Empirical Investigation of COR Theory's Loss Spirals," *Anxiety, Stress, and Coping*, Vol. 25, No. 6, 2012, pp. 679–695.

Helliwell, John, Richard Layard and Jeffrey Sachs, eds., *World Happiness Report 2013*, New York: Sustainable Development Solutions Network, 2013. As of April 24, 2015: http://worldhappiness.report/ed/2013/

Helliwell, John, Richard Layard, and Jeffrey Sachs, eds., *World Happiness Report*, Columbia University, September 2014.

Helpman, Elhanan, "Israel's Economic Growth: An International Comparison," *Israel Economic Review*, Vol. 1, 2003, pp. 1–10.

Hendawi, Hamza, "Donors Pledge $2.7 Billion for Gaza Reconstruction," Associated Press, October 12, 2014. As of April 22, 2015: http://news.yahoo.com/gaza-reconstruction-conference-opens-cairo-082500507.html

Henrich, C. C., and G. Shahar, "Effects of Exposure to Rocket Attacks on Adolescent Distress and Violence: A 4-Year Longitudinal Study," *Journal of the American Academy of Child and Adolescent Psychiatry*, Vol. 52, No. 6, June 2013, pp. 619–627.

"'Historic' Water Deal Signed by Israel, Jordan and Palestinians," Al Jazeera America, December 9, 2013. As of April 27, 2015: http://america.aljazeera.com/articles/2013/12/9/dead-sea-read-seajordanisraelpalestinians.html

Hobfoll, S. E., D. Canetti-Nisim, and R. J. Johnson, "Exposure to Terrorism, Stress-Related Mental Health Symptoms, and Defensive Coping Among Jews and Arabs in Israel," *Journal of Consulting and Clinical Psychology*, Vol. 74, No. 2, April 2006, pp. 207–218.

Horiuchi, Yusaku, and Asher Mayerson, "The Opportunity Cost of Conflict: Statistically Comparing Israel and Synthetic Israel," working paper, last updated September 3, 2014. As of January 11, 2015: http://ssrn.com/abstract=2376032

Horowitz, Adam, "Israeli Settlement Exports from the Jordan Valley Down $29 Million in 2013 Due to International Boycott," Mondoweiss, January 13, 2014. As of April 24, 2015: http://mondoweiss.net/2014/01/israeli-settlement-international

Hufbauer, Gary Clyde, and Barbara Oegg, *The Impact of Economic Sanctions on US Trade: Andrew Rose's Gravity Model*, Policy Briefs PB03–04, Peterson Institute for International Economics, 2003.

Hufbauer, G. C., and J. J. Schott, *Economic Sanctions in Support of Foreign Policy Goals*, Washington, D.C.: Institute for International Economics, 1983.

Hufbauer, Gary Clyde, Jeffrey J. Schott, Kimberly Ann Elliott, and Barbara Oegg, *Economic Sanctions Reconsidered*, 3rd ed., Peterson Institute for International Economics, 2008.

Human Rights Watch, "Lebanon/Israel: Hezbollah Rockets Targeted Civilians in 2006 War," August 29, 2007. As of April 24, 2015: http://www.hrw.org/news/2007/08/28/lebanonisrael-hezbollah-rockets-targeted-civilians-2006-war

ICG—*see* International Crisis Group.

"IDF Strike on Gaza Power Plant to Cost US," *ynetnews.com*, July 2, 2006. As of April 24, 2015: http://www.ynetnews.com/articles/0,7340,L-3269833,00.html

Inbar, Efraim, "Time Is on Israel's Side," Begin-Sadat Center for Strategic Studies, Mideast Security and Policy Studies No. 103, September 2013.

"Increase in Palestinians Treated in Israeli Hospitals," *Algemeiner*, August 2, 2013. As of April 24, 2015: http://www.algemeiner.com/2013/08/02/increase-in-palestinians-treated-in-israeli-hospitals/

If Americans Knew, "Israelis and Palestinians Killed in the Current Violence," undated(a). As of April 24, 2015:
http://www.ifamericansknew.org/stat/deaths.html

———, "Peace Groups and Other Organizations," undated(b). As of April 27, 2015:
http://www.ifamericansknew.org/cur_sit/groups.html

Institute for Middle East Understanding, "Leaked European Union Report," November 24, 2005. As of August 6, 2015:
http://imeu.org/article/leaked-european-union-report

International Crisis Group, *Ruling Palestine II: The West Bank Model?* Middle East Report No. 79, July 17, 2008. As of August 31, 2015:
http://www.crisisgroup.org/~/media/Files/Middle%20East%20North%20Africa/Israel%20Palestine/79_ruling_palestine_ii___the_west_bank_model.pdf

"Israel Begins Forced Removal of Jewish Settlers from Gaza as Deadline Expires," Democracy Now, August 17, 2005. As of April 27, 2015:
http://www.democracynow.org/2005/8/17/israel_begins_forced_removal_of_jewish

"Israel-Jordan Sign $500 Million Natural Gas Deal," *The Times of Israel*, February 19, 2014. As of April 24, 2015:
http://www.timesofisrael.com/israel-jordan-sign-500-million-natural-gas-deal/

"Israel's Assault on Gaza Is 'Collective Punishment of the Palestinian People'" (interview with Paul Murphy), RT.com, July 11, 2014. As of April 27, 2015:
http://rt.com/op-edge/172044-israel-punishment-of-palestinians/

Israel Central Bureau of Statistics, "Gross Domestic Product and Use of Resources, in the Years 1950–1995," undated(a). As of April 24, 2015:
http://www1.cbs.gov.il/shnaton65/download/st14_01x.xls

———, "Gross Domestic Product and Use of Resources, in the Years 1995–2013," undated(b). As of April 24, 2015:
http://www1.cbs.gov.il/shnaton65/download/st14_02x.xls

———, "Table D 2. Trade Countries—Imports and Exports, excl. Diamonds," undated(c). As of April 24, 2015:
http://www1.cbs.gov.il/www/fr_trade/td2.xls

———, *Agricultural Production Quantity and Value*, 2012.

———, *Construction in Israel 2013* [in Hebrew only], Publication 1582, 2013a. As of June 4, 2015:
http://www1.cbs.gov.il/publications14/1582_binuy_2013/pdf/tab10.pdf

———, "Statistical Abstract of Israel 2013—No. 64 Subject 15.4," 2013b.

———, *Tourism 2012*, Publication 1546, February 2014. As of June 4, 2015:
http://www.cbs.gov.il/publications14/1546_tayarut_2012/pdf/e_print.pdf

———, "Price Statistics Monthly—March 2015," 2015. As of April 24, 2015:
http://www1.cbs.gov.il/reader/prices/price_main_division_e.html?MainDivision=a&MyMonth=3&MyYear=2015

Israel Defense Forces, "Rocket Attacks on Israel from Gaza," undated. As of April 24, 2015:
http://www.idfblog.com/facts-figures/rocket-attacks-toward-israel/

———, "Operation Protective Edge by the Numbers," August 5, 2014. As of April 24, 2015:
http://www.idfblog.com/blog/2014/08/05/operation-protective-edge-numbers/

Israel Ministry of Defense, "West Bank Security Fence: Fence Route Map," 2005. As of April 27, 2015:
https://www.jewishvirtuallibrary.org/jsource/Peace/fencemap.html

"Israeli Companies Outsourcing to Palestinians," *ynetnews.com*, December 23, 2010. As of April 27, 2015:
http://www.ynetnews.com/articles/0,7340,L-4000797,00.html

Israeli Ministry of Agriculture and Rural Development, *Economic Report and Evaluation of the Agricultural Sector in 2011*, 2012.

Israeli-Palestinian Interim Agreement on the West Bank and the Gaza Strip, Annex I, Article IX(2 (a), Washington, D.C., 1995.

Israeli-Palestinian Research Group, "Israel-Palestine: Policy Alternatives Given the Infeasibility of Reaching a Final Status Agreement," 2012. As of May 15, 2015:
http://graphics8.nytimes.com/packages/pdf/world/2012/Israeli-Palestinian-Research-Group-summary.pdf

"Israeli Settlements an Economic Choice, Says Study," *ynetnews.com*, March 23, 2010. As of April 24, 2015:
http://www.ynetnews.com/articles/0,7340,L-3866959,00.html

Jewish Press, "Posts Tagged 'Operation Protective Edge," undated. As of January 12, 2015:
http://www.jewishpress.com/tag/operation-protective-edge/

Jewish Virtual Library, "British Palestine Mandate: Text of the Peel Commission Report (July 1937)," 2015. As of May 16, 2015:
http://www.jewishvirtuallibrary.org/jsource/History/peel1.html

Johnson, David E., *Hard Fighting: Israel in Lebanon and Gaza*, Santa Monica, Calif.: RAND Corporation, MG-1085-A/AF, 2011. As of June 4, 2015
http://www.rand.org/pubs/monographs/MG1085.html

Jones, Seth G., "Fighting Networked Terrorist Groups: Lessons from Israel," *Studies in Conflict & Terrorism*, Vol. 30, No. 4, 2007, pp. 281–302. As of January 11, 2015:
http://www.tandfonline.com/doi/pdf/10.1080/10576100701200157

Kaplan, Jonathan, "Introduction: The Diversity of Israeli Society," The Jewish Agency for Israel, undated. As of April 27, 2015:
http://www.jewishagency.org/society-and-politics/content/36171

Karner, Milan A., *Hydropolitics in the Jordan River Basin: The Conflict and Cooperation Potential of Water in the Israeli-Palestinian Conflict*, thesis, Dublin, Ireland: University of Dublin, Trinity College, August 20, 2012.

Katz, Yaakov, "IDF Reveals Hizbullah Positions," *Jerusalem Post*, July 7, 2010.

———, "IDF Declassifies Intelligence on Hizbullah's Southern Lebanon Deployment," *Jane's Defence Weekly*, July 9, 2010.

Kaufmann, Yadin, "The Economic Case for Peace in the Middle East," *Haaretz*, July 9, 2014. As of April 27, 2015:
http://www.haaretz.com/opinion/1.603899

Keinon, Herb, "Livni: Without Peace Progress European Boycott Will Move from Settlements to Rest of Country," *Jerusalem Post*, February 7, 2013a. As of April 27, 2015:
http://www.jpost.com/Diplomacy-and-Politics/
Livni-European-boycott-of-settlement-goods-can-spread-to-all-of-Israel-318307

———, "Netanyahu Disputes Fabius Diagnosis That Israeli-Palestinian Issue Is Region's Central Concern," *Jerusalem Post*, August 26, 2013b. As of April 27, 2015:
http://www.jpost.com/Middle-East/Netanyahu-disputes-Fabius-diagnosis-that-Israeli-Palestinian-issue-is-regions-central-concern-324246

———, "Susan Rice to PM Netanyahu: Only Two-State Solution Can Bring Peace with Palestinians," *Jerusalem Post*, May 7, 2014. As of January 2, 2015:
http://www.jpost.com/Middle-East/Susan-Rice-to-PM-Netanyahu-Only-two-state-solution-can-bring-peace-with-Palestinians-351557

Keller, Linda M., "The International Criminal Court and Palestine: Part I," *Jurist*, January 29, 2013. As of January 11, 2015:
http://jurist.org/forum/2013/01/linda-keller-icc-palestine-part1.php

Kershner, Isabel, "New Palestinian Town in West Bank Awaits Israel's Approval for Water," *New York Times*, August 26, 2014. As of April 27, 2015:
http://www.nytimes.com/2014/08/27/world/middleeast/rawabi-west-bank-palestinians-israel.html?_r=0&gwh=E4E7E033D7738F49D0E271984596B567&gwt=pay

Kessler, Ronald C., and T. Bedirhan Ustun, eds., *The WHO World Mental Health Surveys*, Geneva, Switzerland: World Health Organization, August 2008.

Khadr, Ali, "Chapter 10: Donor Assistance" in Ishac Diwan and Radwan A. Shaban, eds., *Development Under Adversity: The Palestinian Economy in Transition*, Ramallah, West Bank, and Washington, D.C.: Palestine Economic Policy Research Institute (MAS) and the World Bank, 19162, March 1999.

Khalidi, Rashid, "Collective Punishment in Gaza," *New Yorker*, July 29, 2014. As of April 27, 2015:
http://www.newyorker.com/news/news-desk/collective-punishment-gaza

Khamis, V., "Post-Traumatic Stress Disorder Among School Age Palestinian Children," *Child Abuse & Neglect*, Vol. 29, No. 1, January 2005, pp. 81–95.

Khan, Mushtaq Husain, George Giacaman, and Inge Amundsen, eds., *State Formation in Palestine: Viability and Governance During a Social Transformation*, London and New York: RoutledgeCurzon, 2004.

Khoury, Jack, "EU to Reconsider Palestinian Aid If Peace Talks with Israel Fail," *Haaretz*, December 3, 2013. As of April 24, 2015:
http://www.haaretz.com/news/diplomacy-defense/.premium-1.561593

Kinda, Tidiane, "On the Drivers of FDI and Portfolio Investment: A Simultaneous Equations Approach," *International Economic Journal*, Vol. 26, No. 1, March 2012, pp. 1–22.

Kleiman, E., "Is There a Secret Arab-Israeli Trade?" *Middle East Quarterly*, Vol. 5, No. 2, 1998, pp. 11–18.

Klein, Zeev, Hili Yakobi Handelsman, and Hezi Sternlicht, "Financial Toll of Operation Protective Edge: $4.3 Billion," *Israel Hayom*, August 6, 2014. As of April 24, 2015:
http://www.israelhayom.com/site/newsletter_article.php?id=19273

Korn, L., and G. Zukerman, "Affective and Behavioral Changes Following Exposure to Traumatic Events: The Moderating Effect of Religiosity on Avoidance Behavior Among Students Studying Under a High Level of Terror Event Exposure," *Journal of Religion and Health*, Vol. 50, No. 4, 2011, pp. 911–921.

Krakover, Shaul, "Estimating the Effect of Atrocious Events on the Flow of Tourists to Israel," in Rudi Hartmann and Gregory Ashworth, eds., *Horror and Human Tragedy Revisited: The Management of Sites of Atrocities for Tourism*, Chapter 12, Cognizant Communication Corp., 2005, pp. 183–194.

Krugman, Paul, and Alasdair Smith, eds., *Empirical Studies of Strategic Trade Policy*, Chicago: University of Chicago Press, National Bureau of Economic Research Report, 1994.

Kurtzer, Daniel C., "Netanyahu's Right of Way: How the Israeli Left Fell Behind," *Foreign Affairs*, March 26, 2015. As of May 15, 2015:
https://www.foreignaffairs.com/articles/middle-east/2015-03-26/netanyahus-right-way

Kurtzer, Daniel C., Scott B. Lasensky, William B. Quandt, Steven L. Spiegel, and Shibley Z. Telhami, *The Peace Puzzle: America's Quest for Arab-Israeli Peace, 1989–2011*, Ithaca, N.Y.: Cornell University Press, 2013.

Laqueur, Walter, and Barry Rubin, eds., *The Israel-Arab Reader: A Documentary History of the Middle East Conflict*, 7th Edition, Penguin Books, 2008.

Lasensky, Scott, "Paying for Peace: The Oslo Process and the Limits of American Foreign Aid," *Middle East Journal*, Vol. 58, No. 2, Spring 2004, pp. 210–234.

Lavee, D., G. Beniad, and M. Moshe-Jantzis, "Israel's Foreign Trade Policy: The Benefits of Its Reform," *Journal of Policy Modeling*, Vol. 35, 2013, pp. 255–270.

Lavi, I. , D. Canetti, K. Sharvit, D. Bar-Tal, and S. E. Hobfoll, "Protected by Ethos in a Protracted Conflict? A Comparative Study Among Israelis and Palestinians in the West Bank, Gaza, and East Jerusalem," *Journal of Conflict Resolution*, Vol. 58, No. 1, 2014, pp. 68–92.

Lavi, Tamar, and Zahava Solomon, "Palestinian Youth of the Intifada: PTSD and Future Orientation," *Journal of the American Academy of Child and Adolescent Psychiatry*, Vol. 44, No. 11, November 2005, pp. 1176–1183.

Lavie, Ephraim, "The Israeli-Palestinian Economic Agreement and Current Consequences," *Middle East Economy*, Tel Aviv University and the Moshe Dayan Center for Middle Eastern and African Studies, Vol. 3, No. 1, January 2013.

Lazareva, Inna, and Peter Foster, "Israel Issues Figures on Huge Settlement Expansion," *The Telegraph*, March 4, 2014. As of April 27, 2015:
http://www.telegraph.co.uk/news/worldnews/middleeast/israel/10676752/Israel-issues-figures-on-huge-settlement-expansion.html

Lazaroff, Tovah, "Merkel: Boycott Not an Option, Settlement Labeling Acceptable," *Jerusalem Post*, February 25, 2014.

Le More, Anne, "Killing with Kindness: Funding the Demise of a Palestinian State," *International Affairs*, Vol. 81, No. 5, 2005, pp. 981–999.

Lektzian, David, and Glen Biglaiser, "Investment, Opportunity, and Risk: Do US Sanctions Deter or Encourage Global Investment?" *International Studies Quarterly*, Vol. 57, No. 1, 2013, pp. 57–78.

Levinson, Chaim, Gili Cohen, and Jack Khoury, "Palestinian Mosque Set on Fire in Suspected Hate Crime," *Haaretz*, January 15, 2014. As of April 24, 2015:
http://www.haaretz.com/news/national/1.568700

Lieber, Dov, "Majority of Palestinians Still Support 2-State Solution, New Poll Says," *Jerusalem Post*, November 8, 2014. As of April 27, 2015:
http://www.jpost.com/Arab-Israeli-Conflict/Majority-of-Palestinians-still-support-2-state-solution-new-poll-says-381141

Lustick, Ian S., "Two-State Illusion," *New York Times*, September 14, 2013.

Lynfield, Ben, "Israel's Decision to Withhold Tax Money from Palestinians May Impact Security," *Jewish Daily Forward*, January 26, 2013. As of April 27, 2015:
http://forward.com/news/israel/169898/israels-decision-to-withhold-tax-money-from-palest/

MA'AN Development Center, *Parallel Realities: Israeli Settlements and Palestinian Communities in the Jordan Valley*, London: Council for European and Palestinian Relations, 2012. As of May 23, 2015: http://maan-ctr.org/old/pdfs/FSReport/Settlement/content.pdf

Mansour, Antoine, "The West Bank Economy: 1948–1984," in George T. Abed, ed., *The Palestinian Economy, Studies in Development Under Prolonged Occupation*, Routledge Library Editions: The Economy of the Middle East, Routledge, 1988, pp. 71–99.

Maor, Dafna, "Why Are Housing Prices So High in Israel?" *Haaretz*, June 27, 2014. As of April 24, 2015: http://www.haaretz.com/business/.premium-1.601506

Mark, Clyde, *United States Aid to the Palestinians*, Washington, D.C.: Congressional Research Service, CRS Report for Congress, Order Code RS21594, March 4, 2005.

Marten, Kimberly, "Militia Patronage vs. the Diffusion of Professionalism: The PA Security Forces," paper prepared for delivery at the International Studies Association Annual Convention in San Francisco, April 3, 2013.

Matar, Haggai, "The Wall, 10 Years On: The Great Israeli Project," *+972 Magazine*, April 9, 2012. As of January 6, 2015: http://972mag.com/the-wall-10-years-on-the-great-israeli-project/40683/

McMahon, Darrin M., *Happiness: A History*, Grove Press, 2006.

Melhem, Ahmad, "Palestinians Prepare ICC Files," AlMonitor, January 29, 2015. As of April 24, 2015: http://www.al-monitor.com/pulse/originals/2015/01/palestinian-icc-gaza-war-crimes-west-bank-settlements.html

Melvin, Don, "NGOs Petition to Restrict EU Imports from West Bank Settlements," *The Times of Israel*, October 30, 2012. As of April 24, 2015: http://www.timesofisrael.com/ngos-petition-to-restrict-eu-trade-with-west-bank-settlements/

Merkle, Geesche M., Rico Ihle, Yael Kachel, and Ulf Liebe, *Economic Cooperation Despite of Political Conflict: Israeli Traders' Perception of Israeli-Palestinian Food Trade*, Göttingen, Germany: Courant Research Center, Georg-August-Universität Göttingen, Discussion Paper No. 151, September 2013.

Miller, Aaron David, "Israel's Demographic Destiny: Israel Can Be Jewish, Democratic, or a State in Control of the Palestinian Territories. Choose Two," *Foreign Policy*, March 13, 2013a.

———, "Why the U.S. and Israel Are Split Over the Iran Deal," *CNN*, November 10, 2013b.

———, "Bibi Trapped," *Foreign Policy*, February 27, 2014.

Miller, T., M. el-Masri, F. Allodi, and S. Qouta, "Emotional and Behavioural Problems and Trauma Exposure of School-Age Palestinian Children in Gaza: Some Preliminary Findings," *Medicine, Conflict, and Survival*, Vol. 15, No. 4, October–December 1999, pp. 368–378, 391–393.

Muldoon, O. T., "Understanding the Impact of Political Violence in Childhood: A Theoretical Review Using a Social Identity Approach," *Clinical Psychology Review*, Vol. 33, No. 8, December 2013, pp. 929–939.

Nashashibi, Karim, *Palestinian Public Finance Under Crisis Management: Restoring Fiscal Sustainability*, United Nations Development Programme, 2015.

Nasr, Mohamed M., "Chapter 5: Monopolies and the PNA," in M. H. Khan, G. Giacaman, and I. Amundsen, eds., *State Formation in Palestine: Viability and Governance During a Social Transformation*, London: Routledge-Curzon, 2004.

National Institute of Mental Health, "What Is Prevalence?" undated. As of April 24, 2015:
http://www.nimh.nih.gov/health/statistics/prevalence/index.shtml

Naylor, Hugh, and Taimur Khan, "Battered but Not Beaten, Hamas Will Not Stop Building Tunnels," *The National*, July 23, 2014. As of April 24, 2015:
http://www.thenational.ae/world/middle-east/
battered-but-not-beaten-hamas-will-not-stop-building-tunnels#full

Nemes, Hody, "Israel Under Fire Over 'Restrictions' on Palestinian Academics—But What Is Truth?" *Jewish Daily Forward*, January 17, 2014. As of April 27, 2015:
http://forward.com/news/israel/191100/israel-under-fire-over-restrictions-on-palestinian/

Neumayer, Eric, "Visa Restrictions and Bilateral Travel," *The Professional Geographer*, Vol. 62, No. 2, May 2010, pp. 1–11.

———, "On the Detrimental Impact of Visa Restrictions on Bilateral Trade and Foreign Direct Investment," *Applied Geography*, Vol. 31, 2011, pp. 901–907.

"New Poll Indicates Palestinian Public Opinion on Unity and the War on Gaza," *Middle East Monitor*, September 17, 2014. As of April 27, 2015:
https://www.middleeastmonitor.com/news/
middle-east/14196-new-poll-indicates-palestinian-public-opinion-on-unity-and-the-war-on-gaza

Newport, Frank, "Middle East Update: U.S. Support for Israel, Hamas Is Stable," Gallup, August 5, 2014. As of January 12, 2015:
http://www.gallup.com/poll/174305/middle-east-update-support-israel-hamas-stable.aspx

"No One Knows Full Cost of Israel's Settlement Ambitions," Associated Press, August 14, 2005. As of April 24, 2015:
http://usatoday30.usatoday.com/news/world/2005-08-14-israelsettlercosts_x.htm

Numbeo, "Cost of Living in Israel," 2015. As of May 15, 2015:
http://www.numbeo.com/cost-of-living/country_result.jsp?country=Israel&displayCurrency=USD

OCHA—*see* United Nations Office for the Coordination of Humanitarian Affairs.

OECD—*see* Organisation for Economic Co-operation and Development.

Office of the United Nations Special Coordinator for the Middle East Peace Process, "Socio-Economic Report: March 2012; Supplement: The Structure of Gross Domestic Product and Gross Capital Formation in the West Bank and the Gaza Strip in 2011," March 2012.

Ofran, Hagit, "The Price of Maintaining the Territories—Data from 2011–2012 Budget," Peace Now, December 26, 2010. As of January 9, 2015:
http://peacenow.org.il/eng/content/price-maintaining-territories-data-2011-2012-budget

"Olmert's Peace Plan," *Haaretz*, undated. As of January 11, 2015:
http://www.haaretz.co.il/hasite/images/iht_daily/D171209/olmertmap.pdf

Organisation for Economic Co-operation and Development, "Stat Extracts," undated. As of January 14, 2015:
http://stats.oecd.org

———, *Government at a Glance 2011: Country Note: Israel*, June 2011. As of April 24, 2015:
http://www.oecd.org/gov/48215127.pdf

———, "Foreign Direct Investment: Flows by Partner Country," OECD International Direct Investment Statistics database, 2012.

———, "OECD Better Life Index: Israel," 2015. As of August 8, 2015:
http://www.oecdbetterlifeindex.org/countries/israel/

Othman, Mohammad, "Tulkarem and the Factories," undated. As of April 27, 2015:
http://mohammadethman.blogspot.com/p/tulkarem-and-jeicori-factories.html

Palestine Investment Fund, *Annual Report 2010*, 2010.

Palestine Monetary Authority, "Basic Variables in Labour Force Indicators (ILO Standards),"
undated. As of April 27, 2015:
http://www.pma.ps/Portals/1/Users/002/02/2/Time%20Series%20Data%20New/Labor_Force/
basic_changes_in_labour_force_indicators_ilo_standards.xls

———, "Palestinian Economy Main Indicators," 2014. As of January 9, 2015:
http://www.pma.ps/Portals/1/Users/002/02/2/Time%20Series%20Data%20New/
Palestinian_Main_Indicators/main_indicators_palestinian_economy.xls

———, "Statistics—Time Series Data," 2015. As of April 22, 2015:
http://www.pma.ps/Default.aspx?tabid=202&language=en-US

Palestine Trade Center, *The Untapped Potential—Palestinian Israeli Economic Relations: Policy Options
and Recommendations*, The Peres Center for Peace and PalTrade, October 2006. As of August 8,
2015:
http://old.paltrade.org/en/publications/other/
Untapped%20Potential%20-%20Dec%202006%20PRINTED%20(Arabic-English).pdf

———, *Obtaining Visas for Investors*, Ramallah, Palestine, February 2010.

Palestinian Center for Policy and Survey Research, "Index PSR Polls," undated. As of April 28, 2015:
http://www.pcpsr.org/en/node/154

———, "Results of PSR Refugees' Polls in the West Bank/Gaza Strip, Jordan and Lebanon: On
Refugees' Preferences and Behavior in a Palestinian-Israeli Permanent Refugee Agreement," press
release, January–June 2003. As of April 27, 2015:
http://www.pcpsr.org/en/node/493

———, "The Day After: The Likelihood, Consequences and Policy Implications of PA Collapse or
Dissolution," January 2013–February 2014a. As of January 9, 2015:
http://www.pcpsr.org/en/node/114

———, Survey Research Unit, Poll Number 52, June 5–7, 2014b.

———, Survey Research Unit, Special Gaza War Poll, August 26–30, 2014c.

Palestinian Central Bureau of Statistics, "GDP by Expenditure and Region for the Years 1994–2013
at Current Prices," undated(a). As of May 16, 2015:
http://www.pcbs.gov.ps/Portals/_Rainbow/Documents/e-naexpcurr-1994-2013.html

———, "Guide to Palestinian Statistics, A–Z," undated(b). As of January 12, 2015:
http://www.pcbs.gov.ps/site/lang__en/507/default.aspx

———, "Major National Accounts Variables by Region for the Years 1994–2013 at Current Prices,"
undated(c). As of April 24, 2015:
http://www.pcbs.gov.ps/Portals/_Rainbow/Documents/e-namcurr-1994-2013.htm

———, "Percentage Distribution of Employed Persons from Palestine by Economic Activity and Sex,
2000–2012," undated(d). As of April 24, 2015:
http://www.pcbs.gov.ps/Portals/_Rainbow/Documents/employment%202000-2012.htm

———, "Percentage Distribution of Employed Persons from Palestine by Sector and Region, 2000–
2012," undated(e). As of April 24, 2015:
http://www.pcbs.gov.ps/Portals/_Rainbow/Documents/employment%202000-2012.htm

———, "The Total Value of Registered Palestinian Exports and Imports and Net Balance of Goods by Month 2013," undated(f). As of April 24, 2015:
http://www.pcbs.gov.ps/Portals/_Rainbow/Documents/E-Ftrade%202013.htm

———, "Percentage Distribution of Employed Person in the Palestine Territory by Sector and Region, 2000–2011," undated(g). As of August 31, 2015:
http://www.pcbs.gov.ps/Portals/_Rainbow/Documents/Employed%20Person%20by%20sector.htm

———, *Jerusalem Statistical Yearbook 1999, No. 2*, Ramallah, Palestine, November 2000. As of August 31, 2015:
http://www.pcbs.gov.ps/Downloads/book648.pdf

———, *Jerusalem Statistical Yearbook 2000, No. 3*, Ramallah, Palestine, June 2001. As of August 31, 2015:
http://www.pcbs.gov.ps/Downloads/book709.pdf

———, *Jerusalem Statistical Yearbook 2002, No. 4*, Ramallah, Palestine, June 2002. As of August 31, 2015:
http://www.pcbs.gov.ps/Downloads/book789.pdf

———, *National Accounts at Current and Constant Prices (1994–2000)*, Ramallah, Palestine, April 2003a. As of August 7, 2015:
http://www.pcbs.gov.ps/Downloads/book892.pdf

———, "Population Projections," May 2003b.

———, *Jerusalem Statistical Yearbook 2003, No. 5*, Ramallah, Palestine, June 2003c. As of August 31, 2015:
http://www.pcbs.gov.ps/Downloads/book936.pdf

———, *Jerusalem Statistical Yearbook, No. 8*, Ramallah, Palestine, June 2006. As of August 7, 2015:
http://www.pcbs.gov.ps/Downloads/book1263_n.pdf

———, *Jerusalem Statistical Yearbook, No. 9*, Ramallah, Palestine, 2007. As of August 7, 2015:
http://www.pcbs.gov.ps/Downloads/book1354.pdf

———, *Agricultural Statistics 2007/2008*, Ramallah, Palestine, 2009a. As of January 10, 2015:
http://www.pcbs.gov.ps/Portals/_PCBS/Downloads/book1620.pdf

———, *Jerusalem Statistical Yearbook, No. 11*, Ramallah, Palestine, 2009b. As of August 7, 2015:
http://www.pcbs.gov.ps/Downloads/book1561.pdf

———, *Preliminary Estimates for the Economic Losses in Gaza Strip Caused by Israeli Aggression*, Ramallah, Palestine, January 2009c.

———, *Jerusalem Statistical Yearbook 2010, No. 12*, Ramallah, Palestine, June 2010. As of August 31, 2015:
http://www.pcbs.gov.ps/Downloads/book1672.pdf

———, *Labour Force Survey: Annual Report: 2010*, Ramallah, Palestine, April 2011a. As of August 31, 2015:
http://www.pcbs.gov.ps/Portals/_PCBS/Downloads/book1744.pdf

———, *Jerusalem Statistical Yearbook 2011, No. 13*, Ramallah, Palestine, June 2011b. As of August 31, 2015:
http://www.pcbs.gov.ps/Downloads/book1766.pdf

———, *Tourism Activities Report, 2010 Main Results*, Ramallah, Palestine, November 2011c. As of May 1, 2015:
http://www.pcbs.gov.ps/Downloads/book1803.pdf

———, *Jerusalem Statistical Yearbook 2012, No. 14*, Ramallah, Palestine, 2012a. As of August 7, 2015:
http://www.pcbs.gov.ps/Downloads/book1891.pdf

———, *Agriculture Statistics Survey, 2010/2011, Main Results*, Ramallah, Palestine, July 2012b. As of May 1, 2015:
http://www.pcbs.gov.ps/Downloads/book1903.pdf

———, *Jerusalem Statistical Yearbook 2013, No. 15*, Ramallah, Palestine, 2013. As of August 7, 2015:
http://www.pcbs.gov.ps/Downloads/book1983.pdf

———, *Jerusalem Statistical Yearbook 2014, No. 16*, Ramallah, Palestine, June 2014. As of August 7, 2015:
http://www.pcbs.gov.ps/Downloads/book2057.pdf

Palestinian Central Bureau of Statistics and Palestine Monetary Authority, *Foreign Investment Survey of Resident Enterprises in Palestine, 2012, Preliminary Results*, Ramallah, Palestine, November 2013.

Palestinian Economic Policy Research Institute—MAS, "Economic Impacts of Water Restrictions in Palestine, Preliminary Estimates," Ramallah, 2009.

"Palestinian Economy to Shrink in 2014, World Bank Says," *Times of Israel*, September 16, 2014. As of January 2, 2015:
http://www.timesofisrael.com/palestinian-economy-to-shrink-in-2014-world-bank-says/

Palestinian Ministry of Health, Palestine Health Information Center, *Health Annual Report Palestine 2012*, July 2013.

Palestinian Ministry of National Economy in cooperation with the Applied Research Institute—Jerusalem, *The Economic Costs of the Israeli Occupation for the Occupied Palestinian Territory*, September 2011.

PalTrade—*see* Palestine Trade Center.

Pat-Horenczyk, R., R. Abramovitz, O. Peled, D. Brom, A. Daie, and C. M. Chemtob, "Adolescent Exposure to Recurrent Terrorism in Israel: Posttraumatic Distress and Functional Impairment," *American Journal of Orthopsychiatry*, Vol. 77, No. 1, January 2007, pp. 76–85.

Pat-Horenczyk, R., O. Peled, T. Miron, et al., "Risk-Taking Behaviors Among Israeli Adolescents Exposed to Recurrent Terrorism: Provoking Danger Under Continuous Threat?" *American Journal of Psychiatry*, Vol. 164, No. 1, 2007, pp. 66–72.

PCBS—*see* Palestinian Central Bureau of Statistics.

PCBS and PMA—*see* Palestinian Central Bureau of Statistics and Palestine Monetary Authority.

Pew Research Center, "Despite Their Wide Differences, Many Israelis and Palestinians Want Bigger Role for Obama in Resolving Conflict," May 9, 2013.

Picow, Maurice, "Saudi Arabia's Desalination Market a $50 Billion Opportunity," Green Prophet, October 6, 2010. As of April 24, 2015:
http://www.greenprophet.com/2010/10/saudi-arabia-desalination-2/

PMA—*see* Palestine Monetary Authority.

Plitnick, Mitchell, "Polls Show Diminishing Support for Two-State Solution," Inter Press Service, February 1, 2014. As of April 27, 2015:
http://www.ipsnews.net/2014/02/poll-shows-diminishing-support-two-state-solution/

Podolsky, Philip, "Former IDF Chief Indicates Israel Should Withdraw from West Bank Unilaterally," *The Times of Israel*, December 9, 2012. As of April 27, 2015: http://www.timesofisrael.com/ former-idf-chief-says-israel-should-withdraw-from-west-bank-unilaterally/

Popper, Steven W., Claude Berrebi, James Griffin, Thomas Light, Endy M. Daehner, and Keith Crane, *Natural Gas and Israel's Energy Future: Near-Term Decisions from a Strategic Perspective*, Santa Monica, Calif.: RAND Corporation, MG-927-YSNFF, 2009. As of April 17, 2015: http://www.rand.org/pubs/monographs/MG927

Popper, Steven W., James Griffin, Claude Berrebi, Thomas Light, and Endy M. Daehner, *Natural Gas and Israel's Energy Future: A Strategic Analysis Under Conditions of Deep Uncertainty*, Santa Monica, Calif.: RAND Corporation, TR-747-YSNFF, 2009. As of April 17, 2015: http://www.rand.org/pubs/technical_reports/TR747

Populus, "British Attitudes Towards Israel Survey, ONLINE Fieldwork: 10th–12th October 2014," October 2014. As of January 9, 2015: http://www.populus.co.uk/wp-content/uploads/2014/10/OmIsrael_BPC.pdf

Portes, Richard, and Hélène Rey, "The Determinants of Cross-Border Equity Flows," *Journal of International Economics*, Vol. 65, 2005, pp. 269–296.

Portland Trust, *Beyond Aid: A Palestinian Private Sector Initiative for Investment, Growth and Employment*, London, November 2013.

ProCon.org, "Historical Timeline," 2014. As of May 15, 2015: http://israelipalestinian.procon.org/view.resource.php?resourceID=000635

Psaki, Jen, daily press briefing, U.S. Department of State, Washington, D.C., February 3, 2014.

Pullan, Wendy, Philipp Misselwitz, Rami Nasrallah, and Haim Yacobi, "Jerusalem's Road 1: An Inner City Frontier?" *City: Analysis of Urban Trends, Culture, Theory, Policy, Action*, Vol. 11, No, 2, 2007, pp. 175–197.

Punamaki, R. L., "Relationships Between Political Violence and Psychological Responses Among Palestinian Women," *Journal of Peace Research*, Vol. 27, No. 1, 1990, pp. 75–85.

Punamaki, R. L., and T. Puhakka, "Determinants and Effectiveness of Children's Coping with Political Violence," *International Journal of Behavioral Development*, Vol. 21, No. 2, 1997, pp. 349–370.

Punamaki, R. L., J. Salo, I. Komproe, S. Qouta, M. El-Masri, and J. T. De Jong, "Dispositional and Situational Coping and Mental Health Among Palestinian Political Ex-Prisoners," *Anxiety, Stress, and Coping*, Vol. 21, No. 4, October 2008, pp. 337–358.

Qafisheh, Mutaz M., "Bases for the Palestinian Refugees' Right of Return Under International Law: Beyond General Assembly Resolution 194," *Cambridge Journal of International and Comparative Law*, November 26, 2012. As of April 24, 2015: http://cjicl.org.uk/2012/11/26/bases-for-the-palestinian-refugees-right-of-return-under-international-law-beyond-general-assembly-resolution-194-2/

Qouta, S., R. L. Punamaki, and E. El Sarraj, "Prevalence and Determinants of PTSD Among Palestinian Children Exposed to Military Violence," *European Child and Adolescent Psychiatry*, Vol. 12, No. 6, December 2003, pp. 265–272.

Qouta, S., R. L. Punamaki, E. Montgomery, and E. El Sarraj, "Predictors of Psychological Distress and Positive Resources Among Palestinian Adolescents: Trauma, Child, and Mothering Characteristics, *Child Abuse and Neglect*, Vol. 31, No. 7, July 2007, pp. 699–717.

Qurei, Ahmed, *From Oslo to Jerusalem: The Palestinian Story of the Secret Negotiations*, Tauris Press, 2006.

Rabinovich, Itamar, *The Lingering Conflict: Israel, the Arabs, and the Middle East, 1948–2011*, Washington, D.C.: The Brookings Institution, 2011.

Rabinovich, Itamar, and Michael Oren, "Israel's Geostrategic Position at a Time of Regional Instability," 2014 Scholar-Statesman Award Dinner, Washington Institute, December 2, 2014. As of April 24, 2015:
http://www.washingtoninstitute.org/policy-analysis/view/2014-scholar-statesman-award-dinner

Ragozzino, Roberto, "The Role of Geographic Distance in FDI," in Stephen B. Tallman, ed., *A New Generation in International Strategic Management*, New York: Edward Elgar, 2007.

Rahman, Mai Abdul, *Impact of the Israeli Occupation on Palestinian Education*, Washington, D.C.: Howard University, presented at the 18th Annual Conference of the Global Awareness Society International, May 2009.

Ramahi, Sawsan, *The Environmental Impact of Israeli Settlements on the Occupied Palestinian Territories*, Middle East Monitor, March 2012. As of April 27, 2015:
http://www.middleeastmonitor.com/downloads/factsheets/
the-environmental-impact-of-israeli-settlements-on-the-occupied-palestinian-territories.pdf

RAND Palestinian State Study Team, *Building a Successful Palestinian State*, Santa Monica, Calif.: RAND Corporation, MG-146-1-DCR, 2007. As of January 14, 2015:
http://www.rand.org/pubs/monographs/MG146-1.html

Ravid, Barak, "U.S. to Grant Three-Year Extension of Loan Guarantees to Israel," *Haaretz*, January 24, 2012. As of April 27, 2015:
http://www.haaretz.com/news/diplomacy-defense/
u-s-to-grant-three-year-extension-of-loan-guarantees-to-israel-1.409037

Raviv, A., D. Bar-Tal, and R. Arviv-Abramovich, *In the Eyes of the Beholder: Views of the Israeli-Arab Conflict by Jewish Veteran Residents in Israel*, forthcoming.

Regev, E., "Education and Employment in the Haredi Sector," in Dan Ben-David, ed., *State of the Nation Report: Society, Economy and Policy in Israel*, Jerusalem, Israel: Taub Center for Social Policy Studies in Israel, November 2013. As of January 14, 2015:
http://taubcenter.org.il/wp-content/files_mf/stateofnation_013eng8.pdf

"Restriction of Movement: Checkpoints, Physical Obstructions, and Forbidden Roads," B'Tselem, March 11, 2014. As of April 27, 2015:
http://www.btselem.org/freedom_of_movement/checkpoints_and_forbidden_roads

Rosner, Shmuel, "Israel and a Hostile World," *New York Times*, October 8, 2014. As of April 24, 2015:
http://www.nytimes.com/2014/10/09/opinion/rosner-israel-and-a-hostile-world.html?_r=0

Ross, Dennis, *The Missing Peace: The Inside Story of the Fight for Middle East Peace*, New York: Farrar, Straus, and Giroux, 2005.

Rotberg, Robert I., ed., *Israeli and Palestinian Narratives of Conflict: History's Double Helix*, Indiana Series in Middle East Studies, Indiana University Press, 2006.

Rowe, Diana, "Funding Illegal Settlements in the Occupied Territories of Palestine," information brief, Washington, D.C.: The Palestine Center, Jerusalem Fund for Education and Community Development, 2008.

Rubinstein, Danny, "The Case for Letting Palestinian Labor Back into Israel's Workforce," *Al-Monitor*, October 27, 2012. As of January 14, 2015:
http://www.al-monitor.com/pulse/business/2012/10/the-return-of-the-palestinian-wo.html#

Rudoren, Jodi, "Israeli Official Weighs an Imposed Palestinian Border," *New York Times*, May 30, 2012.

———, "Pushing Peace on the Palestinians," *New York Times*, November 19, 2013. As of April 27, 2015:
http://www.nytimes.com/2013/11/20/world/middleeast/pushing-peace-on-the-palestinians.html

———, "In West Bank Settlements, Israeli Jobs Are Double-Edged Sword," *New York Times*, February 10, 2014. As of April 22, 2015:
http://www.nytimes.com/2014/02/11/world/middleeast/
palestinians-work-in-west-bank-for-israeli-industry-they-oppose.html

Ruppert Bulmer, Elizabeth, "The Impact of Israeli Border Policy on the Palestinian Labor Market," *Economic Development and Cultural Change*, Vol. 51, No. 3, April 2003, pp. 657–676.

Rutenberg, Jim, Mike McIntire, and Ethan Bronner, "Tax-Exempt Funds Aid Settlements in West Bank," *New York Times*, July 5, 2010. As of January 9, 2015:
http://www.nytimes.com/2010/07/06/world/middleeast/06settle.html?pagewanted=all&_r=0

S. Daniel Abraham Center for Middle East Peace, *Public Poll Findings: Peace with the Palestinians,* January 2014. As of April 27, 2015:
http://www.centerpeace.org/wp-content/uploads/2014/01/
Israeli-Public-Opinion-Poll-January-2014-Midgam.pdf

Saad, Lydia, "Americans' Mideast Country Ratings Show Little Change," Gallup, February 2014. As of January 12, 2015:
http://www.gallup.com/poll/167474/americans-mideast-country-ratings-show-little-change.aspx

"Saeb Erekat: 'No Partner for Peace in Israel,'" i24news.tv, July 4, 2014. As of April 27, 2015:
http://www.i24news.tv/en/news/israel/diplomacy-defense/
36280-140704-saeb-erekat-we-don-t-have-a-partner-in-israel

Sagy, S., and O. Braun-Lewensohn, "Adolescents Under Rocket Fire: When Are Coping Resources Significant in Reducing Emotional Distress?" *Global Health Promotion*, Vol. 16, No. 4, December 2009, pp. 5–15.

Saïd, N., "Palestinian Perceptions of International Assistance," in M. Keating, A. Le More, and R. Lowe, eds., *Aid, Diplomacy, and Facts on the Ground: The Case of Palestine*, London: Chatham House, 2005.

Santayana, George, "Reason in Common Sense," *The Life of Reason*, Vol. 1, 1905.

Sayre, Edward, "The Labor-Market Effects of Palestinian Return Migration," *Topics in Middle Eastern and North African Economies*, electronic journal, Vol. 5, Chicago, Ill.: Middle East Economic Association and Loyola University Chicago, September 2003.

"Scale of Gaza Destruction Unprecedented, Rehabilitation Will Cost $7.8 Billion, PA Says," *Jerusalem Post*, September 4, 2014. As of April 24, 2015:
http://www.jpost.com/Arab-Israeli-Conflict/
Scale-of-Gaza-destruction-unprecedented-rehabilitation-will-cost-78-billion-PA-says-374460

Schechter, Asher, "Immoral, Ineffective: Destroying Terrorists' Homes Is Nothing But Empty Revenge," *Haaretz*, November 20, 2014. As of April 27, 2015:
http://www.haaretz.com/news/diplomacy-defense/.premium-1.627383

Schlesinger, Liat, *The Settlers' Secret Slush Fund* [in Hebrew], Molad, September 4, 2014. As of June 4, 2015:
http://www.molad.org/images/upload/files/HaHativaLeHityashvut.pdf
English version at http://www.molad.org/en/articles/slush-fund

Schmid, Dorothee, Shai Moses, Alfred Tovias, and Stephen Calleya, *Mapping European and American Economic Initiatives Towards Israel and the Palestinian Authority and Their Effects on Honest Broker Perceptions*, EuroMeSCo, Paper 61, October 2006.

Schmidt, Peter, "Backlash Against Israel Boycott Throws Academic Association on Defensive," *New York Times*, January 5, 2014.

Schocken, Roni, "Chilling Effect of the Nakba Law on Israel's Human Rights," *Haaretz*, May 17, 2012. As of April 27, 2015:
http://www.haaretz.com/opinion/chilling-effect-of-the-nakba-law-on-israel-s-human-rights-1.430942

Shaban, Radwan A., "Palestinian Labour Mobility," *International Labour Review*, Vol. 132, No. 5, 1993, pp. 655–672.

Shalev, A. Y., R. Tuval, S. Frenkiel-Fishman, H. Hadar, and S. Eth, "Psychological Responses to Continuous Terror: A Study of Two Communities in Israel," *American Journal of Psychiatry*, Vol. 163, No. 4, April 2006, pp. 667–673.

Shamah, David, "Keep Israel's Gas at Home, Urge a Growing Body of Experts," *The Times of Israel*, May 28, 2013. As of April 24, 2015:
http://www.timesofisrael.com/keep-israels-gas-at-home-urge-a-growing-body-of-experts/

Sharaby, Linda, "Israel's Economic Growth: Success Without Security," *Middle East Review of International Affairs*, Vol. 6, No. 3, September 2002, pp. 25–41.

Sharon, J. S., *The Arab Boycott Against Israel and Its Unintended Impact on Arab Economic Welfare*, thesis, Bedford, Mass.: The Fletcher School, Tufts University, 2003.

Sharp, Jeremy M., *U.S. Foreign Aid to Israel*, Congressional Research Service, CRS Report RL33222, April 11, 2014.

Shikaki, Khalil, *The Likelihood, Consequences and Policy Implications of PA Collapse or Dissolution: The "Day After" Final Report*, Palestinian Center for Policy and Survey Research, Ramallah, Palestine, February 4, 2014.

Shragai, Nadav, "Disengagement Official: Gaza Settler Families Cost NIS 4.9 Million Each," *Haaretz*, May 12, 2009. As of April 27, 2015:
http://www.haaretz.com/print-edition/news/disengagement-official-gaza-settler-families-cost-nis-4-9-million-each-1.275836

Smith, Charles D., ed., "Excerpts from the Palestine Royal (Peel) Commission Report (July 7, 1937)," in *Palestine and the Arab-Israeli Conflict: A History with Documents*, Bedford/St. Martin's, 2001.

Smith, Rich, "Raytheon Company Rushes to Restock Israel's Iron Dome," The Motley Fool, October 5, 2014. As of April 24, 2015:
http://www.fool.com/investing/general/2014/10/05/raytheon-company-rushes-to-restock-israels-iron-do.aspx

Sobovitz, Dan, *"The Occupation Corrupts"? Quantitative Analysis of Corruption in the Palestinian Authority*, Berlin: Working Paper 50 of the Hertie School of Governance, thesis, June 2010.

Solomon, Z., and T. Lavi, "Israeli Youth in the Second Intifada: PTSD and Future Orientation," *Journal of the American Academy of Child and Adolescent Psychiatry*, Vol. 44, No. 11, November 2005, pp. 1167–1175.

Sousa, C. A., M. M. Haj-Yahia, G. Feldman, and J. Lee, "Individual and Collective Dimensions of Resilience Within Political Violence," *Trauma, Violence and Abuse*, Vol. 14, No. 3, July 2013, pp. 235–254.

Sparshott, Jeffrey, "Obama Signs Law Providing $225 Million for Israel's Iron Dome," *Wall Street Journal*, August 4, 2014. As of April 24, 2015:
http://www.wsj.com/articles/
obama-signs-law-providing-225-million-for-israels-iron-dome-1407193842

State of Israel Ministry of Finance, *The Israeli Economy: Fundamentals, Characteristics, and Historic Overview*, Israel, 2012.

———, *State Budget Proposal for Fiscal Years 2013–2014: Major Provisions of the Budget and Multi-Year Budget Plan*, Jerusalem, Israel, June 2013.

State of Israel Ministry of Industry, Trade, and Labor, "Invest in Israel: Investment Incentives and Benefits," undated. As of January 11, 2015:
http://www.investinisrael.gov.il/NR/rdonlyres/43DB184A-D049-489F-9819-C2E951E4E953/0/
InvestmentIncentivesBenefitsinIsrael.pdf

State of Israel Water Authority, *The Issue of Water Between Israel and the Palestinians*, March 2009. As of January 11, 2015:
http://siteresources.worldbank.org/INTWESTBANKGAZA/Resources/
IsraelWaterAuthorityresponse.pdf

———, *The Water Issue Between Israel and the Palestinians: Main Facts*, February 2012.

State of Palestine, *The National Early Recovery and Reconstruction Plan for Gaza*, International Conference in Support of the Reconstruction of Gaza, Cairo, Arab Republic of Egypt, October 2014. As of January 11, 2015:
http://www.mfa.gov.eg/gazaconference/documents/
finalGaza%20ERP%20report%20ENG30092014.pdf

"Statistics on Palestinians in the Custody of the Israeli Security Forces," B'Tselem, March 31, 2015. As of April 27, 2015:
http://www.btselem.org/statistics/detainees_and_prisoners

Steinberg, Gerald M., "Learning the Lessons of the European Union's Failed Middle East Policies," *Jerusalem Viewpoints*, No. 510, Jerusalem, Israel: Jerusalem Center for Public Affairs, January 1, 2004. As of January 11, 2015:
http://www.jcpa.org/jl/vp510.htm

Stewart, Ain, "Poll: Settlers Split On Leaving West Bank," *The Jewish Week*, March 18, 2014. As of April 27, 2015:
http://www.thejewishweek.com/news/israel-news/poll-settlers-split-leaving-west-bank-0

Stoil, Rebecca Shimoni, and *Times of Israel* staff, "Adelson: Palestinians an Invented People Out to Destroy Israel," *Times of Israel*, November 2014. As of April 22, 2015:
http://www.timesofisrael.com/adelson-palestinians-an-invented-people-out-to-destroy-israel/

Suisman, Doug, Steven Simon, Glenn Robinson, C. Ross Anthony, and Michael Schoenbaum, *The Arc: A Formal Structure for a Palestinian State*, Santa Monica, Calif.: RAND Corporation, MG-327-2-GG, 2005. As of January 11, 2015:
http://www.rand.org/pubs/monographs/MG327-2.html

Swirski, Shlomo, *Is There an Israeli Business Peace Disincentive?* Tel Aviv, Israel: Adva Center, August 2008.

————, *The Cost of Occupation: The Burden of the Israeli-Palestinian Conflict, 2012 Report*, Tel Aviv, Israel: Adva Center, June 2012. As of June 3, 3015:
http://www.adva.org/uploaded/E-kibush1%20page%20by%20page.pdf

Tait, Robert, "Israel Insists on Jordan Valley Presence as John Kerry Pushes Peace Plan," *The Telegraph*, January 5, 2014. As of April 27, 2015:
http://www.telegraph.co.uk/news/worldnews/middleeast/israel/10551677/
Israel-insists-on-Jordan-Valley-presence-as-John-Kerry-pushes-peace-plan.html

Telhami, Shibley, "Does the Palestinian-Israeli Conflict Still Matter?" Washington, D.C.: Brookings Institution, June 2008.

Thabet, A.A., and P. Vostanis, "Post Traumatic Stress Disorder Reactions in Children of War: A Longitudinal Study," *Child Abuse and Neglect*, Vol. 24, No. 2, 2000, pp. 291–298.

Tharoor, Ishaan, "Beneath the Conflict in Gaza Lies the Death of the Two-State Solution," *Washington Post*, July 25, 2014. As of January 11, 2015:
http://www.washingtonpost.com/blogs/worldviews/wp/2014/07/25/
beneath-the-conflict-in-gaza-lies-the-death-of-the-two-state-solution/

"The Separation Barrier," B'Tselem, January 2011. As of April 27, 2015:
http://www.btselem.org/separation_barrier/map

Thrall, Nathan, "Israel and the US: The Delusions of Our Diplomacy," *New York Review of Books*, October 9, 2014.

Tirza, Danny, "Israeli Security Fence Architect: Why the Barrier Had to Be Built," *Al-Monitor*, July 1, 2012. As of April 27, 2015:
http://www.al-monitor.com/pulse/originals/2012/al-monitor/israeli-security-fence-architect.html#

Toameh, Khaled Abu, Herb Keinon, and Tovah Lazaroff, "Palestinians to File First 'War Crime' Case Against Israel on April 1," *Jerusalem Post*, February 3, 2015. As of April 27, 2015:
http://www.jpost.com/Middle-East/
Palestinians-to-file-first-war-crime-case-against-Israel-on-April-1-392697

Tovias, A., "Liberalising Trends in Israel's Trade Policy: Trade Policy Review of Israel," *World Economy*, Vol. 31, No. 11, 2008, pp. 1433–1442.

UN—*see* United Nations.

"UN Constructing Green Schools in Gaza," Voice of America, December 5, 2011. As of April 27, 2015:
http://www.voanews.com/content/un-constructing-green-schools-in-gaza--135090218/149167.html

UNCTAD—*see* United Nations Conference on Trade and Development.

UNDP—*see* United Nations Development Programme.

United Nations, "Statement by Middle East Quartet," February 7, 2011. As of April 27, 2015:
http://www.un.org/press/en/2011/sg2168.doc.htm

————, "General Assembly Votes Overwhelmingly to Accord Palestine 'Non-Member Observer State' Status in United Nations," meetings coverage, November 29, 2012. As of April 27, 2015:
http://www.un.org/press/en/2012/ga11317.doc.htm

————, *Israeli Settlements in the Occupied Palestinian Territory, Including East Jerusalem, and the Occupied Syrian Golan*, A/68/513, October 9, 2013. As of January 11, 2015:
http://unispal.un.org/UNISPAL.NSF/0/0E780293F13D3AB785257C16004C5E78

United Nations Conference on Trade and Development, *Report on UNCTAD's Assistance to the Palestinian People*, Geneva, Switzerland: United Nations, TD/B/52/2, July 21, 2005.

———, *Report on UNCTAD Assistance to the Palestinian People: Developments in the Economy of the Occupied Palestinian Territory*, Geneva, Switzerland: United Nations, TD/B/57/4, July 13, 2010.

———, *The Palestinian Economy in East Jerusalem: Enduring Annexation, Isolation and Disintegration*, New York and Geneva, Switzerland: United Nations, 2013a.

———, *Report on UNCTAD Assistance to the Palestinian People: Developments in the Economy of the Occupied Palestinian Territory*, Geneva, Switzerland: United Nations, TD/B/60/3, July 8, 2013b. As of January 9, 2015:
http://unctad.org/meetings/en/SessionalDocuments/tdb60d3_en.pdf

———, "Inward and Outward Foreign Direct Investment Stock, Annual, 1980–2013," September 2014. As of August 31, 2015:
http://unctadstat.unctad.org/wds/TableViewer/tableView.aspx?ReportId=89

United Nations Development Programme, *Human Development Report 2013—The Rise of the South: Human Progress in a Diverse World*, 2013. As of August 8, 2015:
http://hdr.undp.org/sites/default/files/reports/14/hdr2013_en_complete.pdf

United Nations General Assembly, Resolution 194, *194 (III). Palestine—Progress Report of the United Nations Mediator*, A/RES/194 (III), December 11, 1948. As of May 15, 2015:
http://unispal.un.org/UNISPAL.NSF/0/C758572B78D1CD0085256BCF0077E51A

United Nations Office for the Coordination of Humanitarian Affairs, "Occupied Palestinian Territories Report," September 2008.

———, "Field Update on Gaza from the Humanitarian Coordinator," East Jerusalem, January 27–29, 2009.

United Nations Office for the Coordination of Humanitarian Affairs—Occupied Palestinian Territory, "Oslo Agreement," map, July 2005. As of August 7, 2015:
http://www.ochaopt.org/documents/wb_oslogov&barrier_july05.pdf

———, *Easing the Blockade: Assessing the Humanitarian Impact on the Population of the Gaza Strip*, East Jerusalem, March 2011a.

———, map of Israel, the West Bank, and Gaza, December 2011b. As of August 7, 2015:
http://www.ochaopt.org/documents/ochaopt_atlas_opt_general_december2011.pdf

———, "Land Allocated to Israeli Settlements," map, January 2012a. As of August 7, 2015:
http://www.ochaopt.org/documents/ocha_opt_land_allocated_for_settlements_january_2012_english.pdf

———, *West Bank: Movement and Access Update*, East Jerusalem, September 2012b.

———, *Gaza Initial Rapid Assessment: 27 August 2014*, 2014. As of April 24, 2015:
http://www.ochaopt.org/documents/gaza_mira_report_9september.pdf

———, *Fragmented Lives: Humanitarian Overview 2014*, March 2015. As of April 30, 2015:
http://www.ochaopt.org/documents/annual_humanitarian_overview_2014_english_final.pdf

United Nations Security Council, Resolution 242 (1967), S/RES/242, November 22, 1967. As of April 24, 2015:
http://unispal.un.org/unispal.nsf/0/7D35E1F729DF491C85256EE700686136

United States Institute of Peace, "Clinton Proposal on Israeli-Palestinian Peace," December 23, 2000. As of August 8, 2015:
http://www.usip.org/sites/default/files/Peace%20Puzzle/10_Clinton%20Parameters.pdf

"Urging Political Resolution, UN Agency Chief Laments 'Sheer Unsustainability' of Gaza Crisis," UN News Centre, November 6, 2014. As of April 24, 2015:
http://www.un.org/apps/news/story.asp?NewsID=49274#.VTqO7GZAUbs

"Us and Them," *The Economist*, August 2, 2014. As of April 27, 2015:
http://www.economist.com/news/briefing/
21610312-pummelling-gaza-has-cost-israel-sympathy-not-just-europe-also-among-americans

U.S. Agency for International Development, *The Impact of Israeli Restrictions on the Transfer of Dual-Use Goods in the West Bank*, January 2010.

USAID—*see* U.S. Agency for International Development.

U.S. Census Bureau, "IDB Summary Demographic Data for Gaza Strip," 2003a.

———, "IDB Summary Demographic Data for West Bank," 2003b.

———, "International Data Base," last updated December 2013. As of June 2014:
http://www.census.gov/population/international/data/idb/informationGateway.php

U.S. Department of State, *2012 Report on International Religious Freedom: Israel and The Occupied Territories—The Occupied Territories*, Washington, D.C., May 20, 2013. As of April 27, 2015:
http://www.state.gov/j/drl/rls/irf/2012/nea/208394.htm

U.S. Senate Committee on Foreign Relations, Israel's Disengagement from Gaza and Several West Bank Settlements (S. Prt. 109-36), Washington, D.C.: U.S. Government Printing Office, October 1, 2005. As of August 7, 2015:
http://www.gpo.gov/fdsys/pkg/CPRT-109SPRT23820/html/CPRT-109SPRT23820.htm

Vaiana, Mary E., C. Ross Anthony, and Doug Suisman, *The RAND Palestine Initiative*, Santa Monica, Calif.: RAND Corporation, CP-562, 2009. As of January 9, 2015:
http://www.rand.org/pubs/corporate_pubs/CP562.html

van Hear, Nicholas, "The Impact of the Involuntary Mass 'Return' to Jordan in the Wake of the Gulf Crisis," *International Migration Review*, Vol. 29, No. 2, Summer 1995, pp. 352–374. As of January 14, 2015:
http://www.jstor.org/stable/2546785

Weiss, M. A., *Arab League Boycott of Israel*, Congressional Research Service 7-5700 RL33961, December 19, 2013.

Weissberg, Hila, Nimrod Bousso, and Ronny Linder-Ganz, "Israelis Happy, Says OECD, Despite Low Ranking on Income and Education," *Haaretz*, February 4, 2013. As of April 24, 2015:
http://www.haaretz.com/news/national/
israelis-happy-says-oecd-despite-low-ranking-on-income-and-education.premium-1.512930

Weizman, Stephen, "Israel's Economy and the Arab Spring: Isolation Serves as a Buffer," Washington, D.C.: German Marshall Fund, Mediterranean Policy Program—Series on the Region and the Economic Crisis, policy brief, May 2012. As of April 24, 2015:
http://www.gmfus.org/publications/
israel%E2%80%99s-economy-and-arab-spring-isolation-serves-buffer

Wen, Tiffanie, "Why Are the Israelis So Damn Happy?" *The Daily Beast*, April 14, 2013. As of April 24, 2015:
http://www.thedailybeast.com/articles/2013/04/14/why-are-the-israelis-so-damn-happy.html

Wertheimer, Jack, and Steven M. Cohen, "The Pew Survey Reanalyzed: More Bad News, but a Glimmer of Hope," *Mosaic*, November 2014. As of April 27, 2015:
http://mosaicmagazine.com/essay/2014/11/the-pew-survey-reanalyzed/

White, Adrian, "A Global Projection of Subjective Well-Being: A Challenge to Positive Psychology?" *Psychtalk*, Vol. 56, 2007, pp. 17–20.

White, Ben, "Israeli Government: International Criminal Court Threat 'Potentially Very Significant,'" February 18, 2014. As of April 27, 2015:
https://www.middleeastmonitor.com/blogs/
politics/9819-israeli-government-international-criminal-court-threat-potentially-very-significant

Who Profits from the Occupation, *Financing the Israeli Occupation: The Direct Involvement of Israeli Banks in Illegal Israeli Settlement Activity and Control Over the Palestinian Banking Market*, Tel Aviv, Israel: Coalition of Women for Peace, October 2010.

Wilkie, Christina, "Power Plant Bombed in Gaza Is Insured by U.S. Government," *Huffington Post*, July 30, 2014. As of April 24, 2015:
http://www.huffingtonpost.com/2014/07/30/gaza-power-plant_n_5634723.html

"Winning the Battle, Losing the War," *The Economist*, August 2, 2014. As of January 9, 2015:
http://www.economist.com/news/leaders/
21610264-all-its-military-might-israel-faces-grim-future-unless-it-can-secure-peace-winning

World Bank, *Twenty-Seven Months—Intifada, Closures and Palestinian Economic Crisis: An Assessment*, West Bank and Gaza Office, Jerusalem, Israel, May 2003.

———, *Stagnation or Revival? Israeli Disengagement and Palestinian Economic Prospects: Overview*, Report No. 32972, December 1, 2004.

———, *West Bank and Gaza Investment Climate Assessment: Unlocking the Potential of the Private Sector*, Washington, D.C.: World Bank, March 20, 2007a.

———, Sustainable Development Department (MNSSD) Middle East and North Africa Region, *West Bank and Gaza Energy Sector Review*, Report No. 39695-GZ, May 2007b.

———, *West Bank and Gaza Financial Sector Review*, Finance and Private Sector Group, Social and Economic Development Department, Middle East and North Africa Region, December 2008.

———, *West Bank and Gaza Assessment of Restrictions on Palestinian Water Sector Development*, Washington, D.C.: Middle East and North Africa Region, Sustainable Development, Sector Note, Report No. 47657-GZ, April 2009.

———, *West Bank and Gaza: Towards Economic Sustainability of a Future Palestinian State: Promoting Private Sector-Led Growth*, Washington, D.C.: World Bank, 2012.

———, *West Bank and Gaza: Public Expenditure & Financial Accountability (PEFA), Public Financial Management Performance Report*, Washington, D.C.: World Bank, Report No. AUS3141, June 17, 2013a.

———, *West Bank and Gaza: Area C and the Future of the Palestinian Economy*, Washington, D.C.: World Bank, Report No. AUS2922, October 2, 2013b.

———, "Middle East and North Africa Country Forecasts," 2015a. As of May 15, 2015:
http://www.worldbank.org/en/publication/global-economic-prospects/regional-outlooks/mena#2

———, "World Development Indicators," 2015b. As of January 1, 2015:
http://data.worldbank.org/data-catalog/world-development-indicators

World Bank Technical Team, *Movement and Access Restrictions in the West Bank: Uncertainty and Inefficiency in the Palestinian Economy*, May 9, 2007.

World Health Organization, *International Statistical Classification of Diseases and Related Health Problems 10th Revision (ICD-10)*, Geneva, Switzerland, 2010.

World Health Organization, Occupied Palestinian Territory, *Right to Health: Barriers to Health Access in the Occupied Palestinian Territory, 2011 and 2012*, WHO Special Report, Geneva, Switzerland, 2013.

Wright, Gilly, and Valentina Pasquali, "The Happiest Countries in the World," *Global Finance*, December 30, 2014. As of June 3, 2015:
https://www.gfmag.com/global-data/non-economic-data/happiest-countries

Wurmser, David, "The Strategic Impact of Israel's Export of Natural Gas," *inFocus* (Jewish Policy Center), Vol. 7., No. 1, Spring 2013. As of April 24, 2015:
http://www.jewishpolicycenter.org/4064/israel-natural-gas-export

Yaakov, Yifa, "Shas Will Most Likely Remain in Opposition, Says Yishai," *The Times of Israel*, February 2, 2013. As of April 27, 2015:
http://www.timesofisrael.com/shas-will-most-likely-remain-in-opposition-says-yishai/

Yaar, Ephraim, and Tamar Hermann, *War and Peace Index—November 2008*, Tel Aviv University, 2008. As of April 27, 2015:
http://en.idi.org.il/media/598620/peaceindex2008_11_3.pdf

———, *War and Peace Index—June 2009*, Tel Aviv University, 2009. As of April 27, 2015:
http://en.idi.org.il/media/597848/peaceindex2009_6_3.pdf

———, *Peace Index October 2013*, Israel Democracy Institute, 2013. As of April 27, 2015:
http://en.idi.org.il/media/2792757/Peace%20Index%20October%202013%20-%20Eng.pdf

———, *Peace Index Column, February 2014*, Israel Democracy Institute, 2014a. As of April 27, 2015:
http://en.idi.org.il/media/3091381/Peace_Index_February_2014-Eng.pdf

———, *Peace Index, March 2014*, Israel Democracy Institute, 2014b. As of April 27, 2015:
http://en.idi.org.il/media/3133668/Peace%20Index%20March%202014-Eng.pdf

———, *Peace Index Column, April 2014*, Israel Democracy Institute, 2014c. As of April 27, 2015:
http://en.idi.org.il/media/3164001/Peace_Index_April_%202014-Eng.pdf

Yadlin, Amos, "A Time for Decisions: Toward Agreements and Alternative Plans," in Brom, Shlomo, and Anat Kurz, eds., *Strategic Survey for Israel 2013–2014*, Tel Aviv, Israel: Institute for National Security Studies, 2014a.

———, "The Case for Unilateral Action: Why Israel Needs to Move Now Toward a Division of the Land—Even in the Absence of a Peace Deal," *Mosaic*, September 2014b. As of May 16, 2015:
http://mosaicmagazine.com/response/2014/09/the-case-for-unilateral-action/

Yadlin, Amos, and Gilead Sher, "Unilateral Peace," *Foreign Policy*, March 19, 2013. As of May 16, 2015:
http://foreignpolicy.com/2013/03/19/unilateral-peace/

Yardley, Jim, "Europe's Anti-Semitism Comes Out of the Shadows," *New York Times*, September 23, 2014. As of April 27, 2015:
http://www.nytimes.com/2014/09/24/world/europe/
europes-anti-semitism-comes-out-of-shadows.html

"'Young Jewish Americans Are Less Supportive of Israel,'" *Jerusalem Post*, November 24, 2014. As of April 27, 2015:
http://www.jpost.com/Home/Young-Jewish-Americans-are-less-supportive-of-Israel-382678

Zanotti, Jim, *U.S. Foreign Aid to the Palestinians*, Congressional Research Service, CRS Report RS22967, September 30, 2013.

Zilber, Neri, "The Politics of Rebuilding Gaza," Washington Institute, Policywatch 2314, September 16, 2014. As of April 24, 2015:
http://www.washingtoninstitute.org/policy-analysis/view/the-politics-of-rebuilding-gaza

Zilberman, David, and Richard Carson, "IGCC Policy Brief: Resolving Israeli-Palestinian Water Issues," La Jolla, Calif.: University of California, Institute on Global Conflict and Cooperation, January 1, 1999. As of January 8, 2015:
http://escholarship.org/uc/item/6j51x93q

Index

Abbas, Mahmoud, 94, 96, 147
alternative scenarios, 4–5, 73
    assumptions of, 99–104
    core criteria of, 73
    design of, 73
    economic outcomes of, 161–173
    security outcomes of, 173–174
    See also individual scenarios: two-state
      solution, coordinated unilateral withdrawal,
      uncoordinated unilateral withdrawal,
      nonviolent resistance, violent uprising
analytic framework, 4–6. *See also* counterfactual
  approach
Ansar Bayt al Maqdis, 131
Arab League, 29, 139
Arab Peace Initiative, 74, 75
Arab Spring protests, 87, 88
Arab world
    current changes occurring in, 48
    historical support to Palestine, 139, 140
    Israel's relations with, 77
    Israel's trade with, 29–31
      in coordinated unilateral withdrawal, 116
      costing inputs for, 186
      in nonviolent resistance, 126
      in two-state solution, 77, 106, 108
      in uncoordinated unilateral withdrawal,
        122
      in violent uprising, 130
    Jewish Israeli society's mistrust of, 154
    recognition of Israel by, 76
    regional instability in, 150–151
    See also Middle East
Arafat, Yasser, 52
Arviv-Abromovich, R., 155
assumptions for scenarios, 99–104
    in calculating costs, 73, 183–188
    compared with present trends, 181
    comparison of, 99–101, 103–104

See also individual scenarios: two-state
  solution, coordinated unilateral withdrawal,
  uncoordinated unilateral withdrawal,
  nonviolent resistance, violent uprising

Bahrain, 150
banking industry
    licensing restrictions, 40
    regulations for Palestinians, 24–25
      in coordinated unilateral withdrawal, 116
      costing inputs for, 187
      in nonviolent resistance, 126
      in two-state solution, 78, 106, 109
      in uncoordinated unilateral withdrawal,
        122
      in violent uprising, 98, 130, 132
Bar-Tal, D., 155
Bennett, Naftali, 82
Blue White Future (BWF), 81–83, 86
borders
    tunneling across, 93
    in two-state solution, 74, 75
border security
    as Israeli security cost, 51
    as Palestinian security cost, 53–54
      in two-state solution, 80, 110–111
      in violent uprising, 99
    and recent regional instability, 150
boycott, divestment, and sanctions (BDS)
  movement, 165, 178
    estimated effect of, 69, 71
    as Israeli opportunity cost, 26–28
      in coordinated unilateral withdrawal, 116
      costing inputs for, 186
      in nonviolent resistance, 88, 90, 125, 126,
        128
      in two-state solution, 106
      in uncoordinated unilateral withdrawal,
        122